TALES FROM LANGLEY

The CIA From Truman To Obama

Peter Kross

Adventures Unlimited Press

To the memory of my grandparents,
Cecilia and Sam "Franky" Russack.
We will always remember you.

Books by Peter Kross:

The Secret History of the United States
JFK: The French Connection
Spies, Traitors and Moles
The Encyclopedia of World War II Spies
Oswald, the CIA and the Warren Commission

TALES FROM LANGLEY

Peter Kross

Adventures Unlimited Press

Tales From Langely

by Peter Kross

ISBN 13: 978-1-939149-16-9

Published by:
Adventures Unlimited Press
One Adventure Place
Kempton, Illinois 60946 USA
auphq@frontiernet.net

www.adventuresunlimitedpress.com

TABLE OF CONTENTS

As I was going up the stair, I met a man who wasn't there.
He wasn't there again today, I wish, I wish he'd stay away.

—Hughes Mearns

INTRODUCTION

Throughout its history, the Central Intelligence Agency has been the department that its critics have loved to hate. Called the "Agency," the "Company." or the "intelligence community," the CIA has been part of our lives, for good or bad, since its creation in 1947 via the National Security Act of 1947. The CIA has been linked to the fictionalized group called "The Gang That Couldn't Shoot Straight," for it's sometimes zany and ridiculous schemes aimed at foreign leaders, especially during the cold war years. The CIA plotted against Fidel Castro by putting a bomb laden sea shell in the waters where he liked to swim, and asked a female agent to carry poison which she put in her cold cream jar which melted before she could use it. On the not so funny side, the CIA overthrew countless governments in the world, including Salvador Allende of Chile, aided in the assassination of Rafael Trujillo in the Dominican Republic, helped in the overthrow of Diem in South Vietnam, tried to assassinate Patrice Lumumba in the Congo, etc.

This was not the CIA which President Harry Truman envisioned it would be when he created the agency, two years after the end of World War 11. Truman saw the CIA as an intelligence-gathering group whose sole purpose was to inform the president and his top advisors as to what was going on in the world. It was not until the 1950s when the scope and range of the CIA expanded into the fields of covert operations, assassinations, the ruining of governments, and later on, domestic spying inside the United States, something that is still in the news today.

The abuses of power of the CIA were well documented by the Church Committee in the 1970s, which brought out all the agencies' dirty laundry for the world to see. In the wake of the Church Committee's investigation of the CIA, as well as congressional mandated investigations into the assassinations of Dr. Martin Luther King and President John F. Kennedy, the American people became aware of the plots by the CIA to assassinate foreign leaders, as well as the mysterious ties to a number of people in the assassination of JFK.

In the 1970s, moral in the CIA plummeted as hundreds of long time agents in the DO, Directorate of Operations, that part of the CIA that did the actual spying, quit in droves. It was not until the Reagan administration and its funding of the war in Afghanistan, that the CIA was given a rebirth.

That revival was reduced after the downfall of the Soviet Union when the United States no longer had a common foe to fight.

The moribund condition of the CIA was felt right up to the turn of the century and the lack of attention paid to the increasing rise in international terrorism, culminated in the horror of 9-11.

President Barak Obama has used the CIA in a different way from his cold war successors. The so called "War on Terror," has given the CIA (as well as the other intelligence agencies) a new lease on life, and the president's use of drones to hunt down and kill terrorists in foreign lands, and the selected targeting of certain American citizens, has taken on a life of its own.

This book tells the story of the many, and varied people and events over the past fifty sixty years who played a role in the history of the CIA, and how their actions shaped the modern day agency as we know it. Sometimes the story is not a pretty one, sometimes laughable, but always a factual one, whether we like the outcome or not.

The horrors of 9-11 showed just how dysfunctional the US intelligence agencies, the FBI, the CIA, was, and just how much needs to be done in order to correct the badly flawed system that exists today.

Here then, is the story.

—*Peter Kross,* March 2014

Chapter 1:
Bill Donovan Forms the COI:
America's First Spy Agency

In the years prior to America's entry into World War II, the United States did not have an organized intelligence service. The various armed services and the State Department had only a limited number of people involved in collecting and analyzing information for the use of the President and other top government officials. But as storm clouds of war were developing across the globe, President Franklin Roosevelt decided that the United States was in need of an intelligence agency whose job it would be to keep a watch on America's potential enemies, Japan and Germany. To that effect, FDR appointed an old friend, and World War I hero, William J. Donovan as the head of a new organization directly responsible to him. The name of that covert group was COI (Coordinator of Information). COI would be the predecessor of the wartime Office of Strategic Services, and run by Donovan.

Part of Donovan's job was to "collect and analyze all information and data which may bear upon national security, to correlate such information and data and make the same available to the President and to such departments and officials of the government as the President may determine, and to carry out when requested by the President, such supplementary activities as may facilitate the securing of information for national security not now available to the Government."

Donovan set up his new headquarters in two small rooms in the Executive Office Building just across the street from the White House in Lafayette Park. In its first year, the COI's budget was a measly $1,454,000, most of it coming from a secret fund controlled by the President.

Many of the COI's initial recruits were old friends of FDR's, men who played an instrumental role in the nation's affairs. Among them were Robert Sherwood, a playwright; Archibald MacLeish, the Librarian of Congress; authors such as Edmond Taylor and Douglas Miller; James Roosevelt, the President's son; and future movie producer John Ford.

The COI was headed by three men, chosen especially by Donovan: James Murphy, Colonel Edward Buxton and Otto Doering, Jr. Murphy was in charge of X-2, the counterespionage aspect of COI. Buxton was in charge of the Oral Intelligence Unit whose job it was to interview incoming passengers coming off boats from Europe to the United States. Doering was the de facto chief of COI, supplying new recruits for the agency.

As the COI got started in the intelligence field, they were visited by a number of British spymasters who were sent over to aid the Americans. One with particular expertise in the " second oldest profession" was Commander Ian Fleming of British Naval Intelligence, and the creator of the James Bond character in his later novels. Fleming liaised with COI leaders, passing on his considerable knowledge of the world of espionage. The British were invaluable in training the Americans in the art of secret warfare, imparting wisdom in many areas including radio finding operations, the organization of a successful covert network, the use of codes and ciphers, how to establish a hidden bank account, the use of explosive devices, how to conceal a murder weapon—in short, an encyclopedic knowledge of secret warfare.

In August 1941, the COI initiated a super-secret organization within its ranks called the "K Organization." This group was headed by Wallace Beta Phillips, who previously worked for the Office of Naval Intelligence. Donovan appointed Phillips to run the "K Organization," whose main job it was to establish a network of covert agents in Europe. With the initiation of the "K Organization," the COI became engaged for the first time in actual espionage operations, thus expanding its original mandate.

After the United States entered the war, Britain began to share its most sensitive intelligence information with COI, including the most highly guarded secret of all—ENIGMA. Enigma was the breaking by the British of all German military codes, and the rounding up of all German double agents inside England.

COI's first operational orders came shortly after the Japanese attack on Pearl Harbor. FDR personally gave Bill Donovan instructions 1) to make sure that war between the US and France did not break out in the event of an allied invasion of North Africa,

2) to make sure that the French fleet did not get turned over to the Germans, and 3) to ensure that Spain did not go over to the Nazi side in the war. To that end, Donovan sent his first COI agents to the Iberian Peninsula to establish an arms network, infiltrate suspected fascist groups, set up a direct communications link with his agents in Spain and Portugal, and to stop any German infiltration of these countries by any means.

The COI was the first real, national intelligence organization fielded by the United States. It was replaced by the OSS (Office of Strategic Services) on June 13, 1942.

William J. Donovan

Chapter 2:
William Donovan of the OSS

If any one man could be credited with being the father of the modern American espionage system, it would have to be the all American hero, the winner of the Congressional Medal of Honor for his heroic service in World War I, William J. Donovan. Bill Donovan was born in Buffalo, New York on January 1, 1883. He graduated from Columbia University in New York City and returned to Buffalo to begin the practice of law. In 1916, he joined the National Guard and his unit saw action in the pursuit of the Mexican bandit, Pancho Villa along the US-Mexican border.

He fought in World War I in the famous "Fighting 69th" infantry regiment. He was wounded three times in combat and was awarded the Congressional Medal of Honor. After the war, he left the service with the rank of Colonel. He then returned home to Buffalo where he was appointed to the post of US District Attorney for the Western District of New York. He later served as an Assistant US Attorney General, among other posts. He ran unsuccessfully for the Republican nomination for both Governor and Lieutenant Governor of New York, in 1922 and 1932. In 1929, Donovan founded the law firm that would bear his name, Donovan, Leisure, Newton and Lumbard in New York's Wall Street area.

It was at this time that Donovan began making friends among powerful and influential leaders, both in New York and in Washington. In 1919, while on his honeymoon, Donovan made a side trip to Siberia for the United States government. His main objective was to report on the activities of the anti-Bolshevik White Russian forces under the command of Admiral Alexander Kolchak.

He also went to Europe at the behest of the Rockefeller Foundation to set up a supply line of medical and other vital necessities for war relief victims. During his visit, Donovan went to England where he was introduced to the world of spying, meeting with a number of highly-placed members of the British intelligence services.

In 1939, he traveled to Ethiopia, again working clandestinely for Uncle Sam, to report on the Italian-Ethiopian war. He also made side trips to observe the Spanish Civil War, to the Balkans, and Italy. After the German attack on Poland that began World War I1, Donovan was asked by President Roosevelt to travel to England and report back to him on that country's ability to wage war against Germany. During the trip, Donovan made contacts with many of the top men in British intelligence. He made a detour to the Mediterranean area in order to analyze the military and political situation for Washington. Upon his return, Donovan reported to the President that in his opinion, the British, with enough military supplies at its disposal, would be able to beat back the Nazis.

In an extraordinary step, kept secret from Congress and most of the administration, Donovan went back to England in late 1940 to meet with the high-ranking members of the British government, as well as her intelligence chiefs. Donovan's mission was to assess Britain's secret request for the United States to covertly aid that country in its battle against Germany. Somehow the *New York Times* got wind of Donovan's trip and wrote "Donovan was off on another mysterious mission." Stuart Menzies, known as "C," head of the British Secret Intelligence Service (SIS), took Donovan under his wing by describing to Donovan, then a private citizen, Britain's most sensitive secrets, including Enigma and Ultra. Donovan was so impressed with what he saw and heard in England that he recommended full US aid to England.

On New Year's Eve, 1940, Donovan departed London on what would become a two-and-a-half month trip through some of the hottest spots in the British empire, accompanied on every leg of his trip by agents of the British secret service and other government officials who opened every door for their honored guest.

Donovan's travels took him to Gibraltar, Portugal, Bulgaria, Malta, Egypt, Greece, Cyprus, Palestine, Iraq, Libya, and Ireland. He met with the leaders of all the various nations and local officials, with the exception of Francisco Franco of Spain who said he was too busy to see him, and also French General Maxime Weygand, who was the French commander in Algiers.

Donovan's trip attracted the attention of the German government, which asked its spies to keep a wary eye on his travels. At one point, the German press labeled his trip an "impudent" act.

An embarrassing moment for Donovan took place during his stop in Sofia, Bulgaria. German agents broke into his hotel room and stole a bag of documents that was in the open. Among the items in the bag were questions from the Navy to Donovan that they wanted answered. When the bag was retrieved by the police, the list of questions was missing.[1]

It was during this trip that his British counterparts in the secret intelligence field pointed out to Bill Donovan the need for a centralized American intelligence agency. Donovan told FDR about this new national espionage idea upon his return, and it was met with immediate hostility among the top military leaders in Washington. General Sherman Miles, the head of army intelligence, said such an agency would be "very disadvantageous" to the nation.

Over the objections of both General Miles and more importantly, FBI Director J. Edgar Hoover, President Roosevelt saw merits in Donovan's plan and put the wheels in motion to set up an American espionage agency. The new name of the organization was the OSS, The Office of Strategic Services. FDR chose Bill Donovan to be its first head. Donovan had previously headed the COI, Coordinator of Information post, which was also responsible for intelligence gathering functions. Many of America's elite joined the ranks of the OSS, including authors, businessmen, poets, librarians, adventurers, and a few criminal types. In time, detractors of the OSS would call Donovan's group "Oh So Social."

The initial charter of the OSS was to gather and analyze information that would be sent to the President in order to plan policy toward any potential enemy. Over time, as the United States entered World War I1, the OSS would become a paramilitary organization, conducting both covert and overt missions on behalf of Allied troops in the field.

After the Pearl Harbor attack, the OSS began a new life, becoming an active part in the war in both Europe and the Far East. Specially-trained units were sent behind enemy lines to assassinate German targets, blow up an assortment of industrial and military targets, and train native tribesmen (especially in the jungles of Burma and India) to fight the Japanese invaders. OSS agents were dropped into such places as Italy, Albania and France, linking up, and conducting their own clandestine operations.

Donovan kept a careful watch on all these operations, often going

---

[1] Kross, Peter, *The behind-the-scenes story of how a World War I hero helped to strengthen US-British ties and forged the beginning of today's CIA, WWII Quarterly,* Winter 2013, Page 98.

into the field to oversee his recruits at work. But as the war came to an end, so did the operations of the OSS.

With the end of the war, Bill Donovan cajoled a sick and dying President Roosevelt into agreeing to appoint him the director of whatever new intelligence agency came after the war. Before his death on April 12, 1945, FDR wrote that, "At the end of the war there simply must be a consolidation of Foreign Intelligence between State and War and the Navy."

On April 5, one week before his death, FDR sent Donovan the following note regarding the new intelligence agency:

> Apropos of your memorandum of November 18, 1944, relative to the establishment of a central intelligence agency, I should appreciate your calling the chiefs of the foreign intelligence and internal security units in the various executive agencies, so that a consensus of opinion can be secured.[2]

Donovan's call for a new American intelligence agency was somehow leaked to the press and a number of national papers wrote about Donovan's plan. Among the papers that covered the story were the *Washington Times Herald,* the New York *Daily News,* and the *Chicago Tribune*. The *Tribune* called the scheme a plan for a "super-Gestapo agency" that would spy on "good neighbors throughout the world." No one knows who leaked the news to the papers but the best guess would have to be FBI Director J. Edgar Hoover, who had an animus toward Donovan.

Donovan saw himself as the head of a newly created, peacetime espionage agency, carrying on where the OSS left off. But the sudden death of President Roosevelt, and the ending of the war changed those plans. Bill Donovan retired from active government work and after the war was appointed as the Ambassador to Thailand from 1953-54.

His lasting legacy is evidenced today at Langley, Virginia, the home of the CIA. In 1959, the year of his death, his portrait was hung at CIA headquarters, a reminder to all that it was Bill Donovan who was single-handedly responsible for the modern espionage establishment we know today.

---

[2] Andrew, Christopher, *For the President's Eyes Only: Secret Intelligence and the American Presidency from Washington to Bush,* Harper Collins Publishers, New York, 1995. Page 148.

Chapter 3:
The Stephenson-Donovan Connection

One of the most controversial and important men whom Bill Donovan met as he began his tenure as the head of America's spy agency was William Stephenson, who worked for British intelligence during World War I1. Stephenson was a Canadian by birth, a professional boxer, and a man whose exploits during the war would spawn the myth of "Intrepid" following the end of the conflict. Stephenson's main occupation before and during World War I1, was acting as head of the British Security Coordination (BSC), and developing his relationship with both his own security services and those of the Unites States.

Stephenson was born on January 11, 1896 in Manitoba, Canada. He took an instant liking to anything that had to do with electronics, and made model airplanes and learned Morse code. During World War I, Stephenson entered the Royal Flying Corps as a lieutenant and flew a number of hazardous missions over German-held territory. For his gallantry, he won the Distinguished Flying Cross. During one mission, he was downed by German fire, taken prisoner, and later escaped.

After the war, Stephenson made his fortune by patenting a new can opener and going into the steel manufacturing business, as well as the radio industry. During the interwar years, Stephenson traveled as a private citizen to Germany where he observed its military and industrial capability, and reported all he saw to British intelligence.

With Britain now fighting for her life, it was decided by the top brass in London to send someone to America to act as liaison with the Americans in intelligence gathering operations. William Stephenson was tasked with the job and was sent by Stewart Menzies to Washington "to establish relations on the highest level between the British SIS and the U.S. Federal Bureau of Investigation."

Stephenson's cover in the United States was that of a British Passport Control Officer. However, his real task was to do all in his power to "assure efficient aid for Britain, to counter the enemies' subversion plans throughout the Western Hemisphere, and eventually bring the United States into the war." Accompanied by his wife, he arrived in New York on June 21, 1940.

As the story goes, William Stephenson was sent to the United States in the months preceding the Japanese attack on Pearl Harbor to set up shop in New York to run Britain's espionage operations in the Western Hemisphere. The mission he headed was called the British Security Coordination (BSC) located just across the street from St. Patrick's Cathedral in New York City. New York was chosen because of its easy access to communications to and from England. His mandate was to subvert German activities in South America, to overthrow pro-German governments, watch the ports of the United States for enemy sabotage, and make direct links to the fledgling United States intelligence agencies to ensure their continued support for the war effort.

When Stephenson arrived in New York, his proposed activities were already causing a great deal of talk among the President's advisors. FDR met Stephenson and gave him carte blanche to use U.S. soil in his counterespionage dealings. But if Congress didn't know about Stephenson, two other men who would play a prominent role in the Stephenson-BSC story did. They were FBI Director J. Edgar Hoover and the President's "secret agent," William Donovan. Like kindred soles, Donovan and Stephenson worked faithfully to their mutual advantage. Hoover, on the other hand, saw Stephenson's role in America as conflicting with his own domination over all U.S. intelligence functions.

Donovan was a frequent visitor to Stephenson's BSC headquarters and the two men soon joined forces in an intelligence sharing capacity. Donovan gave an account of his work to the President, and as mentioned in the last chapter, FDR sent Donovan to England as his personal representative.

Realizing that it was imperative for the United States to create an organized intelligence service, the British pulled out all the stops to ensure that that took place. It was decided by the top leadership in London to send a small delegation to Washington to egg the process on. The two men selected for this important trip were Admiral John Godfrey, head of British Naval Intelligence and his aide, Commander Ian Fleming, the creator of James Bond, "007." Donovan and Godfrey had met previously on Donovan's trips to England.

The two men left London in May 1941. They stayed two nights in Estoril, Portugal where the story goes, both spent a profitable might at the gaming tables, taking in a large sum from two Portuguese card players.

They arrived in New York via Pan Am's *Dixie Clipper* wearing civilian clothing so as not to attract attention. They signed their immigration papers as government employees, and settled in at the posh St. Regis Hotel near Central Park. They met with Bill Stephenson at his BSC office in Rockefeller Center. Here, Stephenson described how his BSC operations worked.

Stephenson trusted Fleming and anything he saw, the future Bond novelist shared as well. Shortly before England entered World War I1, Fleming was working as a reporter for the *London Times*. He was regarded as a superb writer, a man who had more than his share of contacts. He traveled to the Soviet Union where he covered the Metro-Vickers trial in which three British citizens were arrested by the OPGU (secret police) on false charges. His reports on the trial gained him a wide following and his name became known in the right circles.

After a stint as a London stockbroker, Fleming began his career in military intelligence working for Admiral Godfrey, the head of British Naval Intelligence. He started working as a part-timer with the rank of commander (the same as Bond). He soon joined full time and worked out of Room 39, the nerve center of Naval Intelligence. His first assignment was to collect information on German naval operations, and he was given the code number 17F.

As time went on, Fleming represented Admiral Godfrey in secret meetings with the SOE (Special Operations Executive) that was responsible for the covert side of the war against Germany. Fleming's first field assignment sent him to France where he was the liaison officer between British intelligence and French Admiral Darlan. He was later sent under civilian cover to Tangier to monitor naval intelligence operations near the Suez Canal.

Fleming's most important contribution during his stay in naval intelligence was his command of a covert group called *Number 30 Assault Unit* or AU-30. Fleming's AU-30s members were all civilians, a sort of "dirty dozen"—men of questionable character, not assigned to any regular army unit. During the D-Day invasion of France, Fleming's men secured vital information on German U-boat pens along the coast.

In a daring mission, 12 of AU-30's men captured 300 German troops complete with a radar system, and destroyed docked U-boats at the port of Cherbourg.

After their brief stay in New York, Godfrey and Fleming traveled to Washington where the most difficult part of the mission began. Their first meeting was on June 6 with the irascible FBI Director, J. Edgar Hoover. For sixteen minutes, Godfrey and Fleming listened to Hoover's opinion of anyone foolish enough to usurp his intelligence domain. They wrote of that meeting, "Hoover received us graciously, listened with close attention to our exposé of certain security problems, and expressed himself firmly but politely as being uninterested in our mission."

Getting nowhere with Hoover, Godfrey pulled strings in Washington, and with the help of Bill Stephenson and Arthur Hays Sulzberger, publisher of the *New York Times,* was able to arrange a meeting with Eleanor Roosevelt. The President listened in, heard what Fleming and Godfrey had to say regarding intelligence sharing, and the result was the appointment of Bill Donovan as head of the Coordinator of Information, COI.

In 1999, noted intelligence writer Thomas Troy interviewed the then 81-year-old Godfrey about his wartime experiences. About his part in FDR's appointment of Donovan as head of COI, Admiral Godfrey said..." the later intervention, namely an hour and a half with FDR, had some effect, because the COI was established within three weeks."

Commenting on William Stephenson, Admiral Godfrey said of the BSC chief, "he had a streak of ambition that caused him to think of himself as a king maker."

The trip by Godfrey and Fleming to Washington aided the British cause in the appointment of Donovan as head of COI, but their claim of being the major instrument in his appointment is not as certain. While they pulled out all stops to get Donovan named to the top spot, President Roosevelt was heading in that direction on his own.

Another historical controversy regarding their trip to Washington was to what extent Ian Fleming played in the organization of America's first intelligence apparatus. In the years after the war, Fleming tried to portray himself as an indispensable player in the creation of what later became the OSS.

One incident involves a memo that he wrote dated June 10, 1941. Years later, Fleming wrote, "In 1941, I spent some time with Donovan in his home writing the original charter of the OSS." In 1962, he related that, "my memorandum to Bill on how to create an American secret service... the cornerstone of the future OSS." While Fleming did write a memo to Donovan referring in principle to how an American secret service was to be created, Donovan did not act on any of his suggestions.

Fleming recommended to Donovan that his office should be set up at FBI headquarters, advised that he appoint as his chief of staff John J. McCloy, and counseled that he appoint Wallace Butterworth as his Economic Intelligence Chief.

007's creator also called on Donovan to "enlist the full help of State Department and FBI by cajolery or other means, to dragoon the War and Navy departments—being prepared to take action quickly if they got no cooperation from Miles and Kirk, and to leave the question of intercept material alone for the time being."

In time, Godfrey and Fleming left the United States. Their influence within the Roosevelt administration was taken over by William Stephenson and his aide, Col. Carl Ellis who worked out of New York at BSC. If anyone on the British side should be given credit for aiding the United States in the creation of the OSS, it was these two men, not Fleming or Godfrey.

Stephenson allowed Donovan the full range of his secret intelligence services, giving Donovan carte blanche to look into his secret files, explaining how the British SIS (Secret Intelligence Service) functioned. Furthermore, Stephenson's BSC was really under the rubric of the highly secret British SOE, Special Operations Executive, created by Prime Minister Winston Churchill to "set Europe ablaze."

Another secret British training facility that was opened to Donovan's secret raiders was a covert training camp run by the British dubbed Camp X, located in Canada, about an hours drive from Niagara Falls.

Stephenson's BSC used the site to operate Special Training School 103, or STS 103, training Allied agents in the techniques of secret warfare for the SOE. Hydra was another operation located at Camp X, a network that communicated secret messages between Canada, the United States, and Britain.

As the camp began its deadly business, agents were sent there from all over the world. Men from the FBI were sent to learn new skills and report back to Mr. Hoover. At various times, Bill Stephenson, William Donovan, and possibly Ian Fleming all arrived at Camp X to take courses and see how their recruits were doing.

On Donovan's part, he sent a number of his top men to London to train with the SOE to learn covert war techniques, and incorporate them into COI and, later, OSS plans.

Now that the Americans were beginning to learn the techniques of covert action, via the British, it was time to incorporate all they had learned. On July 11, 1941, President Roosevelt appointed Bill Donovan to head his nation's first civilian intelligence gathering organization, the COI, or Coordinator of Information.

The concept of COI did not go down well with J. Edgar Hoover. At FBI headquarters, Hoover took an instant dislike to Donovan's new agency, and made his feelings quite clear to the President. Roosevelt, not wanting to offend Hoover too deeply, allowed the FBI to continue the bureau's primary intelligence responsibility in South America.

As mentioned before, a number of men from the British security services aided their COI brethren, giving them invaluable training in the art of secret warfare. Of immense importance to COI was the availability via the British of two powerful short-wave radio services that were under BSC control. One of these transmitters was directed toward Europe, while the other controlled broadcasts coming from the Far East.

After the war, Stephenson would write of how important his BSC was in the working of the COI. "In short, BSC had a considerable part in the upbringing of the agency of which it was in a sense the parent."

The British, who had been scheming all along to get America involved in its own intelligence operations, were thrilled when Donovan was appointed to head COI and later, the OSS. Upon learning the news of his appointment as head of the COI, William Stephenson cabled London saying, "You can imagine how intrigued I am after three months of battle and jockeying for position in Washington, that our man (Donovan) is in a position of such importance to our efforts." Stephenson later recalled that on the day that Donovan's appointment was confirmed, "and that night I took five instead of four hours sleep."

Chapter 4:
The Hoover-Stephenson Relationship

While J. Edgar Hoover was succeeding in creating a growing antipathy between himself and Bill Donovan, the same cannot be said of his relationship with William Stephenson. This cooperation did not stem from the graciousness of his heart, but of pure political necessity. He was first and foremost a believer in his FBI; nothing, or no one could interfere with its survival and domination in the intelligence field. It was to this end that Hoover cemented warm relations with Stephenson who had more to offer him than viice versa.

Hoover, for all intents and purposes, had Stephenson's BSC over a barrel and he knew how to play the political game like a pro. To be frank, Hoover, if he wanted to play hardball, had the BSC in a very tight-fisted noose. Stephenson's BSC was technically working illegally in the United States, in direct violation of the U.S. Neutrality Act. The Congress did not know of its existence and if Hoover felt he was the potential victim of British blackmail, all he had to do was call a press conference and tell the world that British intelligence was working covertly in the United States.

The FBI-BSC relationship was so close, in fact, that Hoover suggested the cover name for Stephenson's organization. In the fall of 1940, the British SIS welcomed two of the Bureau's top agents to a strategy session in London where they were trained in covert activities. A top FBI officer traveled to South America where he met with the SIS chiefs in that region and discussed how the Bureau was going to operate, south of the border. Cooperation went so far as to have certain BSC agents work with their FBI counterparts in the highly technical field of clandestinely opening mail without the recipient knowing about it. Hoover also shared with the British some high-grade intelligence provided by him to the other U.S. intelligence services, namely the Army's G-2 and the Office of Naval Intelligence. Thus, Hoover was able to raise his stock with his counterparts, making him the man to see when it came to counterespionage and other intelligence sharing.

One telling incident of just how far the FBI's involvement with the BSC had gone was an incident concerning 16 German and Italian warships that had been at docks in the Mexican cities of Tampico and Vera Cruz. British intelligence received reports that these ships were planning to run the Allied blockade. Stephenson gave Hoover the authorization to derail the ships by whatever means he thought necessary as long as the FBI kept the British informed. Hoover arranged for a number of limpet mines that would be attached to the hulls of these ships to be sent to U.S. agents in Mexico, but the plan to deploy them was scrubbed.

However, it was decided by the Navy to dispatch a number of U.S. warships off Mexican territorial waters which would report, the movements of the enemy ships. On November 15, 1940, these U.S. Navy ships flooded the Axis ships with their powerful searchlights, illuminating them. The adversary's ships, fearing that an attack was imminent, had one of their own ships sunk (reasons unknown), while the others quickly ran back to port. Days later, the remaining three German ships steamed out of port, and were shadowed by the U.S. Navy who gave their locations to the British blockade runners, who subsequently ran them to ground.

In another series of cooperative ventures, the SIS and the FBI planted bogus deception information inside the German embassy in Washington by using one of their undercover agents who worked inside the embassy.

The genesis of the Hoover-Stephenson relationship came in the form of an introduction from a mutual friend, the heavyweight boxing champion Gene Tunney. At the time of their first meeting, Hoover was 45, one year older than Stephenson. Hoover had been at the helm of the FBI since 1924, and had been appointed by President Harding as the Acting Director. Hoover built up the FBI from a crime-fighting group who pursued such notable criminals as "Pretty Boy" Floyd, Al Capone, and John Dillinger. Hoover's G-men (Government) formed a crystal clear reputation as America's best crime fighters, loyal to both country and to each other.

Tunney wrote of his role in bringing Hoover and Stephenson together:

Through English and Canadian friends of mine, I had

known Sir William for several years. He wanted to make the contact with J. Edgar Hoover and wrote a confidential letter from London. I arranged to get the letter into the hands of Mr. Hoover, having known him quite well. Sir William did not want to make an official approach through well-placed English, or American friends; he wanted to do so quietly and with no fanfare.

J. Edgar Hoover told me on the telephone that he would be quite happy to see Sir William when he arrived in the United States, so when he did come to Washington everything was set up for him; this was sometime early in 1940. Naturally, I had to stay out of whatever business was between them, but it was my understanding that the thing went off extremely well.[1]

As the years went by, mostly after Hoover's death, there were public rumors that Hoover was not the all American figure of repute the newspapers portrayed him to be. There were rumors that Hoover was gay, that he consorted with members of organized crime while he was the Director of the FBI, that when he attended horse races, a fix was in so that he would never lose, and that he used FBI resources for his personal use. There was quiet resentment among some FBI agents that Hoover played favorite when he appointed his long time friend (and possibly gay lover), Clyde Tolson, to be the second in command at the FBI. Both men were constantly in each other's company, and Hoover even left most of his estate to Tolson.

But as war clouds gathered in Europe in 1940, the Bureau turned its attention away from homegrown criminals to keeping America safe from potential enemy spies.

If Hoover and Stephenson were to act as partners, then certain rules had to be laid down right from the start. Hoover told Stephenson that he would not disobey the State Department's order forbidding any open collaboration with British intelligence unless that order came directly from the President. Hoover further stated that even if he got such a guarantee, that under no circumstances would the State Department be privy to their arrangement.

Stephenson gave his OK, and an intermediary was found who

[1] Troy, Thomas, *Wild Bill and Intrepid: Donovan, Stephenson, and the Origin of CIA*, Yale University Press, New Haven, 1996, Page 39.

would relay their arrangement to President Roosevelt. That man was Ernest Cuneo, a New Jersey lawyer who once worked in the administration of New York Mayor Fiorello La Guardia. Cuneo met with the President and reported back to Stephenson and Hoover his response. The President, said Cuneo, agreed to the secret union and stated, "there should be the closest possible marriage between the FBI and British intelligence." The President informed Lord Lothian, the British ambassador to the United States of the special deal.

As the Hoover-Stephenson arrangement grew in scope, so did their covert activities. The range of their actions now included the guaranteeing by whatever means necessary of supplying aid in order for Britain to survive the Nazi onslaught, as well as to counter German espionage operations in the Western Hemisphere. The FBI was already ahead of the game as it was primarily responsible for intelligence gathering activities in South America.

An example of how this new covert relationship blossomed was a case that involved the tracing of funds from the Italian Embassy in Washington to its contacts in Mexico.

In October 1920, the FBI learned that the Italian Embassy was transferring $3,850,000 which was to be sent via diplomatic bags to its various contacts in Latin America. Stephenson believed that the transfer of such a large amount of cash smelled of illegal use by the Italians for possible anti-U.S. or British operations. Hoover's agents followed the couriers as they took the cash to Brownsville, Texas. At that point the couriers split up, one going to New Orleans and the other to Mexico City. Stephenson contacted his section chief in Mexico City and had the Mexican Police Intelligence Department open the Italian diplomatic bag, a patently illegal act. The Italian government was able to get its diplomatic bag back, minus the money that was deposited in a "blocked account" by the Mexican government.

By the end of 1941, Stephenson's BSC had sent the FBI some 100,000 documents relating to intelligence operations, as well as other interesting material. However, all that intelligence sharing now faced a possible halt that would cripple the newly formed BSC-FBI relationship.

The rub of the matter was a highly publicized congressional investigation called the Dies Committee that investigated enemy subversive activities in the United States. A bill sponsored by Senator Kenneth McKellar, a Democrat from Tennessee, called for the transfer from the State Department to the Justice Department regarding the registration of foreign agents operating in the United States.

This looming disaster, if signed into law, would severely limit foreign activities inside the United States and would allow the Justice Department to monitor all expenditures and activities. If the new law was enacted, it would severely disrupt, or put an end to, BSC involvement in the United States. The law would affect BSC-OSS relations as well. Donovan, seeing the calamity that was to follow, had a meeting with FDR in which he explained the perilous intelligence sharing consequences that would ensue if the McKellar law was put into effect. In time, FDR vetoed the bill as it stood, and it was reintroduced and passed on May 1, 1942.

The new law allowed certain exemptions that included agents of foreign governments "the defense of which the President deems vital to the United States, provided that such agents engage only in activities which are in defense of the policies, public interests or national defense, both of such government and of the defense of the United States and are not intended to conflict in any of the domestic or foreign policies of the Government of the United States."

William Donovan, Hoover's public nemesis, had unknowingly not only saved his own ties to the BSC the BSC-FBI covert relationship as well.

William J. Donovan

Chapter 5:
J. Edgar Hoover's Vendetta
Against the OSS

When the United States entered World War 11, President Franklin Roosevelt met with a number of his closest advisors and decided that it was imperative that this country have an official, centralized intelligence service that could meet the challenge of the conflict. From the turn of the century, the various military departments, Army, Navy, etc., were tasked with the job of keeping watch on America's foreign enemies. There was such a mishmash of intelligence gathering and interpretation that one department often did not know what the other was doing, and little if any vital intelligence was shared. As we have seen, FDR replaced that awkward, antiquated system with the COI and later, the OSS both headed by William Donovan. As Donovan coordinated all the various intelligence services into one focused department, his enemies in the military/political establishment in Washington began to grow. Donovan's number one adversary was FBI Director, J. Edgar Hoover.

Hoover saw Donovan's OSS as an infringement on his own intelligence turf, and took his displeasure over the OSS to Attorney General Francis Biddle who met with the crusty director in many private sessions. Hoover tried passionately to get Biddle to try to persuade the White House to drop Donovan and his elite spies, and let the FBI handle all intelligence-related issues.

Over the years, Hoover had been granted the exclusive right to send his agents into South America to keep watch on America's enemies on our doorstep. However, he wanted his jurisdiction to expand to include the rest of the world, now more than ever, with the Unites States engaged in a worldwide conflict. Despite his pleas, the President refused to let Hoover's G-men into Europe, and stayed with the OSS.

Hoover's quest for an expanded role in U.S. intelligence gathering got a huge boost when the British government, with the complete cooperation of the United States (including FDR himself), set up the BSC. This secret US-UK program was kept private from both the American people and the Congress. If word had leaked out that such an arrangement had been made, the political uproar could have led to the President's impeachment. At first, Hoover did not like the idea of British spies having free reign on American soil, and unsuccessfully tried to have the program canceled. In time, though, Hoover decided it was to his best advantage to work with Stephenson's BSC, despite any misgivings he might have otherwise had. BSC operatives taught FBI agents the techniques of mail opening; mail from German and Japanese diplomats was opened in the Main Post Office in Washington and taken to FBI headquarters where it was returned to the mails. This was called "Z-Coverage," and was expanded to include mail openings of supposedly neutral consulates and embassies in both Washington and New York.

While Hoover had an untraditionally good relationship with Stephenson's BSC, the same could not be said of his relations with Donovan and his new organization. Hoover was stung when A.G. Biddle directed that OSS agents could legally operate in the Western Hemisphere but only out of the continental United States. He further stipulated that they must inform the FBI before any such missions began.

The Hoover-Donovan feud came to the surface when OSS agents broke into the Spanish Embassy in Washington, D.C.

Most of the lights were out along Embassy Row in Washington, D.C. on the night of July 29, 1942. But inside the Spanish embassy teams of men from Bill Donovan's OSS were carrying out a covert operation. Their mission was to steal the secret codes used by the embassy to communicate with Madrid and its other consulates around the world.

As the Allied invasion plans for North Africa began in earnest, the prime objective of the United States was to prevent Spain from going over to the Nazi side. Spanish dictator Francisco Franco was not to be trusted when it came to his relationship with Hitler. It was imperative that the Allies be able to keep one step ahead of the Spanish, and that job was given to Bill Stephenson's BSC. Over a long period of time, BSC agents regularly broke into the Spanish embassy in Washington to obtain the keys to the ever-changing Spanish codes. Stephenson was taking a considerable gamble with these highly illegal break-ins. If his spies were caught, their entire

U.S. operation would be in jeopardy. With this in mind, Stephenson asked Bill Donovan to take over these patently illegal activities.

President Roosevelt had ordered Donovan not to conduct espionage activities on U.S. soil and the COI chief was taking a considerable risk in agreeing to Stephenson's request. Donovan got around the President's directive by assenting that the Spanish embassy was indeed located on foreign soil, thus, FDR's mandate was not applicable in this case. Donovan now set to work organizing the raid.

The man he chose to lead the operation was Donald Downes, a 40-year-old graduate of Yale and Exeter, a former schoolteacher in private life. Downes had succeeded in planting a woman informant inside the embassy, but she left after failing to get the combination of the safe that contained the code machine. Next, Downes hired a New York safecracker of some ill repute named G.B. Cohen who refused to be paid for his services. Using a new informant inside the embassy, Cohen was given the exact specifications of the safe; he was now ready to pass on his expertise to his contact inside the embassy.

On the night of July 29, 1942, using the paid services of an embassy janitor, who was in the employ of the OSS, Downes and his party covertly entered the Spanish embassy. Leading the break-in team was José Aranda who was opposed to the Franco regime. Working quickly, the team was able to copy 3,400 photographs relating to the Spanish code. This windfall was a bonanza for British cryptologists who were now able, in real time, to read all Spanish messages.

Just as the burglars thought they had everything under control, sirens broke the nighttime silence. The FBI, which had been staking out the embassy, saw the lights inside the building and created such a ruckus that Downes' men had to flee into the night. The waiting G-men swooped down on the unsuspecting OSS agents and arrested them (including Downes). They were taken to FBI headquarters where they were interrogated. Downes admitted that he was a COI agent and was allowed to call Donovan.

Hoover's G-men were playing the Downes team for all it was worth. They knew who the prowlers were from the beginning, and had the last laugh at their expense. Donovan called James Murphy who managed to have all his men released from custody. To make matters worse for Donovan, the FBI had possession of the Spanish codes, but they were soon to turn them over.

After the fiasco, Donovan met with FDR and said regarding Hoover's raid, "The Abwehr gets better treatment from the FBI than we do."

Downes would later say of Donovan regarding the incident, "I don't believe any single event of his career enraged him more. The next morning Donovan went to the White House to protest. Won't the President do anything about such near treason?, I asked. No, said the Political Advisor of OSS, he won't. No President dares touch John Edgar Hoover. Let alone congressmen. They are all scared pink of him."

Had Hoover deliberately sabotaged Downes' mission for his own personal vendetta against Donovan? That possibility certainly holds water in view of the dislike between the two men. In the aftermath of the Spanish embassy fiasco, Hoover managed to infiltrate the OSS. He kept voluminous files on Donovan, many of which are now in public view. For his part, Donovan ordered a secret probe into the allegations that Hoover and his top FBI aide and confidant, Clyde Tolson, were engaged in a homosexual affair.

Hoover and Donovan would square off again when it came to the debriefing of passengers deplaning from the Pan Am *Clippers'* extensive overseas flights. The COI had set up an Oral Intelligence Unit in New York for the express purpose of talking with these people. The FBI had already been talking with them and Donovan sent a message to Hoover saying he wanted to discuss with these people any "foreign intelligence" information they may have learned. Hoover agreed, but did so yelling and screaming.

Hoover told Donovan "to instruct my Special Agents to obtain any information that you desire from the incoming passengers, and see that this information is probably relayed to you." Hoover sent information of little value to Donovan such as reports of a rice riot in Yokkaichi. For Donovan' s part, he wanted raw intelligence, especially anything to do with Japanese war plans, not the dribble that Hoover was sending.

One of Donovan's spies in the Far East was Edgar Ansel Mowrer who was a writer for the *Chicago Daily News*. Mowrer reported from the Philippines that his sources told him that a Japanese fleet was sailing west, and suggested that the Japanese were going to "do something soon." Jimmy Roosevelt, FDR's son, reported that the War and Navy Departments had told him that the Japanese fleet was preparing for some sort of military action.

A COI agent named Ferdinand Meyer had a meeting with Saburo Kurusu, a special Japanese envoy who was working out of the Japanese embassy in Washington. The two men had a hurried meeting on the morning of December 6, 1941 on the street outside of the Japanese embassy. Kurusu told Meyer that hostilities between the United States and Japan were looming and that "hotheads could upset the applecart at any time."

Hoover and Donovan squared off on the bona fides of a man named Dusan Popov, who came tothe United States with vital information on Japanese interest in the U.S. Naval base at Pearl Harbor, Hawaii.

Popov arrived in the United States on August 12, 1941, disembarking at La Guardia Airport from the Pan Am *Clipper* that had just arrived from Estoril, Portugal. After checking through immigration, Popov took a cab to the posh Waldorf Astoria Hotel overlooking Park Avenue.

Popov had originally worked for the German Abwehr but so disliked the ruin brought upon Germany by Hitler that he offered his services to the British as a double agent. Popov was accepted into British intelligence and was also given $58,000 from the Abwehr to go to the United States in order to set up an espionage ring.

Popov had been recruited into the Abwehr by a German friend, Johann Jebsen. His first assignment was to go to France and report on political leaders who might be helpful to the Nazi's. Popov gave the required information to the Abwehr, and also gave a copy to British intelligence. Popov was run by the so called Double Cross System, a part of British intelligence that was responsible for the running of all captured German spies who were trying to infiltrate Britain. Popov decided to play the double game because of his hatred for the Nazis, and agreed to spy for the British. He was given the code name Tricycle.

Preceding his trip to the United States, the Abwehr gave Popov a vital, new piece of spy paraphernalia. It was a microdot that carried pages of information reduced to the size of a pinhead; a list of questions was written on it. The microdot information carried by Popov was imbedded in a telegram which he kept with him.

Upon his arrival in New York, Popov contacted the FBI and asked that someone come to talk with him. To his chagrin, he had to wait five days until the Bureau responded. He was finally met by Agent James Foxworth who was the FBI's bureau chief in New York. Popov handed over the microdot questionnaire provided to him by the Abwehr. As Agent Foxworth began to read its contents, he knew that he had something important. The paper contained a list of questions that the Germans wanted answered for their allies, the Japanese. Among the queries was information on American defenses at the giant naval base at Pearl Harbor, Hawaii, including the exact locations of the airbases at Hickim, Wheeler, and Kaneohe airfields, sketches of Pearl Harbor, the depths of its waters, and the number and locations of any anti torpedo nets.

Foxworth immediately gave Popov's questionnaire to J. Edgar Hoover. Hoover did not trust Popov, believing he was still working for the Germans. Another strike against Popov was his playboy lifestyle. Popov was a flagrant womanizer, had numerous affairs with women, including the actress Simone Simone (and her mother), and spent the Abwehr's money lavishly.

Popov's actions were watched by the FBI, and what they noticed was that after three months of living the high life in New York, he had not contacted any German agents in the city. The Abwehr too was beginning to have second thoughts about their prize agent and they came to the conclusion that he might have been "turned."

Popov transferred the intelligence information to the FBI under orders from the British SIS, also called MI6 (Military Intelligence Section 6). His case was personally supervised by Stewart Menzies, head of MI6. Menzies contacted Hoover and "loaned" Popov to the Americans.

Hoover did a curious thing with regard to the Pearl Harbor questionnaire. Instead of handing it over to Bill Donovan, or more importantly, to President Roosevelt, Hoover doctored the questions, gave nothing to Donovan, and omitted the Pearl Harbor queries when he finally sent it to the White House.   In   late   November 1941, under the ever-watchful eye of the FBI, Popov received orders from the Abwehr, sending him to establish a radio link between Rio and London. Popov was to concentrate on seeking information on war production, the destination of Allied convoys, and any news he could provide on antisubmarine warfare.

Since the FBI was given responsibility of running the spies in Latin and South America, the Bureau knew all about Popov's adventures and kept one step ahead of him.

Popov was in Rio on December 7, 1941 when the Japanese attacked Pearl Harbor. He returned to the Untied States one week later and handed a second set of microdots to the FBI. A sampling of his second set of questions from the Abwehr concerned the types of powder used for ammunition and a seven-page list of questions concerning America's atomic bomb research.

One of the nagging questions in the Popov case is whether or not he actually met personally with J. Edgar Hoover. FBI documents shed no light on this matter, and persons on each side have differing opinions. In his memoirs, Popov said that he "encountered J. Edgar Hoover at the FBI office in New York." After Hoover's death, the FBI stated flatly that there had been no face-to-face meeting between the two men. Author William Stevenson, who wrote a biography of Sir William Stephenson entitled *A Man Called Intrepid*, wrote of his conversations with "Intrepid" on the Popov case. The BSC chief did in fact say that Hoover met with Popov. "Our conversation was not for publication at that time. But he was very clear. He said Popov had indeed met Hoover—he knew all about it. Stephenson had no doubts about Popov's credibility, and thought the FBI had totally failed to pick up on what Popov was trying to tell them about Pearl Harbor."

The larger question to be asked is this. Like his actions in the Spanish embassy break-in, did Hoover intentionally hold back vital information on Japanese interests in Pearl Harbor, not only from William Donovan, but from President Roosevelt, for his own motives? If so, why? With that information in hand, might not Donovan's COI been able to possibly influence the Navy department to keep a closer watch on Pearl Harbor in the months before December 7, 1941? What *is* clear is that Hoover failed to share Popov's knowledge with Donovan, his erstwhile comrade-in-arms.

Over the years, the FBI has declassified thousands of pages of historical information regarding this time period, especially its voluminous files on William Donovan and the OSS. Here, in no particular order, are the contents of primary source documents from FBI files relating to Hoover's obsession with ferreting out as much dirt as possible on Donovan.

In a memo to the Attorney General dated December 23, 1941, the unnamed writer refers to a decision by President Roosevelt to sett up a Special Intelligence Unit which allowed the FBI to conduct investigations throughout the Western Hemisphere, Mexico, the Caribbean, and Central America dealing with financial, economic, political and subversive activities. One week later, Donovan contacted the White House regarding SIS and was "considerably put out" that he had signed the directive. "Donovan felt the agents of the FBI could not gather material necessary for his purposes, but that his agents should work together with the FBI. It was recommended that Donovan's organization assume responsibility for all intelligence in Mexico, the Caribbean, Central America and South America, and that the FBI be responsible for the continental U.S. and its territories."

Hoover's FBI was given the task of monitoring and stopping all German activities inside the United States during the course of the war. So it was with some real interest that Hoover heard of a case concerning a German war correspondent named Paul Scheffer who tried to contact Donovan. In early 1942, Scheffer was detained at The Greenbrier hotel in White Sulphur Springs, West Virginia. The newsman had an accident and the local FBI office was called in. Scheffer asked the FBI men to keep safe the documents in his possession, one of which was an incomplete manuscript addressed to "Dear Bill." The manuscript dealt with the possibilities of a solution to the menace of Hitlerism, and was intended for Col. William Donovan." A later FBI document on this case says that Donovan "desired to employ Scheffer as a consultant if he was released."

The records show that Donovan cooperated with Hoover in one small way. The OSS produced a weekly secret publication called "The War This Week." Donovan agreed to share this report "…if the Director [Hoover] was interested in having it." He was.

On June 9, 1943, FBI Special Agent in Charge in New York

City, Jerome Doyle, had a chat with Martin Quigley, the owner and publisher of the Quigley Publishing Co., and a friend of Donovan's. "Doyle stated that he was convinced that while Col. Donovan had an excellent personality and could individually handle any project given him, that nevertheless, Donovan was totally unfit temperamentally to administer any such agency as OSS. Mr. Doyle told Mr. Quigley that he had heard a rumor in NYC that Donovan would be made a Major General and placed in charge of MID [Military Intelligence Division]. Mr. Quigley said he had heard nothing along this line... Quigley felt that the presence of many former State Department career men in OSS had deterred rather than assisted it in its operations."

A heavily redacted Memo to the Director, dated October 14, 1943, concerns reports on how fast Donovan's star was falling in the eyes of some people in the Roosevelt administration. The two people informing on this delicate matter were two FBI agents, a Mr. Ladd and a Mr. Pennington. On this date the two men interviewed an unidentified person regarding Donovan. The memo reads in part, "blank stated that Col. Donovan was losing face rapidly with the President and that blank felt that the President would be very receptive to a suggestion that Mr. Hoover take over OSS. Blank—he most anxious to see that FBI take over the operation of OSS inasmuch as he felt that the operation of OSS had been a miserable failure. Blank further stated that on numerous occasions, in connection with blank, he had wired Col. Donovan for instructions, but had not received any instructions or advice from hdqrs. of OSS. It was believed, however blank did not have any particular 'Ax to grind' but that he was exceedingly conscientious and that he believed the Donovan organization was a complete failure and a waste of money."

Hoover's files on Donovan can be summed up in another heavily censored document dated January 15, 1943 which states, "Blank summed this matter up from the standpoint of the War Department by saying, 'Donovan's past sins are at last catching up with him.'"

Hoover even went so far as to infiltrate a number of his most trusted agents into the OSS, and they kept the director up to date on who was being hired, and assembled a detailed personal background on every new employee.

Author Curt Gentry, in his book *J. Edgar Hoover: The Man*

and the Secrets, writes of a possible link between Hoover and the legendary CIA counterintelligence chief James Angleton. After Hoover's death, it was reported that Hoover's closest aides had destroyed most of his personal files on his political enemies that he had accumulated over the years, a portion of which included material on William Donovan.

Gentry writes, "When asked if, as rumored, J. Edgar Hoover's derogatory files on William Donovan had been exchanged for the CIA's investigative files on J. Edgar Hoover's alleged homosexuality, Angleton laughed and said, 'First you have to find out if they're missing.' John Mohr of the FBI told a Senate investigating committee that he saw someone resembling Angleton removing several boxes of spoiled wine from Hoover's home. James Angleton retorted, 'I'll tell you one thing, and this is the last thing I'll tell you, I didn't haul away any spoiled wine.'"[1]

---

[1] Gentry, Curt. *J. Edgar Hoover: The Man and the Secrets,* W.W. Norton & Co., New York, 1991, Page 734-735.

Chapter 6:
The Philby Affair

If there was one man who was considered the most notorious traitor of the Cold War period, loathed by the CIA and British intelligence alike, it would be Harold Adrian "Kim" Philby, a man who at one point was considered a candidate for the position of "C," head of British intelligence. Over his career as a spy, Philby was considered by CIA chief James Angleton to be one of his most ardent supporters in the war against the Soviet Union, and his betrayal shocked him to the core.

Philby's name is associated with the infamous Cambridge Spy Ring comprising his fellow British traitors Anthony Blunt, Guy Burgess, and Donald MacLean. It is ironic that this man, who was trusted with the most sensitive secrets of the British government during World War II and during the height of the cold war, was almost chosen as the head of British intelligence. What would have happened if Kim Philby had indeed been chosen as "C? That prospect is ripe with historical what ifs. With Kim Philby seated in the director's chair at British intelligence at the height of the Cold War against the Soviet Union, there is no telling how the history of those years might have been changed.

If Philby did not achieve his status as "C," he did have a profound effect on both J. Edgar Hoover and James Angleton. In his years as the U.K. representative to the U.S. intelligence services, Philby had more of an influence on Angleton than Hoover, and made Angleton more paranoid than ever in his search for moles inside the CIA.

In his memoirs, Philby wrote that right before he left England for America he was told by his superiors in London, "the news of my appointment to the United States appeared to have upset Hoover who suspected my appointment might herald unwanted SIS activity in the United States. To allay his fear, the Chief had sent him a personal telegram assuring him that there was no intention of a change of policy; my duties would be purely liaison."

Hoover's visceral reaction to Philby's arrival in the United States went back to the days of William Stephenson's BSC operation in

New York. While Hoover worked closely with Stephenson, he did so only under the direction of FDR, and under dire wartime conditions. Now, according to Hoover's view, another foreign intelligence interloper was coming to tread on his own turf, and he vowed to keep a wary eye on Philby and his activities. Hoover was indeed right in keeping a watchful eye on Philby—he was a long time double agent for the Soviet Union.

Harold Philby was born in 1912 in Ambala, India. He was given the nickname of "Kim" after the title character of Rudyard Kipling's novel. His father was the noted spy and adventurer Harry St. John Philby, assistant commissioner in the Punjab district of India, when that country was part of the British Empire. The elder Philby married in 1910 while stationed there.

Kim Philby attended the Westminster school and graduated in 1928. He went on to Trinity College at Cambridge where he was to meet his fellow traitors Anthony Blunt, Guy Burgess, and Donald MacLean. During their time at Cambridge, they were recruited into the NKVD, the Russian espionage service.

His first marriage was to Alice Friedman in Vienna, Austria on February 24, 1934. His new wife was a communist who was on the run from the police. By marrying Philby, she was now a British subject and was given a passport that allowed her to legally leave the country. Philby did not tell his bride of his procommunist connections, one of the first betrayals he was to become so used to.

During the Spanish Civil War, Philby worked for the *Times of London,* covering the war, allowing his pro-Franco sympathies to show. In 1939, he and Alice were divorced. He was transferred to Germany as the *Times* correspondent and spent most of his free time spying for the Russians against the Germans.

When Britain entered the war, Philby joined the British Expeditionary Force as a reporter and was sent to France. After the fall of France, Philby returned to England, and it was then, according to his account, that he was approached by MI6 to become one of their own. Other sources in the know said that St. John Philby pulled strings to get his son inside the bowels of the British Secret Service, an unsuspected double agent who would remain in that role until the early 1960s.

His first posting was with Section V, the counterespionage branch of SIS. He would become the leader of the Iberian subdivision of Section V, responsible for running agents in such countries as Spain, Portugal and Italy, and in North Africa.

Philby, however, had more important cards up his sleeve, and the plan he devised was sanctioned by his controllers in Moscow. As the war grew to a close, both the U.S. and England feared Russia as a potential enemy once the conflict was over. The intelligence services of both countries wanted to keep a close watch on Russia. Philby asked that he be allowed to set up a subsection within Section V, whose primary duties were to monitor Soviet intelligence. This proposal was immediately agreed upon, and Philby was now in a position to funnel highly informative intelligence emanating from the British SIS to Anatoli Lebedve, his Soviet controlling officer.

Philby was aware of the plot by German Admiral Canaris and others to overthrow Hitler, as well as their negotiations with the West to secure a separate peace. This turn of events sent shock waves inside the Kremlin. The last thing the Soviets wanted was a non-Hitler Germany allied with the United States and Great Britain against the Soviet Union.

Philby began to plot against Admiral Canaris, even going so far as to devise a scheme that he proposed to "C," Stewart Menzies, to have the admiral killed while he was in Spain. Behind Philby's pathological desire to see Canaris removed was his fear of an entente between Britain and Germany. This, Philby vowed, would not happen.

In 1945, just at the end of the war, Philby's cover was about to be blown. A Russian named Konstantin Volkov, working as vice counsel in Istanbul, Turkey, defected. He said that he had information about a number of Soviet moles inside British intelligence, one of whom worked inside the London counterespionage section (Philby).

Philby got wind of the Volkov defection and personally took over the file on him. Philby told his controllers about Volkov's allegations and SIS allowed Philby complete discretion in the case. Under mysterious circumstances, Volkov disappeared, never to be heard from again (it is believed that he was killed by Russian assassins).

In 1949, Philby was posted to Washington, where he took over the job as the liaison between the SIS, the FBI and the CIA.

Philby's cover in Washington was that of first secretary at the British embassy. Philby had first met James Angleton during World War 11 but their paths did not cross again until he arrived in the States. His official duty was as the executive assistant to the Assistant Director of Special Operations whose primary responsibility was to act as the liaison officer between the various western intelligence services, like those of Israel and France. In time, Angleton and Philby would dine regularly at the finest Washington eateries, where they would share the latest news coming from their respective capitals. At no time during Philby's stay in Washington did Angleton ever consider that Philby was more than he seemed to be.

Philby's deception cost the CIA the lives of a number of undercover agents who were parachuted into Albania in a futile attempt to overthrow that communist government.

Philby's undoing began in 1951 when he learned that MI5 was about to arrest Guy Burgess and Donald MacLean, who were part of the Cambridge Spies. After Philby alerted them, both men made a quick escape to Moscow on May 21, 1951. Philby received the news of their flight from Geoffery Paterson, who worked in the British embassy in Washington. Philby, trying to sound shocked, offered his services in whatever way he could help. In an elaborate game of chess, Philby informed his contacts at the FBI of the flight of MacLean and Burgess, hoping to deflect their interest in him. But sounder heads in the Bureau soon realized that at one point Burgess lived with Philby in Washington and it did not take too long to suspect that Philby was not only the traitor in their midst, but certainly the person who tipped his friends off.

Philby's prayers were answered when, on June 5, 1951, the head of British intelligence wrote to Philby telling him that his special emissary, John Drew, would be arriving in Washington the following day with orders that he return home. In England, he was confronted by accusations made by another defector named Ismail Akhmedov-Ege, a Turk who had been a colonel in the KGB. Akhmedov-Ege was now working for the CIA, and he told them that Philby was a Russian mole. After a long investigation during which Philby denied he was a Russian agent, he decided to retire from government service. He denied any relationship with either Burgess or MacLean (a lie), and his story was believed by many top men in the British government.

However, the reaction was different in Washington as the CIA and the FBI began their own investigations into the possible intelligence blunders that Philby might have caused them. Shortly after Philby's recall to London, Walter Bedell Smith, the CIA Director, ordered both Angleton and William Harvey to initiate inquiries into the possibility that Philby was a Russian spy.

Both men studied the same evidence but came up with two very different conclusions. Harvey's five-page report detailed Philby's relations with both Burgess and MacLean and ended by saying that Philby was a Soviet spy. In Angleton's four-page narrative, which was not as detailed as Harvey's, he concluded that his old friend was not a Soviet agent. Claire Petty, a high-ranking CIA officer said of both reports that Harvey's document was "lucid and full of hard facts indicating that Philby was a Soviet spy," but that Angleton's report was "fuzzy, strange and irrelevant from an intelligence point of view."

Angleton went on to say that Philby was being duped by Guy Burgess and that Burgess was acting on his own as a Soviet spy. Angleton further told DCI Smith that he should not accuse Philby of working for the Russians.

The Philby affair had now pitted the CIA and the British SIS in direct opposition to each other. If Philby had planned all along to drive a wedge between the two services, it worked out perfectly.

The Philby affair had a profound effect on James Angleton and how he would view other defectors who came calling in the years ahead. Angleton had a deep and profound affection for Philby, a man he called a friend. He now had to face the irrefutable fact that the man whom he gave the deepest secrets of the West to was indeed a Russian mole. Philby's treachery left a personal mark on Angleton's psyche; he felt bitterly deceived that he had gone out on a very long limb for him, and did not want to accept the fact that he had been duped.

After Philby's defection in July 1963, the CIA's counterintelligence staff wrote a detailed report on the entire Philby affair. A person with knowledge of the study said, "The report is conspicuous for its incompleteness and sheer ineptness. It told us nothing. It read like something written by a six-year-old, especially when compared to the quality of the report on Philby sent us by the Brits. Frankly, it read like an attempt by someone to turn the spotlight away from Philby."

Philby's treason was a body blow to Angleton in every respect. Every decision he made regarding the Russians and their spy war against the United States was made with Philby at the back of his mind. Biographer Michael Holzman wrote, "The revelation that his British friend Kim Philby actually worked for Moscow would propel Angleton in the sixties from garden-variety suspicion of the Soviet's to a state that some in the CIA have compared to clinical paranoia. That was a shattering experience for Angleton. [CIA psychiatrist John] Gittinger recalled. From that period on he was the most suspicious man in the agency. My own feeling is the emotional wreckage of that close friendship made him mistrust everybody and colored his life from that point on."[1]

Walter Elder, an assistant to DCI John McCone summed up how the Philby affair affected Angleton's long term thinking about Russian defectors: "Long after Philby's defection in 1963, Jim just continued to think that Philby was a key actor in the KGB grand plan. Philby remained very prominent in Jim's philosophy about how the KGB orchestrated the 'master plan' scenario. To Jim, Philby was never just a drunken, burned-out-ex spy. He was the leader of the orchestra."

However improbable, Philby's career in British intelligence was not over. In 1955, British Prime Minister Harold Macmillian defended Philby in Parliament. In the summer of 1956, he was sent to the Middle East by the SIS under journalistic cover. He moved to Beirut, Lebanon where he spied for the British in that city. While in Beirut, he was finally unmasked by the Station Chief and before he could be arrested, fled to Moscow in January 1963. While in Moscow, he wrote his memoirs called *My Secret War* (1968), was still tailed by his erstwhile partners, and died in 1988, never truly appreciated by the nation he strived so hard to serve.

---

[1] Holzman, Michael, *James Jesus Angleton: The CIA, & The Craft of Counterintelligence*. University of Massachusetts Press, Amherst, 2008, Page. 206.

Chapter 7:
"Operation Valuable"
Self Destructs in Albania

One of the Truman administration's first major covert operations against the Soviet Union took place in Albania in the late 1940s. This joint British-American operation was designed to overthrow the communist government of Enver Hoxha and install an Allied-led government in its place. If there was one strategic objective for "Operation Valuable" it was to prevent Soviet access to the warm water ports on the Adriatic coast, which was vital in controlling the central Mediterranean and its important water routes. The plan was to use internal opposition groups inside Albania, with US-British aid, to overthrow the Hoxha regime. Hoxha was a wartime resistance leader in Albania who took that nation into the Russian orbit after the war ended. The mission was doomed from the start with a top undercover Soviet mole, Kim Philby, passing the plans for the operation directly to the Soviet Union.

During World War II, King Zog of Albania fled his country to escape the dictatorship of Benito Mussolini who virtually took over that nation and brought it into the Axis alliance. Zog spent the war in England, hoping to make a return to a free Albania after the conflict was over. However, once the war ended, Albania came under the brutal domination of Enver Hoxha and his communist government. The British in particular saw in Albania a chance to foment a local revolution that just might overthrow the Hoxha regime and install a pro-democratic administration. To that end, they contacted the American government to discuss possible covert plans to destabilize the governing authority.

As the new Cold War began to heat up in earnest in the late 1940s, it was decided by the Truman administration that a new group was needed to take a tough line against the Soviet Union, checking their worldwide aims. This decision by the President and his intelligence advisors was the beginning of an active, covert program of hit and run raids, the fomenting of revolutions in Soviet dominated areas, and the linking up with anti-Soviet independent groups in areas controlled by Stalin. The name given to this department was the OPC or the Office of Policy Coordination.

The man who brought forth the OPC was a major State Department official named George Kennan. Kennan was an expert on Russia and his views went a long way in the making of U.S. foreign policy vis a vis the Kremlin. Kennan persuaded the president that the United States had to take a much tougher attitude toward the Soviets in world affairs, even going so far as to provide clandestine aid (military or otherwise) to anti-Russian resistance groups in Eastern Europe.

Kennan's proposal was sent up to the members of the National Security Council who, in May 1948, gave their OK for this new venture. The formal agreement to go ahead with this brand new type of covert warfare against the Soviet Union came under the finding called NSC 10/2. Its mandate cited the "vicious covert activities of the USSR, its satellite countries and communist groups to discredit the aims of the U.S. and other Western powers." The new group tasked with taking on the Soviet Union was originally dubbed the Office of Special Projects, but was soon renamed the Office of Policy Coordination. Its original job was to use covert means of confronting the Soviet Union across the globe with one caveat: The missions should be "so planned and conducted that any U.S. government responsibility for them is not evident to unauthorized persons and that if uncovered the U.S. government can plausibly disclaim any responsibility for them." So began the concept of "Plausible Deniability" that would be used so prevalently by the CIA in the decades to come.

The man put in charge of the OPC was Frank Wisner. He joined the Navy in World War II and was subsequently transferred to the OSS where he served in the Soviet Intelligence Branch (SI). After the war, he entered the State Department as an assistant secretary in charge of policy toward the occupied countries. Wisner and his OPC had powerful backers in the government such as Allen Dulles (later to become Director of the CIA under President Eisenhower), General Lucius Clay (who would later become the High Commissioner for Germany), and Navy Secretary James Forrestal. Wisner decided to remake the OPC into a covert fighting force based on the OSS. He derided prior CIA policy toward the Soviet Union, calling it at one point, " a bunch of old washerwomen exchanging gossip while they rinse through the dirty linen."

Wisner's OPC sought help from whatever quarter was available. In an unprecedented move, Wisner made an unholy alliance with one of the top Nazi generals during the war, Reinhard Gehlen. Gehlen was head of the eastern military intelligence section of the German army's high command. He was a fountain of information on Soviet order of battle and was a walking encyclopedia on the disposition and strength of Soviet forces. Before the surrender of Germany, Gehlen made copies of his most important intelligence files and buried them in a safe place. In May 1945, Gehlen surrendered to the occupying American forces and he was quickly put under arrest. He was brought to the Untied States and agreed to share all his intelligence files with the U.S. One of the beneficiaries of Gehlen's records was Frank Wisner's OPC.

In 1947, the first, limited effort to topple the Albanian government was taken by the British without any luck. A small number of men were covertly sent to Albania but nothing significant came out of it. In the wake of this failure, the British contacted the Americans and proposed a far greater, joint effort. To their relief, the Truman administration agreed to their covert campaign.

Joint planning for "Operation Valuable" began in earnest in 1949. The American side of the operation was run by Wisner's OPC, which was the covert end of the newly-created CIA. The British were represented in planning the mission by George Jellico, recently of the elite Special Air Services. The other member of the British delegation was Harold "Kim" Philby. Unknown to the men on the panel, Philby was working for the Russian's as a spy and had been doing so since the war. It was Philby who ultimately betrayed the operation, leading to the deaths of many allied agents. The American delegation consisted of Robert Joyce, who had foreign policy experience, and Frank Lindsay, a veteran of the OSS. The technical name of this allied group was the Anglo-American Policy Committee.

Recruits for the operation were picked from the Albanian refugee camps in Italy, Egypt and other places in Europe where men loyal to King Zog could be found. The CIA and the British

SIS ran the operation behind the scenes, paying the men and giving them training in the covert arts. Their instruction in paramilitary activities took place in such locations as Cyprus and Malta. The CIA officer assigned to oversee American interests in the Albanian operation was Michael Burke. Burke served in the wartime OSS and would, many years later, become president of the New York Yankees baseball team.

The most important of the Albanian opposition groups enlisted in Operation Valuable was the Balli Kombetar, or "National Front." This group was located in Rome and Athens. Many of its leaders had been collaborators with the Germans in World War II, but were now enlisted in the secret war against the Soviets.

Important meetings on Operation Valuable took place in Washington, D.C. in September 1949. One of the participants on the British side was foreign secretary Ernest Bevin. A CIA report that was written during that time period said, "a purely internal Albanian uprising at this time is not indicated, and if undertaken, would have little chance of success." The report ended by saying, "the possibility of foreign intervention, in conjunction with widespread popular unrest and anti-government hostility represents a serious threat to the regime."

During their discussions on the Albanian operation, Ernest Bevin asked Secretary of State Dean Acheson if he agreed thata the United States would be successful in the overthrow of the Hoxha regime. Acheson agreed, and further commented by saying, "Are there any kings around that could be put in?"[1]

Landings of a team of allied agents in Albania took place in the spring of 1950. Subsequent drops of agents followed in the months to come. While the unsuspecting allied soldiers were being parachuted into Albania, Kim Philby was keeping Moscow abreast of every detail of the missions. Upon landing, these unlucky men were immediately captured and underwent tireless interrogation. In time, a few of these men were able to make their way back to allied lines, and reported the blown operations.

During the next two years, further drops of agents into Albania continued but with the same lack of success. It was now obvious in allied intelligence circles that something or someone was betraying

[1] Prados, John, *Presidents' Secret Wars,* Ivan Dee Publishers, Chicago, Illinois, 1996, Page 49.

the airdrops. Due to the lack of any progress in wreaking havoc inside Albania, the operation was ended in 1952.

In the 1960s, the editor of the *London Sunday Times,* Harold Evans, wrote:

> The enterprise was doomed, because at the center of the campaign against Albania, sitting in Washington on the Anglo-American Special Policy Committee, was Kim Philby. We pieced together the story of the Albanian expedition, which had lain secret for seventeen years, by finding survivors: at least 300 men lost their lives.. The first big "drops" of men who would lead the revolution were infiltrated into Albania by sea and air in spring 1950.

"They always knew we were coming," one of the few who lived told the *Sunday Times* researcher. The infiltrators were shot, and the local people who helped them were forcibly resettled in another area."[2]

The Albanian operation was a total failure. However, that did not stop the CIA from making further plans in its covert war against the Soviet Union. Soon, other schemes would come off the drawing board, this time, with better results.

---

[2] Ranelagh, John, *The Agency: The Rise and Decline of the CIA from Wild Bill Donovan to William Casey,* Simon & Schuster, New York, 1986, Page 156.

Chapter 8:
The Berlin Operating Base

On May 2, 1945, what was left of the German armies surrendered, and VE Day was at hand. One week later, on May 8-9, 1945, the official surrender of Germany to the Allies took place and the war in Europe had finally come to an end. Berlin, the once beautiful capital city of Germany lay in ruins, with the four victorious powers, the United States, France, Great Britain and the Soviet Union, carving up their own separate zones of influence in that now divided city. A part of those zones of influence covered intelligence operations against the Soviet Union on the part of the allies, especially the United States.

During the war, the OSS and the Russian intelligence service, the NKVD, grudgingly shared secrets, in spite of the opposition from Bill Donovan. That cooperation suddenly ended when the war was over and it was evident that the Soviet Union now posed a national threat to the United States.

The United States and the other Allies were finally allowed into Soviet occupied Berlin on July 4, 1945 and began setting up their own headquarters. The U.S. section was adjacent to the British zone of control, in the area of Berlin known as Zehlendorf. It was from a sprawling residence there that the CIA, using the cover of the BOB (Berlin Operating Base) set up shop. BOB headquarters was a three-story residence in the suburb of Dahlem and it was once owned by German General Ludwig von Beck, who was executed by the German government in 1944 for his involvement in a plot led by many German generals to overthrow Hitler.

This location had upper and lower floors where new recruits were able to spread out and begin business. Allen Dulles selected the residence but did not spend much time there. He soon left, and control over BOB's intelligence functions was transferred to the War Department and its section, the SSU (the Strategic Services Unit).

Berlin itself was the main target for Soviet intelligence

53

operations. The Soviet Union reigned with an iron fist in its zone of influence, targeting the United States in particular, and mounting a large-scale intelligence gathering operation that included informers, double agents and others of influence in the city.

The city of Berlin was in a very dangerous situation, both politically and militarily by the time the CIA set up BOB as its intelligence headquarters. The city was ringed by 20 divisions of Russian troops not very far away. The Soviet sector was a virtual prison, where the local population was cut off from their relatives only a few miles away. Dissent was dealt with harshly and the people lived without any democratic rights. Berlin was less than 50 miles from Soviet-occupied Poland and any subversive activities by the locals could be crushed in a short period of time. Berlin was at the epicenter of the Cold War, with the Russians having detonated their own atomic bomb, and the communist takeover of China. In June 1950, North Korea attacked South Korea, setting the United States and the Soviet Union on a collision course. Any sudden move on either side might lead to war, with Berlin caught in the crossfire.

Soon, Dulles was replaced by Richard Helms (later to become the Director of Central Intelligence). Helms quickly reorganized BOB with the help of Captain Peter Sichel who ran the intelligence division. Sichel brought in two major units of intelligence: secret intelligence and X-2 (counterintelligence). If anyone was going to counter the Soviets at their own game in Berlin, it would be these two divisions.

At the end of 1945, Helms was reassigned and was replaced by Dana Durand. Durand's main achievement was making the BOB base into a first-class intelligence gathering entity that was at the front lines of the Cold War for years to come.

As the BOB operation took roots, they expanded into fields other than the usual acquiring of military intelligence. BOB agents concentrated for some time on the economic goings on in the vast, Soviet sector of the city. They were able to monitor the shipments of raw materials to various government entities, track the food supply to the troops, gauge the economic capacity of various German businesses, as well as the usual trade craft of bringing on informers and double agents who sympathized with the United States.

Through the use of informers and other covert moves, BOB was able to penetrate the headquarters of Soviet intelligence in Berlin that was located at Karlshorst. In a major coup they were able to read the internal recordings of meetings dealing with the shipment of industrial goods, as well as heavy equipment, in the Soviet zone. BOB's men also picked up important news on the relationship between the Soviets and their puppet government in Berlin.

One of BOB's most important successes was the tracking of the development of the Russian atomic bomb in the late 1940s. It was reported back to Washington that the Soviets were in the process of mining uranium ore, a vital part in the construction of an atomic bomb. They also learned that a number of forced laborers were being used in this area. BOB learned that a company called Wismut was providing the processing for the Russian bomb. BOB used its undercover agents located in a Berlin factory which was operated by I.G. Farben to track the shipments of the necessary parts of the bomb to their ultimate destinations in Russia. The CIA Berlin base used a Russian defector known only as "Icarus" who provided them with detailed information on the technology transfers inside Wismut. Over time though, "Icarus" went back to the Soviet side of the border where he was shot.

In January 1953, BOB was to face a shake-up at its highest order when William Harvey, a tough, ex-FBI agent who now worked for the CIA was made its new station chief. Harvey's ascension to the top of the pecking order in Berlin would remake the base at the CIA's number one espionage operation during the Cold War. William Harvey would make a huge impression not only on the men at the CIA, but in the corridors of official Washington for years to come.

William Harvey was the most famous "defector" from the FBI to the CIA. In time, his critics and supporters alike would call him "America's James Bond." Harvey was a hard-drinking man who often carried a pistol on his person, putting it on the table when he had visitors in order to intimidate them.

Harvey went to Indiana University Law School, went into local politics in Indianapolis, and was an attorney in Kentucky before joining the FBI in December 1940. During World War II, Harvey worked out of the New York office and was intimately involved in counterespionage operations. He worked on the case of German double agent William Sebold, who was turned by the FBI into ratting on his extensive network of Nazi agents in New York. Harvey was later transferred to FBI headquarters where he worked on Soviet counterespionage cases, including the most famous case of Elizabeth Bentley who turned in a large number of Russian spies (whom she ran) to the FBI.

Soon though, Harvey grew frustrated with Hoover's lack of interest in counterespionage cases, and on a summer day in July 1947, he made the hardest decision of his life; he quit the FBI and joined the rival CIA. One former FBI agent said of Harvey's decision to leave the Bureau, "To Hoover, going from the Bureau to the CIA was almost as bad as going over to the Soviets. Harvey was definitely on Hoover's list."

For Bill Harvey and BOB, their most important flashpoint came in the spring of 1953 when the regime of Erich Honecker, the leader of East Berlin, increased work quotas by 10 percent. In April 1953 food prices increased, causing mass demonstrations in the streets. On June 15, fifty thousand workers started a riot in the streets of East Berlin. They vented their anger at government buildings and attacked the feared German police called the Vopos. In Moscow, the Russian government saw the riots as a potential pivotal point in their control over East Berlin and prepared for the worst.

On June 16, a widespread strike began in East Berlin. The government was so scared that the rioters might succeed that they began destroying classified documents.

BOB had no idea what was really going on as they could not get any agents into the eastern zone which was now getting totally out of hand. In order to quench the revolt, the Russians sent T-34 tanks into the city along with two armored divisions. BOB officers sent urgent cables to Washington telling them what little they knew of the rapidly unfolding situation. Only one BOB officer, Deputy Chief of Base Henry Hecksher, cabled Washington asking that the United States arm the strikers. Hecksher waited for a reply from Allen Dulles but Dulles was traveling and did not respond.

Bill Harvey now gave his OK for an urgent message to be sent to CIA HQ asking permission to give stun guns, rifles, and grenades to the striking workers. He even suggested that the United States "mobilize" the Sixth Infantry Regiment, a small force then located in West Berlin. His boss in Washington, John Bross, turned him down.

"When Washington flatly rejected his plan, Harvey privately loosed limitless contempt for the pussyfooting Cold Warriors in Washington, who talked big but chilled when the chips were down, and for the brothers, Allen Welch and John Foster Dulles." After the strikes ended, it was reported that Harvey was given an unofficial reprimand from either Allen Dulles or Frank Wisner.[1]

After Bill Harvey left BOB, he was succeeded by David Murphy, Ted Shackley, Bill Graver, and Herb Natzke. In later years, William Harvey would run the CIA's super-secret Staff D, and later, the Executive Action department which tasked the CIA with the role of assassinating foreign leaders, including Fidel Castro and Patrice Lumumba. Ted Shackley would also run anti-Cuban operations and was put in charge of the CIA's most extensive, covert base in Miami called JMWAVE.

The U.S. Army played a large part in the BOB operation by 1946, providing them with logistical support, as well as transportation facilities in Berlin. BOB worked directly under the Theater G-2 (intelligence) group under the command of General Edwin Sibert. In time, BOB was to become the largest intelligence agency in Europe and was instrumental in keeping Washington abreast of the situation during the Berlin blockade.

The BOB operation was instrumental in keeping the CIA aware of all Soviet moves in the highly charged atmosphere that was Berlin in the infancy of the Cold War.

---

[1] Stockton, Bayard. *Flawed Patriot: The Rise and Fall of CIA Legend Bill Harvey,* Potomac Books, Washington, D.C., 2006, Page.47.

Chapter 9:
Project HT/LINGUAL

As this chapter is being written, there is a huge controversy concerning one of the nation's most secretive intelligence gathering organizations, the National Security Agency and its vast, covert programs of reading and collecting e-mails of American citizens and photographing the front of letters being sent via the post office, all in the name of preventing another 9-11. The man behind the leaking of the NSA program was a high school dropout, a man who was then (somehow) hired by the CIA, Edward Snowden. When Snowden leaked the secret NSA plan, he was working for a private security company in Hawaii. However, this was not the first time in our history that the CIA initiated a secret plan to eavesdrop on unsuspecting American citizens. The project was called HT/LINGUAL, and it was run by both the FBI and the CIA from 1940 to 1973.

Project HT/LINGUAL was a patently illegal mail opening operation based in the United States in direct violation of the Fourth Amendment to the United States Constitution which prohibits unwarranted searches and seizures of Americans and their property. From 1940 to 1973, the two agencies opened mail—mostly from people coming from and going to Russia. In the beginning, the operation, codenamed HT/LINGUAL, was run by the CIA. As the program took shape, the CIA informed the FBI of its operation. The FBI got into the act, calling its own project the Hunter Project. In a sleight of hand, J. Edgar Hoover refrained from informing the CIA that they too were conducting their own mail opening plan until well into operation.

In later years, as the files concerning the HT/LINGUAL program were released, the American public became aware that the mail from a then-unknown former Marine who defected the Soviet Union. Lee Harvey Oswald was being read.

The CIA project began as a sensitive mail intercept program started by the CIA's Office of Security in 1952 in response to requests from the Soviet Russia Division. In 1955, HT/LINGUAL was transferred to Jim Angleton's CI (Counterintelligence Staff). Its original purpose was to obtain the names and addresses of mail going to and coming from the USSR. HT/LINGUAL's operation was a well-kept secret within the CIA known only to a few select people like the DCI (Director of Central Intelligence), the DDP (Deputy Director, Plans), and the DDS (Deputy Director, Security).

Throughout its tenure, a total of twelve mail opening programs, ranging in length from three weeks to 26 years, took place. In one program, a total of 215,000 letters were opened, read, catalogued, and put back in the U.S. mail system. The results of this program were disseminated to the President, as well as the Attorney General, and members of the various U.S. intelligence agencies.

The objective of the CIA was to collect and evaluate foreign intelligence and counterintelligence information. The FBI's target was the collection of counterespionage information. Since the CIA's operation had a domestic component, the FBI, if it chose to, could have blown the program sky high. However, J. Edgar Hoover decided that it was in his best interest to collect whatever information the agency cared to share with him, and still have bribery powers over them if needed.

The historical record of the mail opening operation showed limited success indeed. Only one CIA project and three FBI programs ever produced valuable intelligence. While the initial focus of the program dealt with collecting information during the Cold War years, by the 1960s and the 1970s, it had mushroomed into an illegal surveillance operation of ordinary Americans, including politicians, movie stars, and Vietnam War detractors.

HT/LINGUAL had its genesis in World War 11 when the Untied States and Great Britain shared intelligence on Nazi spies from England's listening post on Bermuda. The Bermuda listening station intercepted mail and radio messages coming from Europe to the Americas and this information was shared with Bill Donovan's OSS. This operation was ended after the war, but was resurrected in the early 1950s.

The CIA set up its secret mail opening center at Federal Building No. 111 (also called the Jamaica Airmail Facility) near the old Idlewild Airport (now JFK) in New York. A six-man team of expert CIA linguists would pour over that night's take, unsealing envelopes and looking for any information from Russia that might be of value. The CIA's Technical Services Division trained these men in the latest techniques of mail opening and closing. Steam would be used to open and then close letters so as not to alert the ultimate recipient.

Besides its New York office, the CIA opened a second branch in New Orleans so as to intercept mail coming from Latin and Central America.

With relations between the CIA and the FBI at loggerheads, Jim Angleton made a conscious decision not to inform Hoover of HT/LINGUAL. His decision was put in jeopardy when in January 1958, U.S. Postal Inspector Stephens told Angleton that the FBI wanted to start its own mail intercept operation.

When the U.S. Congress conducted a study on illegal domestic operations by the CIA, one of the areas of their study was the domestic mail opening program. Their inspection found evidence that the U.S. Post Office, which gave its approval for the use of its facilities for this illegal operation, was duped as to the true nature of what was going on at that time. "The postal officials," said the Select Committee to Study Governmental Operations (1976), "whose cooperation was necessary to implement these programs were purposefully not informed of the true nature of the program, in some cases, it appears that they were deliberately misled. Congressional inquiry was perceived by both the CIA and FBI officials as a threat to the security of their program; during one period of active investigation both agencies contemplated security measures to mislead the investigation and protect their programs against disclosure to Congress. *Only in rare cases did the CIA FBI even inform one another about their programs* [italics by author]."

Jim Angleton reluctantly informed Sam Papich, the FBI liaison, of the existence of the mail intercept program. Hoover feigned abhorrence in being told of HT/LINGUAL but used the CIA's work for his own purposes. The FBI was now able to use the information provided to them by the CIA, especially when it came to their investigation of internal security matters, as well as the identities of illegal agents working inside the United States. As far as Hoover was concerned, the CIA could do the dirty work for him and he would reap the rewards.

With the FBI now on board, they named their own program the Hunter Project. Between 1959 and 1966, the FBI operated no fewer than six programs in eight cities in the United States. The Hunter Project lasted until 1966 when J. Edgar Hoover, seeing the futility of continuing the operation, shut it down.

The FBI's Domestic Intelligence Division had the job of evaluating the mail provided to them by the CIA and over the years it is estimated that the Bureau read 57,000 pieces of information. The material gleaned from the CIA, however, was not up to snuff, and the Bureau got little reward for all its work. The organizations shared technical data, including the use by the FBI of the CIA's New York laboratory.

It wasn't until 1973 that Project HT/LINGUAL was shut down due to the changing political climate in the United States.

In later years, Richard Helms (later to become DCI) and J. Edgar Hoover gave differing interpretations on the mail opening programs they ran. In a terse statement on the matter, Helms said, "Who would have thought that it would someday be judged a crime to carry out the orders of the President of the United States?"

Documents from the Church Committee show just how sensitively the HT/LINGUAL program was viewed at the CIA:

> On the question of continuance, the DDP stated that he is seriously concerned, for any flap would cause the worst possible publicity and embarrassment. He opined that the operation should be done by the FBI because they could better withstand such publicity. Inasmuch as it is a type of domestic surveillance. The D/S stated that he thought the operation served mainly an FBI requirement. The C/CI countered that the Bureau would not take over the operation now, and could not serve essential CIA requirements as we have served theirs; that, moreover, CI Staff sees the operation (blank) foreign surveillance.[1]

Hoover gave his own take on the Hunter Project: "For years and years I have approved opening mail and other similar operations,

[1] Church Committee: Volume 4—Hearing on Mail Opening, May 19, 1971.

but no longer. It is becoming more and more dangerous and we are apt to be caught. I am not opposed to doing this. I'm not opposed to continuing the burglaries, and the opening of mail and other similar activities, providing someone higher than myself approves of it. But I'm not going to accept the responsibility myself anymore, even though I've done it for many years."

Hoover made these remarks during the height of the Watergate affair. He stopped these illegal activities not because he wanted to, but did so in order not to get caught.

Project HT/LINGUAL also sheds light on the activities of the alleged assassin of President John F. Kennedy, Lee Harvey Oswald. On November 9, 1959, the CIA put Oswald on its "Watch List," thus allowing Oswald's mail to be opened via HT/LINGUAL. A person was put on the CIA's "Watch List" for the following reason:

> Individuals or organizations of particular intelligence interest were specified in Watch Lists provided to the mail project by the Counterintelligence Staff, by other CIA components, and the FBI. The total numbers of names on the Watch List varied from time to time, but on the average, the list included approximately 300 names including about 100 furnished by the FBI. The Watch List included the names of foreigners and of United States citizens.[2]

The Warren Commission was never informed of the HT/LINGUAL operation or of Oswald's name being put on it. When the Church Committee was investigating the Kennedy assassination, they asked the CIA for information on why Oswald was placed on the Watch List. They responded by saying he was placed on the List because he was a recent defector to the Soviet Union. One of the reasons Oswald was put on the Watch List was because the CIA opened a letter written to Oswald by his mother Marguerite while he was in the Soviet Union. For some reason, the CIA deleted Oswald's name from the Watch List on March 15, 1960; he was put back on the list on August 7, 1961 by CIA employee Ann Egerter. Why? Possibly because the Soviet Realities Branch Chief of the CIA was investigating the possibilities of Russian women coming

---

[2] Newman, John. *Oswald and the CIA,* Carroll & Graf Publishers, New York, 1995, Page.54.

to the States through marriage to Americans and then working for the KGB in the United States.

One unnamed CIA officer who was privy to Oswald's information on the Watch List said on November 25, 1963, three days after the assassination, "this individual looks odd."

The HT/LINGUAL program also uncovered information on Oswald's use of his nickname "Alik," which was similar to his other nickname "Alex Hidell." The CIA's Counterintelligence Chief James Angleton wrote the following memo to J. Edgar Hoover relating to this issue:

> Your representatives in Mexico advised our representative there that it had not been determined whether Hidell is a person, or an alias used by Oswald. In this connection we refer you to the attached HUNTER items-63 E 22U and 63 A 24 W. These items indicate that Oswald was known to his wife's friends as "Alik," (also spelled "Alick"). While we have no items in which the name Hidell (or Hydell) appears, it is believed that the fact Oswald was known to his Russian friends as "Alik" may be significant.[3]

The entire matter concerning the activities of Lee Harvey Oswald in the years and months prior to the President's assassination is rife for conjecture, but still leaves many unanswered questions about the CIA's interest in him.

The HT/LINGUAL program was just one more domestic power play between the FBI and the CIA, with each agency using the other for its own devious ends.

---

[3] Ibid. Page 286.

Chapter 10:
The Riddle of James Speyer Kronthal

If a screenwriter were writing a story about a CIA agent who died under mysterious circumstances it would probably go something like this. The man in question was a dedicated CIA officer, a man who had the trust and respect of the DCI (Director of Central Intelligence), Allen Dulles. The man was a veteran of the Cold War, having been the head of the CIA's Bern, Switzerland station. However, the person in question had a secret life, one that was not known to anyone else at CIA headquarters; he was a deep cover Russian mole. The day before his mysterious death, he had a hurried conversation at the home of Allen Dulles, although nothing of what occurred at the meeting was ever revealed.

Sounds like a script for a spy novel? No, it was a real incident and the person at the center of the mystery was a real CIA agent. His name was James Speyer Kronthal, whose story is one of the least reported events from the early days of the CIA.

James Speyer Kronthal was a brilliant and dedicated man who came from a well-to-do background. He graduated from Yale where he got at BA in 1934, and an MA from Harvard in 1941. He was fluent in German, French, and Italian.

After the United States entered World War 11, James Kronthal entered the OSS and was stationed in Bern, Switzerland where the Station Chief was none other than Allen Dulles. The Bern station was one of the most highly respected OSS stations during the war. Switzerland was a neutral nation where spies from all the warring powers took up shop. It was an open secret in Bern that Dulles was head of the OSS and he never took pains to hide his position. At the Bern station, Dulles met with any number of anti-Nazis who were covertly trying to overthrow Hitler and end the war. James Kronthal was one of Dulles's men and he proved to be just what his boss needed. He was someone to be trusted and Dulles treated him like a son.

On April 21, 1947, James Kronthal was appointed as Chief of the Bern Station, one of the most prestigious spots at the CIA (the other stations were in London, Paris, Cairo, Lisbon, and Shanghai).

The Russian intelligence agency, the NKVD, took immediate notice of Kronthal's appointment and tried to find out as much about him as possible. The NKVD at that time was headed by the ruthless Lavrenti Beria, a man who ruled with an iron fist. Beria tasked his men to look into Kronthal's background and see what kind of man the CIA had just hired. They soon learned that he was a good friend of Allen Dulles' and that made Kronthal a person of interest within the NKVD. NKVD operatives in its Washington, D.C. headquarters found out that the FBI was doing security checks on new OSS employees, making inquiries about them in the various U.S. government departments to see if there were any derogatory information on them.

The NKVD too did their own background check on James Speyer Kronthal and what they found was most intriguing. The young man got his middle name from a man named James Joseph Speyer, who ran Speyer and Company. It seems that James Joseph Speyer ran one of the most prestigious banking houses at that time. His company was founded in Germany in 1937 in Frankfurt am Main. At one time, the Speyer bank did business with the Tsar of Russia. By the 1930s, the company had its headquarters in Boston and was on par with other huge banks like Morgan, Kuhn and Loeb.

James Kronthal's parents were very friendly with Joseph Speyer and made their son his namesake. Joseph Speyer took an avid interest in the education of James, and he did all he could to aid his friend's son in the business world. After graduation from college in 1934, James Kronthal joined the firm of his old mentor, James Joseph Speyer.

One of James' first assignments was to travel to Germany where he used his business connections to sell the artworks that the Nazis had looted from the Jewish population from 1933 to 1940. While on his various European trips, he met with some of the rising Nazi leaders like Herman Goering, Heinrich Himmler, and Joseph Goebbels.

It was during this time period that James Kronthal realized he was interested in young boys, and on one trip to Germany he was caught by the authorities in a compromising situation. When Goering found out about what the young man had done, he pulled strings to get it released. With that incident, the Russians had blackmail on Kronthal.

When World War II began, Kronthal enlisted in the Signal Corps, and in 1944 he was posted to the OSS. After the war ended, Kronthal scoured Europe on behalf of the OSS (and Dulles) to recover the works of art stolen from the Jews by the Nazis (irony?). In 1947, he was appointed to be the head of the CIA's Bern station. The Russians now had a high-ranking CIA officer at their disposal, if and when needed. Blackmail was an option the Russians would use in the Kronthal case and they kept their options open.

Unknown to Kronthal, his secret trysts with young boys were being filmed by the Russians and they now had the goods on him. He was approached by NKVD agents who blackmailed him into giving them information from the Bern station.

When he returned to the United States in May 1952, the Russians pressed him for information on any changes at the top job at CIA HQ that the new president, Dwight Eisenhower, might make. He didn't have access to that type of intelligence and his Russian masters were becoming exasperated with his low-level intelligence take.

On the evening of March 31, 1953, Allen Dulles invited his old friend James Kronthal to his Washington home to discuss his next assignment for the CIA, rumored to be pretty high level. It was a dinner between friends and history does not have any report of what actually took place that fateful night between the two men. After the dinner was over, Kronthal went back to his Georgetown home which was located at 1662 32nd Street N.W. He then wrote letters to Allen Dulles and Richard Helms. He also wrote a note to his housekeeper informing her that he'd returned home late and was not to be disturbed in the morning.

Early the next day, April 1, 1953, Mrs. Lavinia Thomas, Kronthal's housekeeper, received a call from someone from her employer's office. The man wanted to know if he could talk to Kronthal but she said that he was sleeping and couldn't be disturbed. A few hours later, two men from the CIA's Office of Security, Gould Cassal and McGregor Gray, knocked at the door of the Kronthal residence. Mrs. Thomas answered the door and the two men demanded that she wake her boss; they had urgent information for him. Mrs. Thomas opened the door and they saw the body of James Kronthal lying fully clothed on the bed, a vial of some sort of liquid on the night stand. There were no signs of any struggle and the two CIA officers, as per procedure, called their contact in the Washington, D.C. police department, Lt. Lawrence Hartnett, to dispose of the body.

Lt. Hartnett told the local press that the police found a note by his bed saying that he was "mentally upset because of pressure connected with work." The letters addressed to Dulles and Helms were put in the mail and sent on their way.[1]

CIA analysts said that he died around midnight but did not find the cause of his death; it was ruled an "apparent suicide."

The death of James Speyer Kronthal remains one of the CIA's most enduring mysteries. Like the plot of a good spy novel, the reasons for his demise raise many questions. Did the NKVD, realizing that Kronthal was no longer needed as an intelligence asset, kill him? But what of the rumored promotion in the CIA? What happened the previous night at the home of Allen Dulles? Did James Kronthal confess to Dulles that he was a homosexual who was being blackmailed by the Russians? The only way we'll know what really happened is if the CIA releases their internal files on the Kronthal case. But don't hold your breath.

---

[1] Corson, William, Trento, Susan, and Trento, Joseph, *Widows,* Crown Publishers, New York, 1989. Page 14.

Chapter 11:
CAT: The CIA's Secret Airline

Civil Air Transport (CAT) was a covert airline that was used by the CIA during the Cold War, beginning in 1949 and ending in 1975. The men involved in Civil Air Transport (later to be changed to Air America) saw action including troop and ammunition drops in China right after World War II, well into the war in Vietnam and Laos in the 1960s and 1970s.

In technical terms, CAT/Air America was called in intelligence parlance a "Proprietary Company." These Proprietary Companies have been used by the United States for secret intelligence gathering purposes since the American Revolution. These secret companies were operated by the CIA's Clandestine Service whose main job was facilitating covert operations across the globe. Many of these companies were wholly or partially owned and operated by the CIA.

Claire Chennault was the man most responsible for the formation of CAT. He was born in Commerce, Texas on September 6, 1893. After college, he joined the United States Army in World War 1 and was assigned to the Army Air Corps. After the war ended, he trained pilots at Maxwell Field in Alabama. In 1937 he left the Army and moved to China. He formed his own flying school and trained Chinese airmen, along with being an "air advisor" to the Kuomintang leader Chiang Kai-shek.

The history of how CAT was formed is a murky one. In October 1940, President Franklin Roosevelt asked his advisor Tommy Corcoran to go on a special mission for him. FDR realized that the best way to stop Japanese aggression in the Far East was to arm the government of Chiang Kai-shek. This idea was anathema to the U.S. Congress which did not want any American intervention in a foreign conflict. Corcoran's job was to establish a private entity that would provide arms and equipment to the Nationalists. FDR gave a name to this company: China Defense Supplies. After meeting with Chennault, Corcoran returned to the U.S. and told FDR that Chennault said that if he could get the proper supplies, he'd take

69

the war to the Japanese. Soon, one hundred P-40 fighters were sent to Chennault at his Chinese headquarters and his team, called the American Volunteer Group, was dubbed the Flying Tigers.[1]

Under FDR's direction, men from the various U.S. military services soon joined the Flying Tigers. The pilots of the Flying Tigers harassed the Japanese in the jungles of Burma, cutting off a vital supply road to the Japanese attackers. They also ferried arms and ammunition across the mountains of Burma and India. They destroyed 296 planes and lost 24 men. When word of the Flying Tigers mission went public, there was an immediate outcry from a number of top military men, including General George Marshall and General Joseph Stillwell, who was the American commander in Asia. They complained that Chiang Kai-shek was running a corrupt government and that all further aid to him should be cut off.

In April 1942, Chennault was recalled to the United States and took up duty with the Army as a Brigadier General.

In the 1940s and 1950s, CAT pilots flew missions in support of the Nationalist Chinese and saw action during the Korean War. With the defeat of the Chinese Nationalist forces in 1949, CAT pilots were responsible for evacuating thousands of fleeing Chinese troops to the island of Taiwan.

CAT got some help from an unusual source, Fiorella La Guardia (later to become Mayor of New York City). La Guardia was a friend of Tommy Corcoran, and was serving as the Director General of the United Nations Relief and Rehabilitation Administration. He gave $4 million to deliver relief supplies to China, however, after one year, CAT had trouble delivering the assistance and the contract ended.

In 1950, CAT was bought by the United States and it soon took on a twofold mission. CAT pilots flew regularly-scheduled air routes carrying paying passengers to various spots around Southeast Asia. In order to hide the ownership of CAT, the airline was purchased by the CIA through a number of dummy corporations. In time, CAT became a subsidiary of the Airdale Corporation, which was a Delaware holding company whose directors were all affiliated with the CIA. While this was going on, secret operations were also being conducted by the CIA in Southeast Asia. As the Cold War heated

---

1   "Claire Lee Chennault," *Spartacus Educational.*

up, CAT grew increasingly close to the American military, and had a covert relationship with the Air Force. CAT was also responsible for dropping supplies to the beleaguered French troops in their desperate battle at Dien Bien Phu.

CAT also took part in a failed rebellion in the nation of Indonesia that was run by the strongman President Sukarno. In 1958, the U.S. viewed the Sukarno regime as being in league with the Soviet Union in the Cold War and asked the CIA to try to aid the guerrillas in that nation in overthrowing the regime. The Eisenhower administration tasked the CIA's Clandestine Service under the direction of Desmond Fitzgerald (who later took part in the Castro plots) to aid the rebels in whatever way possible. The CIA gave the rebels some arms and ammunition, as well as a number of B-26 bombers via CAT. One of the pilots was Allen Pope, who was shot down near the town of Ambon in the Celebes after accidently bombing a church and killing many worshipers inside. The Indonesian rebellion was quickly put down and it was one of the few failures the CIA experienced during that time.

In 1959, CAT changed its name to Air America and took on a new assignment: aid the CIA in its secret war in both Vietnam and Laos. In Vietnam, Air America had to carry both men and equipment into the dense jungles to aid regular American "advisors" and loyal Laotian hill tribesmen who were working closely with the CIA against the communists. Air America also ran intelligence missions in the region, dropping off agents in isolated areas of Vietnam and Laos where they would gather intelligence on enemy activities.

Critics of Air America and the CIA during this time have accused the airline and its people of being part of the drug trade that was rampant throughout Southeast Asia. They say that Air America flyers carried illegal drugs from the opium fields of Burma and the Golden Triangle for resale in Vietnam and other parts of the region.

Air America's last official mission took place in 1975 when they participated in the evacuation of the last Americans from South Vietnam.

The exploits of Air America were introduced to a majority of the American people in a film by the same name starring Mel Gibson and Robert Downey Jr. (1980). Over the years, more than 200 brave men worked for Air America/CAT, flying both fixed wing aircraft and helicopters in Southeast Asia. Air America finally went out of business in 1981, bringing to an end one of the CIA's most successful, yet controversial, action arms.

Research Note: Research materials on the history of CAT/Air America are housed in a permanent compendium at the History of Aviation Collection at the University of Texas at Dallas and are open to the public.

Chapter 12:
Project Paperclip

Since its creation, the CIA has been accused of many violations of human rights, as well as conduct contrary to the normal means of statecraft. By far the most outrageous action taken by the wartime OSS and the CIA was called Project Paperclip. It involved the clandestine delivery of Nazi and Austrian scientists, many of them accused of war crimes, with the full knowledge and cooperation of the United States into this country in order to work on our rocket and missile systems. If this action was not bad enough, the military knowingly altered the files of many of these scientists to expunge their participation in atrocities on concentration camp inmates.

In the immediate days after the end of the war in Europe, U.S. and Russian troops began a systematic hunt for all manner of pillaged loot that had been stolen by the Nazis from their concentration camp victims. They were also looking for information on German progress on rockets and any weapons systems that they could get their hands on. But their most important finds were the large numbers of German scientists who had been caught up in the aftermath of the war and were now stateless persons. U.S. military intelligence knew the importance of gaining access to these scientists, before they could be plucked off by the pursing Russians and taken to labor camps in Siberia where they would never be heard from again.

U.S. authorities combed the POW camps in Europe and, little by little, rounded up the cream of the crop of German scientists and secretly brought them back to the United States. Once safely inside the United States, these former Nazi scientists were put to work developing the generation of rockets and missiles that the U.S. would use against the Soviet Union in the new Cold War. There was only one major problem with this secret deal; many of these same German scientists were formally accused of war crimes against the Jews and other inmates in the concentration camps of Europe. The reputations of these people were well known inside the OSS and the infant CIA. However, it was deemed more important to the national security of the country to ignore these wartime atrocities in the new fight against Russian communism.

Even before the advent of Project Paperclip, the Roosevelt administration knew of the scientific work that these men were doing for Hitler and their possible use after the war for the United States. Shortly before his death, President Roosevelt had turned down OSS Chief William Donovan's request that some of these German scientists be allowed to come to the U.S., including "permission for entry into the United States after the war, the placing of their earnings on deposit in an American bank and the like." FDR flatly turned down Donovan's request by saying:

> I do not believe that we should offer any guarantees of protection in the post-hostilities period to Germans who are working for your organization. I think that the carrying out of any such guarantees would be difficult and probably be widely misunderstood both in this country and abroad. We may expect that the number of Germans who are anxious to save their skins and property will rapidly increase. Among them may be some who should properly be tried for war crimes or at least arrested for active participation in Nazi activities. Even with the necessary controls you mention I am not prepared to authorize the giving of guarantees.[1]

FDR was adamant in his statement that we should have no business with any Nazi scientists who were associated in any way with death camp atrocities, but he did not live long enough to put those orders into practice.

The American team that began looking for German scientists who had any knowledge of their fledgling atomic bomb program was called "Alsos." These agents combed Europe looking for any German scientist who had worked on the bomb project. The leader of the Alsos team was Colonel Boris Pash. Aiding Pash on the Alsos team was a scientist named Samuel Goudsmit. When they arrived in Strasbourg, France, Goudsmit, after pouring over captured German atomic bomb records, realized that the United States was at least

[1] Hunt, Linda. *Secret Agenda: The United States Government and Project Paperclip 1945-1990,* St. Martin's Press, New York, 1991, Page 9-10.

two years ahead of their German counterparts. There were only two German scientists, Carl von Weizsacker and Werner Heisenberg, who had any real knowledge of the German atomic bomb project, (In an aside, the OSS tasked Moe Berg, a former major league baseball player turned spy, to find out if Heisenberg knew enough to successfully build a bomb for Germany. If so, Berg was to kill Heisenberg. Berg decided that Heisenberg did not have that kind of atomic bomb knowledge and did not have to eliminate him).

The Alsos team also investigated German scientists who were involved in biological and chemical warfare experiments, often carried out on innocent inmates in the Nazi concentration camps.

Project Paperclip officially opened shop in September 1946 on the instructions of President Truman to develop "a program to bring selected German scientists to work on America's behalf during the Cold War." The President's order had one important caveat which excluded anyone found "to have been a member of the Nazi party and more than a nominal participation in its activities, or an active supporter of Nazism or militarism."

If anyone at the top levels of the CIA read the President's directive, they did not heed his orders. Instead, they deliberately flouted the Chief Executive's instructions and proceeded to bring into this country the butchers from such infamous concentration camps as Auschwitz, Dachau, Mittelwerk-Dora and other places.

One of the first Nazi scientists to come to the Untied States was Herbert Wagner, who arrived by military plane on May 19, 1945. He had been the chief missile designer for the Henschel Aircraft Company, and was the designer of the German HS-293, the first German guided missile that was used in combat in World War II. Wagner was smuggled into the United States by a covert U.S. Navy team who hid him from the prying eyes of the general public. Wagner was a member of the brown-shirted storm troopers, as well as four other Nazi organizations.

During that same month, members of the U.S. Army, Navy and Army Air Force scoured Europe looking for German scientists. At an I.G. Farben plant near the town of Gendorf, Allied soldiers hit the jackpot, finding a slew of major German scientists, including Walter Rappe, an I.G. Farben director and pharmaceutical researcher, and Otto Ambros, also an I.G. Farben chemist. Ambros, it would later be ascertained, oversaw slave labor in the Auschwitz camp. In 1951, John J. McCloy, the High Commissioner of Germany, ordered the release of Ambros, even though he was a convicted Nazi war criminal. He was later hired by companies such as J. Peter Grace and Dow Chemical Company as a consultant in the United States.

The job of investigating the backgrounds of the German scientists was given to the Joint Intelligence Objectives Agency (JIOA) under the direction of Bosquet Wev. Beginning in February 1947, Wev handed over to the State Department the first background dossiers on the original Nazi scientists he wanted to bring to the United States. When the noted writer Dew Pearson penned an unfavorable column regarding some of these men, Wev rejected their past as "a picayune detail," and said that their work for the Nazis was "simply beating a dead horse." He further remarked that if these men had remained in Germany they would "present a far greater security threat to this country than any former Nazi affiliation they may have had or even any Nazi sympathies which they may still have." Unknown to many people at JIOA, its Deputy Director would turn out to be a traitor to the United States.

William Whalen was appointed the Deputy Director of the JIOA in July 1947. For the previous two years, he had been the Assistant Chief of the U.S. Army Foreign Liaison Office, more of a social job than anything else. One of the people whom Whalen met at the various parties he attended was a Russian Colonel named Sergei Edemski, the acting Soviet military attaché and a member of the Soviet GRU, its military intelligence branch. Col. Edemski asked Whalen for unclassified military documents but he refused to hand them over. Whalen was then working in the Pentagon and was privy to quite a horde of U.S. military secrets. Whalen was familiar with many of the Nazis who were then working in the Project Paperclip. Whalen was a braggart who often told his military colleagues that he was going to be appointed to the position of Assistant Secretary of Defense "because my mother delivered so many hundred thousand votes in New York State for John Kennedy." Walter Mueller, who worked at the State Department, said of him, "Whalen griped about being discriminated against and said certain members in the Department of Defense would be sorry someday."

In all, over 700 Paperclip scientists were brought into the United

States. Many of these men were given jobs in such prestigious companies and schools as Duke University, RCA and Bell Labs. Using his top position at JIOA, Whalen lied to the press about the backgrounds of these people.

In March 1959, William Whalen decided to act as a paid spy for the Russians. He met with Colonel Edemski at a shopping center in Alexandria, Virginia and began handing over America's most valuable military secrets. Over a period of time he gave them 30 to 35 U.S. Army manuals, and other information. For his services, the Russians paid him $14,000. Among the other top-secret material Whalen gave the Russians were military plans for troop movements in West Berlin at the time of the 1961 Berlin crisis. He also gave the Russians material on the scientists then working for the United States under Paperclip. He also provided them with information on American Hawk and Nike missiles. While he was secretly working for the Russians, Whalen was appointed Director of JIOA on July 2, 1959. Whalen wrote the following concerning the scientists he brought in under Paperclip: "these aliens are not now, or likely to become security threats to the Untied States."

While he was working as a spy for the Russians, a government fitness report on Whalen was conducted. It was said of this investigation, "Although the investigation reported that he occasionally drank to excess and that between 1952 and 1959 he had recurrent financial problems, it did not uncover evidence that he was a spy."

In February 1960, Col. Edemski was transferred to London and was replaced by Mikhail Shumaev. Whalen continued to meet with his new handler, giving as much information as he could. In return, Shumaev paid him $3,000.

The FBI unmasked Whalen's activities when they conducted an investigation of Colonel Stig Wennerstrom, a Swedish Defense Ministry official who was convicted of espionage in 1964 for giving away material concerning the Swedish air defense system. FBI agent Donald Gruentzel, who was investigating the Wennerstrom case, came across references to Whalen while doing his research. In 1963, Agent Gruentzel interviewed Whalen concerning the Wennerstrom case. Not liking what he heard from Whalen, the FBI agent followed Whalen's activities, subpoenaed his bank records and found that he had accumulated a huge amount of cash from undisclosed sources. Under questioning at FBI headquarters, Whalen finally confessed to being a Russian mole.

On July 12, 1966, a federal grand jury indicted Whalen on charges that he acted as an agent of the USSR. Although the national press got wind of the Whalen case, his participation in Project Paperclip was never mentioned. On December 17, 1966, Whalen was sentenced to fifteen years in prison.

Operation Paperclip included a so-called "Rogues Gallery" of Nazis who came to the United States to work alongside the American military in various scientific endeavors. Among them were:

• Kurt Blome: Blome's crimes against humanity took the form of performing medical experiments on concentration camp victims using plague vaccines. He also performed euthanasia and other, unnamed tests on camp prisoners. He also used Sarin nerve gas on prisoners at Auschwitz. He was tried at the Nuremberg war crimes tribunal and was found not guilty. U.S. Army authorities expunged his record pertaining to the concentration camp crimes, not allowing the court access to this vital material. He came to the U.S., was paid a salary of $6,000 and went to work at Camp King outside of Washington, D.C. where he continued his duties for Uncle Sam.

• Arthur Rudolf: According to U.S. military records, Rudolf was a "100% Nazi, dangerous type, security threat. Suggest internment." Not only was he *not* interned, but Rudolf, the former director of the Mittelwerk factory at the infamous Dora/Nordhausen concentration camp, supervised the deaths of at least 20,000 victims during his brutal reign of terror. The JIOA ignored his sordid past, and when it came time for him to apply for a U.S. entry visa, they wrote that there was "nothing in his records that he was a war criminal, an ardent Nazi, or otherwise objectionable." Rudolf became a naturalized American citizen, was stationed at Fort Bliss, and later joined NASA, the national space agency, working on rocket development.

• Wernher von Braun: Von Braun was, perhaps, the most important Nazi scientist brought over by American authorities under Paperclip. He was mainly responsible for the super-secret German rocket base at Peenemunde from 1937 to 1945. It was from Peenemunde that German V-2 rockets were launched against civilian targets in London, wreaking considerable havoc on the city.

Von Braun also worked in the Dora concentration camp, and had the deaths of countless thousands of prisoners on his hands. His dossier was expunged of this incriminating material upon his entry into the United States. In later years, he was given the important position as Director of the Marshall Space Flight Center, a part of NASA (the National Aeronautical and Space Administration). In 1970, he was named as NASA's Associate Administrator.

In all, some 700 Nazi scientists were allowed inside the United States and were employed by the various military and civilian departments in highly technical and secret work. Project Paperclip was surely the Agency's blackest eye.

Chapter 13:
The CIA and the Corsican Mafia

In the early 1960s, the CIA made an unholy alliance with certain members of the American Mafia to kill Cuba's Fidel Castro. This was not the first time however, that the United States went into business with a criminal organization. In the years following the end of World War II, the CIA began a secret alliance with members of the French Corsican Mafia in the port city of Marseille. This was a Cold War partnership aimed at limiting the power of the Communists and Socialists who threatened to paralyze the docks where military supplies were being loaded for use by the French in their battle in Indochina.

Another consequence of the alliance between the CIA and the Corsican underworld had far-reaching and unintended results not foreseen at that time: the birth of the worldwide heroin industry that would go by the popular term "The French Connection."

The rise to power of the Corsican underworld took roots in Marseille in the 1930s. The two founding fathers of the modern day French Connection were Francois Spirito and Paul Bonnaventure Carbone. Their first business venture was the creation of a brothel in Cairo in the 1920s, which was expanded to Marseille during the next decade. Carbone and Spirito made a deal with Simon Sabiani, the Socialist deputy mayor of Marseille in 1931 to allow their illicit undertakings to flourish in the city through a system of bribes and political payoffs. In return, both men would use their considerable muscle to work against the role of fascism which was spreading across Europe, and was widespread in France. Interestingly, Sabiani later became a facist. During a huge street demonstration in Marseille in February 1934 in which dock workers tried to disrupt the rule of law, gangs in the pay of Carbone and Spirito fired into the crowd, killing many, and disrupting the demonstrations.

Four years later, the power of the two men came to a head when Mayor Sabiani was defeated for reelection, and a socialist, more akin to Carbone and Spirito's politics came into office. With their political base now entrenched in the city, the men turned to new

81

ventures, namely, the importation and production of heroin into Marseille. They used some of the profits from their sale of illegal drugs to purchase a large supply of arms which they sold to anyone with enough cash to lay out.

As war came to Europe, and France fell in June 1940, the fate of both Carbone and Spirito turned once again. They made an alliance with the Germans who now had effective control over Marseille, one of the most important places in France where the Resistance movement flourished. On July 14, 1942, members of the Resistance in Marseille attacked the headquarters of a pro-German group called PPF, and many people were killed. Carbone and his partner became informants for the Germans and supplied them with a list of names of those involved in the attack.

In 1943, Resistance leaders killed Carbone as he was heading into Marseille. Shortly thereafter, Spirito, along with former mayor Sabiani, fled to Spain.

In 1947, two years after the war ended, Spirito made his way to the United States and began the early and lucrative New York-Marseille heroin trade. He was eventually arrested on drug trafficking charges and spent two years in jail. After his release, he returned to France and was subsequently arrested by the government for his collaboration with the Nazis. He spent only eight months in jail, and fled to the French Riviera.

In 1943, the OSS was allied with certain members of the Mafia in Sicily when the United States was preparing its invasion of Italy. The local authorities gave the OSS lists of Nazi collaborators to be dealt with, the locations of German troops, and the best areas for the Allies to land. Upon the successful American invasion, the U.S. army appointed Don Calogero Vizzini, a member of the Sicilian mob, mayor of Villalba. Another Mafia member, Genco Russo, was nominated as mayor of Mussumeli. Dozens of other Mafia-affiliated men were given jobs in local governments in Sicily, all of whom were indebted to the United States. During the war years, these men controlled the rise of the Communists and Fascists in their region.

In Marseille, the Resistance movement was divided into two opposing groups the Communist FTP and the non-communist group MUR. Despite their squabbling, they managed to coordinate their forces into one group by February 1944. Most of the non-communist groups came from the Marseille Corsican syndicates who were not in league with their American and OSS patrons.

Two of the most powerful Resistance leaders were the Guerini brothers, Antoine and Barthelemy. Antoine worked as a rifleman for both Carbone and Spirito, and was closely allied with the OSS. Antoine hid downed Allied airmen on the run from the Nazis, and smuggled arms to the MUR of the French Resistance movement. Barthelemy was instrumental in aiding the Allied cause during the twelve-day liberation battle of Marseille by providing much-needed intelligence and arms to Gaston Defferre's Socialist militia.

In 1946, the United States made one of its most important decisions in its confederation with the mob. In a covert deal between the U.S. government and the Navy, Charles "Lucky" Luciano one of the mob's most influential figures at the time was deported from his jail cell in upstate New York and packed off to Italy, in return for his wartime collaboration in keeping the east coast docks free from Nazi infiltration. Over the next several years, Luciano consolidated control over the worldwide drug trade that imported heroin from the Middle East and Europe into the United States. Marseille was the heroin importing and refining capital of Europe, a distinction that it would keep for years to come.

The CIA and the Corsican gangs further cemented their covert relationship when the Socialist and Communist parties were elected in Marseille and made the Corsicans their number one enemy. In order to divide the two parties, the CIA turned to an unusual ally for help the AFL-CIO, the main labor organization in the United States.

By November 1947, a series of sudden strikes and street demonstrations took place in Marseille over the low wages and high food prices that began to affect the population. Soon, almost three million workers across France walked off their jobs and the economy went into a tailspin. The AFL-CIO had been secretly funding more than $2 million a year to the anti-communist labor leaders in France. In a first for the CIA, they also gave some $1 million to the Socialists in order to split up the labor ranks and end the strike. Working in conjunction with the CIA, French Minister of the Interior Jules Moch ordered the police to take action against the strikers. Fierce fighting between police and the strikers took place in Marseille, led by the Guerini brothers.

The CIA now went into high gear. They furnished guns and ammunition to many of the Corsican gangs who took out their wrath on opposing union leaders, killed a number of strikers and created havoc along the port. A CIA psychological team was sent to Marseille, where they produced pamphlets and made radio broadcasts, all aimed at ending the strike along the docks. The CIA "psy ops" worked, and within a month the strike was broken, and the discouraged men returned to their jobs. Through their cooperation and aid to the CIA during the strike, the Guerini brothers now took total control over organized crime in Marseille, and remained in power for years to come. Antoine Guerini was shot to death in 1967 in an apparent revenge killing by a man named Gaeton Zampa, who was a confidant of a corrupt ex-police official and Marseille heroin smuggler, Robert Blemant.

In 1950, another strike took place in the city when workers refused to load shipments of war material destined for French forces fighting in Indochina. The CIA once again swept into action, giving $15,000 to Irving Brown of the AFL for clandestine purposes. Brown funneled the money to a man named Pierre Ferri-Priani who recruited thugs and strike breakers along the docks. Once more, the Guerini brothers were called in, and through a combination of Guerini gangs and CIA money, quelled anther potential firestorm in the making. In the aftermath of the strike, Gaston Defferre, the leader of the Socialist Party came out on top as the dominant political figure in Marseille, and would be in that position for more than 25 years.

Into this heated mix came Meyer Lansky, the mob's money man, who arrived in Marseille in 1950 where he met with both Lucky Luciano and the Guerinis to coordinate the drug trade from Indochina to the West. From Marseille, the Corsican gangs, with a wink and a nod from both the CIA and the French intelligence service formed the so-called "French Connection." Now, almost 80% of all heroin shipments coming into the United States from Cuba came via Marseille. In their provocative book on the CIA called *Whiteout: The CIA, Drugs and the Press,* authors Alexander Cockburn and Jeffrey St. Clair write, "Between 1950 and 1965 there were no arrests of any executive working in the French Connection."

This author wrote a book called *JFK: The French Connection*

(Adventures Unlimited Press, 2012) in which I tell the story of the so-called French Connection to the Kennedy assassination and the possible role-played by Antoine Guerini in the events leading up to the President's assassination. While it would take too long to relate the entire story, here in a nutshell is the book's thesis.

In 1988, the Arts and Entertainment Channel in the United States aired for the first time a six part controversial documentary called *The Men Who Killed Kennedy*. The second episode, called "The Forces of Darkness," talked about the second assassin on the grassy knoll in Dallas on November 22, 1963. The last part of the episode featured, for the first time on national television, the story of Steve Rivele's private investigation of the Kennedy assassination, featuring the so- called "French Connection."

Rivele's thesis said that the assassination was planned by the Corsican network based in Marseille, France, headed by Antoine Guerini, one of the world's most wanted heroin dealers of the day. The man who gave Rivele the background was a noted French drug smuggler named Christian David. At the end of the hour-long telecast, Rivele gave the names of the three men who allegedly killed JFK, and the entire backstory of the event. Besides Antoine Guerini, Carlos Marcello and Santos Trafficante (who were both used by the CIA in the plots to kill Castro) were also involved in the assassination planning.

Steve Rivele traveled to Dallas to begin his nascent investigation and try to put some of the pieces of the puzzle together. He met with a fellow JFK researcher named Gary Shaw who gave him the name of someone who might shed light on the assassination. That man was Christian David. David was then serving time in jail in Atlanta for his part in the French Connection heroin business. Rivele wrote to David and to his surprise, got a positive reply. Rivele and the late Bernard Fensterwald traveled to Atlanta to interview David in his cell. The men asked David if he could relay any information he had on the President's death. "There was a conspiracy," David replied. When asked how he knew, David replied, "The contract was offered to me." During that first conversation, Rivele and Fensterwald said, "It is not possible to say whether he was bluffing or if he was revealing a secret he had hidden for a long, long time."

When asked who offered him the contract, David responded

by saying, "An important man from Marseille. He made all the decisions. He was the only one who could take on a contract like that one." David gave the name of the man who offered the contract. "It was Antoine Guerini."

David then elaborated further on his conversation with Antoine Guerini. "It was May or June 1963. I was in Marseille. Each evening I went into Guerini's mailbox to see if the man who owed the money were sending it. One evening Guerini asked me to go to his office. He told me he had an important contract. He wanted to know if it would interest me? I asked Guerini, who was the contract out on? An American political man, he told me. A government Senator, I wanted to know? No, he said, much higher up. The big cheese. I felt that he wanted me to reveal more. I asked him where this [contract] would take place, and when? In America, he advised. No thank you, I replied. It's too risky. Not just because of where. I have taken chances [in my life] but in these conditions, I'm not that foolish." [1]

Upon further questioning, Christian David gave the first name of one of the other shooters of the President, a man named Lucien (his name was Lucien Sarti). David said that Sarti was paid for the assassination not in cash but in heroin. Rivele asked if he was paid in heroin because Sarti was a drug dealer and he said no.

Steve Rivele then went on a fact-finding trip to Europe where he interviewed many people in the police, military, and drug trade seeking confirmation of the information that Christian David gave him. One of the men he met with was journalist Karl Van Meter who told him the following story. He said he thought the CIA would have gone through its connections to hire Guerini to engage assassins. Why Marseille? Because they: 1) needed white men who could blend in in Dallas, 2) needed a closed leak-proof milieu, 3) needed people who were not known to the American police, 4) needed experienced professional killers. Cubans, Asians, Middle Easterners and Americans would not do. Marseille mob offered a pool of suitable assassins, and the CIA had longstanding relations with the Guerinis. [2]

Alain Jaubert, a journalist, said the story about the CIA hiring mercenaries out of Marseille was true, but why Antoine Guerini

---

[1] Kross, Peter, *JFK: The French Connection,* Adventures Unlimited Press, Kempton, Illinois, 2012, Page 316.

[2] Ibid. Page 321.

decided to help Sarti and David was "a major mystery."

In a January 17, 1986 meeting between Steve Rivele and Christian David, David gave more information on the Guerini link to the JFK assassination. He said that Antoine Guerini was the only intermediary between Sarti and the Chicago Mafia that was run by Carlos Marcello, "but that once he had put him in touch, he withdrew from the affair." Sarti made his own arrangements with the Chicago mob, deciding it was better for his own security if he did not include anyone else in the affair.

According to Christian David, the real reason that Antoine Guerini entered the plot to kill JFK was because of Guerini's hopes of reestablishing his lost gambling interests in Cuba that had been shut down after Castro came to power. David asserts that this was to come about by making Oswald a convenient patsy Castro agent in Kennedy's death, thus making necessary an American-led invasion of Cuba in retaliation. Once Castro was overthrown, then the mobsters would again have free reign in operating the casinos in Havana.[3]

After considerable time and effort traveling through Europe, Steve Rivele believed he had the rudimentary knowledge of just how the assassination of JFK took place. The hit was offered by Antoine Guerini to Christian David who refused to take part in it. Lucien Sarti, a member of the heroin gang run by Auguste Ricord, a man who was connected to both U.S. and French intelligence as well as the Corsican Mafia, was one of the assassins in Dealey Plaza on November 22, 1963. Sarti was paid in heroin something that he'd never consented to before. David said a man named Nicoli knew a great deal about the assassination but he refused to say more. Once Nicoli was found, said David, the story would come full circle.

Like the CIA's relationship with the German scientists under Project Paperclip, their unholy bond with the Corsican mob was one of the blackest stages in its history.

---

[3] Ibid. Page 331.

Chapter 14:
The CIA and Guatemala

One of the first large-scale operations orchestrated in the CIA's formative years was a covert operation to overthrow the legitimate government of Guatemala. The country's government was led by the popularly elected Jacobo Arbenz who came to office with 50% of the vote in a free election in 1950. When Arbenz tried to restore land to the majority of the peasants, Washington took notice. If that wasn't bad enough, Arbenz took more than 20,000 acres of private land owned by the American-controlled United Fruit Company. United Fruit was the largest foreign company operating in Guatemala, owning more than 50,000 acres of land on which bananas were grown. In addition, United Fruit owned a controlling share in the nation's sole railroad.

The law firm that represented United Fruit was Sullivan and Cromwell, a business owned by John Foster Dulles, the Secretary of State under President Eisenhower, and his brother Allen Dulles, the Director of the CIA. Allen Dulles was the prime mover for the covert operation. Among the other top men in the Agency who had a hand in the coup were Tracy Barnes and Richard Bissell. Barnes was a veteran of the OSS and worked with Dulles during World War II. Bissell, who later in his CIA career was to become one of the most influential men in the history of the CIA, oversaw the technical details from Washington (Bissell would later head the secret U-2 spy plane operation).

United Fruit began a scare campaign in the United States, saying that Arbenz was being controlled by the communists, which was not true. He was an ardent nationalist who detested foreign intervention in his country's affairs. President Eisenhower viewed Arbenz as a "leftist," and began a covert campaign to oust him from power.

Recently declassified CIA documents on the Guatemala affair provide a much larger historical picture of just how far the CIA went in its anti-Arbenz planning. The State Department recommended that a paramilitary force of exiled Guatemalans be established to "persuade military leaders inside the government to cooperate in a coup against Arbenz."

The CIA codename for the Guatemala operation was "Operation Success" or PB/SUCCESS. The operation was led by Albert Haney who was then serving as the CIA station chief in South Korea. The CIA picked as Arbenz's successor Colonel Carlos Castillo Armas, whose only qualification was that he was anti-communist.

A recently declassified narrative released by the CIA gives the historian of today a window into the CIA's thinking as the coup against the government of Guatemala was undertaken. They report that the top brass at Langley headquarters had a dim view of what had occurred in Guatemala before Jacobo Arbenz Guzman came to power in 1951. The study says, "For the first time, Communists had targeted a country in America's back yard for subversion and transformation into a denied area. When comparing what they saw to past experience, they were more apt to draw parallels to Korea, Russia, or Eastern Europe than to Central America. They saw events not in a Guatemalan context but as part of a global pattern of Communist activity. PBSUCCESS, nonetheless, interrupted a revolutionary process that had been in motion for over a decade, and the actions of Guatemalan officials can only be understood in the context of the history of the region."[1]

Using a budget that swelled to $20 million before it was over, propaganda and cash were passed on to certain military officers in the Guatemalan army with the promise of more to come. A secret training base was set up in Nicaragua with the full cooperation of that country's president/dictator Anastasio Somoza. Among those CIA officers who took part in the training of the "rebel" army were E. Howard Hunt and David Atlee Phillips (both men would later be heavily involved in the plots to kill Fidel Castro in Cuba).

To bolster Arbenz's role as a Soviet stooge, the CIA sent Russian arms to the country and a CIA dummy company was established to supply the people with weapons. When Arbenz openly bought arms from the Soviet Union, President Eisenhower believed he had the justification to act.

According to the declassified CIA history of the Guatemalan coup plans, assassination was one of the key components in the operation. Portions of the report concerning the role of assassinations reads as follows:

[1] Haines, Gerald, K. *Operation PBSUCCESS: CIA History Staff Analysis,* June 1995.

The CIA plan, as drawn up by [deleted] Western Hemisphere Division, combined psychological warfare, economic, diplomatic, and paramilitary actions against Guatemala. Named PBSUCCESS, and coordinated with the Department of State, the plan's stated objective was to remove covertly, and without bloodshed if possible, the menace of the present Communist controlled government in Guatemala. In the outline of the operation the sixth stage called for "roll up" of Communists and collaborators after a successful coup.

Training: Although assassination was not mentioned in the overall plan, the Chief of [blank] requested a special paper on liquidation of personnel on 5 January 1954. This paper, according to the [blank] chief, who was to be utilized to brief the training chief for PBSUCCESS before he left to begin training Castillo Armas' forces in Honduras on 10 January 1954. A cable from [blank] the following day requested 20 silencers for 22 caliber rifles. Headquarters sent the rifles. The [blank] chief also discussed the training plan with agent SEEKFORD on 13 January indicating that he wanted Castillo Armas and the PBSUCCESS [blank] officer to train two assassins. In addition, he discussed these "assassination specialists" with Castillo Armas on 3 February 1954.

The idea of forming assassination teams (K groups) apparently originated with Castillo Armas in 1952. Adapting Castillo Armas's concept the [blank] chief routinely included two assassination specialists in his training plans.[2]

The CIA agent named SEEKFORD got in touch with Castillo Armas who gave him a list of people whom he wished to "dispose" of. This was called "executive action" in spy parlance meaning assassination. Fifty-eight names were on the assassination list, and 74 were to be imprisoned. SEEKFORD also reported that General Rafael Trujillo of the Dominican Republic, an ally of Washington, had agreed to help Castillo Armas in return for the "killing of four Santo Dominicans at present residing in Guatemala a few days

[2] Ibid.

before D-Day." SEEKFORD reported that Castillo Armas agreed in principal but said that the assassinations could not take place before the invasion date.

While the behind-the-scenes assassination planning was taking shape, the CIA-backed rebels were ready to pounce. From his base in Honduras, Castillo Armas and his force entered Guatemala. While Armas' men headed for the capital, the CIA propaganda campaign worked brilliantly. News of a huge army descending on the country was broadcast over the radio. The CIA jammed Arbenz' reply that nothing of the sort had taken place. After a short fiasco in which the CIA's recruits mistakenly destroyed a building that was home to a group of American evangelists, and after two of the invaders' P-47 aircraft were shot down, President Eisenhower ordered the CIA to send replacement planes to the Nicaraguan Air Force. (The Nicaraguan government supplied the planes for the exile invasion.) The new aircraft destroyed targets near the capital, and sent the Guatemalan army fleeing in circles.

In the face of the massive "invasion" of his country, Arbenz resigned and headed for the safety of the Mexican embassy. In the name of defeating the communist menace, Operation PBSUCCESS proved a victory in the short term.

The CIA's record of the Guatemalan invasion however, shed new light on the long-term failure the operation had been. By July 1, 1954, the CIA station in Guatemala decided it was time to leave the country and shut down its operation. The first to go was the agency's Voice of Liberation radio station which went off the air early that month. David Atlee Phillips, the propaganda chief for the operation "packed up its mobile transmitter for shipment to the States." An unnamed CIA officer in Guatemala began collecting files and prepared to close up shop. According to one report, "He ordered Guatemala Station to destroy documents pertaining to PBSUCCESS. As Frank Wisner said, it was time for the Agency to return to the tasks for which it was peculiarly qualified. But the agency, "would never be the same after PBSUCCESS. The triumph showed what could be accomplished through covert action, and its lessons, learned and unlearned, would have ramifications for years to come."

The Agency's initial jubilation gave way to misgivings as it became clear that victory in Guatemala had been neither as clear cut nor as unambiguous as originally thought. In Latin America, the Eisenhower administration came under heavy fire for its actions, and Guatemala became a symbol of the stubborn resistance of the United States to progressive, nationalist policies. Castillo Armas's new regime proved embarrassingly inept. Its repressive and corrupt policies soon polarized Guatemala and provided a renewed civil conflict. Operation PBSUCCESS aroused resentments that continue, almost 40 years after the event, to prevent the CIA from revealing its role."[3]

Once the United States left Guatemala, President Castillo Armas turned the country into a dictatorship. He targeted for retribution those influential people who were allied with Arbenz, banning all "subversive literature" including works by Victor Hugo and Fydor Dostoevsky. He then voided the 1945 constitution and gave himself complete executive and legislative power. Over time, Castillo Armas opened up his country to certain members of the American Mafia who joined up with a number of Guatemalan Army officers in establishing gambling halls.

In the immediate aftermath of the successful coup, two members of the CIA's counterintelligence staff arrived in Guatemala City to do a "snatch job "on documents that were relevant to the coup. The men "hoped to find papers that would enable the Agency to trace Soviet connections throughout Latin America and identify people who can be controlled and exploited to further U.S. policy." Another purpose of the trip was to find any papers that would link the Soviet Union to the Arbenz regime. With the help of a number of followers of Arbenz, the two CIA men found 150,000 documents, but most of what they found were only of "local significance." None of the material they found showed any Russian ties to the old regime.

Over the next several years, many participants in the PBSUCCESS operation went on the record, telling of their involvement in the affair. Among those who told their stories were E. Howard Hunt; in his book *Undercover,* he told of his role in the psychological arena. Richard Bissell told John Chancellor in a TV interview "the whole

[3] *Operation PBSUCCESS: Chapter 4: The Sweet Smell of Success.*

policymaking machinery of the executive branch of the government was involved." In 1963, then ex-president Dwight Eisenhower, who was on stage at an event with Allen Dulles, said, "there was one time when we had to get rid of a Communist government in Central America."

As for how things went in Guatemala under the regime of Castillo Armas, his coup, in the end, proved to be a disaster. Anti-American riots sprang up in various parts of Latin and South America in opposition to the U.S.-sponsored coup. Things got so bad that government troops fired on a demonstration, killing many. Castillo Armas declared a state of siege and suspended civil liberties. In 1957, Castillo Armas was assassinated by a member of his own presidential guard. New elections were called for and the presidency went to Ortiz Passarclli, however, his opponent, Ydigoras Fuentes, called his followers into the streets and ultimately the Army took power and invalidated the election.

The Guatemalan coup set the stage for further CIA interventions in other countries around the world, as well as the use of assassination as a means of removing foreign leaders who were anathema to U.S. vital interests around the globe. The next target was Iran.

Chapter 15:
The Plot to Overthrow Iran

In the 1970s, the United States faced one of its most important and long-lasting foreign policy crises in its history. In 1976, the government of Iran captured the American embassy in Tehran and held the occupants hostage for more than 400 days. The crisis drove President Jimmy Carter from office and set the stage for the election of Ronald Regan in 1980. But the United States' interest in Iran did not begin with the hostage crisis. It had its roots in a joint American/British covert operation to topple the government of Prime Minister Mohammad Mossadegh in 1953.

Iran was situated strategically in the Middle East on the border with the Soviet Union, and for that reason it was of vital import to both the United States and Great Britain. The other main factor in the West's interest in Iran was the vast amount of oil it had under its territory. In 1909, the British opened the Anglo-Persian Oil Company, giving the British government a 52% share of the market. They got a 60-year exclusive concession to drill oil in Iran, making Britain the number one power in that nation. In 1941, a joint British-Russian invasion of Iran took place, destroying the Iranian army. The ruler in Iran at that time was Reza Khan, an undistinguished army officer who founded the Pahlavi dynasty. Thinking that Reza Khan was pro-Nazi, the British overthrew him, and put in his place his 23-year-old son. They also kidnapped General Fazlollah Zahedi, a charismatic man who was shipped off to Palestine for his own safety.

Reza Khan's son, the new Shah of Iran, was nothing to talk about. He was easily manipulated by the British who had him under their control.

In 1945, the British and Americans pulled their troops out of Iran, leaving Russian forces in the area of Azerbaijan. The Russians tried to foment a revolt but after a hue and cry from the West, the Russians pulled out, giving access to Iranian oil.

As the Cold War heated up, the United States saw Iran as a buffer against Soviet expansion in the Middle East and gave millions of dollars in both economic and military aid to the Shah. The Shah was wined and dined in both London and Washington and he became a trusted ally of the West.

The Shah trusted two Americans to help him develop a new police force and security services, Kim Roosevelt and Colonel H. Norman Schwarzkopf, the former head of the New Jersey State Police, and the father of the Desert Storm general of the same name. Both men would later play a prominent role in the CIA's efforts to oust Prime Minister Mossadegh.

The basis for "Operation Ajax" came when Premier Mossadegh decided to nationalize the huge, British-dominated oil cartel called the Anglo-Iranian Oil Company, or AIOC. AIOC funneled large amounts of money into the Iranian economy but sent an even greater amount of cash back to England.

On May 2, 1951, the Iranian parliament, or Majlis, approved a bill that turned over complete control of the AIOC to the Iranian government. Mossadegh's actions sent shock waves across the bows in Washington and London, and a covert operation was designed to change the exploding situation.

Recently declassified files held by the CIA pertaining to Operation Ajax are now giving historians and the general public a vastly different view of the events that led up to the Iran coup. According to the new files, the reasons for the coup were: 1) Iran was hedging on its promise to the British and the Americans over a new oil agreement, 2) the regime's disregard of the Iranian constitution, and 3) Mossadegh's desire for power, and his close ties to Iran's communist Tudeh Party. The CIA's ultimate goal was to return the young Shah to power in Iran as a buffer against the Soviet Union.

The first steps in the overthrow of the government took place in the United States in March 1953 when the CIA began drafting a covert plan to remove Mossadegh. In April it was determined that the CIA and the British would join hands in this covert effort and the CIA contacted the British Secret Intelligence Service (SIS). CIA and SIS officers met in Cyprus to begin planning. On June 3, 1953, U.S. Ambassador to Iran Loy Henderson arrived in the United States and was briefed on the coup plans. The plan was completed on June 10, 1953 at which time Kermit Roosevelt, Chief of the Near East and Africa Division, CIA, and Roger Goiran, CIA Chief of Station in Iran, and two CIA planning officers traveled to Beirut, Lebanon to further study the strategy. Kermit "Kim" Roosevelt was the grandson of President Theodore Roosevelt and a distant cousin to President Franklin D. Roosevelt. He was a Harvard University graduate, served in the OSS in World War II, and entered the CIA at its inception.

By mid-July 1953, the U.S. Department of State and the British Foreign Office signed off on the proposal. It was then approved by President Eisenhower. All parties agreed that Kermit Roosevelt would take control of the coup planning, and a CIA liaison officer was sent to Cyprus to act as a go-between for the operations in Tehran, Cyprus and Washington.

The British first froze Iranian assets and imposed a naval blockade to stop the flow of oil out of the country.

The CIA and SIS picked General Fazlollah Zahedi to replace Prime Minister Mossadegh and secretly funneled more than $5 million into his private account to finance the coup. According to the new documents, the CIA did not have a high opinion of General Zahedi and the agency had to develop the coup strategy themselves. An unnamed CIA agent who was working for the Iranian army was named as a cabinet member after the coup, and played a larger role than did General Zahedi. The CIA said that Zahedi was lacking in drive, energy, and concrete plans. Furthermore, most of the leaders of the coup were put in a CIA safe house and kept incommunicado until the revolt was over.

As these events were unfolding, the CIA whisked the Shah's sister, Princess Aahraf, who had been living on the French Riviera, back to Iran. The Shah was livid that his sister had been brought back home and refused to visit with her. Colonel Schwarzkopf, a friend of the Shah, met with the ruler and calmed his agitation regarding his sister's return. The British also had one of their agents, a man named Asadollah Rashidian, meet with the Shah to plan strategy.

The newly released documents on Ajax say that the Shah was very reluctant to go along with the coup, and even refused to sign the CIA-approved decree firing Prime Minister Mossadegh. According to the CIA history, "This meeting was to be followed by a series of additional ones, some between Roosevelt and the Shah and some between Rashidian and the Shah, in which relentless pressure was exerted in frustrating attempts to overcome an entrenched attitude of vacillation and indecision."

In order to get the Shah to cooperate in the coup, a number of attempts were made to have him show some backbone. When the Shah's sister returned home, she told her brother that she had been in contact with various officials from the United States and Great Britain who asked her to pass along the allies' backing of the coup.

Colonel Schwarzkopf arrived suddenly in Tehran to see the Shah. He came with a diplomatic passport and "a couple of large bags containing millions of dollars." The Shah refused to see him and soon, word of the American's arrival had been plastered in the newspapers. The Shah's critics attacked him for being in touch with "brainless agents of international reaction." When Mossadegh learned of Colonel Schwarzkopf's visit, he threatened to hold another referendum, this time to finally depose the Shah.

Kim Roosevelt had now returned to Tehran and stayed in a CIA safe house. The news he received was not good. It seems that the vacillating Shah had fled the country, heading to a retreat on the Caspian Sea, and reneged on his royal decree to replace Mossadegh with General Zahedi. Kim Roosevelt took matters into his own hands and contacted Colonel Nematollah Nassiry and gave him the royal decrees. The Colonel went to the Shah's Caspian retreat where the reluctant Shah signed the documents. Colonel Nassiry returned to Tehran but had to wait for two days before he could deliver the edicts to Mossadegh that would remove him from his post as prime minister.

When Mossadegh learned of Col. Nassiry's arrival in Tehran, he set up a military blockade of his office, giving strict orders to his troops not to allow him into the palace. Nassiry demanded to see the prime minister to deliver his message but was refused entry. The Colonel went behind Mossadegh's back and after an hour-and-a half wait, managed somehow to get a servant in the prime minister's office to sign for the papers expelling him from power. Shortly thereafter, he was arrested by General Riahi, who took Mossadegh to his office.

Prime Minister Mossadegh went on national television and told his people that "foreign elements" were trying to depose him. A hunt for the Shah's agents began, and in all the confusion in the capital, the Shah and his wife fled the country (they went to Baghdad, Iraq). Meanwhile, General Zahedi was encased in a CIA safe house somewhere in the city, temporarily out of harm's way.

Now, things began to move quickly. With the backing of the CIA, General Zahedi called a press conference telling the people that he was the legal prime minister of Iran and that Mossadegh had staged an illegal coup. CIA agents stationed in Tehran began to hand out copies of the royal decree that was signed by the Shah giving Zahedi legitimacy. On August 19, 1953, a series of pro-Shah demonstrations took place in the bazaar area of Tehran, and soon the crowds began to swell. Presently, members of the army joined the demonstrations and the writing was on the wall as far as Mossadegh was concerned. Soon, General Zahedi came out of hiding to lead the revolt. He told the people via radio that he was in charge of the government, and soon Mossadegh's home was seized and he was arrested. The Shah, who was then residing in Rome, quickly returned to Iran where he retook the Peacock Throne.

With the Shah now in power, Kermit Roosevelt was able to freely walk the streets of Tehran. At midnight, August 23, 1953, he entered the Shah's palace for a final meeting. Upon greeting Roosevelt, the man who played such a prominent role in his return to power, the Shah shook Roosevelt's hand and said, "I owe my throne to God, my people, my army, and to you."

In the 1970s, the Shah's continuing dictatorial rule and extravagant lifestyle led the Carter administration to sever its ties with him. An internal revolt led to the Shah's abdication of the throne, and the coming to power in Iran of the Ayatollah Khomeini. The 444-day hostage crisis was a direct reaction to American support of the Shah and his decades-long imperial rule.

Operation Ajax still resonates today. As of this writing, Iran is one of the major players in the politics of the Middle East. Its leaders have made it abundantly clear that they are interested in obtaining a nuclear weapon of their own. If they do obtain the bomb, all bets are off as to how the United States or Israel might react. The dictum that actions have consequences is clearly demonstrated in the events that the CIA began in Iran during the days of the Cold War.

Research Note: For anyone interested in reading the CIA's declassified report on the Iran coup, go to the National Security Archive on the web and look for "*Clandestine Service History: Overthrow of Premier Mossadegh of Iran-November 1952-August 1953.*

Chapter 16:
The U-2 Incident

With the development of highly sophisticated technology during the Cold War years, the United States, using the CIA, was able to conduct large-scale aerial spying operations over the Soviet Union and China. The most important CIA espionage activity regarding the Soviet Union was the development of the super-secret U-2 spy plane which allowed the United States to covertly watch every important Soviet military installation without being detected.

The man who was primarily responsible for the development and overseeing of the U-2 program at the CIA was Richard Bissell. The fancy title for the U-2 program which Bissell headed was the "Development Project Staff." Its headquarters was in Washington but most of the actual development work took place in secret bases and industrial areas across the country.

Richard Bissell was born on September 18, 1909 in Hartford, Connecticut. His father was in the insurance business and their home was once owned by the famed writer Mark Twain. As a young man, Bissell attended the Groton School, the London School of Economics, and got his degree from Yale University in 1932. During the war years, he worked in Washington for the Department of Commerce as an economist.

He joined the infant CIA in 1952 and his hard work and dedication to service caught the attention of the higher-ups in the Agency. His first operational assignment was to prepare the overthrow of the duly elected government of Guatemala, whose foreign policies were not welcome in Washington. The operation was a success and he was soon elevated to a high profile position at the CIA. Two years later, Bissell was given the prestigious job of overseeing the CIA's aerial surveillance program against the Soviet Union and China, the U-2 program. It was the U-2s' job to fly high over the most important military bases in both countries, photographing the constant military buildup of submarines, missiles, and troop concentrations, and return these prize photographs to the military and civilian leaders in Washington for evaluation. When the Eisenhower administration decided it wanted to limit the number of U-2 flights and American involvement in them, Bissell worked out a cover arrangement with the British government in which some Royal Air Force pilots would take over these super-secret flights.

In 1958, Bissell was head of the CIA's Clandestine Service, that part of the agency that was responsible for all covert operations. Bissell was now in the rarefied air of the most important plans the CIA had, and he made the most of the opportunities that were given him. In that capacity, he was a key player in the abortive Bay of Pigs invasion of Cuba in April 1961, and later, the CIA-Mafia plots to kill Fidel Castro. In the fallout after the Bay of Pigs, Bissell and CIA Director Allen Dulles were fired by President Kennedy.

The prototype of the U-2 was to be tested at the atomic testing grounds in Utah where maximum security was assured. Clarence "Kelly" Johnson originally designed the U-2, and had previously built the P-38 fighter/bomber and the F-104 Starfighter. Johnson and the CIA agreed on a budget of $22 million for the U-2 program. Recently released files on the U-2 incident shed new light on this secret agreement. On February 21, 1955, Richard Bissell wrote a check on a CIA account for $1.25 million and mailed it to Kelly Johnson's home. Johnson was the chief engineer at the Lockheed Company's Burbank, California plant. This incident took place just before the CIA was going to sign a contract with Lockheed for the $22.5 million amount for which they would build 20 U-2 aircraft. However, Lockheed needed an immediate cash infusion to keep the work going. The CIA used "unvouchered funds" untraceable money in order to get the U-2 program off the ground. In time, Lockheed built 20 planes at a total lost of $18,977,597, less than $1 million per plane.[1]

Also lending its technical expertise to the project was Edwin Land's camera company, which developed a modern high-altitude camera, which was able to take crystal clear photographs from miles above the earth. Land's cameras would allow the U-2 pilots to shoot high-resolution photographs of Soviet military installations from their planes' cruising altitude of 70,000 feet, and still produce outstanding quality pictures.

On August 6, 1955, the first operational deployment of the U-2s against the Soviet Union began. It consisted of four planes, six pilots, and 200 support staff. This contingent was stationed in

[1] The National Security Archive. *The Secret History of the U-2 and Area 51.*

Turkey, on the border of the Soviet Union. In later years, the U-2s would be stationed at U.S. Air Force bases in Turkey, Germany, Japan, Taiwan, and England. All the pilots were civilians, most with military backgrounds. The first operational flights over the Middle East and the Mediterranean took place in May and June 1956 and were conducted at the time of the Suez Crisis between Egypt and U.S. allies France and Great Britain.

The U-2s could fly more than 13 miles high. As time went on, the U-2s took off from bases in Lahore and Peshawar, Pakistan, Atsugi, Japan (the base where Lee Oswald worked), Wiesbaden, Germany, and Bodo, Norway. The destinations of these flights were the Soviet Union. The Russians were able to pick up these planes on their radar scopes but they had no way of shooting them down.

The CIA conducted a total of twenty flights over the Soviet Union between 1956 and 1960, the time of the downing of pilot Francis Gary Powers. President Eisenhower had to give his permission for any mission of the U-2 and by 1960, Ike had curtailed the frequency of the missions over the Soviet Union and China, fearing that these missions might have a detrimental effect on U.S.-Soviet relations.

By the spring of 1960, tensions between the United States and the Soviet Union had lessened and hope for a new beginning in the Cold War relationship between the two nations was in the air. Russian Premier Nikita Khrushchev made a trip to the United States in September 1959 and made a tour of the country. During Mr. K's trip to the United States, President Eisenhower had fruitful talks with his Russian counterpart, and it was decided that the men would meet in May 1960 for a summit conference in Paris.

President Eisenhower had received word from the CIA that the Russians had developed, or were in the development stage of building, surface-to-air missiles (SAM) that might be able to shoot down the U-2. The SAMs, according to the American military, could not get to the 70,000 feet that the U-2s operated at. Richard Bissell told the President, "if the missile was fired it would be a near-miss, rather than a hit." John Foster Dulles, Secretary of State, told the president, "If the Soviets ever capture one of these planes, I'm sure they will never admit it. To do so would make it necessary for them to admit also that for years we had been carrying on flights over their territory while they had been helpless to do anything about the matter."

103

Despite the risks, the President decided it was necessary to conduct more U-2 flights in order to find out if the Russians were building new ICBM (Intercontinental Ballistic Missile) sites. After the U-2 mission in which Francis Gary Powers was shot down, he said, "the pilots believed the resumption of the flights was due at least in part to the agency's fear that Russia was now close to solving her missile-guidance problem."

In early May 1960, President Eisenhower, flanked by his advisors John Eisenhower (his brother) and General Andrew Goodpaster, studied maps of the Soviet Union, going over the potential flight routes any new U-2 pilot would take. The U.S. had to wait 14 days until cloud cover over the Soviet Union eased enough to send a new plane on its way. When the news of the improving weather over the Soviet Union came to the White House, the President gave his OK for the next flight.

The President was taking a risk in ordering the new U-2 flight at that particular time. He would be meeting later that month with Premier Khrushchev in Paris, and any untoward happening with the U-2 would make for a major international flap. However, he decided that it was worth the risk.

On May 1, 1960, pilot Francis Gary Powers took off from Peshawar, Pakistan, bound for the missile testing grounds called the Tyuratram launch sites in the Soviet Union. Francis Gary Powers was born in Kentucky, entered the Air Force as a cadet in 1951, and received his commission as a Second Lieutenant. He flew F-84 Commandos at his assignment with the 468th Strategic Fighter Squadron at Turner AFB in Georgia. He was transferred to the super-secret U-2 program on "loan" to the CIA in 1956. Powers and five other men were sent to the air base at Adana, Turkey to fly "weather missions." It was from the Tyuratram facility that the USSR was building launch facilities for its new type of intercontinental missile, the SS-6. As he crossed the Soviet Union at 70,000 feet, Powers' U-2 was hit by a Soviet missile near the town of Sverdlosk. Disregarding standard operating procedure, Powers failed to destroy the plane and bailed out instead. He was immediately captured by Soviet soldiers, alive and well.

Later that day, General Goodpaster telephoned President Eisenhower telling him that the U-2 operation he sanctioned was "overdue and possibly lost."

At CIA headquarters there was bedlam after the report that the plane Powers was flying had been lost. No one knew if Powers was alive or dead or if the plane had been destroyed. However, the top brass at Langley mistakenly believed that no pilot could survive a bailout at that height. They put out a cover story that the downed plane was a weather flight staged by the National Aeronautics and Space Administration (NASA) that had crashed. They also fudged when they said that the plane had originally taken off from Adana, Turkey, not Pakistan. Later that day, NASA released a public statement saying that the plane was a high-altitude weather plane that had gone missing on a flight inside Turkey. They added, "the pilot reported over the emergency frequency that he was experiencing oxygen difficulties."

It turned out that as his plane began spiraling out of control, Powers released the canopy, ready to bail out. When he opened his seatbelt, he was quickly sucked out of the plane and was dangling by his oxygen hose. Soon, the hose broke loose and as he fell, his parachute automatically opened. His plane had been destroyed in the crash, but unknown to the CIA, he was alive and well.

According to a declassified CIA report on the U-2 incident that was released in June 2013, Soviet radar began picking up Powers' U-2 when it was only 15 miles south of the Soviet-Afghan border and continued monitor it as the plane flew across the Central Asian republics. When Powers reached the Tashkent area, 13 Soviet interceptor aircraft were scrambled to try to intercept him. Powers' plane was downed when a Soviet SA-1 SAM detonated close to his plane, causing him to lose control.[2]

Oleg Penkovsky, a highly-placed U.S. mole inside the Soviet Union, provided his own account of how Powers' U-2 was hit:

> There were no direct hits, only damage to the tail and wing assembly. The damaged parts were not shown at the Moscow exhibition and your intelligence personnel should have spotted that. He was within the radius of explosion, and as a result of the shock wave from the explosion, the plane was damaged and poor Powers sustained a concussion. I don't know what he reported to his parents or others, but while falling he blanked out several times. He was not conscious when he parachuted to earth or when everything on him was seized. The claims

[2] Pedlow, Gregory and Welenbach, Donald, *The CIA and Overhead Reconnaissance: The U-2 and Oxcart Programs 1954-1972*, CIA History Program.

of a direct hit were, of course, absurd. I reported this to you already on the 12th of August last year, and I reported on the RB-47.[3]

In the Soviet Union, Premier Khrushchev played the downing of the U-2 plane to the hilt. On May 5, he made a statement to the Supreme Soviet that a U.S. "spy plane" had been downed near Sverdlovsk. However, he made no mention of the fact that the pilot had survived. Two days later, he made the shocking announcement that the pilot was alive.

Upon learning of Powers' capture, President Eisenhower lied to the nation when he said that Powers had mistakenly strayed into Soviet airspace while conducting weather research. Soon, Ike was caught in another lie when Powers was incarcerated by the KGB and publicly paraded in front of the world's press in Moscow. It was now obvious that President Eisenhower had been less than truthful about his knowledge of Powers' mission and the Soviets took full advantage of the situation.

The capture of Gary Powers forced the cancellation of the planned Paris summit meeting between U.S., Soviet, British and French leaders meant to seek reductions in worldwide tensions.

After the CIA found out that Powers was still alive, the CIA ordered its pilots out of its base in Turkey, and President Eisenhower cancelled any further overflights of the Soviet Union.

Powers went on trial in Moscow on espionage charges on August 19, 1960. In a forced confession, Powers said that he was "deeply repentant and profoundly sorry" for his mission over Russia. He was found guilty and given a ten-year jail sentence. He served two years and was exchanged for Russian spy Rudolf Abel.

Upon his return to the United States, Powers resumed his duties with Lockheed until 1970. He died in 1977 in a helicopter crash while working for a television station in Los Angeles. Almost forty years after his shoot-down over the Soviet Union, Powers' family was awarded the Distinguished Flying Cross, the Department of Defense Prisoner of War Medal and the National Defense Service Medal for his service to the nation.

---

[3] Schecter, Jerrold, and Deriabin, Peter, S., *The Spy Who Saved the World*, Charles Scribner's Sons, New York, 1992, Page 119.

Chapter 17:
The Defection of Pyotr Popov

In 1953, the city of Vienna, Austria was one of the hotbeds of international espionage, with agents of the allied nations as well as the Soviet Union prowling its dark streets. The city was divided into four enclaves, with the Russians owning their own area of influence, and the U.S., French and British, the others. The spies of each nation watched each other closely, hoping to gain the upper hand. On January 1, 1953, an American vice consul enters his car for the ride home. Once inside the car he notices an envelope, which is addressed to the American High Commissioner. As he opens the letter, he finds a note that was dated on December 28, 1952, only a few days before. The message is brief:

> I am a Soviet officer. I wish to meet with an American officer with the object of offering certain services. Time: 1800 hours. Date: 1 January 1953. Place: Plankengasse, Vienna 1. Failing this meeting, I will be at the same place, same time, on successive Saturdays.

The message was written by a Soviet officer who worked in Russian military intelligence, Pyotr Popov. That clandestine meeting would mark the beginning of the first major CIA penetration of Soviet intelligence during the Cold War. Pyotr Popov would be the first Soviet intelligence office to defect to the United States, but in the end, his story is not a pretty one.

Pyotr Popov was born in 1922 near the Soviet town of Khady, near the Volga River. His family was poor and he did not have much of an early education. When he was 13 his father died, and at age 16 he was sent to a school in Tula, about 300 miles from his home. After Russia entered World War II, Popov was inducted into the army and he attained the rank of Junior Lieutenant, a rank with little privilege. He managed to survive the fighting on the central front, was wounded, and in 1943 he was accepted into the Communist Party.

His superiors saw promise in the young man and in December

107

1944 he was accepted into the Frunze Military Academy that was the Soviet command's staff college. In December 1945, Popov met and later married a woman named Galina and they moved to Moscow. Soon, they had two children and in 1948 he was assigned to the Chief Intelligence Directorate of the Soviet General Staff. At this same time he took classes at a military intelligence school. He'd come a long way from the poor surroundings of his youth, something he had wanted all his life. However, Popov did not really understand the basics of military intelligence, and he was actually not ready to go on the next assignment the Soviets had for him.

He was assigned to Vienna where he lived with his wife at the Grand Hotel, one of the city's best residences. His job was to try to recruit anyone he met who might be willing to serve the Soviet Union. One obstacle was that he could not speak German. Due to his lack of production, he was temporarily recalled to Moscow in April 1954 and sent to GRU (Russian military intelligence) headquarters.

But in 1953, Popov was a strange defector indeed. Previous to his assignment in Vienna, he had never met a Westerner and did not fully comprehend any way of life outside of the confines of the Soviet Union. He was like a fish out of water, trying to make it back to the sea.

Once his bona fides were checked at the CIA, he was hired. For the CIA, Popov was a cheap investment. Unlike the spies of the 1970s and 1980s, Popov was paid the small amount of $100 per month for the bonanza of information he provided. Popov would become in spy parlance, an "agent-in-place," working for the CIA, while still going about his daily work for the GRU. In return for his $100 stipend, the CIA received from their new Russian friend the codenames (and the real ones) of more than 370 Eastern bloc agents who had infiltrated the West.

As Popov's CIA career began to prosper, he had a most unexpected call from his superior. It seems that CIA Director Allen Dulles had been informed of Popov and he wanted to give him a token of his appreciation. Popov's section chief gave him a pair of gold-plated cuff links from the director. But the pair of cufflinks had another purpose: "It was to be used as a recognition device in which an identical pair was held at CIA headquarters, to be used in establishing the bona fides of any emissary who might be sent to contact Popov later, either in the Soviet Union or in some other place." [1]

In 1955, Popov was promoted to full colonel in the GRU. Now back in Vienna, Popov met a woman by the name of Milca Kohanek of Serbian extraction, who soon became his mistress. She was a member of the Austrian Communist Party and her relationship with Popov was encouraged by the GRU. Popov soon fell in love with her and their relationship was noticed by the CIA. One CIA report on them said, "she must, in truth, have hidden charms since it is open to question that even her mother could love her face." Despite his affair, his family soon joined him in Vienna.

In 1955, Popov left Vienna for his next assignment, the Soviet Zone of Germany. He was assigned to the German city of Karlshorst where he worked in the headquarters of the Eastern European Soviet Intelligence. This was a very sensitive assignment for Popov because he now had access to information concerning 288 operations that the Soviets were running. He immediately turned over all of this information to the CIA. His job also entailed the running of "illegals" to foreign countries. An illegal was a Soviet citizen who went abroad and was provided with a new identity in his new country. Once safely in his new home, this person would blend into the woodwork and begin his or her espionage assignment.

One illegal Popov ran was a young Russian woman who was supposed to be a citizen of Austria, but in fact was a Russian. She was sent to Constantinople, Turkey where she operated undercover as the owner of a women's clothing store. Popov told the CIA Station Chief in Turkey all about her.

Another important coup on Popov's part was when he sent a copy of a speech given by Marshal Georgi Zhukov, who was the Deputy Minister of Defense of the Soviet Union. Popov provided the details of this speech to his CIA handler, George Kisevalter. The speech was delivered to a number of top Soviet military officers and it was about Russian strategies for a possible military conflict in Germany. As a matter of routine, the CIA sent all major intelligence finds to the British, and Zhukov's speech was no exception. However, unknown to the British, they had in their midst a double agent named George Blake who read the report

[1] Hart, John. *The CIA's Russians,* Naval Institute Press, Annapolis, Maryland, 2003, Page 42-43.

sent by Popov. It is not known if Blake knew that Popov was the informant.

One of the first agents he successfully infiltrated into the United States was a woman named Margarita Tairova. Tairova went to New York under the watchful eye of Popov. No sooner had she arrived in the city than the FBI was on her case. Hoover's FBI had gotten wind through their intelligence sources that Miss Tairova was visiting the city and put a 24-hour tail on her. The problem at the CIA was whether to give Hoover's G-men the details of why Tairova was in the United States, since their surveillance might alert the Soviets that one of their prized agents was under FBI scrutiny. The matter was settled by CIA Director Allen Dulles who reluctantly told Hoover the operational reasons concerning their interest in the woman.

After her arrival in New York, Tairova met her husband, Walter, and soon they had rented an apartment in Manhattan's fashionable west side. On March 12, 1958, Margarita and Walter disappeared, later to surface in Moscow. The Soviets were alarmed as to why and how Margarita's arrival in New York had been leaked, and they immediately began an investigation. The first person they looked into was Popov himself who had complete knowledge of their travel plans. With Popov now under KGB investigation, the CIA asked him if he wanted to defect. Popov refused. That decision was the costliest mistake he would ever make.

Popov was sent back to the Soviet Union, not a good sign for anyone who might be under covert surveillance by the KGB. Popov had no reason to believe that he was in any danger and he continued working for both sides. His CIA contact in Moscow was Russell Langelle, whose cover was that of an American diplomat working out of the American embassy. George Kisevalter, his old CIA contact, gave Langelle precise instructions as to how to get in touch with Popov. One time Kisevalter wanted to get some items to Popov which included money and operational instructions for future missions. The system of delivery was a "brush contact," a quick handoff (of a brief case, for example) while the men passed each other on the street. In the event that trick didn't work, Langelle would then send Popov the material via mail that would go in care of the U.S. Embassy in Moscow.

Langelle too was now under KGB surveillance and he had to be doubly careful not to be seen in touch with Popov. At one time, Langelle met Popov at a local bus stop and managed to hand over the material without being seen.

Things began to go wrong very wrong almost immediately after the bus incident. Langelle sent a message to another CIA officer working out of the U.S. Embassy by the name of George Winters, telling him that the brush contact had succeeded and not to send the letter by mail. Instead, the inexperienced Winters mailed the letter to Popov. Winters went to the designated mailbox, dropped the letter in, and left. However, he was trailed by the KGB who emptied the contents of the box and took the letter back to headquarters. After reading the note, the KGB put Popov under arrest.

The CIA had no idea that their prized agent was under arrest and made plans to meet him once more. The KGB told Popov to give the CIA bogus information, which he did. Besides giving the CIA the false information, he managed to write a real letter telling the CIA of his arrest. The real information that Popov included was the fact that the Russian army consisted of 3,423,000 men, and that the Russians had 12 nuclear-powered submarines. The inept KGB guards did not fully read Popov's entire note, much to their horror.

It is still unclear how Popov was put to death. Some sources say he was executed by firing squad, others say he was put alive into a burning fire and suffered a horrible death. The case soon became even murkier, when, in 1964, Yuri Nosenko, a Soviet intelligence officer who defected to the United States, said that the KGB had known about Popov's double life long before his arrest. But could Nosenko's information on Popov be believed? Another person who backed up the story of the events leading up to Popov's arrest was a KGB officer named Alexsandr Cherepanov. Cherepanov was a disgruntled KGB officer who took it upon himself to deliver to the CIA 50 pages of the so-called "Cherepanov Papers" from KGB headquarters directly to the CIA at the U.S. Embassy. He was subsequently arrested by the KGB and executed.[2]

James Angleton, the CIA's legendary counterintelligence maven, was highly critical of the circumstances surrounding the arrest of Popov. He didn't believe that Popov had given Langelle a

---

[2] Mangold, Tom, *Cold Warrior: James Jesus Angleton: The CIA's Master Spy Hunter,* Simon and Schuster, New York, 1991, Page 253.

real message concerning the Soviet military at the time of his arrest. He believed that Popov had been blown by the letter sent by George Winters. Angleton, rightly or wrongly, believed that Popov had been blown by a Soviet mole hidden somewhere deep in the bowels of the CIA.

The case of Pyotr Popov, the agency's first defector, still resonates in the history of the CIA as one of its most enduring puzzles.

Chapter 18:
Who Killed Patrice Lumumba?

African nationalism was one of the spreading themes on the Dark Continent shortly after the end of World War II. The old colonial empires, i.e., England, France, and Portugal, were dead in the geopolitical water, only to be replaced by the two superpowers, the United States and the Soviet Union.

One of the countries on the continent of Africa that had its own violent revolution was the Congo, which was previously ruled by Belgium. When the Belgians granted independence, various political factions in the country began to battle each other, separately seeking to become the power. As the situation grew worse, United Nations forces were airlifted into the Congo to try to keep the peace. The civil war in the Congo was made up of three separate groups, all vying for power: the Kasavubu-Mobutu government in Leopoldville, the Antoine Gizenga-Patrice Lumumba organization located in Stanleyville, and the group headed by Moise Tshombe in Elisabethville.

But the flash point as far as the Congo was concerned was the threat of Joseph Mobutu in the Katanga Province to secede from the Congo. The Province of Katanga was rich in diamonds, copper and cobalt, all vital materials needed for weapons and commercial use. It was the threat of the Katanga secession that led to the arrival of UN peacekeepers. Soon though, civil war began in earnest in the Congo and those events were not missed by the Eisenhower administration, then in its final days in office.

In the winter of 1960, a secret meeting of the "54/12 Group" of the National Security Council convened to discuss the ever-worsening situation in the Congo. In further meetings with President Eisenhower, along with CIA Director Dulles, it was decided that "something had to be done" about putting an end to the Congolese crisis and in particular, getting rid of Patrice Lumumba who was by now beginning to become America's new bogy man in Africa. The job was given to the CIA, although it is not absolutely certain that President Eisenhower knew, or gave the order, that Lumumba was to be killed.

At a July 21, 1960 meeting of the NSC between Allen Dulles

and others to discuss the Congo crisis, the note takers in the room made the following remarks: "Mr. Dulles said that in Lumumba we were faced with a person who was Castro or worse. Mr. Dulles went on to describe Mr. Lumumba's background that he described as 'harrowing.' It is safe to go on the assumption that Lumumba has been bought by the Communists; this also, however, fits with his own orientation."

By late 1960, a cable was sent to Lawrence Devlin, the CIA Station Chief in Leopoldville, under the signature of DCI Allen Dulles, to plan an assassination attempt on Patrice Lumumba. Devlin was told to have some individuals try to poison Lumumba. When that attempt failed, Devlin asked the CIA for a "high-powered rifle with a telescopic sight and silencer."

According to declassified CIA documents on the plots to kill Lumumba:

> In November 1962, Mr. Justin O'Donnell advised Mr. Lyman Kirkpatrick that he had, at one time, been directed by Mr. Richard Bissell to assume responsibility for a project involving the assassination of Patrice Lumumba, then Premier, Republic of Congo. According to O'Donnell, poison was to have been the vehicle as he made reference to having been instructed to see Mr. Sidney Gottlieb, in order to procure the appropriate vehicle.[1]

Lawrence Devlin went by the alias "Victor Hedgeman" while he was in the Congo, and in September 1960, he got a call from Washington telling him that he would be getting an important message from "Joe from Paris." The mysterious "Joe from Paris" was Sidney Gottlieb, the CIA's foremost expert in the development of poisons. When Gottlieb arrived in the Congo he told Devlin that the assassination order had been given by President Eisenhower, but that he, personally, had not seen the order. The poison, said Gottlieb, worked in such a way that Lumumba would look to the world as someone who had died of natural causes.

Devlin took an active role in administrating the covert work the CIA Station needed to do in order to drive Lumumba from

[1] Memorandum for the Record: In November 1962 Mr. RIF No. 104-10303-10011.

power. Years later he told a reporter that if he refused to carry out headquarters' orders someone else would just come in and take his place. Once Gottlieb gave him the poison, he put it in his office safe where it would be hidden from view. Devlin did the dirty work for the Leopoldville station, feeding anti-Lumumba stories to the newspapers and bugging the offices of the opposition parties. He often met with Colonel Mobutu, one of the leaders of the anti-Lumumba clique. Mobutu told Devlin that the army was ready to overthrow Lumumba at the proper moment and, after checking with Washington, Devlin gave Mobutu the go ahead with the plan.

The circumstances leading up to the death of Patrice Lumumba are complicated and there is little room in this narrative to give the whole story. Suffice it to say that on November 30, UN sources said that they saw Lumumba somewhere in the northern part of the Congo and he was arrested a few days later. He was placed under arrest near the city of Kinshasa. Lumumba and two others were then transferred to Elisabethville on January 17, 1961, three days before John F. Kennedy was sworn in as President. Sources reported that Lumumba was severely beaten during his transfer. According to several witnesses who were present at the time, Lumumba was killed before arriving in Lumbumbashi. Moise Tshombe said that when he saw Lumumba, he was almost dead.

The CIA wrote of the circumstances surrounding the death of Lumumba:

> The exact circumstances of Lumumba's death remain a mystery, although it is clear he expired his last breath in or around Elisabethville in early 1961. His burial place is unknown. It is also clear that from 9 November, and possibly even from 10 October, this Agency was either unable to determine the whereabouts of Lumumba or was aware that he was under detention by units of the Congolese and UN forces. It seems highly unlikely that anyone within the Agency would have given serious consideration to the assassination of Lumumba when he was, in fact, either virtually incarcerated or his whereabouts were unknown.[2]

---

[2] Memorandum: Alleged Agency Involvement in the death of Patrice Lumumba. RIF No. 104-10310-10201.

Even if the CIA did not itself kill Lumumba, they were knee deep in secret dealings with two elusive agents who were in the Congo at the time of his death. These two mysterious men go by the code names QJ/WIN and WI/ROGUE. Both of these men were part of the CIA's secret assassination project called ZR/RIFLE, which was headed by William Harvey. The House Select Committee on assassinations (HSCA) delved deeply into the ZR/RIFLE project and wrote the following about agent QJ/WIN and his part in the Lumumba plot:

> Shortly after [blank] arrival in the Congo he was joined by a CIA agent with a criminal background who was used by the CIA as part of a program to develop a stand-by assassination capability [the ZR/RIFLE program]. Late in 1960, one of the operatives of the [blank] Station in Leopoldville approached this agent of [blank] with a proposition to join an "execution squad."
>
> Despite the fact that [blank] was initially approached to be part of the plot to assassinate Patrice Lumumba, it is unlikely that [blank] was actually involved in the implementation of that plot by [blank] Station. Whether there is any connection of that plot and either of the two operatives QJ/WIN and WI/ROGUE is less clear.[3]

What is clear is that the CIA hired two men of questionable background; QJ/WIN and WI/ROUGE, to do something possibly take part in the assassination of Lumumba. But just who were these men? There is little concrete evidence in the CIA files, only a lot of tantalizing information as to their backgrounds and how they came to be involved with the CIA.

A CIA document dated March 10, 1975 called "Alleged Agency Involvement in the Death of Patrice Lumumba" is one of many such documents that reveal the back-story of the CIA's involvement in the event. The material comes from the CIA's Africa Division and it refers to QJ/WIN in this regard: "There is traffic originated from FT/D involving the travel to Leopoldville of an asset made available to the CIA by a friendly European liaison service [possibly French

[3] Senate Select Committee Report on Assassinations (Draft), 1975, Page 52.

secret service]. This traffic could lead one to the conclusion that there was a connection between the travel of this asset and Lumumba's death… The conclusion reached is that it is highly doubtful that this individual was connected with any agency planning regarding Lumumba."

Talking about QJ/WIN, the paper goes on to detail how he was recruited by the CIA:

> The European asset in question came to Agency attention for the first time in 1958 as a known smuggler with contacts among illegal traders and petty criminals. His name was surfaced to CIA in response to a request for an individual who could be used in a dangle operation against KGB activities and, particularly, against a known KGB officer. He next came to Agency attention in the spring of 1959 in connection with a reported Chinese Communist attempt to smuggle opium into the U.S. He offered his services on 14 October 1960. FI/D asked the appropriate Chief of Station to see whether the asset can be available the week of 14 October 1960. The reply was affirmative. On October 27, a communication from Europe indicated:

> Some required shots not available and subject must get Paris. Will not complete series until November 1960. On 2 November 1960, Headquarters was informed that the asset was met on 2 November. He accepted offer Leopoldville. Precise mission not conveyed to him. He only informed mission might involve element of personal risk. The cable also indicates that the FI/D case officer who met the asset in Europe was planning to travel to Leopoldville to study the local situation and subsequently to cable European station the details of cover and time of travel, presumably of the asset. On 5 November 1960, the Leopoldville Station asked that the asset should be told to proceed to Leopoldville as soon as his shots were completed. Presumably this would be shortly subject to 11 November. A 6 December cable

117

requested a salary advance be deposited in a European bank for the asset's wife who was ill. This places the asset in Leopoldville on 6 December. On 8 December 1960, a cable from Leopoldville indicates that the asset had developed close relationship with Yugoslav who had agreed to smuggle industrial diamonds for him to Italy. The Station proposed an operation to entrap the Yugoslav pilot for intelligence purposes.[4]

By the tone of the memo, it is safe to say that the CIA's asset, known as QJ/WIN, was sent to Leopoldville at the same time that the plot to oust Lumumba was under way. By the tone of the memo, it is unclear just why QJ/WIN was sent to the Congo, but it was not for the purpose of sightseeing. He was there for some CIA sanctioned operation, not revealed in the abovementioned memo.

According to the CIA memo, QJ/WIN was in the business of diamond smuggling, and if the scenario just described is right, then there is a plausible reason for his appearance in the Congo at the time of the plot against Lumumba, not as an assassin, but in another capacity.

The CIA agreed to pay him $7,200 per year, and he was to be given $600.00 at the end of each month. He was to be paid expenses but not for the purchase of information.

In its investigation into the assassination plots against foreign leaders, the Senate Select Committee divulged the name of a second CIA asset who was sent to the Congo at the time of the plot to kill Patrice Lumumba. Like QJ/WIN, this mysterious person's real identity is still one of the most highly guarded secrets of the CIA. However, there is enough information in the released files to fill in some of the missing blanks in this convoluted story. The codename given to this man was WI/ROGUE. Like QJ/WIN, WI/ROGUE was a soldier of fortune, a man of action, someone whom the CIA would have no trouble hiring for a covert mission like the one in the Congo.

WI/ROGUE was an "essentially stateless" soldier of fortune, a forger and former bank robber. The CIA sent him to the Congo after giving him plastic surgery and a toupee so that any of the other members of the European soldier of fortune community in the

[4]Memorandum: Alleged Agency Involvement in the Death of Patrice Lumumba. 3/10/75. RIF No. 104-10310-10201.

Congo would not recognize him. The CIA called him a man who "learns quickly and carries out any assignment without regard for danger."

When WI/ROGUE arrived in the Congo, he attempted to hire another person to be a member of an "execution squad." That person, believe it or not, was QJ/WIN.

Victor Hedgeman wrote the following about WI/ROGUE. "In sum, the testimony of the CIA officers involved in the PROP operation and the concern about WI/ROGUE's 'freewheeling' suggests that agent WI/ROGUE's attempt to form an 'execution squad' was an unauthorized maverick action, unconnected to any CIA operation. However, the fact that WI/ROGUE was to be trained in 'medical immunization' precludes a definitive conclusion to that effect."

Like QJ/WIN, WI/ROGUE had a checkered past which was known and accepted by the CIA for the work they had planned for him. It seems that the CIA went to great lengths to hide his real identity before shunting him off to Africa. Until the files on both of these elusive men are made public by the CIA, we will not know their true identities.

The CIA's first real assassination plot (called Executive Action-ZR/RIFLE) involving a national leader thus came to an end. However, it was not the last. Both QJ/WIN and WI/ROUGE were later to be named as possible players in the Kennedy assassination.

Research Note: Anyone who is interested in learning more about these two men and the assassination of Patrice Lumumba should see the author's book *JFK: The French Connection*.

Chapter 19:
Disaster at the Bay of Pigs

The April 1961 Bay of Pigs invasion of Cuba by a thousand Cuban exiles had its roots in the last days of the Eisenhower administration. President Eisenhower was in office at the time that Fidel Castro took leadership in Cuba. At first, the Eisenhower administration took a cautious look at the new man in Havana and tried working with Castro, after the corruption of the Batista era. But as time went on, it became obvious that Castro was not the democrat that he proclaimed himself to be. Soon after taking over, Castro took concrete steps that would make the hairs on the U.S. administration's neck stand up. He began to nationalize certain foreign-owned industries and closed down the lucrative Mafia casinos that were run for the most part by American gangsters. The final straw, as far as the Americans were concerned, was drawn when he began overtures toward the Soviet Union. Something would have to be done where Castro was concerned, and to that end, the first covert moves by the Eisenhower administration began.

In March 1960, the Eisenhower team began a secret plan to topple the Castro regime. Richard Bissell was authorized to form a task force called "The Special Group," and later, "Operation 40" to devise an anti-Castro plan of action. A Cuban task force was started, its members consisting of J.C. King of the CIA, CIA Inspector General Lyman Kirkpatrick, and others. A document was worked out that had the following points vis-a- vis the Castro problem:

1) The creation of a united Cuban opposition to the Castro regime located outside of Cuba, 2) the development of a means of mass communication to the Cuban people as part of a powerful propaganda effort, 3) the creation and development of a covert intelligence and action organization within Cuba which would be responsive to the orders and directions of the exile opposition, and 4) the development of a paramilitary force outside of Cuba for future guerilla action.

On March 17, 1960, President Eisenhower signed a secret National Security Council Directive giving "A Program of Covert Action Against the Castro Regime" the green light.

All this was going on during the hotly contested 1960 presidential campaign between Vice President Richard Nixon and Senator John Kennedy. Eisenhower appointed Nixon as the point man in the administration's secret efforts to topple Castro, and the Vice President took on the job with relish. But Nixon was in a dammed if he did and dammed if he didn't situation. As leader of Operation 40, Nixon knew all along about the CIA's secret plans to topple Castro, yet could not state so publicly during the campaign. When Kennedy began attacking the administration's ineffective efforts to topple Castro, Nixon could only bite his tongue.

The administration ordered the CIA to begin covert training of a number of Cuban exiles in the jungles of Guatemala under Agency tutelage. Soon, a number of American military officers and staff were covertly sent to Guatemala to train the ragged but eager troops for an eventual invasion of their homeland. The seeds that were planted in 1960 in the jungles of Guatemala formed the roots of the 1961 Bay of Pigs invasion.

Of all the men in the CIA the newly elected President came to admire the first, was Richard Bissell. Kennedy and Bissell liked each other from the start and Bissell was hoping that Kennedy would appoint him as Dulles's successor. Before being sworn in as the 35th president, Kennedy was briefed on the Cuba project at the home of his father, Ambassador Joseph P. Kennedy, in Palm Beach, Florida on November 18, 1960 by Bissell and Dulles. The men told Kennedy that there was a short window of opportunity if an invasion of Cuba was to take place. They told him that the Soviets were supplying Castro with MIG fighters along with Russian trainers. At the time that they briefed Kennedy, the invasion plan was changing rapidly. It started out as a plan to infiltrate a few dozen men into Cuban jungles where they would conduct hit-and-run raids against Castro's forces. Now the plan was to send hundreds of men into Cuba as per the D-Day invasion of France in 1944.

The first covert effort to supply the rebels was a disaster. On September 28, 1960, an "arms pack" for the men on the ground landed in a dam and the arms were retrieved by the Cuban army. One agent on the mission was shot and killed. Kennedy was skeptical of the operation, but upon taking office on January 20, 1961, allowed the CIA planning for the operation to go ahead.

During a mid-January 1961 meeting of The Special Group, who were tasked with the job of mapping out plans for the invasion of Cuba, a number of questions were posed as to how far the U.S. would go to aid the invasion. Among them was the use of American contract pilots for flights over Cuba, the use of U.S.-based airfields for logistical flights over the island, the use of air strikes one day before the actual invasion took place, and the use of Puerto Cabezas, Nicaragua, as an American staging area. Only the use of Puerto Cabezas was approved. The chief of the CIA's paramilitary division strongly recommended the use of U.S. air power to cover any landing in Cuba, but his recommendation was turned down.

Political necessity, not military planning, was the driving force behind the early CIA planning for the Bay of Pigs invasion. Top CIA advisors were going ahead with a flawed plan even though they did not know whether the new Kennedy administration was going to implement the invasion or cancel it.

By the time the Kennedy administration came to office, the invasion scenario was dramatically changed. The original plan called for the invaders to land near the Escambray Mountains in Cuba where conditions were ripe for a guerilla-type war against Castro's army. Instead, the new landing site was to be along the beaches of the Bay of Pigs, a flat area surrounded by large bodies of water, open to a counterattack by Cuban forces. After the invasion took place, the CIA conducted a thorough review of the events leading up to the invasion and they summed up this part of the planning by saying, "The lack of contingency planning for either survival or rescue of the brigade has never been satisfactorily explained."

Soon, the CIA sent their ragtag brigade for intensive training at a secret base in Guatemala called Camp Trax. Most of the men had little or no military experience and it was a hard job for their CIA instructors to mold them into some semblance of a fighting force. The Agency also began operating a clandestine radio station called Radio Swan, which sent anti-Castro propaganda into Cuba.

As training for the invasion began, the exiles were given their own name—Brigade 2506. The official name "2506" was born when one of the exiles with that membership number—Carlos Santana, died in a training exercise at the secret camp in Guatemala. It was decided by the brigade's CIA case officers to name the attack force "Brigade 2506" in honor of their fallen comrade.

Into this fluid mix, the CIA sent a number of men to train the exiles. They were a cast of characters out of a B movie, some of whom did not speak Spanish, some who were openly contemptuous of the exiles, and others who did not get along with their fellow agents. Among them were:

• Frank Bender. His real name was Gerry Droller. He came from Germany, and served in the OSS during World War II. He did not speak any Spanish but was assigned to be the agency's political action arm to the newly created Cuban government-in-exile. The CIA sent E. Howard Hunt to help Bender care for the Cubans whom the administration wanted to see in power once Castro was gone. Hunt and Bender never got along, with each man trumpeting the virtues of their own favorite Cubans. Hunt even went so far as to have Droller banned from taking part in Agency operations in Miami.

The two Cuban exile leaders Droller and Hunt were most receptive to were Manuel Artime and Anthony "Tony" Varona. They did not like each other and their own feud only added to the battle between Bender his CIA colleagues. At one point in the early exile training in Guatemala, it was announced by Hunt and Richard Bissell, after visiting one of the secret camps, that it would be wise to print some pictures of the soldiers and publish them in an American newspaper. Bender was given the job of producing the photos of the agency's secret troops training to overthrow Castro that were shown in a Miami newspaper for all the world to see (including Castro's spies in the city).

• Jack Hawkins. Jack Hawkins was a Marine Colonel who aided the CIA in the planning of the exile invasion. He traveled to the CIA-run camps in Guatemala where he worked with the other CIA trainers to get the exiles into fighting shape. At first, Hawkins was positive concerning the Cuban invasion, working hand in glove with Jacob Esterline, who was the project director. He sent a glowing letter to Richard Bissell saying that the exiles were in fighting shape and were bound to succeed. This letter was sent to JFK. As plans for the invasion went along, he believed that air power could do the trick in toppling Castro. But as the invasion planning got into high gear, and the obvious faults became evident, Hawkins changed his mind and saw the invasion for what it was: a defeat ready to happen. After the invasion's failure, he went back to active duty.

• Jacob Esterline. By 1960, Esterline had been promoted to director of the Eisenhower administration's secret operation to overthrow Castro at the Bay of Pigs. He worked closely with Marine Colonel Jack Hawkins who was assigned to the CIA to train the cadre of Cuban exiles then in their secret training base in Guatemala. Soon though, he began to have doubts that the plans being developed for the overthrow of the Castro government would work, and threatened to resign. Instead, he was persuaded by Richard Bissell to remain on the team. Now, with the passage of time, it seems that Esterline and Hawkins' reservations concerning the Bay of Pigs invasion were correct. According to newly declassified documents, it is evident that even before Bissell pleaded with both Esterline and Hawkins to remain on the team, he had admitted to President Kennedy that he (JFK) should cut off any air cover for the Cuban exiles then trapped at the Bay of Pigs. Esterline was dumbfounded concerning the Kennedy administration's cutting off of any further military aid to the invaders, and was heartsick over the entire operation.

• Tracy Barnes. Tracy Barnes was one of the original CIA officers who began preparations for the Agency's plans to kill Fidel Castro. By 1961, Barnes had risen to the post of DD/P, Deputy Director of Plans for the CIA. Richard Bissell, his boss, asked him to take over the task of creating an Agency operation to topple the Castro regime. Working closely with the anti-Castro groups in the U.S., Barnes directed two of his most trusted men to act as liaisons with them, Gerry Droller and E. Howard Hunt.

Barnes dove into his new job with relish, establishing CIA training bases in Guatemala, creating an anti-Castro, CIA owned and operated radio station on Swan Island that broadcast propaganda into Cuba and ordering Droller and Hunt to choose a government-in-exile among the leaders of the U.S. Cuban community. One of Barnes's tasks was to find ways to destroy Castro personally, psychologically, and otherwise. Barnes was a fan of Ian Fleming's fictional spy, James Bond. Early in the Kennedy administration,

Fleming and his wife visited the White House where they had a personal meeting with the new President and his wife (Kennedy, too, was a Fleming fan). When Fleming proposed ways to do in the "Beard," the CIA took up some of the author's proposals—all with Barnes' approval. One of the Agency's plans was to find a way to make Castro's beard fall off, thus making his image as a rough and macho guy seem irrelevant.

• E. Howard Hunt. Of all the names that stand out in the Eisenhower-Kennedy administrations efforts to eliminate Fidel Castro, the name of E. Howard Hunt comes to the front. Hunt was one of the most influential CIA officers in the Cuba Project, who was linked to the early Bay of Pigs invasion of Cuba. Later he was in the spotlight as an infamous Watergate burglar.

In his early years, Hunt was a dime novelist, writing adventure yarns about secret agents. During World War II, he served in the OSS, and was assigned to Detachment 202 in China where he learned lessons on the life of a spy that would stay with him the rest of his life. He joined the CIA in the late 1940s, and took up duty stations in Mexico City, Washington, D.C. and Europe, among others.

Hunt was sent to Miami where he used the cover name "Eduardo" and was the Agency's liaison officer to the exiles. Hunt became friendly with a number of the most important of these exiles, like Enrique "Harry" Williams, a favorite of Robert Kennedy, and Manuel Artime. It was his closeness to these and other men that the Kennedy administration trusted that eventually got Hunt in trouble with the higher-ups in the Agency who supported another faction of the Cuban exiles.

It has been reported by many people associated with the CIA at the time of the Castro plots that it was Hunt who first originated the idea of assassinating Castro. Frank Sturgis, one of the mercenaries working with Gerry Patrick Hemming in the Interpen Organization, said that Hunt was responsible for various agency operations where "disposal" was carried out. "Disposal" is a CIA code word for assassination.

The landings at the Bay of Pigs were scheduled for April 17, 1961. However, before those could take place, the Cuban air force had to be taken out. On April 15, nine B-26s took off from Nicaragua.

Eight of the planes bombed Castro's air force, but did not destroy all of it. One plane made it to Miami with bullet holes in its fuselage. The bullet holes were fake, and the pilot said that he was a Cuban who defected (not true). A second air strike was supposed to have taken place on April 16, but JFK, who did not want any American participation in the raid, called it off.

The exiles landed at the Bay of Pigs on April 17 and were met with heavy resistance from Cuban forces. A number of ships carrying ammunition and medical supplies were destroyed offshore by Cuban fighters, dealing a heavy blow to the men on the beach. The USS *Essex,* an American carrier was offshore in international waters, ready to give aid and assistance to the men on the beach. According to Jake Esterline and Sam Halpern, also of the CIA, the *Essex* was not sent there by the President. The order had come from the Chief of Naval Operations, Admiral Arleigh Burke. The top brass at the Pentagon mistakenly believed that the President would not let the exiles die on the beach, and sent the Marines in to rescue them.[1]

While Brigade 2506 was fighting for its life on the beaches, President Kennedy was hosting a gala affair at the White House. Most of his top civilian and military advisors were in attendance and at one point they left to discuss the ongoing crisis. Both Richard Bissell and Admiral Burke asked the president to order another air strike, but he said no. JFK received heated messages from the exiles on the beach saying they were about to be overrun. Reluctantly, JFK ordered the military to send six unmarked planes to cover the beach to protect the invaders. However, the planes did not get there in time due to a horrible misstep. The men at the CIA forgot that there was a one-hour time difference between Cuba and Nicaragua. The planes never made it to the Bay of Pigs in time to save the exiles.

In an interesting aside to the Bay of Pigs planning, the CIA detained four men who were working in support of the invasion. These unidentified men were held in a detention facility shortly before the invasion. "The individuals were three Cuban trainees held in jail from 9 April until 20 April 1961 and a [blank] ship captain held from 29 March 1961 until 20 April 1961. The captain, who jumped ship on 28 March 1961, was in charge of a ship, which was

[1] Von Tunzelmann, Alex, *Red Heat: Conspiracy, Murder, and the Cold War In the Caribbean,* Henry Holt and Company, New York, 2011, Page 220.

transporting ammunition in support of the Cuban invasion. It was determined that the individuals' knowledge of the [blank] operation presented a security problem for the entire Cuban invasion operation. The three Cubans were jailed for several reasons, all relating to their reluctance originally to carry out their training. Release from the project site was determined to create a security hazard and they were also held in the jail until after the invasion. Upon their release each of the individuals was given a small amount of money and allowed to return to their choice of residence in the United States."[2]

In the end, more than 1,000 men from Brigade 2506 were captured and the rest were killed. The survivors were treated badly by the Cubans and a deep resentment toward President Kennedy took root. It took almost a year before they were ransomed by the U.S. government.

On December 29, 1962, President Kennedy spoke before the now freed brigade members at Miami's Orange Bowl. A crowd of 40,000 was on hand when Brigade 2506's chief Pepe San Ramon presented Kennedy with the brigade flag. In the heat of the moment, JFK told the audience, "I can assure you that this flag will be returned to this brigade in a free Havana."

In the congressional report on the Kennedy assassination they wrote of this time:

> Nevertheless, it is difficult to finalize an assessment of the brigade's collective attitude toward the U.S. Government and the Kennedy administration following the Orange Bowl event. Kennedy's resolution to the Cuban missile crisis, in which he promised Castro that raids against Cuba from the U.S. mainland would be halted, was considered an act of betrayal to their cause by many of the exiles in the anti-Castro communities. Yet most of the members of the brigade seemed to maintain a basic confidence in the U.S. Government's resolve to topple the Castro regime, and, in fact, nearly half of them enlisted in the U.S. Armed Forces through a special arrangement made by President Kennedy himself.
>
> In the perspective of an investigation of the Kennedy

[2] Background Material Re: CIA Activities Prior to the Bay of Pigs, 5/75. RIF No. 157-10011-10069.

assassination, the members of Brigade 2506 had to be considered of primary interest if only in terms of motivations and means. As one member, who later became involved in anti-Castro terrorist activity, explained: "We learned from them. We use the tactics that we learned from the CIA because we were trained to do everything. We were trained to set off a bomb, we were trained to kill.[3]

The Bay of Pigs defeat was the first major drubbing of the young Kennedy administration and set the stage for the administration's later efforts to oust Castro, including the use of the mob and the CIA's covert/overt plans called Operation Mongoose.

---

[3]V1. Brigade 2506-Manuel Artime-Movimiento De Recuperacion Revolucionaria (MRR).

Chapter 20:
The Plot to Kill Fidel Castro

In the late 1970s, the Church Committee investigating CIA abuses at home and abroad revealed one of the most important operations the organization ever undertook. In the last year of the Eisenhower administration the president ordered the CIA to take whatever steps were necessary to "get rid" of Cuba's leader, Fidel Castro. Numerous books, both official and private, have detailed the entire story of the CIA plots to kill Fidel Castro. All these years later historians are still arguing the merits of the plans to kill Castro and the tenuous relationships they spawned.

The Castro assassination plots began in 1960 and ended in the early years of the Johnson administration. Most of the active attempts to kill Castro took place in the Kennedy years and involved the use of the Mafia. There has been considerable speculation over the decades that the CIA-Mafia plots to kill Castro may have been linked in some way to the assassination of President Kennedy on November 22, 1963, and that the President's alleged assassin, Lee Harvey Oswald, was a pro-or anti-Castro operative in the assassination.

When the CIA proposed a plan to get rid of Castro in 1960, all they were interested in at the time was to discredit his regime and lay the groundwork for his eventual overthrow. The later stages of the plot involved extensive military planning, culminating in the Bay of Pigs invasion that took place in April 1961, during the early stages of the Kennedy administration. Why did the United States want to commit itself to overthrowing Castro?

When Castro took power in Cuba after the revolution that ousted the American puppet Batista, the U.S. turned a wary eye toward the bearded strongman. In the beginning, Castro said he was a defender of democracy. But that soon changed as he publicly espoused communist doctrine, made an arms and economic pact with the Soviet Union, and more importantly, as far as the American mob was concerned, closed down the lucrative casinos that had been flourishing in Havana for years. The Eisenhower administration saw in Castro a fundamental threat to America's political and economic interests in the Caribbean, and took steps to end the terror.

At CIA headquarters, harebrained schemes to kill Castro were hatched. Among them were the spraying of LSD at the radio station where he was to speak, poisoning his cigars and/or food, placing exploding seashells in an area where Castro liked to go skin diving, and using assassins inside Cuba.

But the most ambitious plot to kill Castro directly involved the CIA and members of organized crime. The mob suffered hundreds of millions of dollars in losses when Castro closed down the gaming houses and was most interested in getting them reopened. J.C. King, the head of the Agency's Western Hemisphere Division, originally gave Richard Bissell the idea of contacting the "Gambling Syndicate." Utilizing resources from the ranks of the CIA, a meeting was set up with Los Angeles crime boss Johnny Rosselli.

It should be noted that while all this was going on, Vice President Richard Nixon (who was running for President against JFK), was actually in charge of the Eisenhower administration's secret plans to eliminate Castro. Whether or not Nixon knew of the unholy alliance between the Agency and the mob is still open for debate.

In November 1960, John Kennedy won the election and became the 35th president of the United States. Once he took office in January 1961, the CIA-Mafia plots began in earnest. Unknown to Kennedy, the Cuban connection would haunt his presidency and its aftermath would forever change the way historians would look at his assassination two years later.

But back to the beginning — "Big Jim" O'Connell was the CIA's liaison with members of organized crime in the original plots to kill Castro. When it was decided by the CIA that certain members of the mob were going to join the secret effort to remove Castro from power, Richard Bissell was asked how to go about contacting these men. Bissell asked Sheffield Edwards to ask Jim O'Connell, one of his most trusted aides, to make the first covert moves. James O'Connell had been a member of the FBI for many years before coming over to the CIA. He was good friends with Robert Maheu, who had worked for the FBI. O'Connell brought Maheu, who he knew had covert contacts with members of the mob in the United States, into the picture. In a private meeting, O'Connell told Maheu under the strictest confidence that the U.S. was going after Castro and asked him if he could recommend someone in organized crime who might be willing to help.

Maheu gave him the name of Johnny Rosselli, a top mobster in L.A. Maheu met with Rosselli and told him that certain people were willing to pay hundreds of thousands of dollars to kill Castro and they needed a go-between to cement the deal. Would Rosselli be interested? Rosselli said yes and a meeting was arranged between him and O'Connell. O'Connell met with Rosselli using the alias "Jim Olds," an Englishman who told Rosselli about a secret group of businessmen whom he represented.

The meeting was held in New York on September 14, 1960. Rosselli was not fooled and knew right away that "Mr. Olds" was no Englishman, and probably worked for the CIA. Who else would have the moxie to create such a bizarre scenario? According to the CIA's IG (Inspector General) report, only two people in the Security Division, Sheffield Edwards and Jim O'Connell, knew of the Maheu-Rosselli connection.

The Inspector General's Report has this to say regarding Rosselli's relationship with James O'Connell: "By this time, Rosselli had become certain that O'Connell was an Agency employee, not a subordinate of Maheu. He told O'Connell that he was sure that O'Connell was a 'government man' — CIA — but that O'Connell should not confirm this to him. Rosselli said that as a loyal American he would do whatever he could and would never divulge the operation."

Subsequently, Rosselli brought into the scheme two other top mobsters: Santo Trafficante and Sam Giancana. A price of $50,000 was offered to Rosselli and his partners to kill Castro. At subsequent meetings between Rosselli, Giancana, and Trafficante the first operational plans to kill Castro were discussed. One of the first plans was a strict assassination operation in which a sniper would kill Castro. In December 1960, O'Connell and Rosselli discussed this topic but the mobster told O'Connell that the CIA needed to have a plan in which the assassin would have the chance to escape once the hit was carried out. What they came up with was a delayed-action poison that the assassin would slip into Castro's food or drink, and still be able to escape.

The man who was the given the pills was Juan Orta who was

working at the time in the office of Fidel Castro. After the failure of the Orta mission, Rosselli told O'Connell that Santo Trafficante had another man who might be willing to take on the Castro hit, Manuel "Tony" Varona.

Soon after the failure of the Bay of Pigs invasion in April 1961, Edwards sent word to Rosselli through O'Connell that any more assassination attempts were to be ended. Both Edwards and O'Connell testified that Phase One of the plans to kill Castro was called off right after the Bay of Pigs and things remained quiet until April 1962. The IG's Report says regarding O'Connell, "He believes that there was something going on between April 1961 and April 1962, but cannot recall what." Regarding the poison pills he gave to Rosselli, "O'Connell believes that he got them back but can't be certain. He thinks he must have flushed them down the toilet."

Phase Two of the CIA's plots to kill Castro got underway in April 1962 when Rosselli made contact with Varona and an associate of his named Maceo. This plot involved poison pills, as well as sending a three-man hit team to Cuba to kill Castro or recruit someone to do the job for them. In reality, the team never left Florida and by February 1963, the plan was ended.

The CIA learned of other plots by the Mafia or Cuban exiles working independently of each other to kill Castro:

> For example, the Schweiker Report cites an October 18, 1960, FBI memorandum which quotes Sam Giancana to the effect that Castro would be assassinated in the immediate future. According to Giancana, the Mafia had a girl who was going to poison Castro. Since the October 18 date it is rather early in the development of Phase 1 and since the pills to be used in Phase 1 were not delivered until February 1961, this would seem rather premature for Giancana to make such a categorical statement.
>
> However, a series of articles which appeared in the *New York Daily News* in 1975 and 1976 provide the basis for speculating that there was an independent plot which did involve a girl who planned to poison Castro.[1]

---

[1] Security of Mafia Assassination Plotting Against Castro. RIF No. 1993.07.19.18.28:40:280390 3/8/77.

The girl mentioned in the report is Marita Lorenz, who was once Castro's girlfriend.

According to the articles, she returned to Cuba on two occasions in 1960. On the first occasion, circa March 1960, she allegedly photographed documents in Castro's private office, and on the second occasion, date not specified, she intended to poison Castro. She reportedly had two poison pills with her, hidden in a jar of cold cream, but she was unable to use them because the pills dissolved in the cold cream. Lorenz alleged that these activities were undertaken on behalf of the CIA, but she further alleged that her case officers were Frank Sturgis and Alex Rorke. Frank Sturgis (Fiorini) was one of the Watergate burglars who took part in anti-Castro activities in the early 1960s. There is no record of Lorenz, Sturgis, or Rorke ever having been associated with the Agency:

> In addition to the possibility that the Lorenz plot was connected, it is noteworthy that Sturgis, Orta, and Varona are all known to have had some connections with the Mafia.[2]

This report regarding the Mafia and Castro's murder plots ends by saying, "It thus seems probable that the Mafia was connected with several operations against Castro." While we have no positive indication that Castro was aware of these operations, we likewise do not know positively that he was not aware of them. Even though the cover used in the Agency-connected operation was that of private companies interested in plotting against Castro, there is no guarantee that if Castro became aware of any of these plots he did not assume that they were U.S. government sponsored. It can only be concluded that it appears there where several plots going on, some Agency-connected and some not, which conceivably could have created a desire on Castro's part to retaliate in some fashion against the Untied States.

Another CIA officer who had direct responsibility as far as the Castro plots were concerned was William Harvey. Harvey was a thorn in the side of Robert Kennedy who did not care for Harvey's brash, abrasive style. Harvey was a former FBI agent who had changed allegiances to the CIA years before. Harvey often was seen at his desk at CIA headquarters, or in the field, wearing a pistol on

[2]Ibid.

his belt. He was a hard-drinking, no-nonsense man who disliked anyone treading on his own turf. When RFK made his frequent trips to the CIA base in Florida dubbed JMWAVE, he always had run-ins with Harvey, who disliked the Attorney General's presence at the base. Often, the men were seen in shouting matches over how the secret war against Castro was being run, and one time, fists were almost thrown.

More importantly to the story of the Castro plots, Harvey was put in charge of a secret unit called ZR/RIFLE which was a CIA-run assassination plot that was to be used against certain foreign leaders the United States did not like (among them were Castro and Patrice Lumumba of the Congo. This assassination unit was never put to use.

Harvey stated that when he took over the Castro plots, he was working on an ongoing operation. Harvey was given the job as the chief operating officer in a briefing with Richard Helms in late 1961, or early 1962. He met with Sheffield Edwards in February 1962 and was briefed on the full aspects of the Castro operation. The Assassination Report has this to say concerning Harvey's taking over the Castro function:

> After Harvey took over the Castro operation he ran it as one aspect of ZR/RIFLE; however, he personally handled the Castro operation and did not use any of the assets being developed in ZR/RIFLE. He says that he first came to think of the Castro operation and ZR/RIFLE as being synonymous. The overall Executive Action program came to be treated in his mind as being synonymous with QJ/WIN, the agent working on the overall program. He says that when he wrote of ZR/RIFLE, QJ/WIN the reference was to Executive Action capability; when he used the cryptonym ZR/RIFLE alone, he was referring to Castro.[3]

In April 1962, Harvey contacted Edwards in order to set up a meeting with Rosselli. Edwards then contacted Richard Helms, who gave his approval. Before and after his covert meetings with Rosselli, Harvey informed Helms on their discussions and plans.

"Edwards' statement that he 'verified Helms" approval is the

[3] *CIA Targets Fidel: The Secret Assassination Report,* Ocean Press, 1996, Page 50.

earliest indication we have that Mr. Helms had been made witting of the gambling syndicate operation against Castro. Harvey added that, 'when he briefed Helms on Rosselli, he obtained Helms' approval not to brief the Director.'"

What is of particular interest in the entire area was the fact that the CIA, in the persons of Edwards and Lawrence Houston, met with Robert Kennedy on May 7, 1962 and informed him of the wiretapping case that involved the mob, the CIA, and the initial plans to kill Castro. According to the IG's Report, Edwards, "briefed him all the way." This is the first instance we know of that Robert Kennedy learned of the CIA-mob plans to kill Castro. It is inconceivable that Robert Kennedy failed to tell his brother, the President, of this astonishing news. The men were so close in all respects, both personally and on such an important policy decisions, that he could not have kept such a secret from him.

While the CIA and the Mafia were working together to kill Castro, the various reports indicate that they may not have been on the same timetable. The CIA's involvement with the Mafia ended in April 1961 and was reactivated in April 1962. One of the CIA case officers involved in the plots believed that some mob actions were going on despite the calling off of the Castro plots by the CIA:

> It is possible that the CIA found itself involved in providing additional resources for independent operations that the syndicate already had underway. The criminal syndicate had important interests in Cuba, and to recover them may well have sought on its own to eliminate Castro. In a sense, the CIA may have been piggybacking on the syndicate and in addition to its material contributions was also supplying an aura of official sanction. It is unlikely that Castro could have distinguished the CIA plots with the underworld from those plots not backed by the CIA. In fact, the methods of the CIA used in these attempts were designed to prevent the Cuban government from attributing them to the CIA.[4]

Sam Giancana was one of the Mafia bosses who was selected by the CIA to take part in the Agency's assassination plots against Fidel

[4] New CIA Consideration of Syndicate Operation Against Castro, RIF No. 1993.07.19.18.38.03.930390, 3/31/1977.

Castro. In 1960, Sam Giancana was the top mob boss in Chicago, the successor to the legendary hoodlum Al Capone. During the days of the Batista regime in Cuba, Giancana was heavily involved in casino operations and had his hand in the very lucrative money the casinos brought in. He was involved in the skimming of millions of dollars from the vice, gambling, and prostitution industries that thrived in pre-Castro Havana. When the CIA began looking for allies to oust Castro, one of them was Sam Giancana.

Called "Sam Gold" by the CIA, Giancana went along with the plot not out of any patriotic zeal, but simply as a matter of high finance. Giancana believed, along with his associates, Santo Trafficante and Johnny Rosselli, that once Castro was gone, the casinos would reopen and their enormous profits would start to flow again.

But now a new and important wind blew into the tempest that was already brewing. Sam Giancana was also being investigated by Robert Kennedy's Justice Department. How would it look if word got out that Giancana was working secretly for the CIA while RFK was prosecuting him? Somehow, that fact had to be kept secret.

Giancana also had tenuous links to the Kennedy family. It has been reported that during the 1960 presidential election, Giancana funneled much-needed cash to John Kennedy in his race against Nixon. If this is the case then Giancana probably saw his participation in the Castro plots as insurance, and possibly blackmail fodder to be used against the Kennedy administration. Giancana was also involved with Judith Campbell Exner, one of JFK's lovers. It has also been alleged that she was a conduit between JFK and the mob for cash payments to them.

Sam Giancana died a violent death, as was his way of life. On June 19, 1975, while he was cooking dinner at his Chicago home, unidentified gunmen entered his residence and shot him with a .22 caliber automatic, placing the bullets in a row near his chin and mouth. This was undoubtedly a mob hit, a warning to others who may have wanted to talk to the Feds. In the end, Giancana's unholy alliance with the CIA cost him his life.

Another member of the mob to take part in the Castro hit was Santo Trafficante, Jr., the powerful mob boss in Tampa, Florida. With the death of his powerful father, Santo Senior, the younger

Trafficante took over all the illegal activities in Florida, including gambling, loan sharking, vice, etc. Over time, Florida became one of the most important entry points of illegal narcotics, especially heroin, into the United States.

In 1946, Trafficante moved from Tampa to Havana where he oversaw his father's gambling interests. It was while he was in Havana that Trafficante made a covert deal with Cuba's longtime dictator and president, Fulgencio Batista.

When Batista fled the country in 1959 after the successful Castro revolution, Trafficante remained in Cuba for a while, even when the majority of the other mobsters had fled with their ransom to Florida. It was during this time that Trafficante would, some Congressional investigators say, make contact with a man who would, a few years later, play an integral part in the assassination of JFK, Jack Ruby.

After the recruitment of Rosselli and Giancana, Trafficante was brought into the CIA assassination plot. His code name was "Joe the Courier" and it was his job to be the messenger who would make all the arrangements with his contacts inside Cuba.

It is also believed by some Kennedy assassination researchers that throughout this time in the Mob-CIA plots to kill Castro, Trafficante was a double agent working for Castro, informing him of every facet of the scheme.

When the HSCA undertook its investigation of the Kennedy murder, one of the areas they looked into with interest was Santo Trafficante's relationship with Jack Ruby. What they found was most interesting.

After Castro took over, he jailed Trafficante, along with a number of other mob figures who did not leave for the U.S. Ruby's visit to the jailed Trafficante was reported to the Warren Commission by a British journalist named John Wilson-Hudson, who said that "an American gangster type named Ruby" visited Cuba in 1959. Wilson-Hudson was in jail with Trafficante and said that he saw Ruby visit the mob boss during that time. Trafficante was released from the Trescornia jail on August 18, 1959 and was deported to the U.S. While this alleged incident took place well before John Kennedy's election in 1960, and probably has no bearing on his death, if it is true, then a positive Ruby-Trafficante link is established, which could have far-reaching consequences relating to the Kennedy

139

assassination.

On September 28, 1979, Santos Trafficante testified before the committee that was investigating the Kennedy assassination and said that he played no role in the event. The HSCA did however say this concerning the relationship between Santo Trafficante and the assassination of the president: "The committee found that Trafficante, like Marcello [Carlos Marcello, the mob boss of Chicago] had the motive, means and opportunity to assassinate President Kennedy."

Students of the CIA-Mafia plots have been very suspicious regarding whether Trafficante was a double agent for Castro, or had some ties to his government. Johnny Rosselli, who worked with Trafficante in the early plots, had this to say regarding his former colleague:

> This whole thing has been a scam. Santo never did anything but bullshit everybody. All these fucking wild schemes the CIA dreamed up never got further than Santo. He just sat on it, conned everybody into thinking that guys were risking their lives sneaking into Cuba, having boats shot out from under them—all bullshit.

Santo Trafficante, like Johnny Rosselli, might have been using the CIA and its plots to kill Castro as leverage against the Kennedy administration's activities regarding his long mob history. Rosselli himself was living in the United States under an assumed name. It seems obvious that Trafficante played a more cryptic role than that depicted in the official story we have been told.

Chapter 21:
Operation Mongoose

The failure of the CIA's not so secret invasion of Cuba at the Bay of Pigs in April 1961 was a turning point in the Kennedy administration's attitude toward Cuba and the Castro regime. Cuba had become the number one priority of the new administration and the defeat of the CIA-backed rebels only hardened the policymakers in Washington as to what future steps would be taken to rid the hemisphere of Castro.

What followed was Phase Two of the secret war against Castro called "Operation Mongoose," run entirely by the CIA, according to the documents that have come out over the past decade. The new documents paint a completely new canvas on which we view Operation Mongoose and the Kennedy administration's secret war against Castro.

The documents show a widespread, all points press by almost every department in the Kennedy administration to get rid of Castro, including State, Defense, Justice, the Army, the CIA and the Voice of America, among others. Most of Kennedy's top advisors, like Arthur Schlesinger Jr., backed the President on more "appropriate" measures to be taken against Castro.

In 1962, JFK decided to take on a new, direct action oriented policy toward Cuba. To that effect he asked two of his most trusted advisors, Presidential Assistant Richard Goodwin and General Edward Lansdale (who was an expert in counterinsurgency operations) to take the lead. The name of the new plan was Operation Mongoose.

Richard Goodwin was informally assigned to work with Robert Kennedy to oversee the U.S. government's anti-Castro policies. The documents released by the CIA show that Goodwin wrote many important internal memos regarding the Kennedy administration's policy concerning Cuba. One memo dated November 1, 1961, read as follows: "I believe that a command operation for Cuba, as discussed with you by the Attorney General, is the only effective way to handle an all out attack on the Cuban problem. The beauty of the operation over the next few months is that we cannot lose. If the best happens, we will unseat Castro. If not, then at least we will emerge with a stronger underground, better propaganda and a far clearer idea of the dimensions of the problem which affect us. I believe that the Attorney General would be the most effective commander of such an operation. Either I or someone else should be assigned to him as Deputy for this activity, since he obviously will not be able to devote full time to it. His role should be told to only a few people at the very top with most of the contact work in carrying out his decisions being left to this deputy."

A November 2, 1961 Goodwin memo to both JFK and RFK makes his role in the Castro plots more evident. Goodwin outlined a plan in which the CIA would lend a topflight counterinsurgency expert to work with the Cuba Group. Goodwin outlined a five-point plan of operations against Cuba including, "intelligence collection and evaluation, guerilla and underground operations, propaganda, economic warfare and diplomatic relations."

He suggested that writer Tad Szulc, who worked for the *New York Times,* would be a good candidate for propaganda purposes.

The man tapped by the President to by the top counterinsurgency expert for Operation Mongoose was Edward Lansdale. He served in the OSS in World War II, rising to the position of Intelligence Chief for the U.S. Army. He joined the CIA in 1947, winding up in the Far Eastern Division. At the time of the insurrection in the Philippines in the early 1950s, he became one of the most important proponents of using psychological warfare against the Huk tribesmen.

After ending his job in the Philippines, Lansdale was transferred to Vietnam where he worked to bolster the Western-leaning government. His flamboyant style attracted certain journalists, among them Graham Green, a British writer who modeled his main character in his novel called *The Quiet American* after him. Lansdale worked closely with South Vietnamese President Ngo Dinh Diem, bolstering up the South Vietnamese armed forces and carrying out intelligence missions against Diem's enemies.

By now, Lansdale's star had been rising in the Pentagon and he was given the job of Deputy Director of the Pentagon's New Office of Special Operations, a post that would put him right in the middle of the new counter warfare strategy that the Kennedy administration was now pursuing. The President was told glowing things about Lansdale and he even thought about giving him the job of U.S. Ambassador to South Vietnam. It was not offered. But if Lansdale was not to get the Saigon post, he was about to be thrust into the Kennedy brothers' efforts to oust Castro under Operation Mongoose.

Lansdale was not in favor of the ill-fated Bay of Pigs invasion and right after the fiasco, JFK wanted near him men who would tell him the truth as far as military operations were concerned, not yes men like those who had caused the debacle. To that end, Lansdale was offered the job as head of the Cuba Project.

Lansdale told the President that he envisioned as a first step the development of "a very necessary political basis" among the Cubans who were opposed to Castro. He also sought to develop "means to infiltrate Cuba successfully and to organize cells and activities inside Cuba who could work secretly and safely."

In order to get the ball rolling on Operation Mongoose, the President set up a control group called the Special Group (Augmented) (SGA). Its members consisted of McGeorge Bundy, the President's National Security Advisor, Alexis Johnson from the State Department, Roswell Gilpatrick of the Department of Defense, John McCone, the Director of the CIA, and General Lyman Lemintzer of the Joint Chiefs of Staff. Attorney General Robert Kennedy and General Maxwell Taylor also attended the meetings.

At one of the early meetings of the SGA held in the fall of 1961, notes taken by the Assistant to the head of Task Force W reveal that Richard Bissell, who attended the meeting, "was chewed out in the Cabinet Room of the White House by both the President and the Attorney General for, as he put it, sitting on his ass and not doing anything about getting rid of Castro and the Castro regime." Later, Bissell was asked whether he considered that to be an instruction for proceeding with the assassination of Castro, and he said no. He said that "formal and explicit approval" would be required from higher-ups. Bissell also recalled that there was in fact no assassination activity between the pre-Bay of Pigs/Rosselli operation and his departure from the CIA in February 1962.

In late 1961 or early 1962, William Harvey, who also ran the

Executive Action/ZR/RIFLE program, was put in charge of the CIA's Task Force W, the CIA unit that ran Operation Mongoose. There were more than 400 members of Task Force W, which was run out the CIA's secret base in Miami called JMWAVE. Harvey's team worked separately from the Agency's Western Hemisphere Division, which was headed by J.C. King. In this new relationship, Task Force W and William Harvey were directly under the supervision of the Kennedy administration, especially Robert Kennedy who made Operation Mongoose his personal fiefdom.

One of Bill Harvey's trusted aides on the staff of Task Force W was Desmond Fitzgerald (who would later take over from Harvey). Fitzgerald worked in the propaganda section where he and his staff worked overtime sending various leaflet drops into Cuba containing false information concerning the Castro regime, and trying to instill fear among the Cuban population of life in Cuba under Castro.

After numerous failures by Task Force W's agents to inflict major damage to their Cuban military and economic targets, William Harvey was sacked and was replaced by Desmond Fitzgerald, a Kennedy administration ally.

On January 18, 1962, General Lansdale assigned 32 tasks to the respective agencies involved in Operation Mongoose planning. These included intelligence collection and planning for the "use of U.S. military force to support the Cuban popular movement and developing an operational schedule for sabotage actions inside Cuba." Lansdale sent a memo to the other members of the SGA saying, "It is our job to put the American genius to work on this project, quickly and effectively. This demands a change from the business as usual and a hard facing of the fact that we are in a combat situation-where we have been given full command."

General Lansdale sent a handwritten copy of these 32 tasks in a note to Robert Kennedy on January 18, 1962. The Church Committee later questioned Lansdale about this communication, especially one interesting sentence quoted in the report: "'My review does not include the sensitive work I have reported to you; I felt you preferred informing the President privately.' Lansdale testified that the sensitive work did not refer to assassination, and that he never took up assassination with either the Attorney General or the President. He said that he could not precisely recall the nature of this sensitive work but that it might have involved a special trip he made under cover to meet Cuban leaders in Florida to assess their political strengths."[1]

In a later memorandum to the Attorney General on January 27, 1962, Lansdale talked about the possibility that "we might uncork the touchdown play independently of the institutional program we are spurring." Lansdale later said that the phrase "touchdown play" was a "breezy way of referring to a Cuban revolt to overthrow the regime rather than to Castro's assassination."

One additional task that he wanted incorporated in Operation Mongoose was a plan to "incapacitate" Cuban sugar workers at harvest time by the use of chemical warfare. This involved the use of a non-lethal means of putting the workers to sleep and away from their tasks.

The SGA approved Lansdale's 33 points on January 30, 1962. On February 29, Lansdale detailed a new six-phase schedule for Mongoose planning which included "an open revolt and overthrow of the Communist regime." One of the "Resistance" phases listed "attacks on the cadre of the regime, including key leaders. This should be a '"Special Target"' operation. Gangster elements might provide the best recruitment potential for actions against police-G2 [intelligence] officials."[2]

We don't know what he meant by "gangster elements" in this regard. Maybe he was talking about local gangsters in Cuba who were working for the CIA under cover, or he might have been referring to the Trafficante-Marcello-Giancana-Rosselli faction that was already underway. In all the records of the CIA-Mafia link there is no mention that Lansdale knew of that secret relationship. Although that may be the case, we can't be sure if either JFK or RFK might have told Lansdale of the secret alliance.

Besides the collection of intelligence, only one major military operation took place, an attack on a large Cuban copper mine. Lansdale described the sabotage acts as involving "blowing up bridges to stop communications and blowing up certain production plants."

Despite the calls by Lansdale for more attacks inside Cuba, by

---

[1] Church Committee: Interim Report-Alleged Assassination Plots Involving Foreign Leaders.

[2] Ibid.

1962, the SGA was changing course and called for a lessening of sabotage and other violent actions inside Cuba. Richard Helms, who attended one of the SGA's meetings, wrote in a memo dated October 16, 1962, "Robert Kennedy, in expressing the general dissatisfaction of the President with Mongoose, pointed out that [Mongoose] had been underway for a year [and] that there had been no acts of sabotage and that even the one which had been attempted had failed twice."

In the wake of the Cuban Missile Crisis of October 1962 in which the United States and the Soviet Union almost came to nuclear war, JFK took a more cautious approach to Mongoose operations.

In two meetings, dated October 19-20 and November 14, 1962, between William Harvey, Richard Helms and John McCone, the following was noted: "Harvey states, it should be noted that all action operations which could be put on ice by the CIA, in accordance with the instructions, were put on ice."

In notes from a November 14, 1962 conference regarding Operation Mongoose, the following points were made:

> Lansdale states, On October 30-31 for an eyes-only background memorandum requested by Roswell Gilpatrick, information was requested from the CIA on the current status of all operations. CIA reported all militant operations have been ordered held at a stop, although the volatile Cubans were frustrated and not under complete control.

On November 5, 1962, George McManus wrote the following regarding Cuba, Mongoose and the Special Group:

> McManus states that if these agreements [between Kennedy and Khrushchev] are carried out, it seems clear that Cuba will be dealt with as another denied area in a manner differing not really from that in which CIA handles other areas. If the agreements are not carried out, military action cannot long be delayed. In either event, the Mongoose structure as it has existed in government is through.

In notes from a November 5, 1962 meeting between President

Kennedy, Robert Kennedy, Defense Secretary Robert McNamara, General Maxwell Taylor, William Bundy, Roswell Gilpatrick, and others, "McManus states, when the President, in his letter to Khrushchev on October 27 gave assurances against the invasion of Cuba in consideration of the Soviet removal of offensive weapons in Cuba under UN supervision, Operation Mongoose was on its deathbed. When the President stated in a letter of October 28 to Khrushchev, 'I consider my letter to you of October 27 and your reply of today as a firm undertaking on the part of both our governments which should be promptly carried out,' Operation Mongoose died."

As the tensions between the United States and the Soviet Union lessened after the Missile Crisis, new calls for further military action via Mongoose were called for.

The minutes of an SGA meeting on March 19, 1963 say:

> Fitzgerald states that the consensus of observers is that a popular uprising will overthrow Castro. Current policy included the overt use of U.S. military force to overthrow Castro. He suggests that economic strangulation program will follow in near future with a request for policy approval to mount sabotage operations against Cuban ships and cargo vessels. CIA proposes to devote main effort against key officers in the armed forces and militia who are disenchanted with Castro's management of Cuban affairs. Effort will be to identify these officers and convince them that their future lies only in disposing of Castro.

While these covert activities were going on, a so-called Track Two policy toward Cuba was being developed. This program was discussed at a June 6, 1963 meeting between CIA Director John McCone, Mac Bundy, and others regarding Mongoose, Castro and the SGA:

> On June 6, 1963, SGA discussed various possibilities of establishing channels of communication with CASTRO. All members of the group agree that this is a useful endeavor. Mr. Bundy emphasized of keeping any such approach entirely secret.

On November 6, 1963, Bundy told the SG [Special Group] that it has come to the attention of the White House that Castro would like to have a talk designed to bring about some arrangement with the U.S. To hear what Castro has to say and to know on what basis he might wish to negotiate would be of some use to the U.S. After discussion, it was decided by the SG members not to try to reach a firm decision at this time but to study the problem for several days and to attack it again.

On November 6, 1963, President Kennedy disapproved all Cuban operations scheduled to be run before November 12. Two such operations dated November 8 and 10 were cancelled.

JFK's interest in lessening the political and military tensions between not only Cuba but the Soviet Union as well, began to take shape in the summer of 1963. The resolution of the Cuban Missile Crisis the year before left an indelible impression on the young President. The world had come ever so close to nuclear war and Kennedy never wanted to let that happen again.

JFK's thoughts on what action to take regarding Cuba and Castro are reflected in discussions he had with two men whose views he respected: Senator George Smathers of Florida and *New York Times* reporter Tad Szulc.

On November 8, 1961, Robert Kennedy met with Szulc to discuss the situation in Cuba. It was now seven months since the Bay of Pigs invasion, and Operation Mongoose was in full swing. The meeting was off the record, just a chat between two old friends. RFK wanted to feel out Szulc to find out what the reporter thought of the administration's current policy toward Cuba. At no time was the word assassination brought up. Before the meeting broke up, RFK asked Szulc if he would like to meet the President the next day. Szulc agreed and a meeting was set up. The next day, Szulc was escorted into the Oval Office by JFK's Special Assistant, Richard Goodwin. Just before the meeting ended, JFK asked Szulc the following question: "What would you think if I ordered Castro to be assassinated?" Szulc told the President that if Castro were killed it would not necessarily change the political situation in Cuba, as someone else would take his place. He also said that the U.S. should have no role in political assassinations. Szulc testified to Congress that President Kennedy then said, "I agree with you completely."

Szulc remarked further concerning his conference with the President:

> He then went on for a few minutes to make the point how strongly he and his brother felt that the United States for moral reasons should never be in a situation of having recourse to assassination. JFK then said he was testing me, that he felt the same way—he added, I'm glad you feel that same way—because indeed the U.S. morally must not be part of assassinations. JFK said he raised the possibility because he was under terrific pressure from advisers (think he said intelligence people, but not positive) to okay a Castro murder, and he was resisting pressure.

Another person JFK talked to in regard to assassinating Castro was then-Senator George Smathers (D-Florida). Smathers was not one of the President's Boston buddies but JFK was friendly enough with the Florida politician to invite him to the White House for a round of drinks and a walk in the Rose Garden. Smathers was well connected to the anti-Castro leaders who lived in his home state and was called "the Senator from Cuba" by friends and foes alike.

During one of Kennedy and Smathers' walks on the White House lawn in 1961, the President broached the subject of assassinating Castro because the topic had come up in discussions among his advisors. Smathers said that if that took place, the U.S. should also proceed with a staged invasion of Cuba. Eventually, Kennedy got so fed up with Smathers' war talk over Cuba that he stopped discussing the subject with him.

Smathers discussed his conversation with President Kennedy concerning Cuba and Castro in his Assassination Report testimony: "President Kennedy asked me what reaction I thought there would be throughout South America were Fidel Castro to be assassinated. I told him that even as much as I disliked Castro that I did not think it would be a good idea for there to be even considered an assassination of Fidel Castro, and the President of the United States completely agreed with me, that it would be a very unwise thing to do."

A document on Operation Mongoose dated November 5, 1962 sums up the Kennedy administration's attitude toward Castro: "Looking back to the origins of Mongoose, one finds the AG [Attorney General] and Mr. McNamara seeking primarily to remove the political stain left on the President by the Bay of Pigs failure. Both the AG and the Secretary of Defense felt it necessary for political reasons that some action be taken with respect to Cuba to ensure the President's future. In a nutshell, they were out to dump Castro or make him cooperate."

Chapter 22:
The CIA's Secret JFK Probe

Less than twelve hours after the assassination of President John F. Kennedy in Dallas, the CIA was alive with activity as analysts were called in to learn all they could about the alleged assassin, Lee Harvey Oswald. The man who was given the job of investigating the activities of Lee Harvey Oswald was John Whitten, who went by the codename "John Scelso." Whitten's role in the CIA's investigation in the aftermath of the shooting of JFK and his probe into Oswald's activities are paramount in our knowledge of how the agency fudged its conclusions and decided not to let Whitten and his staff of 30 trained analysts learn all they could about what transpired on November 22, 1963.

John Whitten was born in 1920 in Annapolis, Maryland. He graduated from the University of Maryland, and entered the U.S. Army where he was posted to an intelligence unit interrogating German POWs. After the war ended, he returned to school and graduated from the University of Virginia's Law School. In 1947 he joined the CIA and for many years served in both Washington and Vienna. By March 1962, he was promoted to the agency's Western Hemisphere Division. In March 1963, he was promoted to be chief of all the CIA's covert operations in Mexico and Central America. So it was to John Whitten that the CIA turned in the early hours of November 23, 1963 to look into the activities of Lee Oswald.

As Whitten began his investigation he was immediately stymied on two fronts: by James Angleton in the CIA and by the FBI. The Bureau sent his team thousands of documents that they knew Whitten and his staff could never read. Whitten called the information given to him by the FBI "weirdo stuff." Among the information that Whitten was not told by the FBI was Oswald's association with both pro- and anti-Castro people in New Orleans, his alleged attack on right wing general Edwin Walker in Dallas in 1963, and the contents of Oswald's "historic diary" which he supposedly penned while he lived in Russia. Even more surprising was the fact that Whitten, who was supposed to have been knowledgeable of all the CIA's activities in Latin America and Mexico (where Oswald was in September-October 1963), had never been made aware of Oswald before November 22, 1963, even though the various U.S. intelligence agencies had a file on him since his defection in 1959. Whitten had been on the phone with the CIA Mexico Station Chief Winston Scott when Scott told him that the CIA had on file a photograph of Lee Oswald entering the Cuban consulate that October. Whitten asked Scott to send the picture to him as soon as possible. What the picture showed was that Oswald had visited both the Cuban consulate and the Russian embassy. What was Oswald, a former Marine, doing at the embassies of America's enemies?

As Whitten continued his investigation it soon became apparent that he was being stymied in his search by none other than Richard Helms, who stopped him from looking into Oswald's Cuba-related activities in New Orleans in the summer of 1963, information that the FBI had on hand for months. In the end, Helms' decision to withhold vital information from John Whitten forced him to end his investigation and stop an avenue of inquiry that may have altered what the public knew about the activities of Lee Oswald, and clouded the investigation of the JFK case for decades to come.

More important to his investigation, Whitten was not told of George Joannides, a CIA officer who took over as the CIA's liaison with the DRE (an anti-Castro group) in Miami in 1963. Joannides was the paymaster to that anti-Castro group and followed closely Oswald's activities in New Orleans, including his meeting with Carlos Bringuier and other DRE members in the Crescent City, It was Richard Helms who deliberately withheld the Joannides file from Whitten so the latter could not delve into Oswald's anti-Castro activities. Both Angleton and Helms desperately wanted to keep any mention of the Castro-Oswald connection secret, and (especially Angleton) put the blame for the assassination of the President squarely on the shoulders of the men in Moscow.

In a frantic search for whatever tidbits of information he could find, Whitten, using only the information provided to him by the CIA, was able to report to Helms that Oswald was the sole assassin of the President and that he had no confederates at large. Whitten's preliminary findings were sent to the new President, Lyndon Johnson. Whitten thought his investigation was over. However, that was not the

152

case, as he would soon learn — to his chagrin.

On December 6, 1963, Whitten was sent to the White House to look at an FBI report that had been prepared on Lee Oswald. To his shock he found that Helms had not been forthcoming with him about all of Oswald's activities. The most important information that Helms withheld from Whitten dealt with Oswald's associations with anti-Castro people in New Orleans, as well as his membership in the pro-Castro Fair Play for Cuba Committee. Whitten was shocked to learn of Oswald's Cuban connections and he voiced his objections to Helms in a no-nonsense manner. To his amazement, Helms relieved Whitten of his duties and the investigation was turned over to the office of James Angleton, the head of the counterintelligence division.

Angleton, it seems, had his own, hidden agenda when it came to informing the Warren Commission on Oswald's links to both the Soviets and the Cubans. Angleton worked closely with Commission member Allen Dulles who had been fired by JFK after the abortive Bay of Pigs invasion. The ace up Angleton's sleeve was a Russian defector named Yuri Nosenko who had come out from the cold and was taken in by the CIA. During his debriefing, Nosenko told his CIA handlers a rather intriguing story. He said that he was the KGB's controlling officer who handled the Oswald case when the ex-Marine defected to the Soviet Union. Nosenko said that the KGB had no operational interest in Oswald in the two and a half years that he lived in Russia. Angleton believed that Nosenko was a disinformation agent sent by the Russians to fool the CIA into believing his tale was true. Nosenko also said that the Soviet Union had no role in the President's assassination.

Earlier, another Soviet defector named Anatoly Golitsyn told the CIA that the Russians would send another agent to the United States to discredit Golitsyn. Angleton believed that agent was Yuri Nosenko.

Angleton worked with Dulles, feeding him all the information that came out of the debriefing sessions with Nosenko. In their deliberations, Dulles never once told the other Commission members of the ties between the Mafia and the CIA to kill Castro.

A cryptic remark made by Angleton years after the assassination left many people wondering what he really meant to say. Angleton said regarding the Kennedy assassination, "A mansion has many rooms and there were many things going on. I am not privy to who struck John."

When he later testified before the House Select Committee on Assassinations (HSCA) in 1978, Whitten said that if he had been informed of Oswald's Cuban ties he would have focused his investigation on the "possible involvement of the [CIA's] Miami station." He told the HSCA that he did not believe that Oswald was in any way connected to the CIA, but after he learned of the Executive Action operation, he remarked that he could no longer rule out any agency ties to Oswald. When his 192-page deposition was declassified in 1996, readers learned that after his discovery of the FBI files in December 1963 he tried to retract his early opinion that Oswald had acted alone since "it was obviously, completely irrelevant in view of this Bureau information."

In his testimony before the HSCA, Whitten pulled no punches in his condemnation of the actions of Richard Helms and William Harvey. He called Harvey, the head of ZR/RIFLE-Executive Action, "a thug." He had harsh words for his old boss Helms, saying that Helms violated "every operational precept, every bit of operational experience, every ethical consideration."

When asked by the committee if he thought William Harvey was involved in the President's assassination he said probably not. When he was told that immediately after Harvey's death, his wife destroyed his personal papers, believing that Harvey may have had a "smoking gun," he said of Harvey, "He was too young to have assassinated McKinley and Lincoln. It could have been anything."

The "Scelso Deposition" shows how far the CIA went in its internal investigation of Oswald, a fact that was deliberately withheld from the Warren Commission. When questioned about the Oswald file at the CIA, Whitten's remarks were more than interesting. He told how the CIA did not have a substantial file on Oswald (not true) before the assassination; he called it a "scan file" made up mostly of information given to the CIA by the Navy, the Marine Corps, and information provided by the agency in Mexico City. He said that he had dealt with many other defector cases in the past and that the Oswald incident was just "a typical defection case."

Whitten further stated that there was a fair amount of intelligence sharing cooperation between the CIA and the FBI and other U.S.

intelligence agencies in Mexico City in the months preceding President Kennedy's death. The CIA passed along all information to J. Edgar Hoover's G-men on any American citizens in Mexico City who appeared around the Soviet and Cuban embassies, and anybody who was possibly trying to defect. A similar arrangement was formalized with military intelligence.

Whitten had some very interesting comments to make on a number of the principal actors in the U.S. intelligence community whose names played a prominent role in the investigation of the Kennedy assassination, to whit, James Angleton, David Atlee Phillips, William Harvey, and Richard Helms.

According to Whitten, who was related to David Atlee Phillips through marriage, Phillips was "one of the most brilliant, capable officers that I have ever known, and nothing has happened since then that has changed my judgment."

When asked if it were possible that David Phillips ever sent out disinformation concerning the JFK assassination, Whitten stated, "No, but I can conceive that it might have happened in the Mexico station. Perhaps they did, in their propaganda efforts that were going full-blast all the time, put in newspaper articles and so on to discredit somebody, some foreign power, in connection with the operation. I do not believe it was ever a policy to do so, but they were pretty much independent in formulating their propaganda."

What Whitten failed to say, or maybe he wasn't aware of the fact, is that many researchers believed that his relative, Mr. Phillips, may have been the mysterious CIA officer known as "Maurice Bishop." Bishop, it is noted, is said to have been Oswald's case officer who met him in Dallas a few weeks prior to the assassination.

Whitten also commented on the famous "mystery man" photograph that the CIA took in Mexico City that proved not to have been Oswald. He told his interviewer that the CIA had not received this photograph prior to the assassination, and when it was finally received, he did not know if the picture was the real Lee Oswald or not. While it seems that Whitten was kept out of the loop of information concerning who the mystery man was, he did say that he was certain that the CIA surveillance team did not photograph everyone who entered the Soviet embassy. He said that the case officers he personally spoke to regarding the mystery man's photo were Win Scott and David Phillips but cannot recall if Phillips was physically in Mexico City at the time of the assassination. The only clue to this man's identity, according to Whitten, was that the CIA "conjectured that it was a Mexican seaman."

Another twist in the CIA's covert espionage game in Mexico City also directly involves Lee Oswald. Recently discovered documents reveal a CIA message dated September 16, 1963, informing the FBI that "the agency [CIA] is giving some consideration to countering the activities of the FPCC, Fair Play for Cuba Committee, in foreign countries."

Oswald was the lone member of the FPCC in New Orleans during the summer of 1963 and was arrested in a scuffle with Carlos Bringuier, an anti-Castro Cuban. Oswald had previously approached Bringuier offering his services in anti-Castro operations, while he was handing out pro-Castro leaflets only a short time later. It is interesting to note that the day after this CIA memo dealing with a covert action program against the FPCC, which had a direct Oswald connection, Oswald was applying for a Mexican tourist visa card. Is there any connection?

What is obvious is that the covert arm of the CIA was very active in tracing developments of the Oswald case in Mexico City and committed many of its top personnel to that task.

One of the most interesting aspects of the Scelso interview with the HSCA is his impressions of and working relationship with the head of the CIA's CI (counterintelligence) Division, James Angleton. Whitten says that in his opinion, Angleton was not an easy person to get along with, and he ran his CI branch with an iron fist. Often during his CIA career, Whitten said that he was ordered by his superiors, either Helms or Thomas Karamessinas, to investigate some of the operations that Angleton was running and "this always caused bitter feelings, the most bitter feelings."

According to Whitten's testimony before the HSCA, "Angleton ignored Helms' orders that no one was to discuss the case [the Kennedy assassination] without my being present. He ignored that. I tried to get Helms to make him obey and Helms said, you go tell him."

Angleton, according to Whitten's testimony, kept on meeting clandestinely with the FBI and also certain members of the Warren Commission, which was in direct violation of Helms' orders. But, continued Whitten, Helms refused to stop Angleton from conducting these secret meetings. Angleton did not invite Whitten to these affairs, since they were done under the table, without official CIA sanction.

While Whitten was in the middle of his investigation, Helms suddenly shifted the probe into the hands of Angleton's CI Staff. This was done because of the Soviet angle that had been discovered, i.e., Oswald's two-year sojourn in the Soviet Union. Thus, the Soviet connection now took over from the almost-as-important Cuban connection that most likely would have led to even more important clues as to why President Kennedy was killed.

Whitten dropped another possible bombshell regarding James Angleton's potential ties to organized crime. He testified, "Back when I was branch chief, the Department of Justice, Mr. Hunley, who was working against organized crime, asked people from the agency to come over and asked us if we could find out the true names of holders of numbered bank accounts in Panama because the Mafia was depositing money there, cash money skimmed off the top in Las Vegas. And we were, indeed, in an excellent position to do this and told them so, whereupon Angleton vetoed it and said that it was the Bureau's business. Unless the Bureau requests us to do it, we are not going to do it, so we did not do it. And I told J.C. King this and he smiled a foxy smile and said well that's Angleton's excuse. *The real reason is that Angleton himself has ties to the Mafia and he would not want to double cross them, or something like that.*" (Italics by author.)

When it came to his assessment of William King Harvey, Whitten pulled no punches. When asked by Mr. Goldsmith, who was an investigator for the HSCA Staff, what he thought of Harvey, Whitten said, "Well, he is dead now. Harvey was a really hard-boiled, unstable, ruthless guy who was, in my opinion, a very dangerous man. I had run-ins with him several times. I also had to investigate one of his big cases and although I was already on friendly terms with him—we never slugged it out with each other—he never liked me and I never liked me."

Whitten continued his thoughts on Harvey: "The very thought of Helms entrusting Harvey to hire a criminal to have the capacity to kill somebody violates every operational percept, every bit of operational experience, every ethical consideration. And the fact that he chose Harvey—Harvey could keep a secret, you see. This was one way to make sure that nobody ever found out about it."

Whitten put the nail in Harvey's coffin by saying, "Harvey was not the kind of personality who appeals to me and I certainly was not the kind of personality that appeals to him. I have wondered—I wonder if the government has ever looked into the possibility that Harvey did not knock off Giancana. He lived in the same area, when he was retired. He was a great one with guns. I read it [the murder of Sam Giancana] in the newspaper, I was overseas and I said to myself, I wondered if they looked into Bill Harvey."

Turning his attention to Richard Helms, Whitten said that he was shocked that he had appointed Harvey to create the secret assassination plots called Executive Action. "I think," continued Whitten, "on the fact that Helms did not inform the Warren Commission on the Castro assassination plots, that was a morally highly reprehensible act, which he cannot possibly justify under oath of office, or any standard of professional public service."

Asked why he thought Helms failed to tell the Warren Commission about the Castro plots he said, "I think that Helms withheld the information because he realized it would have cost him his job and would have precipitated a crisis for the agency, which could have a very adverse effects on the agency."

After departing the CIA, John Whitten and his family left the United States and moved to Vienna, Austria. There, he took up opera and joined the Vienna Men's Choral Society. In Vienna, he never revealed his secret past. He died in 2000.

It is clear that the "Scelso Deposition" is one of the most important documents to be released by the Assassinations Record Review Board (which was responsible for the release of all relevant JFK assassination documents). We now have a clearer picture as to the mechanics of the early CIA probe into President Kennedy's assassination, which people were assigned to perform certain tasks, the failure of the CIA to cooperate fully with the Warren Commission, and Whitten's revealing comments on the key figures inside the agency and how they conducted their own parts in the Kennedy assassination probe.

Research Note: For those people interested in obtaining the full Scelso Document, refer your queries to the National Archives for the following information. Record Number: 180-10131-10330. Agency File Number: 014728.

Chapter 23:
The Man Who Kept the Secrets

Richard Helms was one of the most secretive, cunning, and devious men who walked the halls of CIA headquarters at Langley, Virginia. He stood more than six feet tall, had a ramrod bearing, did not take much to criticism, and was part of some of the most important missions that the CIA carried out. From his days in the OSS, and later the early CIA, he participated in operations in Berlin, took part in the Gehlen operation, Vietnam, Cuba, and the Watergate affair which finally ended his career under a cloud of smoke.

Richard Helms was born in 1913, graduated from Williams College and became a foreign correspondent in Europe for the United Press. He was commissioned in the Naval Reserve in July 1942 and served in the OSS under William Donovan beginning in August 1943. During the war, he worked as an analyst in such places as New York, London and Washington.

When the CIA was founded in 1947, Helms worked under the direction of Frank Wisner who headed the covert arm of the agency, the Office of Policy Coordination under State Department management. When the OPC was incorporated into the CIA, Wisner became Deputy Director for Plans. Helms became acting chief of operations for the DDP in July 1952. In 1958, Wisner left his post as DDP, and the rumor at headquarters was that Helms was to be promoted to take his place, Instead, Allen Dulles appointed Richard Bissell. In 1962, after the fiasco at the Bay of Pigs, President Kennedy fired Dulles and replaced him with John McCone as the new DCI. McCone in turn, appointed Helms as his deputy.

When the Kennedy administration decided to take action to topple Castro after the Bay of Pigs, Helms was asked to provide service. Helms, like the good soldier he was, followed his orders to the letter, even though he deeply disagreed with many of the policies he was asked to carry out. Helms had been skeptical to say the least about the Bay of Pigs planning and wisely stayed out of the plans for the invasion. He was so disliked during the Bay of Pigs planning that Richard Bissell later said that "he would not have welcomed"

Helms's participation—but it was no secret in the DDP that Helms was getting out of the way in this one.

Richard Bissell was the man who ran the pre-Bay of Pigs planning and he and Helms had been friends. There is no evidence that Helms, at any time, protested to Bissell about the invasion plans. In a puzzling incident, Bissell twice asked Dulles to remove Helms from any dealings with the invasion actions.

Bissell gave his own account of this incident. He went to Dulles early in 1961 and, according to author Thomas Rowers, "protested Helms's foot-dragging and noncooperation; they couldn't work together; Helms had to leave; perhaps a transfer to London as chief of station would ease the situation. Dulles then raised the matter with Helms, who said the tension between him and Bissell was as much of a mystery to him as it was to Dulles. He had tried to get along with Bissell, was sure they could settle their differences, and proposed an attempt to patch things up before disrupting in the middle of a major operation."[1]

As the design of the Bay of Pigs unfolded, Helms was to meet a man with whom he became very good friends throughout his life, E. Howard Hunt. Hunt, a longtime CIA officer and pulp fiction writer, was made the liaison officer between the CIA and the FRD, the top Cubans who were to lead the Bay of Pigs invasion. Helms first met Hunt in 1956, when Hunt was in Washington en-route to a new assignment in Uruguay. Though they did not see each other for a long period of time, both men kept in touch. In his memoirs of the Bay of Pigs operation, Hunt gave Helms the code name "Knight." David Phillips, a top CIA propaganda officer, wrote, "Bestowing the name of Knight was the ultimate accolade—people who have worked in the CIA will recall that pseudonym belonged to one of the Agency's most senior officers, a man Hunt idolized."

What is not widely known by mainstream readers or the general public is that on the morning of November 22, 1963, the day President Kennedy was shot, a secret meeting was held in Washington, D.C. which was attended by a number of high ranking CIA officers in which another attack on Cuba was discussed. Among those in attendance were the CIA's Executive Director Lyman Kirkpatrick, Richard Helms, Howard Hunt, and a prominent Cuban exile leader

[1] Powers, Thomas, *The Man Who Kept the Secrets: Richard Helms and the CIA,* Alfred A. Knopf, Inc. New York, 1979, Page 108.

named Enrique "Harry" Williams. Harry Williams was a close friend and confidant of Attorney General Robert Kennedy and the AG had Williams to his home on numerous occasions. The subject of the meeting was another attack on Cuba by a highly trained Cuban exile force, which was slated for December 1963. Upon the President's assassination, the plan was scrubbed as the new President, Lyndon Johnson, did not want any more hanky-panky as far as Cuba was concerned.

If Helms did not want anything to do with the Bay of Pigs planning in 1961, that cannot be said as far as the further plots to kill Castro were concerned. By 1963, Helms was the CIA's Deputy Director of Plans and he was knee-deep in the Castro plots.

During his testimony to the HSCA, Helms, now under oath where he could not hedge his bets, said the following, "All I am trying to say is the U.S. Government had a policy for many months of trying to mount a coup against Fidel Castro in 1963." He said that "these operations against Cuba were known to the Attorney General of the United States, the President of the United States, all kinds of people high up in the government." He continued by saying that the operations went nonstop during 1963. When asked by the Committee staffers if he was talking about a coup or an assassination attempt he said, "When one government is trying to upset another government and the operation is successful, people get killed. I don't know whether they are assassinated or whether they are killed in a coup." When asked how far-flung the plots to kill Castro were he said, "If you go through the records of those years, you will find the whole U.S. government was behind this one."

Helms told writer Richard Reeves, "Robert Kennedy ran with it [the Cuba plots], ran those operations and I dealt with him almost every day." Helms later told another journalist, Jim Lehrer (for his TV show *Newshour* on PBS): that President Kennedy had "organized his entire administration to get rid of Castro." He further told historian and writer Michael Beschloss in 1988, "There are two things you have to understand: Kennedy wanted to get rid of Castro, the Agency [CIA] was not about to undertake anything like that on its own." Helms further told the HSCA, "If President Kennedy had not been the motivating force, then the Cuban effort wouldn't have taken on the size and character it did." He also told the Discovery

Channel in 1997, "There isn't any doubt as to who was running that effort. It was Bobby Kennedy on behalf of his brother. It wasn't anybody else."[2]

Richard Helms did not tell then-CIA Director John McCone the entire story of the CIA-Mafia plots to kill Castro. He decided, for whatever reason, not to inform the Director on all aspects of the plans. Maybe he did it in order to protect the agency or to protect himself if the story ever came to light.

In 1967, Helms, who was then Director of the CIA, became directly involved in the Castro plots when he was asked by President Lyndon Johnson to report to him the facts surrounding the CIA's attempts to kill Castro. President Johnson first got wind of the plots when he was approached with story by the noted Washington reporter Drew Pearson. Pearson wrote the popular "Washington-Merry-Go-Round" column that had a nationwide audience. Pearson was friendly with President Johnson and when LBJ heard the story, he wanted to find out more. The gist of the story, as told to Pearson, came from Johnny Rosselli, one of the men who was hired by the CIA to kill Castro. Rosselli told Pearson that Kennedy was killed by a group of men who were sent by Castro in retaliation for an attack on him.

On January 13, 1967, Jack Anderson, also a noted Washington, D.C. reporter and a colleague of Pearson's, arranged for Pearson to meet with famed attorney Edward Morgan who was the lawyer for Jimmy Hoffa, and was now working with Johnny Roselli. Pearson, Anderson said would "meet with attorney Morgan and hear from a client of his who was on the fringe of the underworld [how] Bobby Kennedy had organized a group who went to Cuba to kill Castro; that all were killed or imprisoned... that subsequently Castro decided to utilize the same procedure to kill President Kennedy."

On January 16, 1967, Pearson met with President Johnson for an hour in the White House and told him the entire story as it was related to him. Pearson wrote in his diary, "I told the President about Ed Morgan's law client [Rosselli]. Lyndon listened carefully and made no comment. There wasn't much he could say." Johnson did not know about the CIA-Mob plots to kill Castro and shut down

---

[2] Waldron, Lamar with Hartmann Thom, *Ultimate Sacrifice: John and Robert Kennedy, the Plan for a Coup in Cuba, and the Murder of JFK*, Carroll & Graf, New York, 2005, Page 44.

any further CIA-related activity once he became President. Pearson said he wasn't going to write the story until November of that year. The President asked him to call Chief Justice Earl Warren and tell him what he'd told the President. They met on January 19, 1967. According to Pearson, Warren was "decidedly skeptical" about the report and the matter was dropped. However, Earl Warren was in a difficult situation. He was the chairman of the Warren Commission which looked into the assassination of JFK and he was not informed of the CIA-Mob plots by then-DCI Allen Dulles.

During his meeting with Lyndon Johnson, Helms did not reveal the entire story of the Castro assassination. Once again, Helms had his own reasons for not telling LBJ the whole truth about the Castro plots, the primary one, it can be argued, is that if they were revealed in their entirety, the CIA would take a major hit and he would possibly lose his job. Before leaving the Oval Office that day, LBJ asked Helms to make further inquiries regarding the Castro plots, and tell him if there was any connection between Robert Kennedy and the CIA that might have had the undesired effect of a blowback operation against JFK.

To further complicate matters for Helms, in 1963 he had been juggling another Castro assassination plot devised by the CIA, the so-called AMLASH operation.

Besides the CIA's external efforts to oust Fidel Castro, the agency used a number of internal assets in Cuba for their own purposes. One of their most important agents, and one that would prove to be the most controversial in their efforts to remove Castro from power, was one of the Prime Minister's most trusted aides, Rolando Cubela, a.k.a. AMLASH. The AMLASH story is a very complicated and long one, and there is no time in this chapter to tell the whole story. Here, in a nutshell, are the important facts.

In 1961, Cubela was the second-ranking member of the Directorio Revolucionario (DR), a revolutionary group of students who worked for the overthrow of the Batista regime. It is believed that Cubela was part of the team of men who killed Lt. Col. Antonio Blanco, then head of Batista's military intelligence unit in 1956. Cubela's DR group, while working for the same goals as Fidel Castro's 26th of July movement, did not see eye to eye with that group, and they kept each other at a distance. In the final days of the

Cuban Revolution, Cubela's DR group took over the presidential palace, refusing to turn it over to Che Guevara, but finally, and reluctantly, gave it over to Castro. When Castro finally took power, Cubela held the rank of Major in the Cuban armed forces.

The CIA's Inspector General's Report on the early days of the Cubela operation and his relationship to Castro reads as follows: "Prior to his appointment to the post of Cuban Military Attache to Spain and his subsequent departure for Madrid on March 27, 1959, Rolando Cubela frankly expressed to Prime Minister Castro his dissatisfaction over the present situation in Cuba. Cubela privately told intimates that he was so disgusted with Castro, that if he, Cubela, did not get out of the country soon, he would kill Castro himself."

The first meeting between the CIA and Rolando Cubela took place in Mexico City on March 9, 1961; the CIA wanted to find out his views on the Cuban revolution. Cubela did not give the questioner any favor and the meeting ended.

After the CIA learned of Cubela's anti-Castro remarks, new covert dispatches were sent to him and further meetings were arranged. Thus, the AMLASH operation was born. Cubela wanted to defect but the CIA said no. As time went on, CIA representatives met with Cubela in such places as Helsinki, Madrid, Copenhagen, Stockholm and Paris. Cubela told his CIA contacts that there were only two ways of getting rid of Castro. The first was an invasion of Cuba by U.S. forces and the second was an "inside job."

Cubela wanted to meet with Robert Kennedy but that idea was nixed. Instead, he met with Desmond Fitzgerald who ran the Special Affairs Staff, which was the CIA branch that ran all Cuban affairs, including Cubela. Fitzgerald met Cubela in Paris on October 29, 1963, and told him that he was a personal representative of Robert Kennedy. He told Cubela that the U.S. was prepared to give him all necessary assistance and would support any anti-Castro group of his choosing in Cuba that would succeed in toppling Castro from power. He told him that American support would continue after a successful coup.

Fitzgerald's talks with Cubela in Paris were sufficiently positive for him to recommend to his superiors at CIA headquarters to trust the Cuban. In a CIA memo of November 18, 1963, the CIA approved of Cubela's planned coup attempt. Headquarters gave the go-ahead to provide him with the rifles and scopes he previously requested. On November 20, 1963, the CIA sent a message to Cubela asking him to postpone his trip back to Cuba in order to see case officer "O." The purpose of the discussion was to inform him that the "technical support," i.e., guns, scopes, etc., that he had requested had been approved. The next meeting would take place in Paris on November 22, 1963.

In what started out as just an ordinary day between the CIA case officer and his agent, Fitzgerald met AMLASH in a secret location in the late afternoon. Since Desmond Fitzgerald is now deceased, and Cubela is not talking, we have to rely on the CIA's IG Report to reconstruct the events of the day. Cubela had previously stated that while he wanted to do away with Castro, he was not willing to lay his life on the line. Cubela was also a medical doctor and he had suggested that Dr. Gunn (who was the "Q"—James Bond's technical expert—of the CIA) come up with an exotic weapon to eliminate the enemy. What they came up with was a poison called Black Leaf 40, a common enough insecticide containing about 40% nicotine sulphate. The drug could be given to the victim either by injection or by absorption through the skin. By November 20, two days before the Fitzgerald-Cubela meeting in Paris, the device for administering the poison, a ballpoint pen rigged as a hypodermic syringe, was ready for shipment, and it went out on the next plane to Paris. The pen was given to Cubela, who, according to the Report, did not take it. He said that as a medical doctor, he was well aware of how Black Leaf 40 worked but would not take it to Cuba with him. He then said that the CIA should come up something more sophisticated for him to use.

"As they were coming out of the meeting [blank] and Cubela were informed that President Kennedy had been assassinated. Cubela was visibly moved by the event. He asked, 'Why do such things happen to good people?' The contact report does not state the time nor the duration of the [blank] Cubela meeting, but *it is likely that at the very moment President Kennedy was shot, a CIA officer was meeting with a Cuban agent in Paris and giving him an assassination device for use against Castro.*"

Helms, who knew all about the Cubela assassination operation never told Robert Kennedy that he was having Fitzgerald meet with him in Paris. This seems inconsistent because RFK was running the Castro operations and would have a need to know that such a meeting was taking place. The Church Committee said that Helms told Fitzgerald that he should tell Cubela that he was the personal representative of Robert Kennedy. Helms said the reason he didn't tell RFK about the Cubela meeting was "because it was so central to the whole theme of what we had been trying to do."

During the Johnson administration, the President, facing an ever-growing chorus of anti-Vietnam War demonstrators, began a secret campaign called "Operation Chaos" against the antiwar leaders (American citizens). Helms was the man who ran the operation on LBJ's behalf, and he did it without questioning the legality of the program. Operation Chaos also was run during the Nixon administration and was one of the CIA misdeeds that were made public in the early 1970s.

Helms had been appointed to the top spot at the CIA by President Johnson in June 1966 and when the Church Committee began its investigations, Helms' name was up front. They wanted to know all about his role in the Watergate affair, in the CIA's efforts to oust the freely elected President of Chile, Salvador Allende, and his part in the Phoenix Program during the Vietnam War. Speaking to the Committee, Helms was unrepentant, defying the Senators, not allowing his beloved CIA (or himself) to take the fall. (The investigations brought forth by Congress in the 1970s was called the "Family Jewels" by the press and the CIA.)

Helms told the Committee how President Nixon asked him to persuade the FBI not to dig too deep into the CIA connection to the Watergate burglary. To his credit, Helms refused and was fired by President Nixon in February 1973. He was later appointed Ambassador to Iran in 1973.

As the result of the Church Committee investigation, Helms was convicted of lying to Congress during Senate confirmation hearings into his appointment as Ambassador to Iran. He lied when he said that the CIA played no role in the ouster and death of Allende in Chile. He was fined $200,000 and left government service.

Chapter 24:
A Death in Saigon

In the last summer of his life, President John F. Kennedy was focusing more and more on the ever-changing situation in South Vietnam. At that time, there were almost 16,000 U.S. "advisors" training the South Vietnamese Army and already there were casualties among the U.S. contingent. U.S. advisors were even going on search and destroy missions with the South Vietnamese, a fact that was held back from the American public. If a poll was taken among the American people at the time, most of them would not have been able to find Vietnam on a map, let alone tell what we were doing in that country. However, as time and events would unfold, that attitude would change dramatically.

South Vietnam was run by its corrupt and ruthless President, Ngo Dinh Diem who ruled the nation with an iron fist. He was aided by his brother, Ngo Dinh Nhu, and his flamboyant wife, Madam Nhu. As a member of Congress, Kennedy watched as the French lost its war against the communists in Vietnam and knew that it would be a mistake for the United States to intervene militarily in Southeast Asia. Speaking in Congress, Kennedy said, "that no amount of American military assistance in Indochina can conquer an enemy or the people which has the sympathy and covert support of the people. For the United States to intervene unilaterally and to send troops into the most difficult terrain in the world, with the Chinese able to pour in unlimited manpower, would mean that we would face a situation which would be far more difficult than even that which we encountered in Korea."

As President, Kennedy would face an ever-unraveling political and military situation in Vietnam which he had little control over, and where the stakes were extremely high.

By the summer of 1963, it was obvious to the Untied States that their ally in South Vietnam, President Diem, was running a corrupt and leaderless government. Corruption ran rampant inside his administration, and more importantly, the war against the North Vietnamese and their Viet Cong allies was going badly. The Kennedy administration and its military mission were more interested in combating the National Liberation Front (Viet Cong) than the government of President Diem. Diem was prepared to rule his country without regard to the will of the people and he did everything in his power to do so.

Diem came to office in an election in 1954, becoming the prime minister of a divided Vietnam (North and South). He later consolidated his power by rigging elections, banning political parties and eliminating any opposition to his autocratic rule.

In November 1960, Diem survived an attempted coup by dividing the opposing military generals and circumventing the coup before it took place. In February 1962, a second coup attempt took place when a number of disgruntled air force pilots bombed the presidential palace in hopes of killing him. However, Diem was in another part of the palace and escaped injury.

Between 1961 and 1963, the United States increased its military assistance to South Vietnam in the hope of giving the military a fighting chance to beat back the Viet Cong. Back in Washington, the President was getting conflicting information from his military and political aides as to what was really going on in South Vietnam.

On May 8, 1963, an unforeseen event took place in South Vietnam that changed the entire political/military situation as far as the Kennedy administration was concerned. During a demonstration in the city of Hue, South Vietnamese forces under the direction of President Diem fired into a crowd of Buddhist monks who were celebrating the Buddha's 2,527th birthday. In the ensuing gunfire, nine were killed and 14 were wounded. This incident triggered a nationwide Buddhist protest and a decline in support among the people for the Diem regime.

Things got so bad that a number of Buddhist monks openly killed themselves in public by dousing their bodies with gasoline and setting themselves on fire. The horrific scenes went around the world via TV, and the Kennedy administration had no choice but to back a coup that was planned by the dissident generals opposed to Diem's dictatorial rule. Madame Nhu, Diem's sister-in-law, clapped openly as the pictures of the Buddhist monks self-immolating were shown on TV. She showed glee when the monks were, in her words, "barbecued" and said that she hoped the same fate awaited the American newspaper correspondent David Halberstam who was writing critical news accounts of the war in Vietnam. Her husband,

Ngo Dinh Nhu, told Morris West, who was an Australian novelist, that the Americans should leave the country and that he was in touch with some communists in Hanoi (North Vietnam).

In the wake of the Buddhists deaths, the United States Ambassador to South Vietnam, Frederick Nolting, met with President Diem to read him the riot act. Ambassador Nolting told Diem that he had to take certain steps to alleviate the crisis. They included admitting responsibility for the Hue incident, compensating the victims, and backing religious freedoms to all the people of the country.

One of the most important CIA officers who worked in Vietnam at the time was Lucien Conein who was called "Black Luigi" by his colleagues. He served in Vietnam during the buildup of American troops under the Kennedy administration and played an essential role in the overthrow of the Diem regime in South Vietnam in November 1963. He served in the OSS during World War II in the Special Operations Branch. He also took part in the Jedburgh Operation, which consisted of a three-member team comprised of Allied agents who parachuted into Nazi-occupied Europe to carry out sabotage and guerilla operations against enemy positions. In 1944, he left Europe and made his way to Asia where the OSS had a large intelligence base. In Indochina, Conein linked up with French troops who were waging their own war against Japanese forces who were threatening to overrun the region. It was during his stay in Indochina that Conein met a number of local resistance fighters like Ho Chi Min and Nguyen Giap, two men who would later be the leaders of the North Vietnamese government.

In 1954, by now a member of the CIA, he went back to Southeast Asia under the command of Colonel Edward Lansdale who headed a CIA support team that was aiding the French in their war against the Communist forces. Conein remained in Vietnam throughout much of the 1950s and 1960s, and would make friends with many of the up- and-coming South Vietnamese generals who would later play an important role in the American-led war in Vietnam.

Conein later testified that the Buddhist uprisings were the catalyst that ultimately brought down the Diem regime: "These events led the United States to apply direct, relentless, and table hammering pressure on Diem such as the Untied States has seldom before attempted with a sovereign friendly government."

On July 4, 1963, a meeting took place between Generals Minh,

Don, Kim, and Khiem in which they all agreed that it was time to stage a coup against Diem.

President Diem told a reporter that he had no resentment against the Buddhists and would respect their religious rights forthwith.

After midnight on August 21, 1963, Nhu ordered forces loyal to him to attack Buddhist pagodas in all parts of the country. Many monks were arrested and there was widespread looting of religious buildings. Over 30 monks were hurt and 1,400 arrested. This was a shattering blow to U.S. policy and JFK knew that something drastic had to be done vis-a-vis Diem and his brother.

Over the preceding six months, Ambassador Nolting asked to be relieved for personal reasons and JFK nominated Henry Cabot Lodge, the vice-presidential candidate on the Republican ticket in the 1960 presidential election, as his replacement. Kennedy had defeated Lodge in 1952, and even though they were not close, JFK respected his talents. The nomination of Lodge as the new ambassador was also political. The President knew that if the situation worsened in Vietnam, part of the blame would fall on Lodge, and thus, the Republican party. Nolting still backed Diem despite the Buddhist uprising and said, "trying to separate the members of that family [Nhu and his wife] would be like separating Siamese twins."

On August 24, 1963, a telegram from the State Department to Ambassador Lodge arrived:

> It is now clear that whether military posed martial law or whether Nhu tricked them into it, Nhu took advantage of its imposition to smash the pagodas with police and Tung's Special Forces loyal to him, thus placing the onus on military in eyes of world and Vietnamese people. Also clear that Nhu has maneuvered himself into commanding position.
>
> U.S. Government cannot tolerate situation in which power lies in Nhu's hands. Diem must be given chance to rid himself of Nhu and his coterie and replace them with best military and political personalities available.
>
> If, in spite of all of your efforts, Diem remains obdurate and refuses, then we must face the possibility that Diem himself cannot be preserved.[1]

[1] Telegram Department of State: Action: AmEmbassy Saigon-Operational Immediate August 24, 1963.

Newly released documents show just how frustrated the President and his advisors were with President Diem. A meeting was held on August 26, 1963 between President Kennedy and his top advisors concerning the situation in Vietnam, and the following quotes come from the memorandum from that meeting. The President asked if the United States had a military plan to remove and/or protect U.S. citizens in Vietnam if an evacuation was called for. He was told that a battalion landing team was at sea, only 24 hours from Saigon at that time. The President "observed that Mr. Halberstam of the *New York Times* is actually running a political campaign; that he is wholly non-objective, reminiscent of Mr. Matthews in the Castro days. He stated that it was essential that we not permit Halberstam unduly to influence our actions."

"The President observed that Diem and his brother, however repugnant in some respects, have done a great deal along the lines that we desire, and, when we move to eliminate this government, it should not be as a result of *New York Times* pressure.

During that talk, General Maxwell Taylor told those present that "in Washington we would not turn over the problem of choosing a head of state to the military."

The discussion then centered on whom the CIA and the U.S. military were talking to among the South Vietnamese generals. Contact had been made with three senior officers, Generals Khiem, Khan, and Minh. The next topic of discussion was President Diem and his brother. "The President commented that he did not believe that Diem would let his brother be ejected from the scene. The President asked what would happen if we find we are faced with having to live with Diem and Nhu, to which Hilsman replied this would be horrible to contemplate because of Nhu's grave emotional instability. The President asked if we are being blamed in Vietnam for the situation, to which Hilsman responded that we may be suffering slightly but that mostly the people seem to want to get rid of the Nhu's, but clearly need U.S. support to do so. He stated that, on these terms, it is imperative that we act." [2]

The newly declassified documents shed new light on President Kennedy's thinking regarding how to deal with President Diem

[2] Memorandum for the Record of a Meeting at the White House, Washington, August 26, 1963, Noon.

and the political ramifications if a coup against Diem took place. Concerning the possibility of a U.S.-sponsored military coup against President Diem, the President believed that if Diem's brother Ngo Dinh Nhu remained a major influence, the action might not succeed. Recognizing that Congress might get "mad" at him for supporting coup-minded Vietnamese generals, Kennedy said that "it will be madder if Vietnam goes down the drain." The President also said that for the situation to get better in Saigon, President Diem had to get rid of his brother and Nhu's wife, Madame Nhu, from the South Vietnamese government. There was a growing agreement in the administration that U.S. aid to Saigon might have to be cut off in order to weaken Diem.

On August 29, a message was sent from the White House to General Harkins in Saigon to tell the dissident generals in Saigon that the United States would support a coup if it had a good chance of succeeding, but that it would not include U.S. troops. The President sent a cable to Ambassador Lodge reaffirming the message to General Harkins.

However, the coup attempt at that time did not take place "because the Generals did not feel ready and did not have sufficient balance of forces. There is little doubt that GNV [South Vietnamese government] aware U.S. role and may have considerable detail."

In order to assess the situation in Vietnam, the President sent Defense Secretary Robert McNamara and General Maxwell Taylor to Saigon for talks with President Diem. Upon their return, they reported that the military effort was going reasonably well, but warned that increasing pressure on Diem had to be kept up. They also recommended the President announce the withdrawal of 1,000 men by the end of the year.

In a TV interview, the President said the following about the situation in Vietnam: "In the final analysis, it is their war. They are the ones who have to win it or lose it. We can help them, we can give them equipment, we can send our men out there as advisers, but they have to win it, the people of Vietnam."

On October 5, CIA officer Lucien Conein met with General Minh. Minh explained that a coup was being planned, and asked for assurances of American support if it were successful. Minh said that one part of the plan was the assassination of Diem and his brother,

Nhu. CIA Director McCone cabled the Saigon station saying that the United States did not condone assassination but that the U.S. could not be held responsible for the violent actions of others. McCone later said "he did not discuss assassination with the President, but rather whether we should let the coup go or use our influence not to. He left the meeting believing that the President agreed with his hands off recommendation."

In Saigon, Ambassador Lodge could not get President Diem to meet with him and told Washington that he was powerless to stop a coup.

Events came to a head on the morning of November 1, 1963, when units of the army surrounded the presidential palace. The U.S. embassy was given only four-minutes' notice of the coup. CIA officer Lucien Conein brought three million piasters ($42,000) to his office that would be given to pay for food for the troops and pay death benefits to those killed in the coup.

The generals met with Diem and guaranteed him and his family safe passage if they left immediately. Diem called Ambassador Lodge and asked what the U.S. position was. Lodge said that as far as he knew, the U.S. had no view and said he was concerned for his safety. After Diem refused to resign, the air force began bombing the palace and troops quickly moved in.

No one is sure what happened next, but by 10:30 that night, the bodies of President Diem and his brother Nhu were found. Conein opined that the brothers escaped to a Catholic Church in Chalon. He said that they might have been recognized and shot. It is also possible that they took their own lives, but as they were Catholics, that is doubtful. An Inspector General's Report on foreign assassinations said that on November 8, "a field-grade officer of unknown reliability gave the CIA two photographs of the bodies of Diem and Nhu, in which it appeared their hands were tied behind their backs. The source reported that Diem and Nhu had been shot and stabbed while being conveyed to the Joint General Staff headquarters."

Three weeks later, President Kennedy himself was assassinated in Dallas, Texas while riding in an open motorcade. No one knows how the history of the Vietnam War might have been changed but for that horrible act of violence.

Chapter 25:
The CIA's Spy in Moscow

One of the top agents the West used in the early 1960s was a Soviet army officer named Oleg Penkovsky. Penkovsky was instrumental in aiding the CIA during some of its most turbulent times, from the building of the Berlin Wall to the Cuban Missile Crisis. In espionage lore, he was dubbed "The Spy Who Saved the World."

Penkovsky's father served with the White Russian forces fighting the Bolsheviks during the Russian Revolution of 1917 (his father's choice of sides would later affect his son's career in the GRU, Soviet Military Intelligence).

As a young man, Penkovsky attended school in Kiev and later joined the Russian army in 1917. During World War II, he was commissioned as an officer in 1939 and saw action against Finland. Later in the war he was given a job as a political officer and did some intelligence work. After the war ended, he married the daughter of a high-ranking Soviet army officer and attended the famous Frunze Military Academy. In 1949, Oleg joined the GRU, or the Soviet Military Intelligence branch where he would work for the rest of his military career.

He got his training at the Military Diplomatic Academy where he studied the art of espionage and intelligence and was soon assigned to his first overseas post, Ankara, Turkey. While stationed in Turkey, Penkovsky got into an altercation with his boss, and he was reassigned back to Moscow. From then on his promising career in the GRU went downhill, and he stagnated in uninteresting positions when his father's White Russian background became known. But, for whatever reason, the top members of the GRU decided not to fire him. It was about this time (1960) that Penkovsky decided to contact the West and offer his services.

Penkovsky's first attempt to contact Western intelligence came in August 1960 when he was stationed in Moscow. One evening, he approached two Americans who were taking a stroll. He went up to them and asked if he could join them on their walk. The two strangers said yes, and the trio looked like old friends having a good time. He then told the startled foreigners that he was a Russian military officer who wanted to make contact with someone in the American embassy. He then gave them a letter to forward to the embassy. Not knowing what to do, the two strangers took the letter and delivered it as promised.

Penkovsky's note was given to Paul Garbler, who read it with interest. Garbler instantly recognized Penkovsky's name and sent the letter up the chain of command to his superiors in Washington. Penkovsky's note stirred interest at the CIA and they cabled Moscow to pursue the lead. Richard Helms wanted British intelligence to get Penkovsky first, before the CIA would take on the case. After a quick study, British intelligence told the CIA that Penkovsky had a cover job as Deputy Chief of the Foreign Section of the State Committee for Science and Technology. This agency was responsible for gathering all scientific information from sources outside the Soviet Union. His real job was to meet businessmen from all countries outside of the Soviet Union to try to recruit as many of them as possible.

In December 1960, while attending a trade fair in Moscow, Penkovsky met a British businessman named Greville Wynne. Wynne represented many British companies that sold industrial equipment to Eastern Bloc nations including the Soviet Union, Poland, and East Germany. Penkovsky pulled Wynne aside and told him that he was fed up with Prime Minister Nikita Khrushchev and wanted to make contact with either MI6 or the CIA. Unknown to Penkovsky, Greville Wynne was working undercover for British intelligence under commercial cover. MI6 ordered Wynne to talk with Penkovsky, which he did. The men agreed that they'd meet with each other when the Russian made his next trip to London. Richard Helms agreed to go along with MI6, and they began a joint operation to "run" him.

When Penkovsky turned up at the Mount Royal Hotel in London as the head of a Soviet delegation doing scientific research, a joint meeting between Penkovsky, the CIA and MI6 was arranged. One of the CIA men at the meeting was George Kisevalter who was fluent in Russian. The session lasted 12 hours, and Penkovsky gave the agents a wealth of information on all aspects of military/political developments in Russia. He said that he'd do whatever he was asked to do if it would lead to the downfall of the current Russian regime. He startled the CIA-MI6 team by saying that there were rumors flying around Moscow that Khrushchev was about to send Soviet missiles to Cuba. He was told that Greville Wynne would be his cut-out (the man who would pass along information between himself and London).

Penkovsky asked that he be photographed wearing the uniforms of both the U.S. and British armies. The CIA gave him the codename "Hero," while the British called him "Yoga."

The CIA supplied him with a small camera, which he used to take pictures of sensitive documents. They also instructed him as to how to contact them while he was in Moscow without being detected.

During one lengthy session with the CIA, Penkovsky said that Premier Khrushchev was determined to win the cold war against the West and that he believed that JFK was a weak man who could be bullied. However, the most important piece of intelligence that Penkovsky passed along was that the quality of Soviet missile technology was far less superior to that of the United States. This was a crucial piece of information, which would be of great value during the Cuban Missile Crisis of October 1962.

As Penkovsky's intelligence began to flow into CIA headquarters, the top brass knew they had a winner on their hands. Just how important Penkovsky's information was can be seen in a memo dated May 10, 1963 to the Chief, SR Division regarding Penkovsky:

> On the first point there is no doubt that many GRU and KGB officers realize that the CIA was able to run a highly successful operation in a professional manner. Their respect for CIA must have gone up. They do not know what interest CIA has for the security and well-being of anyone who collaborates. If indeed word should be spread about that U.S. intelligence is trying to save Penkovsky's life, this is bound to have a tremendous impact on many in the ranks. The need for other Oleg Penkovsky's, as the Director expressed to you, is greater now than ever. We must do all we can to achieve this.

On the second point, we all know of the tremendous contribution that Oleg Penkovsky made to our Government and to our Agency. We were at one point prepared to give him an unusually large sum of money whenever it was feasible for him to defect. As a professional intelligence officer, he was well aware of the risks he was taking for himself and for us. I feel we owe him a tremendous debt. For us not to consider ways and means of saving his life is to me a reflection of low morale level.[1]

Allen Dulles gave President Kennedy an up-to-date briefing on the news that Penkovsky was telling the CIA, among which was that the Russian's believed the West was not willing to go to war over Berlin and that the Soviets were also trying to avoid a conflict. President Kennedy even used some of Penkovsky's information in a hard-hitting speech he gave to the nation concerning the Berlin crisis. Penkovsky handed the President's speech to his Russian handlers so they would know how the President stood on the potentially explosive matter. JFK was also given a copy of the minutes of an internal Soviet report on the summit meeting between Kennedy and Khrushchev that had taken place a few months before. Penkovsky learned four days in advance that the Russians were going to begin building a wall in Berlin to separate the Western and Eastern sections of the city. However, the U.S. ambassador did not want to get involved in Penkovsky's report and did not inform Washington of the Soviets' preparations to divide the city. When President Kennedy was finally informed that the wall was going up, he was livid. He was quoted as saying to Secretary of State Dean Rusk, "How come we didn't know about this? How long have you known? Was there any warning in the last few days?"

On August 22, Greville Wynne arrived in Moscow where he met with Penkovsky. The Russian handed him six rolls of film, which included secret documents relating to the Berlin Wall.

While in Moscow, the CIA told Penkovsky that his contact in the city was a woman named Janet Chisholm whose husband worked as the attaché at the British embassy. On a crystal clear day in September 1961, Penkovsky approached a few children who were playing in a nearby park. Penkovsky casually walked up to

[1] Oleg Penkovsky-Soviet Double Agent-CIA Files.

178

the children and gave one of them a box of candy, which the child immediately gave it to his mother, Janet Chisholm. Chisholm, in spy parlance, was his "cut-out," the person who would act as his courier.

On September 20, 1961, Penkovsky arrived in Paris and was met by Greville Wynne. Penkovsky had with him fifteen rolls of film, which covered all sorts of military intelligence ranging from missile designs, military memorandums, and scientific and technical information. Over the next month, he was debriefed by four members of allied intelligence in a Paris safe house. Just before leaving Paris for Moscow, Penkovsky had second thoughts about returning home. He was clearly enjoying his life in the West, temporary as it may have been. He did though, have a family back in Russia and he just couldn't leave them alone. At the departure gate he almost changed his mind but returned home, a troubled man. Penkovsky returned to Moscow on October 16, 1961.

For the next year, Penkovsky worked secretly for the U.S., trying to keep a low profile in Moscow. However, by September 1962, the CIA had lost contact with him. President Kennedy was told by the CIA that the Russian was "under suspicion" and "possible surveillance" by the KGB. However, he showed up at a diplomatic reception in Moscow on August 27 where he handed over films that were developed with his Minox camera. He told his contact that he believed he was under surveillance and would have to be careful. He met again with his handlers on September 5 at the American embassy and at a British film show the next day. At that meeting he told this contacts that the Russians were sending huge amounts of arms to Cuba and the CIA should watch the situation carefully.

Penkovsky's biggest contribution to the CIA came in the days leading up to the Cuban Missile Crisis of October 1962. On October 14, 1962, a U-2 reconnaissance flight over Cuba took photos of a number of SS-4 medium range missile sites that had been delivered to Cuba by the Soviet Union. The missiles had the capacity to carry nuclear warheads, which were already in Cuba and could strike the continental United States in a very short period of time. In 1961, Penkovsky had given the CIA the manual of the specifications of the SS-4 missiles through Janet Chisholm. The Kennedy administration now had enough information to devise its strategy to monitor the missile delivery to Cuba and plan the appropriate response. The manual provided by Penkovsky gave JFK three extra days to counter the missiles if a U.S. air strike was to be launched. Richard Helms said of the information provided by Penkovsky during the missile crisis, "It gave President Kennedy time to maneuver. I don't know of any single instance where intelligence was more immediately valuable than at this time. Penkovsky's material had a direct application because it came right into the middle of the decision making process." It is not going out on a limb to say that the technical material provided by Penkovsky to the CIA during the missile crisis was hugely valuable in the peaceful outcome of the situation.

On October 22, 1962, right in the middle of the Cuban missile crisis, Oleg Penkovsky was arrested by the KGB. His original contact, Greville Wynne, was arrested in Hungary on November 2, and would be exchanged in 1964 in a spy swap for Soviet agent Gordon Lonsdale. Oleg Penkovsky was executed by the Soviets in May 1963.

Chapter 26:
Peter Karlow and
the Search for SASHA

In December 1961, a Russian KGB Major named Anatoly Golitsyn, approached a top CIA officer in Helsinki, Finland and asked his shocked counterpart for political asylum. Instantly recognizing who he had, Frank Friberg, the CIA's Station Chief, went into action, contacting his superiors in Washington. Golitsyn was soon on his way to the United States. If Golitsyn was a real defector and not a Soviet plant, then the United States would have in its hands an important intelligence catch.

Upon his arrival in the United States, Golitsyn bean telling all he knew about the spy game between East and West. Operating out of a safe house in Virginia, Golitsyn began to regale his listeners with the most fantastic stories imaginable. One item of particular interest caught their full attention. He said that the Russians had infiltrated a mole inside CIA headquarters, someone who had been there for a long time. All CIA counterintelligence plans were known to Moscow Center as fast as they were put in motion. When asked who this mysterious mole was, Golitsyn said he did not know his real name. But he gave some tantalizing clues. The person had previously served in Germany, the man was of Slavic background, and went by the codename SASHA. Golitsyn added that the man's last name began with the letter K. He also said that he believed that the man's name probably ended with the letters "sky." With these alluring clues, the CIA began a year-long mole hunt looking for the sleeper agent who had penetrated the inner sanctum of the CIA. By the time the search for the mole ended, the CIA's Counterespionage Section would be torn apart and many innocent men's lives would be in ruin.

As soon as Golitsyn was safely ensconced in a CIA safe house, the hunt for the mole began in earnest. Anyone connected with foreign counterintelligence was gone over with a fine tooth comb and the field was soon narrowed down to a few suspects. One person who seemed to fill all the categories laid out by Golitsyn was

Peter Karlow, whose real name was Klibansky, the same "sky" as mentioned by Golitsyn. Was Karlow/Klibansky the mole?

The Klibansky family came to the United States from Germany in 1910. The elder Klibansky got a job as a singing teacher. Both mother and father became naturalized American citizens in 1921, and their son, Serge Peter, was born the same year. Serge's father's teaching career took off during the 1920s, and he was often tutoring aspiring vocalists at the Metropolitan Opera House in New York City. During this time, the family made numerous trips back to Germany, but soon stopped as the political situation in that country deteriorated. The Depression in the United States hit the Klibansky family especially hard, and on September 17, 1931, Serge, the father, committed suicide by putting his head in an open oven while the family was in a separate room.

In 1937, Peter officially changed his name to Karlow, and graduated from the McBurney Prep School. He was awarded a scholarship to Swarthmore College, and joined the Navy when the United States entered World War II. He soon found himself in the OSS and remained in that capacity until the conflict was over. His most important duty while posted to the OSS was carried out on the island of Corsica, where he was assigned to a PT boat base. Karlow was part of a 15-man radar intercept platoon located near the island of Elba. One of his duties was to locate German planes that made attack runs against the U.S. military in Corsica. In February 1944, while on a mission aboard a boat, an explosion from a German mine tossed him over the side and killed most of his crew. In the ensuing hell, Karlow lost his left leg above the knee. At age 22, he now had to wear an artificial limb for the rest of his life. After the war, he and many other veterans of the OSS joined the CIA (he was accepted in 1947).

In 1946, one year before his entry into the CIA, Karlow was asked to write a history of the OSS. He worked on the narrative with legendary OSS officer. Kermit Roosevelt, a grandson of former President Theodore Roosevelt. The classified study was an in-house publication that was read by only those invited to view its secrets. Many years later, the manuscript was finally released to an eager public under the name *War Report of the OSS*.

Karlow had an affinity for all types of gadgets, liked to tinker with all sorts of mechanical applications, and asked that the CIA place him in an area where he could utilize his special talents. He pushed the CIA to begin a crash program to improve its technical means of spying, to make high-tech a reality, not something belonging to science fiction. He soon got his wish and was posted to the CIA's Special Equipment Staff where he refined bugs (listening devices), and made improvements to all sorts of espionage articles.

It soon became obvious that Karlow's technical talents were wasted in Washington, and in 1950, on orders from Richard Helms, he was sent to Frankfurt, Germany to set up a technical lab where he would refine his espionage/technical talents. He worked out of the CIA station in Karlsruhe, and within six months, had a prosperous business up and running.

One of his duties was to supply clandestine espionage tools for the secret agents whose job it was to parachute into Soviet-held parts of Eastern Europe. His team made lock picks and specialized guns, forged identity papers, all the necessary items needed for clandestine warfare. Karlow's specialty was to create to perfection forged identity papers that he and his team called the "7922nd Technical Aids Detachment of the United States Army."

One of his wilder schemes was to steal a Russian MIG-15 airplane. An elaborate plan was put in place wherein a Czech defector would fly the plane from East Germany to West Germany where it would then be disassembled and flown in parts to the U.S. Unfortunately, the operation was canceled.

During his stay in Germany, Karlow married a woman named Elizabeth Rausch, who later joined the CIA. She too connected with her husband in the technical gadgets department in Germany. Elizabeth also worked in the counterintelligence division, leaving in 1953 when their first child was born.

Peter Karlow left Germany and by 1956 was back in the United States. He now had a job in the Eastern European Division as the Deputy Chief of the Economic Action Division. By 1959, he was Secretary of the Technical Requirements Board.

For the next two years, Karlow performed his duties unencumbered by the secret events that were going on around him. As 1962 arrived, he did not know that Anatoly Golitsyn had defected in Helsinki and that the information he brought would collide with his peaceful life.

As the CIA began to piece Golitsyn's information together, they came to the conclusion that their main suspect was Serge Peter Karlow. Not wanting to tip him off, they decided that he was to be transferred to a new job, one that did not allow him access to really sensitive information. He was called into the office of Richard Helms who told him that the Kennedy administration was starting up an office that would handle foreign policy crisis, and that Karlow had been picked to represent the CIA. As Karlow began his new assignment, he had no idea that he was under investigation as a Russian mole.

As time went on, Karlow received a sudden and unexpected visit from two FBI agents. They came to see him on an unrelated case concerning a German forger he had known. They said that this person wanted to defect to the Russians, and could he tell them anything about him. Karlow wasn't very helpful and he was mystified why the Bureau had bothered to see him. Later, other agents came to his home and told him that they believed a person on his block might be a German spy. They asked if it would be OK for the Bureau to set up a listening device in Karlow's garage. Karlow agreed to their request. Soon, he realized that his own phone was tapped and knew something untoward was going on.

When Karlow traveled to Philadelphia to get a new artificial limb (the CIA believed he was going to meet a Russian contact), he was followed by FBI agents, who were dumbfounded when they realized what he was actually doing in the City of Brotherly Love.

For Karlow, the signs were all beginning to make sense. He was being followed for some reason of which he was not aware. Another blow to his psyche came when he was turned down for a job in the Technical Services Division.

On February 11, 1962, he was told to report to the Washington Field Office of the FBI where he would assist agents on a sensitive yet unnamed case. When Karlow showed up, he was greeted by two FBI agents, Aubrey Brent and Maurice Taylor. He was told up front that he had "the right to remain silent," a sure indication that he was being accused of some crime. He was dumbfounded when the agents told him he was accused of being a Russian mole. His flawless 22 year career in the CIA was now at an end.

He was interrogated by government agents who wanted to know all about his family ties to Germany and tried to cajole him into admitting that he was SASHA, all to no avail. Shortly before he left the Agency, Karlow confronted Richard Helms and his boss, James Angleton, the head of the CIA's Counterintelligence Section. Angleton told him, "there is more that goes on here than I can possibly explain to you. It has to do with a Russian defector." Stalking out of Angleton's office, Karlow now realized where the accusations had come from. As he left the CIA for the last time, he vowed to clear his name.

After leaving the CIA, Peter Karlow worked in the private sector, still doing everything to clear his reputation. By the 1980s, 20 years after he was forced out of the CIA, the nation's mood, as far as the intelligence community was concerned, had changed. In the 1970s, the Congress held open hearings on the CIA's abuses, both at home and abroad. The Congress passed a special bill on Karlow's behalf called "The Mole Relief Act." With new access to previously classified CIA files, Karlow got the help of then-CIA Director William Webster. Webster, after reviewing the evidence against Karlow, decided that he had been unjustly relieved of his duties. He was awarded $700,000 in back pay and reparations for his loyal service to the country, and now had his good reputation back.

Two other top-level CIA agents besides Karlow were also investigated and compensated after the fact. They were Paul Garbler, the CIA's first station chief in Moscow, and Richard Kovich, who had helped "run" Pyotr Popov, and was instrumental in recruiting many foreign nationals for the CIA. He was investigated because his last name began with the letter K.

In a secret CIA ceremony, Peter Karlow was awarded the Intelligence Commendation Medal and an award that was signed by DCI Webster.

In an ironic twist to the Karlow case, James Angleton, the CIA's chief spy catcher, was himself believed by some of his CIA colleagues to be the elusive SASHA.

Chapter 27:
Igor Orlov- The Next SASHA

Not content with hounding Peter Karlow as the elusive SASHA, James Angleton and the counterintelligence staff turned their attention to another possible mole inside the CIA. Their next potential victim was Igor Orlov, who had the same characteristics as Peter Karlow.

Igor Orlov's real name (or so he said) was Alexander Kopatsky, containing the same "K" and"sky" that Golitsyn talked about. He was born in Kiev, Russia on January 1, 1922.

According to Orlov, he attended military school in the Novosibirsk region of Russia. He liked to hunt tigers in the wilds of Siberia, fish, and was a dashing ladies man. He also said that he served with the Russian intelligence service during World War II. (1944). He also related that he had been wounded during a parachute landing when he dropped behind German lines. According to his military biography that he gladly gave to the CIA, he was captured by a German patrol and recuperated in a field hospital.

After regaining his health, Orlov took sides with General Andrei Vlasov and became the official liaison between the Germans and Vlasov's forces. Vlasov was one of the most powerful Russian military officers during the war, but what happened after his capture by the Germans tarnished his reputation. He was a Lt. General during World War II, who surrendered his forces to the Germans in July 1942. Vlasov, despite being of Russian heritage, was a political opponent of the Russian government and he now switched sides, taking his troops to fight his one-time countrymen. He formed a group called the Army of Russian Liberation (ROA), even using newly-freed Russian POWs to fight the Soviets.

During this time, Orlov became a German intelligence agent and served in the same capacity on Vlasov's staff (from April 1944 to March 1945). After the war ended, he was captured by the Americans and spent a short period of time in the infamous Dachau concentration camp. In a bit of irony, his future wife was also at Dachau at the same time.

The Orlov resume is sketchy, but he is believed to have joined the

CIA in 1947 and was stationed in Pullach, near Munich, Germany. He was part of the CIA's secret liaison with German General Reinhard Gehlen who switched sides after the war in order to keep himself out of jail or being hung as part of the Nazi hierarchy. It was during this time in Germany that Igor met Eleonore Stirner. They were married in July 1948. Eleonore had been a member of the Hitler Youth Organization, thus, her imprisonment by the Allies for five months at Dachau. At the time of their marriage, Eleonore said that her husband told her that his real name was Alexander Kopatsky. He picked that Polish-sounding name to ensure that he would not have to endure a one-way trip back to the Soviet Union. If he was captured by the Russians and they learned of his work for General Vlasov, his end would be swift.

In 1949, while on assignment in Berlin, Eleonore and Igor again changed their names, this time to Franz and Ellen Koischwitz. Part of his Berlin assignment was to recruit women from the bars and streets of the teeming city. He also took to drinking and many a time had to be taken in by his colleagues. Orlov's CIA case officer while in Berlin was Paul Garbler, and the two men shared a fond friendship and many a night on the town.

In 1956, the couple was sent from Berlin to Frankfurt (by now Mrs. Orlov was working in a small capacity for the CIA, and also had a two year old son). Something curious now happened to them. It was decided by the CIA that they should have American passports in order for them to travel legally to and from the United States. It seems that "Franz Koischwitz" at one time had been arrested for a traffic offense and their travel documents were not approved. In order to overcome that minor problem, the CIA gave them a new name: Orlov. Igor Orlov now had three identities; Orlov, Koischwitz and possibly, Kopatsky. To make matters more interesting, he had ties to three intelligence services: the CIA, the Russians and the Germans.

By April 1957, the Orlovs left Germany and arrived in the United States. Their second child, a boy named George, was born on August 9, 1957 and was a bona fide American citizen. Soon, Orlov was sent back to Frankfurt.

While on a CIA-inspired trip to Vienna, Austria, an incident took place at the Orlov home that caused considerable friction between him and Nicholas Kozlov, like Orlov, a Russian who worked for the Agency.

Upon his return home, Eleonore said that their home safe had been rifled. Orlov reported the incident to his boss, Sasha Sogolow (Sogolow would later be considered a traitor to the CIA because of his association with Orlov). In the meantime, Mrs. Orlov had met a man with whom she traded materials from the PX for opera tickets. The CIA accused her of black market dealings. Igor confronted his wife about her illicit meeting, but she denied any illegal activities.

With this unpleasant incident now swirling around them, the Orlovs were sent to the United States in January 1961, one day before JFK was to be inaugurated as the 35th President of the United States.

The CIA told Orlov that he would be posted to an important position in the newly created Defense Intelligence Agency (DIA). They were put up in a home in Manassas, Virginia, about 30 miles from Washington, D.C. Soon, life began to get quite unpleasant for the Orlovs, as the high expectations that the CIA promised them, did not pan out.

Like Peter Karlow, the Agency began to suspect Igor Orlov as being SASHA. The fact that he worked in Germany, that his name ended with "sky," and that he was of Russian (Slavic) heritage made him a prime candidate as the mole. They never intended to give Orlov any job within the American intelligence community, let alone allow him to access the DIA's secrets. When he wasn't called to come in to work, Orlov began to get concerned. One person he contacted was Sam Wilson. When Orlov asked why the DIA had never heard of him, Wilson said that he was unable to give him any help. Alone in a new and unfriendly country, Orlov and his wife were in limbo.

Over the next half year, Orlov still hadn't been hired by the CIA or any other branch of the American intelligence establishment. However, the CIA did find the time to help them enroll their children in a Lutheran school and gave them money for resettlement purposes.

Needing desperately to earn a living, he obtained a job as a furniture mover on a van. Orlov soon tired of the backbreaking work and got a job as a driver delivering newspapers for the

Washington Post for 60 dollars a week. The couple soon began their own business and opened up a picture gallery in nearby Alexandria, Virginia. They managed to make a decent living, making picture frames and selling paintings. The FBI kept a keen eye on their Alexandria facility, believing that the store was a front for their espionage activities.

In order to try to make more money, Eleonore Orlov and her sons went back to Germany where she tried to get a job. She wanted Igor to join her but he stayed in Virginia.

Back at CIA headquarters, Jim Angleton set up a team of investigators to look into Orlov's background. He appointed Bruce Solie, who worked in the Office of Security, and Pete Bagley, a good friend on the CIA staff. They believed that he was a Russian intelligence officer from the day he joined the CIA and was sent to the United States to penetrate the Agency. Solie and Bagley turned their attention to members of the Berlin staff who worked with Orlov, including Paul Garbler and David Murphy, believing that they were in cahoots with Orlov.

By now, the FBI was getting into the Orlov investigation. In 1955 they brought him in for questioning but came up empty. On May 10, 1965, while working on his paper route, Orlov sneaked into the Soviet embassy. His picture was not taken by the ever-present FBI cameras that constantly monitored the building. Orlov's official story was that he sought out the Russian's help by asking them if they could keep an eye out for his mother, then living in the Soviet Union. He was convinced that she might face reprisals because of his ties with the CIA. In a bit of irony, the Russians contacted the State Department regarding Orlov's visit.

When Angleton learned of Orlov's surreptitious entry into the Russian embassy, he flipped out. He was now convinced that Orlov had made contact with the Russians in order to help him escape back to the motherland.

Another person who believed that Orlov was the mole named SASHA was a Russian agent named Igor Kochnov, who was acting as a double agent for the CIA. Kochnov worked in the foreign counterintelligence section of the KGB's First Chief Directorate that was responsible for foreign intelligence. He approached the CIA and offered his services, saying he wasn't being appreciated by the KGB and was denied promotion. He said he came from Russia to recruit a man named Nikolai Artamonov, who was living in the United States under the alias of Nicholas Shadrin. He told the CIA that if they helped him in catching Shadrin, he'd act as a spy for the CIA inside the KGB. He also tantalized the CIA by saying that one of his reasons for being in the States was to locate Anatoly Golitsyn and Yuri Nosenko and possibly lure them back to the Soviet Union.[1]

Orlov made arrangements with Eleonore to take care of their children, as he was convinced he was about to be arrested by the FBI. He told her to be at a certain location in Alexandria, Virginia with their sons and that the Russians would take care of them. Instead, Mrs. Orlov balked, contacted her pastor and never showed up at the prearranged location.

Orlov was questioned on a daily basis by the FBI but they were never able to crack the case. In the end, they had no definite proof that Igor Orlov was the elusive SASHA.

---

[1] Bagley, Tennent H. *Spy Wars: Moles, Mysteries, and Deadly Games,* Yale University Press, New Haven, Connecticut, 2007, Page 198.

Chapter 28:
Anatoly Golitsyn: The First "Dangle"

In spy parlance, a "dangle" is an agent who is sent to supply deliberately misleading information. Was Anatoly Golitsyn just such a character?

In the annals of the CIA, the most contentious defector to come to the West was a topflight Soviet intelligence officer named Anatoly Golitsyn. When Golitsyn first contacted Western intelligence in 1961, no one in either the American CIA or the British SIS would have believed the hornets' nest they were about to enter. For, with the defection of Golitsyn to the West came a decades-long search for a top Soviet "mole" inside both the CIA and the British intelligence service, a witch-hunt that would tear the CIA apart and ruin the careers of many decent men.

Anatoly Golitsyn first made contact with the CIA on December 15, 1961 in Helsinki, Finland. Without any fanfare, he arrived at the doorstep of CIA Station Chief Frank Friberg. Friberg was shocked to see the Russian at his home and immediately knew who the visitor was. Golitsyn told the surprised CIA officer that he wanted to seek political asylum in the West for himself and his wife and child. Friberg immediately realized that he had to act quickly, and he instantly contacted his superiors in Washington for advice.

Who was this prize catch and why did he show up at Friberg's door? Golitsyn was born in the Ukrainian village of Poltava. The family soon moved to Moscow and at age fifteen he joined the young Communist Youth movement (Komsomol). He missed World War II and in 1945, attended the officers' artillery service school in Odessa. Upon graduation, he joined the Soviet intelligence service.

Golitsyn had a long career in Soviet intelligence, joining the KGB in 1951; he began his vocation as an agent in the First Chief Directorate's Anglo-American Division. In the mid 1950s, he served in Vienna, Austria, a top city for spies in continental Europe. It was in that posting that he got into a fight with his KGB resident in charge of operational matters. At the time of his original contact with Frank Friberg in Finland, Golitsyn was serving as a Major in the KGB's First Chief Directorate, which was responsible for foreign operations on NATO and its military command.

At CIA headquarters, the men in the Soviet Russia Division pulled out all the stops to find out who Golitsyn was and if he could be trusted. Their first bit of information came from Peter Deriabin, a KGB officer who had defected to the United States. In their files, the CIA had found out that Deriabin was not happy with life in the Soviet Union and thus, was a possible target for recruitment, which turned out to be correct.

Friberg got permission from Washington to bring Golitsyn in, and after a convoluted voyage from Frankfurt, West Germany to London, and a one-night stopover in Bermuda, they finally arrived in New York a few days later. With his CIA escorts in tow, Golitsyn and his family were put up in a CIA safe house for debriefing. He was given the codename "AE/LADLE." For the CIA and Golitsyn, it was just the beginning of a long and frustrating dance of conflicting egos.

In the winter of 1962, the CIA moved Golitsyn to a safe house near the Choptank River in Maryland for the long debriefing process. During his interrogations, Golitsyn began to spill the beans on any number of Soviet penetrations of U.S. and allied intelligence services. He began by saying that the Soviet's had a number of highly placed moles inside the French intelligence agency SDECE. He went so far as to describe an assassination plot on the life of Phillippe de Vosjoli, the French liaison to the CIA.

This information was given to President Kennedy who passed it along to French President Charles de Gaulle. Golitsyn surprised the CIA even further when he said that the KGB was using its French spies in the United States to mount a clandestine operation to gain information on U.S. missile sites.

As his interrogations continued, his questioners asked him about the possibility that the Soviet Union had penetrated the CIA, a query that had the deepest consequences if answered in the affirmative. Golitsyn, to everyone's surprise, said yes, but he could not give any further details, nor could he provide any names. Friberg said of Golitsyn's news regarding a potential mole inside the CIA, "That's all he had, there was no meat on the lead. Golitsyn didn't know anything more himself."

Golitsyn was able to give the U.S. the names of three other

Russian agents in the West: John Vassall, a British Admiralty Clerk, John Watkins, a one-time Canadian diplomat, and Hugh Hambelton, a Canadian teacher. As far as any Soviets in the CIA was concerned, the only vague hint that Golitsyn gave was the name of a suspected mole called SASHA, a man who formerly worked in Berlin, and was of Slavic heritage. He also said that this person's last name began with the letter K and probably ended with "sky."

As we have seen, the hunt for SASHA began, the CIA zoomed in on an officer named Peter Karlow. Karlow had previously run a CIA laboratory in Hochst, he was of Slavic background, and had a name that might have ended in the letters "sky." It seems his real last name was Klibansky, and his father said he had been born in Russia. In January 1962, wiretaps were placed on Karlow's home, and the CIA called him the "principal suspect" in their investigation. Karlow was interrogated by the FBI but was never told why he was being questioned.

In order to find out what was going on, Karlow had a meeting with James Angleton, chief of the CIA's counterintelligence staff. Angleton said to him regarding his case, "This is a very uncertain and highly dangerous situation. There is more that goes on here than I can possibly explain to you. It has to do with a Russian defector. Please don't discuss this with anyone."

Karlow was eventually forced to resign from the CIA on July 5, 1963. He was exonerated years later under the "Mole Relief Act."

As time went on, Golitsyn began to show paranoid characteristics, telling different versions of stories he had earlier spun, which now did not make sense. He also demanded to have a face-to-face meeting with President Kennedy. He was allowed to see Robert Kennedy instead. He also asked for a secret slush fund of $1.5 million for his own use that would be used in the overthrow of the Soviet government.

In time, James Angleton himself took over the day-to-day debriefing sessions with Golitsyn. He had help from one of his most trusted aides, Newton "Scotty" Miller, a 14-year veteran of the CIA. What Angleton was looking for from Golitsyn was proof that the Soviets had penetrated the CIA. He wanted to know what specific sections of the CIA had been burrowed into. In response, Golitsyn told Angleton that the wealth of material he had seen in

Moscow relating to the CIA could not have come from one source, therefore, there had to be a number of Soviet moles hidden inside the agency. The one piece of information that shocked Angleton the most was when Golitsyn said that Soviet Union would eventually send another person to the United States to discredit everything he told the CIA. That man would come to the States one year later.

Showing paranoid tendencies himself, as Angleton listened to Golitsyn spin his stories about Soviet penetration at Langley, he ordered searches for the suspected moles. One of the possibilities centered on David Murphy, the head of the CIA's Soviet Division. Another person of interest was Pete Bagley, the deputy director of the Soviet Bloc Division. Things got so bad inside the CIA that in 1967, Angleton asked DCI Richard Helms to stop the Soviet Division from running important missions, which Helms agreed to do.

Golitsyn also persuaded Angleton that another top-ranking, well-respected Soviet double agent working for the United States, Oleg Penkovsky, was under Soviet control, and was giving the United States false information pertaining to the state of Russia's nuclear arsenal.

He also astounded Angleton by telling him that the KGB had been secretly divided into two separate KGBs, an "inner group" that planned and carried out covert operations, and an "outer" KGB whose agents who were deliberately sent to make contact with the West. These agents were "doomed spies," people who, if they were caught, were on their own.

Speaking on the reorganization of the KGB, Angleton said, "If Golitsyn was correct, it meant that we knew virtually nothing about the KGB's capacity for deception."

The Soviets knew of Golitsyn's defection and were not too pleased with his decision to turn to the West. A revealing CIA document on Golitsyn and the Russians shows exactly how far they were willing to go to exact retribution.

It seems that in 1966, the Russians were looking for three of their prime defectors, Yuri Nosenko, Anatoly Golitsyn and Peter Deriabin "in order to carry out liquidation operations against them" ("liquidation" meant death). However, said researcher Michael Holtzman:

196

The KGB considered Golitsyn an average officer. They believed that he probably did not provide American intelligence with much information, as he was working in the Information Department before his defection and therefore did not have access to operational matters and also was assigned to the 14th (Counterintelligence) Department for only a short study of operations. In this regard, they concluded Nosenko's defection much more damaging to the KGB.

In looking back at what powerful information Anatoly Golitsyn provided to the CIA, and Angleton in particular, it is not too much to ask if all these messages were on the level. After all, Golitsyn told Angleton that another Soviet agent would soon come to discredit him. Yuri Nosenko arrived one year later. He also discredited Top Hat and Fedora, as well as Oleg Penkovsky, who some writers of 20th century espionage called "The Spy Who Saved the World." By describing the division of the KGB into an "inner" and "outer" organization, Golitsyn made the CIA question all the counter moves it took against the Russians during this time. Was Golitsyn sent ahead of even Nosenko to soften up the CIA, and initiate inside Langley a mole hunt for bad spies who didn't exist?

It was the FBI's turn to interrogate Golitsyn and they went at it full bore. The U.S. government set Golitsyn up in New York City and paid him a handsome salary of $200,000 for his help.

Unlike Angleton, J. Edgar Hoover did not believe anything that came out of Golitsyn's mouth. Hoover was astonished when the defector asked for U.S. files on Soviet operations. Hoover flatly refused to pass over any of these sensitive documents. Despite the FBI's distrust of Golitsyn, a secret meeting between the top brass of the FBI and the Russian was arranged. In 1962, a number of FBI counterintelligence specialists met with Golitsyn at the Mayflower Hotel in Washington. In the end, nothing of substance came of the meeting.

During these meetings Golitsyn told the Bureau that there were a number of unidentified communist spies inside the FBI. Since he did not have the names of these alleged moles, Hoover chose not to believe him. Hoover also held to the view that Angleton was being taken in by Golitsyn's notion of a "Monster Plot," wherein Soviet moles were infesting the West's intelligence services.

For all the tug-of-war statements between the agencies regarding the bona fides of Golitsyn, the FBI had as one of its main jobs the role of investigating moles inside the CIA and of getting access to any defector, real or fake, who came calling. For the CIA's part, it did not want any FBI agents looking into its sensitive counterintelligence functions, even if it meant creating deep divisions between them. Golitsyn was just the first of the defectors in the 1960s who would create a split in the U.S. intelligence community. Soon, another Soviet defector would come knocking on our doorstep, and he would bring with him very potent allegations regarding the Soviet Union and its possible ties to the Kennedy assassination. His name was Yuri Nosenko.

Chapter 29:
Yuri Nosenko Comes Calling

Three months after the assassination of President Kennedy, the CIA and the FBI were to begin a high level investigation of Yuri Nosenko, a high-ranking Soviet KGB officer who defected to the West. For historians, the Nosenko case had all the ingredients of a good spy thriller: espionage, fake defectors, political assassinations, and the incarceration of a defector in harsh conditions. The ramifications of the Nosenko case are still being debated by historians and journalists of the 21st century and it is a good bet that their investigations will go on for some time to come.

At the time of his defection, Nosenko was one of the highest-ranking Russian intelligence officers to come westward. Nosenko worked for the Seventh Department—the section that oversaw all visiting American tourists to the Soviet Union during the 1960s. At the time that Nosenko was monitoring the few Americans to set foot on Russian soil, his branch was keeping tabs on a recent American defector, a former Marine radioman named Lee Harvey Oswald.

The Oswald case would come to haunt both the CIA and the FBI, and would perpetuate the ever-growing feud between James Angleton and J. Edgar Hoover. They had two different views on Nosenko and the information he brought with him.

Nosenko first made contact with the CIA in 1962 while he was in Geneva, Switzerland in his capacity as chief of security for the Soviet delegation to the disarmament talks. In a bit of bad luck, Nosenko lost all the money he was given by the KGB on his first foray to the West. He had to get the money back before his KGB friends could discover his indiscretion. In a hasty decision, he decided to approach the CIA and offer to sell information to the U.S. for 900 Swiss francs.

The CIA was very much interested in what Nosenko had to offer and he was soon debriefed by two officials: Pete Bagley, a CIA case officer, and George Kisevalter, who arrived to act as Nosenko's interpreter.

Nosenko arrived at a CIA safe house a bit tipsy from all the liquor he had been consuming. Still, he had quite a tale to tell. One of the things he said was that the walls of the American embassy in Moscow were bugged by the KGB, After intensive interrogations, Bagley sent a cable to Washington saying, "Subject has conclusively proved his bona fides. He has provided info of importance and sensitivity. Willing to meet when abroad and will meet as often and as long as possible (until) his departure from Geneva on June 15."

Nosenko told the CIA men that they should not try to contact him once he returned to the Soviet Union-it would be too dangerous. Instead, the CIA gave Nosenko a secure telephone number as well as a codename, AE/FOXTROT.

Before their sessions ended, Nosenko told his astonished listeners that the CIA was infested with moles which were feeding the KGB all sorts of top-secret information coming out of Langley headquarters. For the members of James Angleton's CIA staff, Nosenko was the devil incarnate, a man who came to destroy the CIA. Furthermore, he was the man Golitsyn had said would follow him in a massive disinformation campaign to destroy the CIA.

As Nosenko began to be quizzed by the CIA his story was met with deep suspicion by James Angleton, chief of the CIA's counterintelligence unit. From the beginning of the Nosenko saga, Angleton was deeply suspicious of the newest Russian defector. He was certain beyond a reasonable doubt that Nosenko was on a disinformation mission as spelled out by Golitsyn. As time went on, Angleton became more and more paranoid, seeing conspiracies beyond every corner and distrusting the people he had worked with for years.

As the Nosenko interrogations began in earnest, he dropped a bombshell that made Angleton even more distrustful of him. He said that while he was in Moscow, he had seen the KGB file on Lee Oswald, the alleged assassin of President Kennedy. Under further questioning Nosenko said that there was no connection between the Russians and the assassination of the President. Nosenko said that the Russians had no interest whatsoever in a loner like Oswald and the only reason they allowed him to stay in the country was his attempt at suicide.

The possible Russian connection to the Kennedy assassination involved Yekaterina Furtseva, who was Nikita Khrushchev's lover. The story of Yekaterina Furtseva is told by journalist Joseph Trento in his book *The Secret History of the CIA*. Furtseva served as the Russian Minister of Culture and also as a member of the Soviet Presidium under Khrushchev.

According to Trento's account, Furtseva was given a high degree of power over the KGB, and her son-in-law was promoted to become a KGB officer. Soon, Furtseva and a number of high-ranking KGB officers, including Vladimir Semichastany, plotted against Khrushchev, believing his harsh, anti-American rhetoric was working against Soviet interests. Trento writes that Nosenko told his CIA interrogators that it was the decision of Yekaterina Furtseva rather than the KGB's not to recruit Oswald.[1]

The message that Mdm. Furtseva was sending to the CIA was that the Russians had no operational interest in Oswald. Thus, they had no part in the President's death.

In a convoluted way, the message sent by Mdm. Furtseva gave Angleton fresh proof that the Soviet Union was in some way connected to the Kennedy assassination. Angleton may have believed that since the highest levels of the Russian government were aware of who Lee Harvey Oswald was, then they must have deliberately dispatched him to the U.S., so they were somehow involved in the Kennedy assassination.

Despite the fact that the Warren Commission decided that there was no conspiracy, foreign or domestic, in the Kennedy assassination, Angleton was convinced that Oswald was a "dispatched agent," sent to the U.S. to absolve the Russians of guilt in any plot to kill Kennedy. Furthermore, Angleton believed that Oswald was groomed as an assassin by the KGB during his three-year stint in the Soviet Union; that he was sent to the United States to kill Kennedy; and lastly, that the Nosenko mission was meant to excise any possible involvement by the Soviet's in the President's death. The real culprit in the whole, sordid mess was none other than Yuri Nosenko.

As the Nosenko interrogations went on, a number of officers in both the CIA's Soviet Russia Division and the Counterintelligence Division had doubts about Nosenko's reliability. For example, they believed that the information he gave them was out of date and of no operational value; that he lied about his military career, as well

[1] Trento, Joseph, *The Secret History of the CIA*. Prima Publishing Co., New York, 2001, Page 279.

as his schooling; that he was giving them a "legend," a fake story about his past; and that some of his answers concerning Lee Oswald might have been made up.

When Nosenko arrived in the U.S. in February 1964, he was placed under CIA custody, most of the time in solitary confinement. He was subjected to extensive interrogation, and took a number of polygraph tests: April 4, 1964, October 18, 1966, and August 6, 1968. In each session, Nosenko said that he had never been interested in Lee Oswald and had never used him as an agent of the Russian government.

The man who conducted the first two polygraph tests said that on the first test Nosenko had lied, though not on the Oswald question. On the second, he had lied to two of the Oswald questions. Another polygraphist conducted the third test. He concluded that Nosenko was telling the truth.

In the 1970s, the CIA conducted an internal investigation of the Nosenko case and had the following to say about the polygraphs he had been given. The first two tests were considered to be "invalid or inconclusive" because of deficiencies in the way they were conducted. The first exam was meant to create a hostile atmosphere for Nosenko. The questioner was told to tell Nosenko that he was lying, even if the evidence proved otherwise. The CIA said that the third examination was valid "and that the results could be considered credible." [2]

The Soviet Russian Division at CIA headquarters wrote a 900-page report on Nosenko that was pared down to 447 pages in February 1968. Their conclusions were that:

1) Nosenko did not serve in the naval reserve as he said he did.

2) He did not serve in the American Embassy section of the KGB at the time he told the CIA he did, and did not serve as a case officer or deputy chief of the seventh department as he claimed.

3) He did not join the KGB at the time he reported.

4) He wasn't the chief of the American Embassy section.

---

[2] The Analysis of Yuri Nosenko's Polygraph Examination, HSCA, March 1979.

The disparity of opinion inside the CIA regarding Nosenko is seen in the testimony of Harold Osborn, the Director of Security who stated on October 5, 1972:

> Mr. Nosenko has been an extremely valuable source, one who has identified hundreds of Soviet intelligence officers, and he has otherwise provided a considerable quantity of useful information on the organization of the KGB, its operational doctrine, and methods. He has conducted numerous security reviews on Soviet subjects of specific intelligence interest and he has proven himself to be invaluable in exploring counterintelligence leads. In effect, Mr. Nosenko has shown himself to be a productive and hardworking defector who is rehabilitated and favorably disposed towards the Agency.[3]

Angleton was not the only top level CIA official to doubt Nosenko's statements on Oswald. Richard Helms, the Deputy Director for Plans, was not convinced that Nosenko was telling the truth concerning the ex-Marine. Helms made this comment on Oswald's defection: "Since Nosenko was in the agency's hands this became one of the most difficult issues to face that the agency had ever faced. Here a President of the United States had been murdered and a man had come from the Soviet Union, an acknowledged Soviet intelligence officer, and said his intelligence service had never been in touch with this man [Oswald] and knew nothing him. This strained credulity at the time. It strains today."

Over at the FBI, the defection of Yuri Nosenko was seen differently. Nosenko's defection fit right in with the mindset of J. Edgar Hoover, who wanted to create from the beginning that Oswald was the lone assassin of President Kennedy. Hoover needed a backer who would deflect any unfavorable suggestions that the Bureau was not diligent enough in investigating the possibilities of conspiracy in the Kennedy assassination. In Nosenko, with his assertion of no Soviet involvement with Oswald during his time in the Soviet Union, Hoover had, in his own mind, positive proof that

---

[3] Duffy, James, R., *Who Killed JFK? The Kennedy Assassination Cover-Up,* Shapolsky Publishers, New York, 1988, Pg. 78-79.

Oswald was a lone nut, who had no confederates in the death of the President.

The Nosenko affair was going on at the same time that the Warren Commission was investigating the Kennedy assassination, and Hoover wrote a letter to the Commission informing them of Nosenko's defection and his startling revelations about Oswald

Richard Helms met with Warren Commission lawyer J. Lee Rankin concerning the Oswald-Nosenko case. Helms explained that the CIA was dubious of Nosenko's story, no matter what contradictory information the FBI might offer. The Nosenko problem grew so large that Helms had a private meeting with Chief Justice Earl Warren, the Commission's head. Helms laid out the CIA's case against Nosenko, saying that there were too many irregularities in his testimony. The matter came to a head in July 1964 when a top contingent of CIA officers including Helms, Pete Bagley, and David Martin met with the entire Warren Commission. They said in no uncertain terms that Nosenko was a plant of the KGB and that if that information came to light, the public might connect the Russian government with the assassination of the President.

CIA documents relating to Nosenko and the Warren Report are very revealing as to the damage that might occur if the public were made aware of Nosenko's "Oswald connection." The CIA wrote the following:

> B. Nosenko is very likely to be uncovered publicly as a KGB plant at some point in the future. When this occurs, unsophisticated readers of the Commission's report will be inclined to read his statements through a mirror and to assume that the reverse of what he said was true: i.e., that Oswald was a KGB agent, perhaps dispatched on a mission to kill President Kennedy.
>
> C. The inclusion of Nosenko's information followed by the revelation that he was a Soviet plant, would cast a shadow over the reliability of the report and the judgment of the Commission.
>
> D. Revelations that Nosenko had any specific knowledge of Oswald's case in the Soviet Union would be seized upon by an alert press as the most intriguing news

item in the whole report. It would make Nosenko into a public figure again and would raise demands for public appearances and testimonies. This would have catastrophic results on our current plans to get to the bottom of the Nosenko affair and, among other things, would lessen our chances of eventually learning the true story behind his Oswald information. If we do, we might be able in this way to contribute significantly to the work of the Commission.[4]

The Nosenko case now took a new turn due to an FBI informant with knowledge of the goings-on inside the KGB Residency in New York. This unidentified informer was interviewed by SAS Vincent Cahill and Harry Morris, Jr., regarding what the Russians knew about Nosenko's defection. The informant said that he learned that meetings took place headed by Colonel Boris Ivanov, the Chief of the KGB, New York Residency on the eight floor of the Soviet Mission at 136 East 67th Street in New York City. Ivanov met with the Security Branch on February 18, 1964 as well as with men from the Scientific Branch on the same day. Ivanov told them that he had received a message from KGB headquarters that Nosenko had defected. He was told that arrangements were to be made for a meeting with some Soviet official from the Embassy, namely a member of the KGB:

> Ivanov stated that they decided that when a man from the Soviet embassy had a chance to confront Nosenko, that this man should be a KGB employee and that he should be assigned the task of killing Nosenko. In reply to a direct question, informant stated it was his understanding that this KGB employee would kill Nosenko by shooting him. According to Boris Ivanov, Alexandr Pomin suggested that the man to carry out this assignment was Alexsei P. Kosikov.
>
> Informant described Kosikov as a member of the Consular Group of the Soviet Embassy in Washington, D.C. He stated that Kosikov is a KGB employee. Informant said that he did not know whether Kosikov is an employee of the 13th Department (assassinations), 1st Directorate KGB.

[4] Use of Nosenko Informant. RIF No. 104-10429-10028, 7/17/64.

205

Colonel Boris Ivanov explained to KGB personnel he felt that Kosikov would not be arrested and detained by US authorities for killing Nosenko inasmuch as Nosenko is a Soviet citizen, and that Kosikov, in killing Nosenko would not be committing a crime against the US or any citizen of the U.S.[5]

This document goes on to say that Ivanov received two telegrams from Moscow regarding the possible Nosenko hit and that "the Nosenko matter contained a statement near the beginning to the effect that our intelligence service is strong enough to destroy anyone in the world. It was stated that the KGB Headquarters felt that now was not the proper time to destroy Nosenko and that this could be accomplished later."

Why would the KGB want to kill Nosenko? Was it because of the important Oswald information he gave to the CIA? Or was it because he knew too much about Soviet espionage missions around the world that could be compromised by his defection?

Late in 1968, the CIA did an about-face and termed Nosenko the genuine article. They gave him a "consulting" job with the agency, relocated him to a new home, and said a final goodbye to their most controversial "defector." Yuri Nosenko died in the U.S. in April 2008, age 81.

---

[5] No Title, Subject: Nosenko, Oswald and JFK: Fedora. RIF No. 124-90153-10010.

Chapter 30:
James Angleton and the Mole Hunt

James Jesus Angleton was a skeleton-like man with horned rimmed glasses and a top hat on his head on even the warmest of days. He was a charter member of a bygone era, when one's country was always right and the enemy, always wrong. His persona has been depicted in numerous espionage novels and films, yet this complex man who ran the CIA's most sensitive unit, the counterintelligence department (the division tasked with the job of capturing enemy spies, often called the "mole hunting" branch at Langley headquarters), set off a firestorm of activity and recrimination at the CIA which lasted well after his death.

By the time his long and complex career at the CIA ended in the 1970s with his unexpected dismissal, Angleton would launch a paranoid search for a suspected Soviet mole hidden deep in the bowels of the agency. In the end, no Soviet traitor was ever found, with the notable exception of Aldrich Ames. By the time he left in disgrace, some top-level people at the CIA even thought that Angleton himself was the long buried Soviet mole.

Angleton grew up in Idaho, born of an American father and a Latin mother. He went to Yale University where he distinguished himself as the editor of a literary magazine called *Furioso,* then attended Harvard University. After World War II broke out, Angleton was recruited into the OSS headed by William Donovan. It was from the OSS that Angleton was to begin his lifelong career in the American espionage establishment. During the war, he was placed in X-2 (counterintelligence) that was under the command of the British Secret Intelligence Service, MI6, Section V. It was during this time that he met Harold "Kim" Philby who was the liaison between MI6 and the Americans. This friendship would continue through the next two decades until Philby was exposed as one of the most notorious British double agents in history. Angleton served in London with the OSS and learned a lot from his British counterparts.

He also served in Italy, working in the X-2, where he took part in an ill-fated espionage operation concerning the placement of a potential agent inside the walls of the Vatican. Angleton was tasked with the job of going over the man's bona fides, and it turned out that the potential American agent was nothing but a fraud.

After the war ended, he entered the fledgling CIA, and quickly befriended the tiny state of Israel that had been given its independence from Britain in 1948. Over the decades, Angleton was Israel's best friend at Langley headquarters, courting the men who were in charge of Israel's highly rated intelligence unit, the MOSSAD. Angleton's interest in Israeli affairs at the CIA made him an outcast with a number of the top-level men at the State Department who were violently anti-Semitic. He began his CIA career working in the Central Intelligence Group and then CIA's new Office of Special Operations (OSO) where he took on foreign intelligence duties. When the OSO was organized into four units in 1949, Angleton was asked to head one of them. By 1948, he was assigned to "Staff C," as the counterintelligence unit was then called.

It was in this capacity that he was reunited with Kim Philby, whom he had met during the war. Adrian Harold "Kim" Philby was then England's top liaison officer with the CIA, while, at the same time, working as the Soviet Union's number one spy in the United States. The men became fast friends and confidants, and throughout Philby's long career as a Soviet penetration agent, his good pal Jim Angleton had no idea of his double life. When two of Philby's counterparts in British intelligence, Guy Burgess and Donald MacLean, defected to Moscow on Philby's orders, Angleton still refused to believe that Philby had anything to do with the defections (Philby himself would depart to the Soviet Union in 1963).

Working as he did in the so-called "Wilderness of Mirrors" at the CIA, Angleton became paranoid about the Soviet threat to the United States, even dismissing the Sino-Soviet split as a disinformation campaign by the Russians and the Chinese to weaken the West. He also deeply distrusted any Soviet defector who came knocking on the CIA's door. Yet, by the early 1960s, Angleton would be up to his neck in "defectors." He would now have to decide who was bogus and who was for real.

Angleton's deep distrust of the Soviet Union began during World War II. In 1976, he gave an interview to John Hart, a former

CIA officer, about his time in the OSS: "when OSS found that the Soviets were involved in major espionage operations against their allies, we were living in a dream world. We had broken Enigma and could track German agents, but when Igor Gouzenko defected he opened our eyes about the KGB Rote Kapelle and Rote Drei operations."

In 1976, he told two interviewers, Cleveland Cram and Richard Drain, about his wartime experiences in Italy. He told of a KGB penetration of the OSS and said that hundreds of cases in X-2 showed Soviet penetrations. He said that "through research analysis we re-created over 400 cases under Felix Dzerzhinskly, which controlled all information from Russia to the Western allies for some 15 to 20 years; the Trust and everything else. We were so god-dammed proliferated with Communist Party members."[1]

One of the unintended consequences of Angleton's vast conspiracy theory concerning Russian infiltration of both the CIA itself and the counterintelligence unit was the deep division that was created between the men and women who were responsible for Russian affairs. Angleton's defector theory, which postulated that the Russians would send bogus defectors to infiltrate the CIA, e.g., Golitsyn, found disciples in both camps. The once solid CI camp whose main job was to stop Russian infiltration of the agency was now at war internally. Angleton's hunt for SASHA, the mysterious Slavic Soviet mole, ruined the careers of many fine, upstanding CIA officers. The group who swore by were called "Intelligence Fundamentalists," and worked not only for the CIA but in other friendly intelligence circles. Angleton's obsessive mole hunt also divided the CI staff from their counterparts in the Soviet Russia Division, whose lines of work often overlapped. These men, whose job it was to know every aspect of Soviet politics and life, attacked Angleton and his CI staff for their lack of fluency in the Russian language, the fact that they never broke a spy before, and the notion that his staff was more important in the overall scheme of things concerning anti-Russian developments in the agency.

Angleton also believed that the Sino-Soviet split was a huge KGB deception operation. He had no conclusive proof for his charge,

---

[1] *James J. Angleton, Anatoly Golitsyn, and the "Monster Plot"; Their Impact on CIA Personnel and Operations,* Studies in Intelligence, Vol 55, No. 4 (December 2011).

only the word of a number of defectors who came to the United States over a period of years. Among them was an FBI undercover agent, a Russian named Dimitri Polakov who was a KGB colonel, and Aleksey Kulak, a Soviet science officer. The men were given the codenames of TOP HAT and FEDORA by both the FBI and the CIA. Angleton also took the word of a Soviet scientist by the name of Mikhail Klochko, who defected to the Canadians in 1961. All three men, according to Angleton, had been used to support the story of the Russian-Chinese ideological split.

The hunt for the mole also created an almost decade-long interruption of CIA operations inside the Iron Curtain, looking to penetrate the Soviet intelligence services. The case officers who ran agents in the Russian sphere of influence were now gun shy when it came to recruiting new agents, for fear that one or more of them might turn out to be a Russian plant.

The CIA itself was so obsessed with Angleton's mole hunt that in 1977, they recalled Cleveland Cram, a Harvard PhD, and a one-time senior CIA officer to write an internal history of Angleton's career using classified materials available at CIA headquarters. Upon its completion, the study came to 11 volumes which must have been interesting reading, to say the least. Cram wrote in his study, "Angleton was obsessively theoretical, obsessively ambitious, and obsessed about Philby. When Philby defected, Angleton suffered severe psychic damage. If Philby had achieved nothing else in the Soviet service he would have earned his keep by the peculiar thralldom he obtained over Angleton's thinking." Angleton's wife, Cicely, said that Philby's defection to Russia affected her husband "terribly, deeply—it was a bitter blow he never forgot."[2]

Under President Lyndon Johnson's orders, Angleton began a covert CIA domestic spying campaign called "Operation Chaos" in which the agency illegally opened the mail of ordinary American citizens.

The end of James Angleton's career at the CIA came when Seymour Hersh, a reporter for the *New York Times,* wrote a front-page article that appeared in the paper on December 22, 1974. The headline read: HUGE C.I.A. OPERATION REPORTED IN U.S.

---

[2] Brown, Anthony Cave, *Treason in the Blood: H. St. John Philby, Kim Philby, and The Spy Case of the Century*. Houghton Mifflin Co., New York, 1994, Page 551.

AGAINST ANTI-WAR FORCES.

Hersh had gotten this information a few days earlier when he had an interview with CIA Director William Colby, who told him the gist of the story. After the story broke, Colby tried to protect the CIA by laying the blame for the operation on the doorstep of James Angleton. Colby summoned Angleton to his 7th floor office and fired him. The most powerful man in the CIA was now out in the cold for the first time in his life.

After his retirement, Angleton was called to testify before the Church Committee, headed by Idaho Senator Frank Church, who was investigating domestic spying operations by the CIA. The noted espionage writer David Wise wrote the following about Angleton's appearance before the Committee: "The feared former chief of the CIA's Counterintelligence Staff looked for all the world like someone who had emerged from a damp underground cave where he had spent three decades of Cold War creeping among the stalagmites."

James Angleton died in 1987, a shell of the powerful man he once was, a real life character who could never have been dreamed up by even the best fiction writers.

Tales From Langley

Chapter 31:
E. Howard Hunt: The Elusive Spy

Of all the names that stand out in the world of contemporary espionage over the past four decades, Howard Hunt comes to the front. Hunt was a prolific writer of espionage novels, worked for the OSS during World War II, and was most infamous for his participation and arrest in the Watergate affair that drove President Richard Nixon from office. He participated in such hot spots as China, Latin America, and has even been linked by some writers to the Kennedy assassination.

E. Howard Hunt was born in Hamburg, New York on October 9, 1918. He graduated from Brown University in 1940, and then joined the Navy one year later, after the attack on Pearl Harbor by Japan. He served on a destroyer but was soon released from service due to an injury while on board ship. After he left the military, he worked for a while as a writer for *Life* magazine. By 1942, he was back in the military as a member of the U.S. Army Air Corps and held the rank of Second Lieutenant. He was later transferred to the OSS, and was assigned to Detachment 202 in China where he cut his teeth in the life of a spy and learned lessons that would stay with him for the rest of his life. Part of his assignment with Detachment 202 was to join the local resistance jungle fighters who were battling the Japanese.

After hostilities ended, Hunt returned to civilian life and began a part-time career as a Hollywood screenwriter. By 1948, he was back in government service getting a job with the Marshall Plan in its Economic Cooperation Administration. In 1949, Hunt joined the CIA and took up duty stations in Mexico City, and at agency headquarters in Washington, D.C. Hunt also worked as the propaganda chief in the CIA-backed effort to overthrow the government of Guatemala. By 1956, he was in Uruguay as station chief, and by 1960, he returned to headquarters.

Between his CIA assignments, Hunt was able to fashion another career as a writer of spy novels, writing under the pen name "David St. John," among others. In fact, Hunt was asked by Richard Helms, when he was CIA Director, to write a series of novels about the CIA in order to raise the public's opinion of the agency. Among the books he wrote were *The Berlin Ending* and *The Hargrave Deception*.

Hunt returned to Washington in the spring of 1960 to take over another top-secret assignment, one that would dominate his time for the next several years. He was to be given the job of "Chief of Political Action" in the Eisenhower administration's plan to remove Castro from power. Hunt was given the job by his boss and friend, Tracy Barnes. He told Hunt that his job was to create an alliance among the various Cuban exile leaders and bring them into a cohesive group. These men would constitute a new provisional government-in- waiting that would take the reigns of power in Havana once Castro was gone.

In his memoirs, Hunt wrote that his immediate supervisor in the Cuba Project told him, "The only question raised about you is whether you're too conservative to handle guys like these. A lot of them are way to the left of you, socialists, labor leaders, and so forth." Hunts' reply was, "My own political views, whatever they may be, don't enter into it." Those words would soon come to haunt Hunt as the Cuba Project unfolded.

Hunt was known by his Cuban exile buddies as "Eduardo." It has been rumored over the years that it was Hunt who first originated the idea of assassinating Fidel Castro. Frank Sturgis, one of the men who was also arrested at the Watergate complex, and who was also a CIA contract officer, said that Hunt was responsible for various agency operations where "disposal" was carried out.

This was two years from the start of the CIA-Mafia alliance to kill Castro and Hunt's idea was met with certain skepticism among the top brass at the CIA. There was no hint of any plans at that time by the Eisenhower administration to even contemplate any assassination attempt on Castro's life. At that time, the U.S. still had not run its course with Castro and there were still some men in power in Washington who believed that an accommodation with Castro could be achieved. All that would change, but for now, Hunt's idea was quickly nipped in the bud.

Writing about his early idea of killing Castro, Hunt said, "As the months wore on I was to ask Barnes repeatedly about any action on my principal recommendation, only to be told that it was in the hands of a special group. So far as I have been able to determine, no coherent plan was ever developed within the CIA to assassinate Castro, though it was the heart's desire of many exile groups."

Hunt is not telling the complete truth about there not being any "coherent plan ever developed within the CIA to assassinate Castro." A plan was decided upon in 1960 by President Eisenhower, which eventually involved certain members of the mob. Why Hunt forgot that historical fact is clearly not known.

Another man who worked with Hunt during the Bay of Pigs planning was Bernard Barker (Barker was also arrested during the Watergate burglary). As the planning for the invasion intensified, Hunt was soon at loggerheads with his agency colleagues and he was sent to work with David Atlee Philips, preparing agency propaganda for the invasion.

Despite Hunt's assurances that he could work with the myriad people forming the anti-Castro leadership, he never felt comfortable in his daily tasks. He left after spending one year trying to reconcile all the different anti-Castro groups into one cohesive force. He held so many rightist views that he made more enemies than friends.

After leaving the Cuban operation, Hunt was sent to Madrid, Spain where he told his friends he was going to write his books. However, one of his assignments was to try to recruit the Cuban Military Attaché, Colonel Ramon Barquin. Barquin told Hunt that he still believed in the Cuban revolution and turned down his offer.

There has been considerable speculation as to the exact reason Hunt was sent to Madrid and by whom. In the concise biography of Howard Hunt by Tad Szulc called *Compulsive Spy: The Strange Career of E. Howard Hunt*, the former *New York Times* reporter writes that Hunt was given the Madrid assignment as a reward for helping former CIA Director Allen Dulles write his book called *The Craft of Intelligence*. No one truly knows if Hunt was the ghost writer for Dulles, but he was well known among his colleagues at CIA headquarters as a proficient writer of pocket books, mostly adventure stories. In fact, Hunt said that he accepted the Madrid post was so that he could "play golf and write books."

In a CIA memo dated December 20, 1973, with the title: "Subject: E. Howard Hunt—Madrid assignment," Edward Ryan, Chief, Staff D, Deputy Director for Operations, remarked about

Hunt's Madrid posting, "Mr. Ryan was asked specifically whether or not he was under the impression that Mr. Hunt's writing activities were either being encouraged or subsidized directly by this agency in any official effort. Mr. Ryan responded that he was personally not aware of any such assignment. He added as an expression of personal opinion that Mr. Hunt had no operational function and was simply granted the opportunity to write books for his own personal gain at Government expense during this period."[1]

Hunt spent the time period from July 1965 to September 1966 in Spain. Maybe his job was in recognition of his role in helping Allen Dulles write his book, but if that is so, why did Richard Helms, one of the most powerful men in the CIA at that time, insist that Hunt be given the Madrid assignment? Did his role in Madrid have some other operational nature that we don't know about? Could that secret assignment have something to do with Cuba?

The question of whether Hunt was up to something regarding Cuba was pondered by author Tad Szulc in his book *Compulsive Spy*. In the book, Szulc writes that the United States was going to attempt a second invasion of Cuba that would include the assassination of Castro. Szulc writes that the codename for the invasion was "Second Naval Guerilla," that it was sponsored by the CIA, and that training camps had been secretly opened in both Nicaragua and Costa Rica where some 700 Cuban exiles would be trained. According to Szulc, a number of CIA people who had been involved in the Bay of Pigs invasion were also taking part in Second Naval Guerilla, including such Hunt friends as James McCord and Bernard Barker.

As told by Szulc, while Hunt was in Madrid, he was in contact with the CIA-sponsored assassin Rolando Cubela, a.k.a., "AMLASH" who would later play his own, unique role in the Castro assassination plots. As the story goes, Cubela was brought to Madrid and Paris where he had secret meetings with certain CIA officers. Another person who was brought to Spain was Manuel Artime; in February 1964, he met with Cubela to plot strategy. Cubela later went to Cuba where the CIA provided him with an FAL automatic rifle, which was to be used in the Castro, hit.

Szulc writes that both Hunt and Artime traveled to San Jose, Costa Rica, which was the jumping off point for their travels to check on the status of the training camps then in progress. Rumors

[1] E. Howard Hunt-Madrid Assignment. RIF No. 104-10103-10040.

had it that they arranged for the use of a C-46 cargo plane that came from U.S. officials in the Panama Canal Zone where the U.S. had a large military installation. Hunt's Madrid sojourn is still one of the lingering questions about his time in the CIA.

In 1973, Howard Hunt's personal memoir of the Bay of Pigs invasion and his participation in it called *Give Us This Day* was published by Arlington House publishers in New Rochelle, New York. When the book was underway, the CIA got wind of it and took an active interest in just what Hunt had to say. A detailed critique of the working manuscript was written by CIA officer Walter Pfersheimer, the Curator of the Historical Intelligence Collection Department. A lengthy memo which was dated February 16, 1970, was sent to the Director of Security at CIA headquarters under the title: "Comments on Manuscript Give Us This Day: CIA and the Bay of Pigs Invasion by Edward J. Hamilton" (Edward Hamilton was Hunt's pen name).

Mr. Pfersheimer writes in his opening page that Hunt said that he "has taken up his pen reluctantly and in a mood of nostalgic bitterness." The CIA Curator chides Hunt, saying "the author's claim that his book would provide no information not known to Castro's intelligence services, or that details this late are of no value to the opposition, is my view, seriously open to question."

He notes that in his opinion, the contents of the book are favorable to the CIA and points out the villains in the story are Arthur Schlesinger Jr., Richard Goodwin and Adlai Stevenson, all of whom Hunt accused of being "liberals," and to some extent, the President himself. In his concluding chapter, the author's bitterness is "undisguised against those in the Administration and the press who took the opportunity of the Bay of Pigs incident to attack and denigrate CIA."

In 1970, he "retired" from the CIA and took a job with Robert Mullen & Co., a Washington, D.C. public relations firm that had direct ties to the CIA. In 1971, one year before President Nixon ran for a second term, Hunt joined a secret unit operating out of the White House called the Special Investigation Unit, a.k.a. "Plumbers." He helped orchestrate the Plumbers' burglary of Daniel Elsberg's psychiatrist's office after Elsberg had stolen a copy of the Pentagon's secret report on U.S. involvement in the Vietnam War, called the Pentagon Papers.

With the Nixon reelection campaign now in full swing, Hunt joined with his other ex-CIA and Cuba pals to burglarize the office of the Democratic National Committee Headquarters located at the Watergate Apartment Complex on June 17, 1972. After being arrested, Hunt was indicted and pled guilty to charges including wiretapping, burglary, and conspiracy. He spent a few years in jail and was released in 1977.

After the break-in, heated discussions took place in the Nixon White House regarding the arrest of the Watergate burglars. Hunt's name was right up front when reviewing the possible ramifications that might affect the Nixon presidency.

One meeting centered around the aftermath of the Watergate affair would focus on the activities of the CIA, the men involved in the matter, the 1961 Bay of Pigs invasion, and its possible connection to the events of June 17.

President Nixon began by saying, "Well, we must protect Helms from one hell of a lot of things." Then the President mused about how to control the CIA. He said, "Hunt will uncover a lot of things. You open that scab there's a hell of a lot of things… tell them we just feel that it would be very detrimental to have this thing go any further. This involves these Cubans, Hunt, and a lot of hanky-panky that we have nothing to do with ourselves."

Nixon continued by saying of Hunt, "…just say (unintelligible) very bad to have this fellow Hunt, he knows too dammed much, if he was involved—you happen to know that? If it gets out that this is all involved, the Cuba thing, it would be a fiasco. It would make the CIA look bad, it's going to make Hunt look bad, and it is likely to blow the whole Bay of Pigs thing which we think would be very unfortunate both for the CIA and the country."

President Nixon's statement is ripe with possibilities. What was so dreadful about reopening the "whole Bay of Pigs thing," and what did it have to do with Howard Hunt?

Howard Hunt died in 2007, taking whatever secrets he could have revealed with him to the grave.

Chapter 32:
Karl Koecher Penetrates the CIA

In the past 20 years a number of high-level Soviet double agents have been unmasked working inside the U.S. intelligence community. The most recognizable names are John Walker, Aldrich Ames, and Robert Hanssen. The first eastern block spy to worm his way into the CIA was a Czech intelligence agent, a person who, with his wife, attended open sex parties in both New York and Washington, Karl Koecher.

Koecher was a native of Czechoslovakia and joined that country's intelligence service, CIS, in 1962. It was in 1965 that Koecher and his wife, Hana, decided to "defect" to the United States. Over the years, the dominating theme among Western intelligence agents is that the Koecher's "defection" was nothing but a plot to gain admittance into the CIA. Their first stop was a debriefing session in Austria where their story was checked out. Believing that the couple was indeed defecting for purely political reasons, the CIA allowed them entry into the United States. They entered the country on December 4, 1965.

Karl was accepted into Indiana University and later the couple moved to New York where he entered Columbia University and got a PhD in philosophy. At the same time that Karl was attending Columbia, he got a job as an assistant professor of philosophy at Wagner University on Staten Island. They took the oath as American citizens in 1971. But if the Koechers were to lead an upstanding life in the United States, they kept their secrets to themselves.

Before leaving Czechoslovakia, Koecher's KGB handlers ordered him to seek employment in the CIA once he arrived in the United States. In New York, Koecher donned an elaborate cover. He told friends that he was rabidly anti-communist in his politics, and that he had been fired from the official Czech radio network for his anti-state political views. The couple lived briefly in West Nyack, New York. To earn a living, Karl worked as a freelancer for Radio Free Europe.

In October 1967, Karl was hired on a full-time basis by Radio

Free Europe specializing in Czech affairs for $10,000 a year. One of his duties was to provide news broadcasts in Czech to his brethren behind the Iron Curtain. In time, the Koechers moved back to New York where he did book translating. The CIS gave the Koechers $20,000 to pay for their expensive apartment.

In 1972, Karl applied for a job at the CIA and despite his coming from an Eastern state, his application was accepted. He was given a job as a translator and began his illegal career as a Soviet double agent. As part of his cover at the CIA, his colleagues knew him only as a Pentagon employee.

His wife Hana took part in her husband's illegal activities, often acting as his courier. She also had a job as a diamond merchant with a firm called Harry Winston, Inc., which gave her ample opportunity to meet their KGB advisors in other parts of the world to pass on delicate information.

At the time that Karl was working in Washington for the CIA he had clandestine meetings with a member of Czech intelligence in Washington, D.C., Vesek Kralik, the First Secretary of the Czech embassy. In an elaborate ploy to beef up his bona fides, Koecher told the FBI about the contact and said that the Czechs were trying to recruit him. Soon though, the Bureau asked Karl to stop his clandestine meetings with the Czech agent. What Koecher didn't tell the Bureau until after his capture, was that Vesek Kralik was his case officer. The entire episode was just a huge ruse to make him look better in the eyes of the U.S. intelligence community.

Apart from the daily grind at CIA headquarters, the Koechers led a double life. For years, they attended sex parties in New York and Washington, D.C. It was at these nocturnal assignations that Karl would use his wife and her great beauty to lure other couples into orgies that ran all night. The Koechers used these parties to gain information from other partners who participated in the orgies. Despite long months of sex swapping, the CIA was unaware of these activities.

Karl worked at CIA headquarters from 1973 to 1975. He was then reassigned to New York until 1977. The Koechers attended sex parties at New York's premier underground club, Plato's Retreat.

The Koechers came under suspicion by the FBI when they were seen meeting with a member of the CIS in New York. One of the most damning pieces of information they gave to the KGB was the identity of a Soviet official named Alexander Ogorodnik who was a deep cover CIA mole operating out of Moscow. Ogorodnik worked in the Soviet Ministry of Foreign Affairs and was given the code name TRIGON. TRIGON was one of the most important spies the CIA had inside the KGB and his identification would be a major blow to U.S. intelligence. The information he sent back to Washington wound up in the files of the White House, the National Security Council, and the State Department.

At the CIA, Koecher translated material supplied by Ogorodnik and also wrote progress reports on his secret duties. The trail of evidence led the agency right to Koecher and he was put under covert surveillance.

Upon learning of Ogorodnick's duplicity, the KGB put him under watch and caught him in the act of espionage in 1977. Before he could stand trial, he poisoned himself with a CIA- supplied pen, a Mont Blanc.

On November 27, 1984, as they were beginning a trip to Switzerland, the Koechers were arrested by the FBI and charged with espionage. In February 1986, Karl and Hana were secretly taken to Berlin where, in a prearranged spy swap with the Soviet Union, they were exchanged for Soviet dissident Anatoly Shcharansky.

E. Howard Hunt

Chapter 33:
What Happened to Nicholas Shadrin?

On June 25, 1959, a short article was printed by Reuters News Service: "RUSSIAN AND POLE GET ASYLUM. Stockholm, Sweden, June 25, 1959. A Soviet naval captain and a 22-year-old Polish woman medical student who escaped to Sweden this month in a launch from the Polish Baltic port of Gdynia have been granted political asylum in Sweden, the Aliens Commission announced today." That short piece began one of the most controversial spy stories of the year, one that is still being debated by historians and spy enthusiasts today. The case of Nicholas Shadrin was just one more "defection" by a Soviet military officer who offered his services to the CIA and continued the great debate inside the agency, mired as it was in its search for "moles" hidden inside its wilderness of mirrors.

Captain Nikolay Fedorovich Artamonov was one of the most promising young naval officers coming out of the Soviet Navy. He was highly connected in the Russian Navy, as his wife's father was Sergei Gorshkov, an admiral in the Soviet fleet. He could have had any posting he desired, and if he wanted, his future was as secure as one can imagine. But the route he eventually decided upon took him away from his wife Elena and their ten-year-old son Sergei Nikolay, and his home in the Soviet Union, to an unknown life in the United States.

In March 1958, Artamonov was given command of a two-destroyer squadron and ordered to carry out the transfer of a number of ships to the Indonesian Navy as part of a military assistance deal. He left his family and traveled with the ships to the Polish Naval Base at Gdynia, stopping for repairs and the training of the Indonesian crew who would take over the ships.

Artamonov and his fellow Russians were not welcomed in Poland due to the animosity between the local population and the Russian sailors. However, that was soon overcome when he met a 22-year-old beauty named Ewa Gora, whom he soon began dating. Ewa's parents did not like the fact their daughter was dating an older Russian Naval Captain and they told her so in no uncertain terms.

However, she was infatuated with handsome Nikolay and soon a romance blossomed. As their romance grew, he even had a special phone set up from his sea cabin on board his ship to Ewa's home. The ever-watchful GRU knew all about his infatuation with the girl, but due to his powerful position in the Navy, they did not stop the couples' dates.

On May 19, 1958, Nikolay proposed marriage to Ewa and she accepted. However, what he now told her was nothing but a shock out of the blue. He told her that he wanted to leave Poland and seek political asylum in the West. Ewa was stunned but she agreed to go along with him, as long as they could be together.

They planned to escape on a 22-foot launch at night, supposedly going on a late night fishing trip. They planned to leave Gdynia enroute to the Swedish port of Oland Island, located on the southeast coast of Sweden. It was a trip of 115 nautical miles, but Captain Artamonov was certain they could make it safely.

On the night of their departure, Captain Artamonov had the assistance of Ilay Popov, a young sailor who would accompany them on their trip (Popov had no idea what they were planning and would eventually be freed once they arrived in Stockholm). The night's voyage was plagued with heavy seas, but Artamonov was able to navigate using all his skills; after a 17-hour trip, they landed at the Swedish port of Farjstaden. Once on land, they contacted local officials who let them stay in the town's jail for the night. The next day, they were interviewed by a Swedish naval official named Commander Sven Rydstrom. During their talk, Captain Artamonov asked for political asylum for both himself and Ewa in Sweden.

Captain Artamonov was subsequently interviewed by members of Swedish Naval Intelligence. While he was being interviewed, Ewa made her way to the American embassy where she met with Lt. Col. Anthony Caputo, the assistant naval attaché. She told him her story, including the naval background of her fiancé, and said they wanted political asylum in the West. Col. Caputo referred her to Paul Garbler who was the embassy's second secretary, but was in reality, a CIA agent assigned to the embassy. Garbler, in fact, was leaving for reassignment back to the States and he handed her off to his replacement, Edward Goloway. Goloway contacted CIA headquarters and it was agreed that the couple would be sent to the

United States as soon as possible. The Artamonov case was sent to the office of the Director of the CIA, Allen Dulles, who gave his permission for their transfer to the United States. They whisked the couple quickly back to Washington and gave their new prize a fresh name: Nicholas Shadrin. Soon, the couple was married and both became naturalized American citizens.

Shadrin went to work for U.S. intelligence, finally gaining a position with the Office of Naval Intelligence. Over the years, he worked in ONI, helping U.S. intelligence with any problems they might have had concerning Soviet naval affairs. But as the 1960s wore on, the case of Shadrin's defection made its way toward the CIA's mole hunting unit headed by James Angleton, the head of the CIA's counterintelligence (CI) branch.

In June 1966, a bizarre incident took place that muddied the Shadrin case. By that time, President Johnson had relieved Admiral William Raborn as DCI and replaced him with Richard Helms. Over the years Helms had presided over many secrets and now he would add the Shadrin case to his pile.

On June 18, 1966, a phone call came to the former residence of Richard Helms, who had separated from his wife of many years. Mrs. Helms answered the phone and the man on the other line identified himself as Major Igor Kozlov. The Russian said he wanted to speak to Director Helms but he did not know that Helms had moved out some time previously. Mrs. Helms told him to call the Congressional Country Club where her husband could be found. Major Kozlov was put through to Helms and what the Russian told him was nothing but explosive. He told Helms that he was a Major in the KGB and that he wanted to work for the CIA. He told Helms that in years past he had made contact with a CIA officer in Pakistan by the name of Gardner "Gus" Hathaway. Helms told Major Kozlov that he would get back to him with an answer. Helms immediately contacted James Angleton who (for obvious reasons) did not trust Major Kozlov, and said he was another Soviet penetration agent come to disrupt the CIA. Angleton asked CIA agent Bruce Solie to meet with Major Kozlov and find out what he wanted. Solie in turn, contacted FBI agent Bill Branigan and told him of his impending meeting with Major Kozlov.

Solie and Major Kozlov met at a CIA safe house a few miles

outside of Washington. Kozlov said he was willing to work with the CIA but not the FBI. He said that he was going to be transferred back to the Soviet Union but was positive he'd be back in the States some time soon. In the meantime, he'd be willing to act as an agent-in-place for the CIA while he was in Moscow. Solie agreed and the CIA now had a new, promising agent in Russia with whom they could work.

Kozlov then said something to Bruce Solie that made him flinch. Major Kozlov told him that his assignment in the United States was to recruit a former Soviet naval officer who defected to the United States some time before. His name was Captain Nikolay Artamonov, a.k.a. "Nick Shadrin." The Major asked for the CIA's help in finding him! Why would the Russians ask for the CIA's help in finding one of their own former military officers they knew was now working for some part of the U.S. intelligence establishment? It would make no sense for the Americans to help the Russians get Shadrin back after all the intelligence he had provided them on all sorts of Russian naval matters. The whole thing was bizarre and the CIA knew it. To make matters more interesting, Anatoly Golitsyn told the CIA that he had met Shadrin before, and could vouch for the man's bona fides. "The consensus in CI was the KGB wanted to show that no defector was unreachable. But to Angleton, the real point was that Nick Shadrin was simply bait for information the CIA wanted from Kozlov about the KGB. He would be run, after all, by the FBI. Angleton had no reason to object. Nick Shadrin would be an FBI case." [1]

The Shadrin case was now to be handled by the FBI and he met with a number of Bureau agents to get the ball rolling. Shadrin was now working in a small unit with the DIA, the Defense Intelligence Agency, in its translation unit. His office was in the Old Post Office building, the same building in which the FBI had its offices. The FBI gave the Shadrin-Kozlov case the code name KITTYHAWK and in effect, Shadrin was now acting as a double agent for the FBI.

In one of his interviews with FBI agent Bert Turner, Kozlov dropped another bombshell. He said that he had information that Yuri Nosenko was assigned to the Oswald case by the KGB, but

---

[1] Corson, William, R., Trento, Susan, and Trento, Joseph. *Widows,* Crown Publishers, New York, 1989, Page 202.

because Oswald was so unstable, the KGB never recruited him.[2]

Shadrin met with Kozlov five times before Kozlov returned to Moscow for reassignment. During Kozlov's absence, Shadrin met with another Soviet officer. Over a 10-year period, Shadrin also met with KGB officers in Montreal and once in Vienna.

Other high-profile events took place in Vienna at the same time Shadrin was meeting with his Soviet agents. Carlos the Jackal had kidnapped the OPEC Ministers only a few miles away, and Richard Welsh, the CIA Station Chief in Athens was murdered.

It was 1975 when Shadrin and Ewa went to Vienna on a supposed skiing trip. They checked into the Bristol Hotel in Vienna. The next day, Nick told Ewa that he was going to meet a KGB contact and that he'd return later that night. When he failed to return home by 1:00 a.m. a shaken Ewa called Cynthia Hausmann, a CIA contact at the American embassy. Hausmann was curt, saying that she should not worry about her husband—he could take care of himself.

According to authors Susan Trento, Joseph Trento and William Corson in their book *Widows,* the following events took place relating to the disappearance of Nick Shadrin. He took his car to the city of Neualbein where he parked at the Restaurant Winter. He was met by Oleg Kozlov and Mikhail Kuryshev. The two Russians gave Shadrin keys to a car and a safe house. He was also given a KGB passport and new identity cards in the name of Nikolay Artamonov. He was told to take a boat down the Danube to Bulgaria. He was then to go to Hungary for some unspecified mission.

The case of what really happened to Nick Shadrin took an interesting twist with the "defection" of yet another Soviet intelligence officer, Vitaly Yurchenko. Yurchenko defected to the United States under unusual circumstances in 1985. Under interrogation, he told the CIA that Shadrin had been kidnapped in Vienna in 1975. He said he was accidentally killed while being subdued by KGB agents. Over the years, though, reports came in from various sources that Shadrin was still alive. One sighting put him quite alive at the funeral of Admiral Sergei Gorshkov on May 17, 1988. It can safely be said that the case of Nick Shadrin is a riddle wrapped up in an enigma.

---

[2] Ibid. Page 204-05.

Yuri Nosenko

Vitaly Yurchenko

Chapter 34:
The Troubled "Defection"
of Vitaly Yurchenko

The so-called "Year of the Spy" (1985) would see the exposure of such traitors as the Walker Family Spy Ring, ex-CIA officer Edward Lee Howard, Larry Chin, Jonathan Jay Pollard of the Naval Investigative Service, and Ronald Pelton of the NSA. But the most embarrassing event in that painful year involved the defection of a top Russian intelligence officer, Vitaly Yurchenko. The Yurchenko affair had the same unpleasant characteristics as other high-profile defections by Soviet intelligence officials over the years, namely, the cases of Anatoly Golitsyn and Yuri Nosenko. If Yurchenko was indeed a bona fide turncoat, then the CIA would have in its grasp one of the most important Russian defectors to come their way. The information he could provide on the inner workings of the KGB would be enormous. On the other hand, if Yurchenko proved to be nothing more than an impostor, than the CIA would be burned, with all the unintended consequences involved in such a ruse. Little did the top brass at Langley headquarters know that when the fallout from the Yurchenko affair was complete, the CIA would be the laughing stock of the world's intelligence agencies.

Vitaly Yurchenko was a veteran of the Soviet Navy (its submarine service), receiving his degree in navigation in 1958. He rose to the rank of lieutenant and took patrols with his sub in the Pacific. He lost the tips of his middle and ring fingers on his right hand when it was caught in a winch accident. He sported a bushy moustache, which gave him the look of a grizzled old warrior.

In 1959, he changed professions, joining the KGB as a counterintelligence officer. He was assigned to the KGB's Third Directorate and later moved to Washington as Chief of Security at the Soviet embassy between 1975 and 1980. During his stay in Washington, the FBI kept track of Yurchenko and even made a pitch to recruit him as a double agent (the plot failed).

As one of the top men in the KGB, he was sent back to Moscow where he was given the assignment of chief counterintelligence officer for internal security. One of his major responsibilities was to debrief and work with a number of Western spies who defected to the East, notably, Adrian "Kim" Philby, and George Blake, who was instrumental in giving up the CIA-run Berlin Tunnel operation in the 1950s. In 1985, he was awarded one of the most prestigious duties in all of Soviet intelligence, deputy chief of the First Department of the First Chief Directorate of the KGB, whose function was to oversee all intelligence operations in North America, especially in the United States. He also supervised KGB agents burrowed inside the Canadian intelligence services, namely the Royal Canadian Mounted Police (RCMP).

One of his responsibilities was to organize and review the backgrounds of all potential agents that were to be recruited by the KGB. Thus, Yurchenko would be privy to all the deep penetration agents the KGB planted inside the various Western intelligence services.

In June 1985, while Yurchenko was serving in Rome, Italy, he startled both the Soviet Union and the United States when he asked the U.S. for political asylum. The CIA Station Chief in Rome was contacted via pay phone, and the parties agreed on a mutual rendezvous point a few weeks hence. CIA headquarters was contacted regarding the Yurchenko offer and the go-ahead was given to bring him in.

On August 1, 1985, Yurchenko left his office at the Soviet embassy, telling his colleagues that he planned a visit to the sights of Vatican City. Instead, he walked into the U.S. embassy and defected. The following day he arrived via a U.S. Air Force C-5-A cargo jet and deplaned under tight security at Andrews Air Force Base outside of Washington, D.C. Yurchenko was whisked to CIA headquarters where he was met by three of his initial interrogators: Aldrich Ames, Colin Thompson and FBI agent Mike Rochford.

Yurchenko's debriefing by Aldrich Ames is a story in itself. At the time of his defection, Ames was secretly working as a mole inside the CIA for the Russians. If, as Yurchenko told his questioners, he knew all the Soviet penetration agents inside the CIA, why didn't he immediately inform the CIA that Ames was a traitor? Or, was he lying just to trick the CIA into believing he was more than he

230

seemed?

Yurchenko told his eager listeners that in order to keep watch on Soviet agents in Moscow who were making covert contact with Americans in the city, the KGB implanted an exotic "spy dust" on the clothing of the suspected Americans and were able to trace their movements and see who they came in contact with.

Under further interrogation, Yurchenko said that he knew of a Western source who worked for the Soviet Union who went by the name of "Robert." Although he didn't know the man's real name, he did give some interesting clues as to his identity. "Robert," it seems, was now an ex-CIA officer who paid a visit to the Soviet embassy in Washington in 1983. This man was supposed to have been sent to the U.S. embassy in Moscow but his orders were canceled due to his drug habit. "Robert" also made a trip to St. Anton, Austria where he met his KGB contacts.

The mysterious "Robert" turned out to be Edward Lee Howard who had a history involving drug use and the theft of a woman's handbag, information he hid from the Agency upon entering the service. Howard was dismissed from the CIA in 1983 and subsequently contacted the KGB where he offered to supply them with whatever secrets he knew.

Howard was investigated by the FBI, and in an elaborate deception operation, eluded his FBI pursuers at his New Mexico home, and fled to the Soviet Union. In 1986, Howard appeared publicly in Moscow, holding a press conference to announce his defection.

Yurchenko also exposed Ronald Pelton who worked for the NSA (National Security Agency). But here the Yurchenko "defection" begins to break down. Yurchenko said that as far he knew, the KGB was frustrated because they couldn't recruit any full-time CIA agents. If that was the case, what about Aldrich Ames? Some theorists postulate that Yurchenko "gave up" Howard and Pelton in order to protect Ames. If that is correct, then his entire "defection" story goes up in smoke. The CIA even tried to entice Yurchenko into revealing the names of Soviet moles by offering him a million dollars. President Reagan, who was being kept informed of the Yurchenko case commented, "The information he provided was not anything new or sensational."

He also provided information on the case of Navy radioman John Walker and his family of spies. He said that when he handled the Walker case he was asked by the KGB if Walker had been compromised by the FBI, which was taking a very active interest in Walker's increasingly erratic conduct. After a thorough review, he reported that Walker had not been compromised.

Once inside the United States, Yurchenko was wined and dined and even took a trip out west at the CIA's expense to see the Grand Canyon and Las Vegas. In time, he brought his wife and adopted son to live with him in Alexandria, Virginia in a townhouse apartment. At one point, the FBI took Yurchenko to visit Thomas Jefferson's home at Monticello.

At the counterintelligence branch at CIA headquarters, the defection of Vitaly Yurchenko was proving to be problematical indeed. There were doubts about his bona fides from the beginning of his defection. Was his defection real, or was his just another Soviet plant sent to penetrate the CIA? The past defections of such Soviets as Yuri Nosenko, Anatoly Golitsyn, Nick Shadrin, Karl Koecher and others weighed heavily inside the CIA. The last thing they needed was another fake defector. Despite all the questions relating to Yurchenko, he was given a one-on-one meeting with DCI William Casey.

Over time Yurchenko's information began to dry up. His bona fides began to be questioned by some top level CIA officers and he became more and more disenchanted. In September 1985, he startled the CIA by requesting that he be taken to Canada in order to meet with a woman he had once had an affair with. In Canada, the woman wanted nothing to do with Yurchenko and he returned to the United States deeply depressed.

On November 1, 1985, barely three months after his defection in Rome, the case of Vitaly Yurchenko came to a dramatic and sudden end. On that fateful evening, Yurchenko and his inexperienced, young agency handler went to the posh Au Pied du Cochon restaurant in the Georgetown section of Washington for dinner. Just before the meal was over, the Russian said that he had to use the facilities, and that the young man should not feel slighted if he did not come back.

Yurchenko walked out the door and made a beeline to the Soviet embassy where he "redefected." In a hurriedly called news conference, Yurchenko said he had been kidnapped and drugged by the CIA in Rome and kept a virtual prisoner these past three months. In a further brazen attempt to upstage the CIA, he asked to be taken to the U.S. State Department where he said that he was returning to the Soviet Union under his own volition.

Vitaly Yurchenko returned home, no worse off for his American sojourn. In front of a packed press conference in Moscow he gave a rendition of his time in the United States. Among the tidbits he gave the reporters was his opinion that William Casey, the new DCI, was a pill-popping "old man with his pants unbuttoned." He said that if the meeting with Casey had gone well, he might have been allowed to see President Reagan. He also said that he played golf with his CIA handlers who feared for his health.

If Yurchenko had indeed come to "protect" the identity of Aldrich Ames, the Soviets' most important mole, he succeeded brilliantly. Henry Brandon, an FBI counterintelligence officer told the noted espionage writer David Wise, "It is possible that they [the KGB] doubted Ames and sent Yurchenko here as a test to see if Ames would report Yurchenko's debriefing? Once it was determined that Ames was reporting on Yurchenko's disclosures, they told Yurchenko to come home. The Yurchenko thing is still extraordinarily puzzling."

Chapter 35:
The Strange Saga of John Paisley

As the decade of the 1970s ended, the CIA was rocked by yet another unexplained death of one of its top officers, John Arthur Paisley. Paisley was connected to both the counterintelligence division and, the Office of Security where he played a minor role in the Watergate affair with the "Plumbers."

September 24, 1978 dawned with a bright sky and a warm breeze that skipped over the waters of the Chesapeake Bay. On that bright day, John Arthur Paisley, a 55-year-old former CIA officer, a man privy to the nation's highest secrets, left the mooring at Solomons Island near the Patuxent shore of the Chesapeake Bay. Before leaving, Paisley asked the harbormaster to leave the lights on at the dock, as he would be back that night.

His ship, the 31-foot *Brillig,* named after a character in Lewis Carroll's book *Through the Looking Glass,* set sail for a routine day at sea.

Paisley, an expert sailor, navigated the *Brillig* on the historic waters, past the nation's capital. One of the spots he passed was a secret CIA safe house used to interrogate Soviet defectors. One of these defectors was Yuri Nosenko. There had been talk after the death of Paisley that he might have met with Nosenko at the safe house along the Bay. All apparently went well on Paisley's voyage, and between 5:00 and 6:00 p.m., he received a call via ship-to-shore radio from and an old friend, Colonel William Wilson. Paisley told Wilson that he would be back after dark. That call from Colonel Wilson proved to be the last time that anyone would hear from John Paisley.

The next day, September 25, the Coast Guard received a call from a pleasure boat that a sloop had been sighted near Point Lookout on the Bay. A cutter was sent out to investigate and upon boarding the ship they found a blood-soaked deck, a highly sophisticated radio transmitter, a nine-mm bullet, but no body. Also discovered were numerous classified documents belonging to the CIA, including the name and phone number of David Young, the head of President Nixon's infamous Plumbers unit. Despite the paper trail, no body was found.

That same day, John Paisley's wife, Maryann, herself a one-tine CIA employee, and two other CIA officers, arrived at the Bay and took possession of the *Brillig* and its contents. The agents inspected the boat and took into their care materials they later labeled "for internal use."

The first person to come aboard the ship when it had been found was Gerald Sword, a Park Ranger. Looking around the empty ship, he found a piece of paper with the name John Paisley on it and he wrote down the name and called the Coast Guard. Sword would later say of the events after he left the *Brillig,* "two CIA agents and a lieutenant colonel from the Pentagon had gone aboard. Apparently the information was of a higher classification than the agents were permitted to handle, so the colonel took possession of the papers."

On October 1, 1978, the Coast Guard found the body of John Arthur Paisley near the same Solomons Island mooring from which the *Brillig* set sail only a week before. The body was taken to the Maryland State Medical Examiner's Office for an autopsy. The Medical Examiner, Dr. Russell Fisher, found that a bullet had entered from the left ear (Paisley was right-handed), the body was weighted with two sets of diving belts, and it was badly decomposed.

Another baffling set of facts was that the bodies contained no blood or brain tissue, nor were any weapons or spent cartridges found on the boat. Most of the skin had been peeled away, making fingerprint identification almost impossible. There were also marks on the victim's neck that could not be explained. These facts promote the theory that Paisley was killed some place else and then returned to the vicinity of the ship. The official cause of death was a gunshot wound to the head. Yet, despite these numerous inconsistencies, Dr. Fisher ruled the death a suicide. In another inconsistency, the coroner stated that the body he was examining was indeed John Arthur Paisley.

This seems to be an inconsistency because there are other interesting facts concerning the curious corpse. The body discovered by the Coast Guard was four inches taller and 26 pounds lighter than Paisley. Dr. Fisher listed Paisley's height as 5'11 when his medical records state him to be 5'7. The body wore size 30" shorts while Paisley's waist was 34". When Paisley's fingerprints (they were severely damaged by the crabs in the Bay and the hands were almost falling off) were sent to the FBI for positive identification, the CIA replied that Paisley's fingerprint file had been lost.

After the autopsy was finished, the body was sent to an Agency-approved funeral home where it was cremated. It is interesting to note that no one who knew Paisley in life was allowed to view the dismembered torso before cremation.

Maryann Paisley was convinced that her husband had died of unnatural causes and hired a prominent Washington, D.C. attorney, Bernard Fensterwald Jr. to look into the case. At one time, Fensterwald represented James McCord who was one of the Watergate burglars. Fensterwald would later organize the Assassinations Archives and Research Center, a nonprofit group that looked into political assassinations, especially those of John and Robert Kennedy.

Who then was John Paisley?

At the age of 25 in 1948, he went to Palestine as a radio operator for the United Nations. There, he was recruited by James Angleton into the CIA. He began his agency career working on Soviet strategic research, learned Russian, and was privy to one of the most highly classified secrets in the agency, the methods of obtaining information on Russia's nuclear program.

Paisley helped to develop a variety of U.S. reconnaissance and spy satellite systems, including the KH-11, capable of reading the license plates of vehicles from miles in space. But his most important duty at CIA HQ, was to debrief two Soviet defectors, Yuri Nosenko and Nicholas Shadrin.

As a technical advisor, he was also involved in early CIA mind control experiments with LSD and hypnotism in the 1950s.

After his retirement from the CIA in 1974, Paisley was offered a post as a "consultant" to various CIA Directors, including George Bush and Admiral Stansfield Turner. As a consultant he worked in an analysis section codenamed Team B from August to December 1976. Team B's work included a determination of the United States' evaluation of Soviet nuclear forces and the nuclear capabilities of the U.S.S.R. Paisley had access to the highest codes and information about the Untied States and Soviet nuclear power, even though one CIA officer called Paisley "a rather unimportant intelligence officer and analyst."

When the *Brillig* was found, it contained a highly sophisticated radio that enabled Paisley to send and receive thousands of words a minute of top-secret communications used by the CIA and the National Security Agency. Why, after his retirement, was Paisley privy to such important information if he was just a "rather unimportant intelligence officer and analyst?"

The motive for Paisley's death is the stuff of modern-day spy fiction. For years, reports of a Soviet mole hidden in the upper echelons of the CIA had been actively investigated.

Dick Russell, the author of *The Man Who Knew Too Much,* tells the story of Richard Case Nagell (a military intelligence officer from 1955 to 1959, and a CIA contact agent from 1962 to 1963) with whom he was a friend over a long period of time. Nagell gave Russell many tips on the world of intelligence, as well as his direct knowledge of Lee Harvey Oswald. In October 1978, Nagell sent Russell a clipping from a newspaper regarding the death of John Paisley. Under the headline, Nagell wrote the following words, "Was he nash? He was nash."

When the two men met for lunch, Russell asked Nagell what "nash" meant. Nagell replied that it was a Russian phrase meaning "ours and nobody else's." What Nagell was implying was that John Paisley was a Russian agent. Was Paisley the Russian mole, a trusted confidant of Agency directors and knowledgeable of their inner secrets? Or was he a CIA double agent, sent to penetrate the KGB? Was Paisley found out by the Russians who had him killed?

James Angleton took an active interest in the Paisley case because of the strange circumstances surrounding his death. "He suggested that if it had not been for some of the weights slipping off the body and consequently its surfacing, Paisley's disappearance would have been written off as a presumed suicide. Because Paisley had obtained a crucial overview of the credence given by the CIA to the different methods of assessing Soviet developments, Angleton speculated that Paisley's knowledge would have been of great value to the KGB, and that if they had obtained it they might also have had an incentive to hide his success by disposing of Paisley."[1]

The answers to all these questions lie at the bottom of the Chesapeake Bay, begging for a plausible solution, but unwilling to reveal its deadly secrets.

---

[1] Holzman, Michael, *"James Jesus Angleton, The CIA, & The Craft of Counterintelligence,* Page 317.

Chapter 36:
William Colby and the "Family Jewels"

William Colby took over the CIA during one of the most tumultuous times in the history of the agency. He was appointed to be America's top spy during the Nixon administration and spent most of his time doing battle with his critics inside the agency. He was responsible for bringing to right many of the wrongdoings of the CIA that took place during the 1960s and 1970s, including the so-called "Family Jewels," a listing of more than 300 questionable activities that was brought to light during the Church Committee hearings of the middle 1970s.

William Colby got his first taste of the espionage craft during World War II. He was born in St. Paul, Minnesota on January 4, 1920, and as a young man, attended Princeton University, graduating in 1941. After Princeton, he attended Columbia University Law School in New York. Like many other young men of his age, he stopped school after the United States entered World War II and joined the Army. He was commissioned as a Second Lieutenant and was assigned to the airborne and artillery units. He took airborne training at Fort Benning, Georgia, but after a jumping accident, he was assigned to other duties. In time though, he was chosen to become a member of the OSS.

By 1943, Colby was assigned to the OSS Special Operations Branch where he took part in commando training in Scotland and England. He was given instruction in the military arts by specially trained members of the British Special Operations Executive (SOE).

Colby joined the Jedburgh Operation in which teams of three men were covertly sent into France directly after the Allied landings in Normandy on June 6, 1944. It was their job to meet up with local French Resistance fighters and pave the way for the Allied push into France. Colby served well and after a few months in the field, he returned to London where he took command of a unit called the OSS Operational Group. The purpose of the unit was to send a number of agents into Norway in order to sabotage German industrial and military plants. Colby and his OSS group spent many months evading the ever-present German patrols that hunted them down; he stayed in Norway until the end of the war. After the conflict ended, he left with the rank of Major, and was awarded the Silver and Bronze Stars for bravery.

He returned to Columbia to get his law degree and then joined a Wall Street law firm headed by his old wartime boss at OSS, William Donovan. He later got a job with the Legal Aid Society and the American Civil Liberties Union. He then worked for the National Labor Relations Board in Washington.

In June 1950, Colby joined the newly-created CIA and was posted to such countries as Sweden and Italy, and served as Chief of Station in Rome from 1953 to 1958. The years 1959 to 1962 saw Colby in America's new international hot spot, South Vietnam, where he also served as Station Chief. During his tenure in South Vietnam, Colby was to oversee a secret CIA-run assassination and pacification program called "Operation Phoenix." In this controversial program, Viet Cong and North Vietnamese agents were picked out for assassination by U.S. authorities. Colby was also responsible for running the secret war in Laos in which CIA officers trained and equipped Meo tribesmen who fought the Communists in Laos and Thailand. In time, more than 30,000 men of *L'Armee Clandestine* (the secret army) fought the Pathet Lao communists and North Vietnamese soldiers in the dense jungles of Southeast Asia.

Working his way up the CIA ladder, Colby was appointed to the important post of Deputy Director for Operations in 1973. That same year, Colby was appointed by President Nixon to the top job at the CIA, becoming its Director during the Watergate scandal that was threatening to unravel the Nixon presidency.

Upon taking over as DCI, Colby made it his business to make the CIA more human, going so far as to give out disabled parking spaces, and hiring more women and minorities. He even ate lunch in the main cafeteria and mingled with the regular staff.

Colby's institutional changes inside the CIA rankled many of the old timers who disliked the way he was doing his job. For instance, Colby made peace with FBI Director Clarence Kelley who took over the Bureau on July 7, 1973. Colby invited Kelley and his top advisors to come to Langley headquarters for lunch and proceeded to institute a better working relationship between the two, often times, antagonistic agencies. Colby and Kelley worked out an arrangement whereby the FBI was given the job of watching Americans abroad, a job that was sometimes shared by both agencies. The FBI also agreed to send one of its own agents to serve as a liaison between the Bureau and the CIA. The FBI agent who took on this thankless job was William Cregar, a one time pro football player for the Pittsburgh Steelers. Cregar was a specialist in Soviet counterintelligence affairs and worked closely with Jim Angleton's CI staff at the CIA. Another organizational change initiated by the two men was that now certain CIA and FBI officers were able to train at the others' training facilities—"The Farm" and there were CIA agents at the FBI's facility at Quantico, Virginia. Intelligence and document sharing was put into place and the FBI's counterintelligence division was now given up- to-date CIA information on current Russian projects.

Colby's biggest internal fight came at the expense of James Angleton and his CI Staff. Colby was often critical of the way Angleton used the information brought in by such Soviet defectors as Golitsyn and Nosenko. In a decision unparalleled in agency history, Colby took some of Angleton's counterintelligence duties away from him and "decentralized" the way the CI department worked. In time, Colby fired Angleton when he decided the long time spook was becoming a hindrance to agency morale.

It was during Colby's tumultuous term as DCI that a number of scandals rocked the agency. *New York Times* reporter Seymour Hersh revealed a secret CIA operation called "Operation Chaos," an illegal CIA mail-opening scheme against certain American citizens. This was an unlawful operation, and when questioned by Congress, Colby said it was a necessary counterintelligence operation. Colby blamed the program on CIA Chief James Angleton.

Colby got caught up in the so-called "Family Jewels" case begun under his predecessor, James Schlesinger who served as DCI from February 2, 1973 to July 2, 1973. In 1972, President Nixon suddenly fired Richard Helms as DCI and packed him off to Iran as our new ambassador. In his place, he chose James Schlesinger who had served under President Nixon as the deputy director of the U.S. Office of Management and Budget. Nixon asked him to write a report on how the U.S. intelligence community could be reorganized to bring about a more efficient organization. The result of the investigation was a 47-page paper called "A Review of the Intelligence Community." He recommended a number of institutional changes including the creation of the post of Director of National Intelligence (which was not accepted). His report also severely criticized the way intelligence was handled and called for a new position named the Coordinator of National Intelligence. This person would be in overall charge of all U.S. intelligence gathering methods and procedures (this position is now in use).

During his tenure as CIA Director, Schlesinger was about to become involved in Watergate and other scandals that rocked the Nixon presidency. News stories had been printed regarding the CIA's association with the Watergate affair, including a revelation by the Justice Department to the presiding judge in the trial of the Watergate burglars that some of these same men, including Howard Hunt, had broken into the office of Dr. Lewis Fielding (he was the psychiatrist for Daniel Elsberg who released the Pentagon Papers). Schlesinger asked William Colby to initiate an investigation to see if there were any more misdeeds of the CIA that were still locked away. Thus was born the "Family Jewels."

The "Family Jewels" was a long list of covert, sometimes illegal, CIA operations dating back to the 1950s. Among the "Jewels" were the CIA's part in the Watergate affair, the illegal wiretaps placed on reporters, including Operation Mudhen, which put noted journalist Jack Anderson under surveillance in 1971-72, the CIA's use of journalists as informers, the mail opening program that the CIA and the FBI collaborated on in the 1950s, the infiltration by the CIA of the Bureau of Narcotics and Dangerous Drugs, Project Merrimac. This operated from February 1967 to November 1971; its sole purpose was to keep watch on domestic groups and individuals whom the agency believed to pose a threat.

Also exposed was the Huston Plan, which was shot down by J. Edgar Hoover, that involved the use of hallucinogenic drugs on unsuspecting victims, the so-called brainwashing experiments, all under the umbrella of Operation MK/ULTRA. Among the most shocking revelations were CIA attempts to kill foreign leaders such as Patrice Lumumba of the Congo, Fidel Castro of Cuba, and Rafael

Trujillo of the Dominican Republic.

After Schlesinger left the agency, his successor, William Colby, had the dubious distinction of taking possession of the Family Jewels/Skeleton information. Colby decided it was best for the CIA and the nation at large to reveal the CIA's past sins. He decided to impart this information to Congress and let them take the ball.

In unveiling the Skeletons, Colby was taking on a large part of the CIA old boy establishment, including his predecessor, Richard Helms. Much of the CIA's illegal activity took place under Helms' watch and Colby took a huge gamble in bringing that information to light. In his book *The Agency: The Rise and Decline of the CIA,* John Ranelagh writes about this time. 'Helms never forgave Colby for the disclosures,' said one retired clandestine-service chief. Helms could never have done what Colby did. There are two camps among CIA people: pro-Colby and anti-Helms and vice versa, and they'll never really come together."

Another victim of the Family Jewels fallout was CIA legend James Angleton. Angleton had been part of the CIA for so long that it was hard to think of the agency without him. When Colby took over at the CIA, he met with Angleton and had a heart-to-heart talk with him. Colby was not enamored of Angleton's obsession with finding moles, or his overall paranoia when it came to anything Russian. As far as Colby was concerned, Angleton's treatment of Golitsyn and Nosenko had pitted factions of the CIA staff against each other, and it was now time to end the bickering once and for all.

Colby met with Angleton on December 17, 1974, and told him that it was time for him to retire, that other people in the agency would now be taking over the CI department, as well as his liaison with the Israeli Mossad. Colby did offer Angleton a consulting position if he so chose. Before Angleton could make up his mind, an event took place that seemed to seal his fate, and brought the CIA's past misdeeds out into the open for all to see.

On December 18, 1974, *New York Times* investigative reporter Seymour Hersh called Colby at CIA headquarters and asked for an interview. He said that he was going to write a blockbuster article on the CIA and he wanted to tell him about it. Hersh had gained a solid reputation as a muckraking journalist when he uncovered the My Lai massacre during the Vietnam War. Hersh told Colby that he was about to break the story of the CIA's domestic spying activity called Operation Chaos, which was directed against the anti-war movement. In subsequent conversations with Colby, Hersh said he was also prepared to reveal the CIA's years-long mail opening operation. Colby told Hersh that the anti-war surveillance ended when no foreign involvement was ascertained, and admitted that the mail opening operation was strictly against the CIA's charter.

After speaking with Hersh, Colby fired Angleton. Admirers of Angleton charged Colby with creating a climate wherein Angleton was forced to resign in light of Hersh's story.

On December 22, 1974, the *Times* published Hersh's story under the banner headline, "Huge CIA Operation Reported in U.S. Against Anti-War Forces, Other Dissidents in Nixon Years." The lead paragraph said, "The CIA directly violating its charter conducted a massive illegal domestic intelligence operation during the Nixon Administration against the anti-war movement and other dissident groups in the Untied States, according to well-placed Government sources."

Instead of denying the *Times* story, Colby told the nation that the article was correct. He later said that he withheld the so-called Family Jewels/Skeletons from both President Nixon and Ford. In the ensuing furor over the Hersh article, Colby brought a 58-page report to the Ford White House where the President read the tale of CIA culpability and deception with amazement.

President Ford tasked Vice President Nelson Rockefeller to chair an independent commission to look into the CIA's illegal domestic activities. By 1975, however, it was revealed that the CIA was involved in the assassination plots against foreign leaders.

Helms returned from his role as ambassador to Iran to testify before the Rockefeller Commission. He lashed out at CBS *Evening News* reporter Daniel Schorr who broke the assassination story to the nation.

In the wake of the Hersh-Skeletons-Rockefeller Commission report, the Congress of the United States opened its own investigation of the CIA's illegal activities in January 1975. Its formal title was the *"Select Committee to Study Governmental Operations with Respect to Intelligence Activities."* The Committee was headed by Democratic Senator Frank Church from Idaho, and soon came to be known as the Church Committee. The Church Committee held 60 days of live hearings, airing the CIA's assassination plots, as well as all the other crimes of the CIA.

At the height of the hearings, Senator Church said that the CIA was a "rogue elephant on a rampage." When the hearings ended on April 26, 1976, the commission made hard-hitting recommendations on how the CIA should act when carrying out its mission. Among the items banned were assassinations of foreign leaders, stopping illegal wiretaps against domestic targets, and illegal mail openings. The Congress now created its own committees to oversee CIA operations and had CIA directors report to both the House and Senate Intelligence Committees for funding and reporting of future clandestine operations.

In the end, no proof of any CIA involvement in the deaths of any foreign leader could be demonstrated.

Colby left the CIA on January 30, 1976, and wrote a book about his career called *Honorable Men: My Life in the CIA*.

On April 27, 1996, William Colby left his home for a canoe ride along the Potomac River. When he failed to come home, a search was initiated. His body was found nine days later. Conspiracy theorists have speculated that Colby's death may have been the result of foul play (just like the death of John Paisley under similar circumstances), but no evidence to that effect was ever proven.

William Colby

Chapter 37:
"Dewey" Clarridge Tracks a Terrorist

If the CIA were to present someone who resembled William King Harvey, their legendary agent from the decades of the 1950s and 60s, it would have to be Duane "Dewey" Clarridge, a no-nonsense, cigar stomping, hard driven man who took part in CIA operations ranging from the Middle East to Latin America and Europe. Clarridge was a trusted advisor to later day DCI's, and was responsible for the creation, and running of the Counter Terrorism Center (CTC) whose job it was to monitor the actions of America's enemies across the globe. While operating out of the CTC, Clarridge mounted a covert operation to catch one of the most wanted terrorists of the 1980s, Fawaz Yunis.

Duane Clarridge was born on April 16, 1932 in Nashua, New Hampshire. He still has his distinctive New England accent, all these years later. In his formative years, his family spent many a summer on the beautiful shores of Lake Winnipesaukee, New Hampshire where Duane went fishing and explored the pine-laden forests. He attended a prep school in New Jersey called Andover, and later graduated from Brown University. He was accepted by Columbia University in New York for graduate school, and majored in international affairs. Between semesters he worked in Washington, D.C. for the State Department's Passport Office.

Clarridge was married on April 2, 1955, and soon thereafter took a step that would mold the rest of his life. While he was at Columbia, the CIA came to the campus looking for new recruits. In the early 1950s, not many people had ever heard of the CIA, and its operations were hardly spoken of in the public media. He was accepted into the CIA in 1955 and he and his wife moved to Washington where he would receive his training. His original posting was in the Clandestine Service, the Directorate of Operations whose primary duties were the collection of foreign intelligence and covert action.

While in the CIA, Clarridge had to undertake his military responsibilities, and in a joint CIA-Army program, he entered military service. He soon rose through the ranks to Sergeant, enrolled in Officers Candidate School, and was commissioned as a Second Lieutenant assigned to the U.S. Army Reserve. Throughout his military duties, no one he came in contact with realized he was a member of the CIA.

Over the next three decades, Clarridge rose high up in the CIA's covert operations division. He was chief of the Latin American Division (1981-84), chief of the European Division (1984-86), and headed the Counter-terrorism Center (1986-88).

As the Reagan administration came to power, the new chief executive reordered the CIA into its post-World War II covert arm of the country. Clarridge directed the agency's not so secret war against the Sandinista guerillas in Nicaragua, and was the man responsible for the mining of Nicaraguan harbors, which got the CIA in hot water with Congress. He was also responsible for the infiltration of a woman agent into the tiny Caribbean island of Grenada just prior to the U.S.-led invasion in October 1983. He then spent an unrewarding stint as chief of the European Division and found the assignment boring. However, Clarridge was to oversee a much more interesting assignment when he was tasked with the job of running the newly created CTC, which took the covert war on terror to America's enemies around the globe. One of his most complex and dangerous assignments was to catch the Middle Eastern terrorist, Fawaz Yunis.

Fawaz Yunis was a Lebanese Shiite, who, on June 11, 1985, hijacked a Royal Jordanian Airliner from Beirut, Lebanon. Yunis and his men disarmed the passengers, commandeered the plane, and diverted it to Tunisia. Yunis subsequently blew up the plane, and eventually let the terrorized passengers go free. Even though no one was killed, there were three Americans on board the jet and the FBI, under the powers of the Omnibus Crime Act, now had jurisdiction.

After the Jordanian incident, Yunis took part in another plane hijacking, the taking of TWA Flight 847 which was carried off from Athens, to Beirut, and finally to Algiers. During that incident, an American hostage named Robert Stethem was killed, his body thrown onto the bloody, hot tarmac.

Over a long period of time, the DEA (Drug Enforcement Administration) had compiled a large dossier on Yunis who was being investigated for drug violations in Cyprus. The DEA had a source named Jamil Hamdan who was close to Yunis and contacted him concerning Yunis' whereabouts.

In a show of interagency cooperation, the covert arms of U.S. intelligence concocted an elaborate scheme to lure Yunis out of Beirut and capture him. The CTC was to head the assignment, with Clarridge in command.

The codename for the extraction was "Operation Goldenrod" and it involved the Justice Department, the FBI, and the CIA. Since the CIA was not allowed by law to arrest people for crimes committed, the FBI would have to take on that job. Once Yunis was safely in custody, they would prosecute the case. The CIA would be the hidden brain behind the operation, with Dewey Clarridge riding shotgun.

The CIA's plan called for Hamdan to reach Yunis and tell him that he had a contact named "Joseph" who was one of the richest drug dealers in the world. Hamdan would link Yunis up with "Joseph" and a huge drug deal would be completed aboard a yacht owned by Joseph. The plan called for Yunis to be taken by Hamdan to the yacht, which would be anchored in international waters, and would be manned by a team of covert FBI agents (including, it turned out, bikini-clad women to lure Yunis even further). Once aboard the yacht, he would be arrested and taken back to the United States for trial.

The CIA, under Clarridge's direction, rented a yacht called the *Skunk Kilo* for "Joseph's" use. The U.S. Navy also got into the act by sending the USS *Butte,* which was a munitions ship operated by the Sixth Fleet to transfer Yunis to U.S. Justice Department officials.

The operation would go down in Cyprus and Clarridge headed a covert team of CIA agents coordinating the mission.

On September 11, 1985, Hamdan and Yunis arrived in Larnaca, Cyprus and checked into a hotel, which was already part, occupied by CIA personnel masquerading as guests. In an operation that went off without a hitch, Hamdan and the unsuspecting Yunis rendezvoused with the FBI Hostage Rescue Team on board the *Skunk Kilo.* Instead of providing "Joseph," the FBI team slammed Yunis to the ground, read him his rights, and placed him under arrest.

Hamdan and Yunis were transferred to the *Butte, which* sailed to meet the USS *Saratoga* in the Med. Here, Yunis and his FBI watchers boarded a long and grueling flight to the United States. Clarridge and his team silently left Cyprus, their mission accomplished.

Unfortunately for Dewey Clarridge, his 30-year CIA career ended with a cloud hanging over his head. He was caught up in the Iran-Contra affair when he aided Lt. Col. Oliver North in his covert shipment of Hawk surface-to-air missiles to Iran in exchange for U.S. hostages being held in Lebanon. Clarridge was indicted three years later on seven counts of perjury and false statements by the Independent Counsel, Lawrence Walsh. Clarridge never saw his case go to trial as he was given a presidential pardon by President George H.W. Bush on December 24, 1992.

In 1997, Clarridge penned his memoirs of his life in the CIA in a book called *A Spy for All Seasons*. After leaving the CIA, he made the most of his notoriety by appearing on many television documentaries concerning his years in the CIA.

Chapter 38:
The CIA vs. Abu Nidal

Before Osama bin Laden thrust himself into the role as the world's most notorious terrorist, that undistinguished mantle belonged to a militant Middle Eastern revolutionary and killer. Named Sabri al-Bana, or "Abu Nidal," he wrecked his vengeance across the world in the decades of the 1970s and 1980's. Like Osama bin Laden was, Abu Nidal was in the crosshairs of the CIA's CTC, which did all it could to penetrate his organization and kill him.

Over the years, Abu Nidal's terrorist organization called ANO was responsible for murderous acts across the globe, mostly targeting Western and Israeli interests. Only recently Abu Nidal has been linked by many Western intelligence agencies to the downing of Pan Am Flight 103 over Lockerbie, Scotland with the resulting deaths of 270 people. In a trial, agents of Libya were convicted of the crime. He had ties with many of the so-called terrorist states of the Middle East, including Syria and Iraq. The CIA and the FBI also tracked Abu Nidal sleeper cells inside the United States.

In August 2002, less than a year before the U.S.-led invasion of Iraq, a stunning report came from the Palestinian newspaper *Al-Ayyanm* that Abu Nidal, 65, had been found dead in Iraq, supposedly of self-inflicted wounds. It seems that he had blown off the back of his head using a Smith & Wesson by shooting himself in the mouth. He then, the story goes, was able to put three bullets into his head. The how and why of the death of one of the world's most wanted men is not really important. What is relevant is to what extent the CIA and the Israeli Mossad tracked down Abu Nidal and possibly used him for their own intelligence purposes.

Sabri al-Bana was born in Jaffa in May 1937, which was then under the control of the British. He was one of 16 children of a prosperous family who owned a number of citrus farms. His schooling was limited to the third grade but that did not stop him from learning the harsh realities of life under British, and then Israeli, occupation. During the War of Independence in 1948, the al-Bana family was forced from their home and made various moves, first to the town of Majdal, and later to a refugee camp in the city of Nablus in the West Bank, which was then under Egyptian control. He soon joined the Ba` ath party in Jordan which was a recruiting ground for those mostly poor youths whose dream was to drive Israel out of the lands it conquered in the 1948 War of Independence.

He soon moved to Saudi Arabia, and then to Cairo, where he organized a group of like-minded young men called the Palestine Secret Organization. In 1960, he decided to send two men to Beirut to set up shop, but they determined they'd rather enjoy the nightlife and relative freedom of the city and dropped out. It was during this time that he joined the Fatah, the militant, anti-Israeli group headed by Yasser Arafat. Over the next years, Nidal would join with Arafat's PLO (Palestine Liberation Organization) to wage his own, personal war against Western interests in the Middle East.

In 1973, however, Abu Nidal decided to split away from Arafat's PLO and set up his own organization. He called his new group the Fatah Revolutionary Council (FRC). For the next several years, his group was just a blip on the intelligence screens of the CIA. By January 1978, all that changed, as the FRC began a decades-long campaign of assassinations, bombings, and killings against its enemies across the globe.

On January 5, 1978, the PLO representative in London was shot dead. This was followed by the PLO representatives in Paris, Rome, Madrid, Brussels, and being killed.

On June 2, 1982, Nidal's men shot and critically wounded Shlomo Argov, the Israeli Ambassador to England. British writer Alec Collett who was working for the U.N. Relief and Works Agency, was kidnapped and killed in Beirut. On August 7, 1985, Nidal's gunmen killed thirteen innocent tourists in a hotel in Athens.

Ninety-seven people were on board an Egyptian airliner that was hijacked on November 23, 1985, and diverted to Malta. Egyptian commandos stormed the plane the following day, which resulted in the deaths of six passengers.

Their most brazen assault took place on December 27, 1985 when eighteen travelers were killed and more than 120 wounded at the El Al ticket counters in Rome and Vienna airports.

On September 6, 1986, 22 people were killed and six wounded in a machine gun attack on the Neve Shalom synagogue in Istanbul, Turkey.

These horrific attacks quickly got the attention of the CIA. The CTC appointed Dewey Clarridge to head the team that would take down Abu Nidal. A CIA psychological profile of Abu Nidal said that he "is the textbook loner. He has one ambition—to become supreme at the profession he had chosen. He is dangerously special." Since it was almost impossible to penetrate the FRC, the CIA decided to implement a large-scale disinformation campaign against him. CIA agents on the ground in the Middle East passed along disinformation saying that a number of Abu Nidal's most trusted advisors had secretly made contact with the CIA. These unfortunate people were confronted and summarily killed. During this successful campaign against Nidal, he ruthlessly killed more than three hundred of his own men who never had anything to do with the CIA.

While the CIA was acting against Abu Nidal overseas, the FBI was penetrating its U.S.-based sleeper cells. During the 1980s, FBI agents arrested a number of Nidal's inactive agents living in St. Louis, Mo.

Over the years there had been reports that the Israeli Mossad had secretly recruited Abu Nidal himself sometime in the 1960s. The reason (if this was actually done) was to provide a buffer against Yasser Arafat's PLO and possibly use Nidal's killers to act against the PLO, if the call ever came.

The CIA kept track of Nidal's operations in the late 1980s, according to intelligence provided by a secret arrangement between Morocco and the United States. Members of their respective intelligence services worked together in a special spy school, which concentrated on Palestinian affairs. The CIA helped train men from North Africa who were recruited in Europe. These men would then keep track of the goings-on in the PLO, as well as Nidal's group.

By the 1990s, the political landscape of the Middle East had changed. Egypt made a peace treaty with Israel and the terror attacks against Western interests in the region abated.

In ill health, Nidal found refuge in Saddam Hussein's Iraq, where the dictator gave him shelter (and little else). His end came in August 2002, but by whose hand is uncertain. It is possible that the one-time king of terror took his own life, or that he was executed on the orders of Saddam Hussein. If the latter is true, then the CIA has at least one good thing to say about the late "butcher of Baghdad."

Chapter 39:
The Murder of William Buckley

During the Reagan administration the United States found itself involved in an arms for hostages scandal called Iran-Contra. Numerous civilians were captured in Lebanon and held, sometimes for years, by militant terrorists who wanted to show their disapproval of the United States. One of the men who fell into their deadly hands was the CIA Station Chief in Beirut, William Buckley (no relation to the writer of the same name).

William Buckley was born in Bedford, Massachusetts in 1928. He began his military career as a member of the Army Special Forces and it was in that position that he was recruited into the CIA. He saw limited action at the end of World War II, and also served a tour of duty in Korea where he won a Silver Star.

He covertly joined the CIA in 1954 while still in the Army. He kept his identity secret while in the Army, and only a few of his trusted officers and colleagues knew of his agency links. During the Cold War years, Buckley served in Berlin and worked on the secret CIA-led Berlin Tunnel operation. After a stint back at CIA headquarters, Buckley served in various international hot spots over the following three plus decades, which included Egypt, Syria, Vietnam, Pakistan, and finally, Lebanon.

In the early 1980s, Buckley came to the attention of then-CIA Director William Casey. Casey, who was given the job of combating Middle Eastern terrorism by the new Reagan administration, asked Buckley to head back to Lebanon even though he was known to our enemies in the country. Part of his job was to oversee counterterrorist policies in Lebanon after the U.S. embassy in West Beirut was attacked on April 18, 1983. Sixty-seven people were killed, including a number of CIA personnel.

On Friday, March 16, 1984, William Buckley left his room at the Al-Manara apartment building where he resided. This was just like any other day, one of danger and boredom, all wrapped up in one.

A few months previously, Buckley met covertly in Beirut with an undercover member of the Israeli Mossad at a seafront restaurant. At that meeting, the men developed a plan to rescue the American hostages then being held in the city. The plan called for a team of American Green Berets to be flown from the United States to Tel Aviv, Israel where they would join up with members of an Israeli Special Forces unit on gunboats, which would be stationed offshore. The plan further called for a number of Mossad officers to plant bombs in the homes of known terror suspects in the city. Once the explosions began, the joint U.S.-Israeli team would attempt to free the hostages. One day earlier, the plan had been approved by DCI William Casey.[1]

On the 16th, under circumstances that are still not clear, William Buckley was captured in Beirut by members of the radical group called Islamic Jihad. In the wake of the Buckley kidnapping, Director William Casey, a veteran of the OSS during World War II, and Ronald Reagan's 1980 campaign chairman, set up an inter-agency task force to plan Buckley's rescue; members included people from the FBI, the CIA, and the NSC. One plan called for the ransoming of Buckley to the tune of two million dollars, some of which would be supplied by Ross Perot, the wealthy Texas businessman with worldwide intelligence connections. However, the design was scrubbed as too impractical to succeed.

Another operation called for the U.S. to kidnap Imad Mugniyed, a powerful Lebanese Shiite leader who was in charge of the Islamic Jihad (the same group who captured Buckley) while he was on a trip to France. It was decided to cancel the plan because of the likelihood of French displeasure over the fact and that the operation was to be conducted on their soil.

Immediately after Buckley's abduction, a joint FBI-CIA team was sent to Beirut to find out what had happened. The team came up with the following conclusions about what happened to the Station Chief. He left his home in his Renault and was waved past a number of Hezbollah checkpoints. At some point in his trip, he was forcibly taken from his car by unidentified members of Hezbollah in West Beirut. With Buckley now hidden in an undisclosed place, the joint CIA-Mossad plan to free the hostages, and possibly rescue Buckley, was cancelled.

---

[1] Thomas, Gordon. *"The Spy Who Never Came in from the Cold,* October 25, 2006, world-wide web.

At CIA headquarters, there was consternation and shock that Buckley had been abducted. He was privy to so much top-secret information on CIA activities in the Middle East that his abduction was seen as a disaster in the making.

On May 7, 1984, the United States embassy in Athens, Greece received a package that contained a VHS tape. The tape was sent to Washington where it was viewed by CIA personnel. On the tape was a horrid picture of William Buckley being tortured.

Twenty-three days later, another video was sent to the U.S. embassy in Rome. In it was a second tape of William Buckley, looking gaunt, bruised and bloody, a man in terrible pain. A third tape was received on October 26, 1984, which showed Buckley near death.

As the months passed and there was still no word of where Buckley was, rumors spread about where he had been taken. It was said he was in the Beka'a Valley of Lebanon or maybe in Tehran.

At the CIA, internal squabbling went on as to whom was responsible for Buckley's abduction. During his service at the CIA, William Buckley had made many enemies due to his abrasive style and personality. One CIA contract employee said that "Buckley wasn't liked, he wasn't liked at all."

While he was in captivity, the U.S. tried to win his freedom by contacting the Israeli government, which was working with both Israeli and Iranian arms dealers. These arms dealers tried to broker an arrangement to free Buckley through their contacts with the terrorists groups that were holding Buckley. However, he had already died when these talks were going on.

William Buckley eventually died by contracting pneumonia while in captivity. Before he passed away, he was forced to admit to "crimes" he carried out against the Islamic peoples. The death of William Buckley was a black mark on the agency, coming at a time when the rise of Islamic terrorism was gaining strength across the Middle East.

Chapter 40:
William Casey—From OSS to the CIA

When Ronald Reagan was elected President of the United States in 1980, one of his first appointments was that of his old friend and campaign manager, William Casey, to be the head of the CIA. This was a political appointment, to be sure, but what the critics did not know, or chose to forget, was that William Casey's roots in espionage went back to his participation in the early days of the OSS, under William Donovan.

Bill Casey was born and bred in New York City, living in the borough of Queens with his family. He attended Fordham University, soon married, and began his career as a lawyer. One of young Bill Casey's hobbies was to read spy novels and he kept that interest throughout his life. He was an avid collector of books and magazines and after his death; his wife found literally thousands of books and periodicals stuffed around his home. His family's politics were that of the New Deal of Franklin D. Roosevelt but soon Bill gravitated to the Republican Party. He campaigned for Wendell Wilkie, against Franklin Roosevelt.

As the war spread in Europe, it was obvious that eventually the United States would have to enter the conflict. Casey was offered a job by his friend Leo Charne in a think tank called the Research Institute of America. The RIA's work was to debate and write about the pressing international problems facing the world. Casey helped write a book that came out of this work called *The Business of Defense Coordinator*.

On February 22, 1941, Bill married Sophia Kurz and the couple spent their honeymoon in Cuba and the Caribbean. But soon, Bill Casey and the rest of America would be caught up in the whirlwind of war. To that effect, on June 5, 1943, two years after the U.S. entered the war, Casey was commissioned as a lieutenant junior grade in the Navy. His first assignment was with the Office of Naval Procurement in Washington. As the war progressed, Casey, who had poor eyesight and was not allowed into a combat theater, made a call to a man he knew to be somehow involved in secret work, Jerry

259

Doran. Doran's former law partner was Otto Doering, then working in Bill Donovan's newly created OSS. Doran got Casey an interview with Doering and Doering sent Casey to meet a man named Colonel Vanderblue. The secretive Vanderblue was a recruiter for the OSS. The two men spent hours talking and the Colonel said he'd get back to Casey. Two weeks later, Casey met with Otto Doering again and got good news—he was accepted into the OSS. His first posting was to London in November 1943. It was there that his first daughter, Bernadette, was born.

Casey and a few other men worked in a section that read and handled cables that came in during the previous night from OSS agents and outposts across the globe. It was their job to filter each piece of information, catalogue it into priority sections, and decide which piece of the intelligence nugget was sent to Donovan's desk. While working with Donovan in those early years in London, Casey said this regarding his new boss, "I was just a boy from Long Island. Sure, I had worked with high-level government officials, generals, and admirals. But never had I been in personal contact with a man of Donovan's candlepower. He was bigger than life. I reveled in my association with that man. We all glowed in his presence."

In late 1944, with Allied victory in sight, Donovan ordered his London station to draft a report on how the United States could develop a permanent intelligence organization. Bill Casey's job was to serve as the secretary to this committee, and when the report was completed, he went to Washington to deliver its recommendations directly to Donovan.

Once back in Europe, Casey was promoted to chief of intelligence in the London station, and traveled to Paris to oversee the liberation of the city from Nazi rule. He wrote an important policy paper vis a vis the agency's German operations called "An OSS Program Against Germany." Its most basic subject was the scope and detail of OSS covert operations against the German army in the field. One of his jobs, as the war neared its end, was the recruitment of agents among all categories of people: communists, POWs, etc. Casey obtained their services, oversaw their training, and was on hand when they were sent behind the lines.

The end of the war saw the dismemberment of the OSS and the (temporary) end of the road as a spy for Bill Casey. He returned to civilian life, and went into the legal publishing business. When someone asked him of his time as an OSS agent he replied, "It was the greatest experience of my life." Little did Casey know that 25 years later he would get a second chance in the intelligence business, this time as head of the CIA, the successor to the OSS, and enter into another covert battle against the enemies of the United States.

In the intervening years between the ending of the OSS and his ascendancy as DCI, Casey lost an election for Congress from Long Island, was appointed by President Nixon as head of the Securities and Exchange Commission, and was president of the Import-Export Bank.

With the election of Ronald Reagan over President Jimmy Carter in the 1980 election, Casey had met his ideological soul mate. Reagan won the election determined to restore America's role in the world as the number one superpower. The United States had been humiliated in the 444-day Iran hostage incident, and its covert action arm failed to get the hostages freed in a bungled rescue operation. The new President was determined to restore vigor to the CIA, and he tasked that very important job to Bill Casey who was now to serve as DCI.

At age 67, Casey was the oldest man to head the CIA. He was not a prepossessing man wearing old, unpressed suits, his white hair asunder, sometimes slurring his words. It was these personal qualities that kept him from becoming either Secretary of State or Secretary of Defense. However, he was rewarded with cabinet rank as head of the CIA. As DCI, Casey reverted to the old style business at CIA headquarters where secrecy was paramount and the ever-inquisitive press would not be able to pry into the agency's affairs.

Casey was not long at the CIA when he was the object of an investigation in the so-called "Debategate" affair. As far as scandals went, this one had no legs. In short, Casey was accused by James Baker, the White House Chief of Staff, of providing him with a copy of Jimmy Carter's briefing papers before a debate between the President and Ronald Reagan. Despite his denials of any wrongdoing, the FBI, under the direction of William Webster, initiated an investigation. Casey was interviewed by the Bureau and he was eventually cleared of any wrongdoing.

With the approval of President Reagan, the CIA under Bill

Casey's direction asked for, and was given, permission to a limited expansion of CIA operations inside the United States. This enlargement of previously forbidden activity was authorized by Executive Order 12333, signed by President Reagan on December 4, 1981. The agency was now able to "conduct counterintelligence activities within the United States, in coordination with the Bureau [FBI], as required by procedures agreed upon by the Director of Central Intelligence and the Attorney General." During the Reagan administration, both FBI and CIA agents collected information on groups who were opposed to the war in El Salvador, and other domestic groups who expressed opposition to the administration's positions in Nicaragua.

Casey's tenure as DCI came during the year that was dubbed the "Year of the Spy." As we have seen, in 1985 Casey had to watch in horror as numerous high-level members of the CIA and other U.S. intelligence services were arrested for selling U.S. secrets to the Soviet Union. For Casey, the hardest blow came with the defection and redefection of KGB officer Vitaly Yurchenko, who accused the CIA of kidnapping him and forcing him to undergo drug testing against his will.

While the other intelligence services giggled at CIA bungling, Casey took the covert war directly to the Soviet Union, then America's main enemy. Casey was a firm believer in the old OSS adage of taking the fight directly to the enemy, which meant the infiltration of agents into the other side's camp. So what if some of or all of these men were caught? The best defense was the best offense, and to hell with the consequences.

William Casey and President Ronald Reagan shared the same Cold War mentality when it came to rolling back the communist menace, and to that effect, Casey wrote a daring report which would allow the United States to aid, militarily and otherwise, the various resistance groups anywhere in the world. Throughout the Reagan administration, the CIA, through Casey's watchful eyes, began a widespread covert war aiding the Contras in Nicaragua, propping up the government in El Salvador which was fighting domestic dissidents, and most importantly, as far as Casey was concerned, taking the covert war directly to the terrorists in the Middle East, and supervising the so-called Iran-Contra affair which would embroil him in his last days. Another international hot spot which had its roots in the Reagan administration was Afghanistan, where the massive CIA-backed war to aid the anti-Soviet forces who were battling the Russians was launched when they invaded Afghanistan. The not so covert war, which was headed by the CIA, saw the United States deliver tons of military supplies, including the very effective Singer anti-helicopter missile, to the Afghan rebels. Through the CIA's intercession, the agency made covert deals with a number of local Afghan groups who had no love for the United States. If the U.S. was willing to give them military aid in order to eliminate the Soviet invasion of the country, they would accept it. But to these hard-driven men, the U.S. was still the infidel, and once our usefulness was over, we would once again become their bitter enemy. This policy on the part of the U.S. was nicknamed "Blowback," which would have unintended consequences for the United States with the culmination of the terrorist attacks on September 11, 2001.

One crazy scheme that was concocted by the President regarding the Soviet invasion of Afghanistan concerned the French spy chief Count Alexandre de Marenches. The Count met with President Reagan shortly after his election to the White House. He asked the President what the United States did with all the illegal drugs seized by the DEA, Coast Guard, and Customs. Count de Marenches devised a scheme to use all these drugs, offering the Soviet soldiers in the Afghan city of Kabul the opportunity to buy them, in order to undermine their ability to fight. The President agreed and asked Marenches to meet with Bill Casey to discuss the matter. Casey said it would be a good idea and set the plan in motion. Casey asked the Count if the French would carry out the mission if the United States provided the funds. He agreed. The plan specified, "Pakistani operatives and Afghan freedom fighters would be responsible for infiltrating the country with the contraband."

Before the plan was put into effect, the French spy chief became worried about the growing number of Americans who were aware of their secret deal, and he came to Washington to see Casey. The Count said that if the plan went south, his name should not be mentioned in any after-action fallout. Casey said that he could make no guarantees, and "Operation Mosquito" was scrubbed.[1]

As the Soviets became more bogged down in Afghanistan,

---

[1] Beaty, Jonathan, and Gwynne, S.C., *The Outlaw Bank: A Wild Ride into the Secret Heart of BCCI,* Random House, New York, 1993, Page 305-306.

President Reagan gave Casey the job of funneling weapons to the Afghan resistance. The CIA made a secret deal with Saudi Arabia to funnel more than $4 billion in weapons to the rebels during the war. Casey used the services of Aga Hasan Abedi, the founder of the clandestine bank called BCCI, Bank of Credit and Commerce International, whose secret tentacles were used by the CIA to supply arms and money all across the globe. It is not precisely known just when Casey first met with Aga Hasan Abedi, but published accounts say they first met in the latter part of 1983 or the beginning of 1984. They supposedly met for a period of three years; in Washington, they met at the Madison Hotel where the CIA-BCCI funding agreement was made.

The CIA, under Casey's direction, purchased arms for the Afghan resistance and shipped them to the Pakistani city of Karachi. It also supplied money to the secretive ISI, Pakistan's Inter-Services Intelligence agency, which passed along the arms to the rebels (the ISI also had direct links to the Taliban in Afghanistan).

As the worldwide terrorist threat reared its ugly head during the Reagan administration with the brutal attacks against the U.S. Marine barracks in Lebanon, the kidnapping of CIA Station Chief William Buckley, and the abductions of a number of innocent Americans living in the Middle East, a Restricted Interagency Group for Terrorism (RIG-T), was established. Members of the group came from the CIA, the FBI, and the National Security Council. Casey was the nominal head of the RIG but he placed the daily operations of the panel in the capable hands of Duane Clarridge, who had been the point man of the CIA's covert war in Nicaragua.

During the Iran-Iraq war, the CIA decided to back the authoritarian regime of Saddam Hussein in its brutal conflict against Ayatollah Ruhollah Khomeni whose Islamic revolution had toppled the longtime ally of the U.S., the Shah of Iran, Reza Pahlavi. The CIA gave more than $100,000 a month to the anti-Khomeni faction called the Front for the Liberation of Iran that was based in Paris. Thousands more were funneled to Radio Liberation which sent anti-Khomeni propaganda into Iran. As the long and bloody war between the two nations slugged on, Casey met with a number of high ranking Iraqi military officers to cement their covert relationship, and made sure that the CIA supplied aerial and photographic intelligence on Iranian military positions to the Iraqis. One of Casey's secret middlemen in the American intelligence bureaucracy vis a vis Iraq was a then little-known lieutenant colonel assigned to the White House, Oliver North.

William Casey's demise came about because of the Iran-Contra affair wherein the United States sold weapons in exchange for the release of American hostages being held in various parts of the Middle East. Monies from the sale of these arms were then diverted to aid the Contras in their war against the government of Nicaragua.

In the scandal that followed, Lt. Col. North testified before Congress that Casey had been the engineer of the arms-for-hostages scheme. Just before Casey was to be called to testify in an open session before the Iran-Contra Committee, he suffered a massive stroke in December 1986. One month later, Casey was dead, and any chance of him telling his side of the story in the scandal that almost ended the Reagan presidency died with him.

In a still-debated side plot to the story of William Casey, author Bob Woodward wrote in his book called *Veil: The Secret Wars of the CIA 1981-1987,* that shortly before Casey died, he had a final conversation with Casey while he lay in his hospital bed. Woodward says that Casey revealed to him his part in the Iran-Contra affair. Other people close to Casey refute Woodward's assertions, saying that Casey was too sick to respond to the reporter's questions, and that security at the hospital was too tight to allow Woodward, a stranger, entry into Casey's room.

CIA HQ, Southern Building, Washington DC

Chapter 41:
Edward Lee Howard Goes East

The Year of the Spy saw the successful defection to the Soviet Union of ex-CIA officer Edward Lee Howard who was named as the elusive "Robert" by the Russian defector Vitaly Yurchenko. As far as defections go, the information that Howard divulged to the Russians was not as damaging as the cases of Aldrich Ames and Robert Hanssen; however, it is believed that the information disclosed by Howard led to the death of an important CIA double agent in Moscow named Alfred Tolkachev. The case of Edward Lee Howard may also have been a well-planned operation on the part of the KGB to protect its number one source inside the agency, Aldrich Ames.

Edward Lee Howard was born in Albuquerque, New Mexico in 1951. He graduated from the University of Texas in 1972 where he majored in international business and was fluent in German. After graduation, he joined the Peace Corps and did work in South America. By 1974, he was back in the United States where he did Peace Corps recruiting in Dallas. He furthered his education by obtaining his MA degree from the American University in Washington, D.C. in 1976. Howard married Mary Cedereleaf whom he met while in the Peace Corps. He soon left the Pace Corps and found a job in Washington, working for the Agency For International Development which, over the years, had been a CIA front organization.

In 1981, Howard was recruited by the CIA and was assigned to the "Farm" where all new undercover recruits took intensive training in the clandestine arts. During the rigorous background checks that all new CIA employees must endure, he said that he had indulged in various illegal substances like marijuana and cocaine, and was a "moderate" drinker. All these warning signs were ignored by the CIA who saw in Howard a smart, streetwise potential agent. During this time period, when the Cold War against the Russians was still in its heyday, the CIA tended to ignore many indiscretions by its employees in the hope that their exposure to the real world would temper their youthful practices (the CIA also ignored Aldrich

Ames' habitual drinking while he was still an active agent).

After his basic training at the "Farm," Howard was assigned to the sensitive Soviet/East European Division, which was responsible for the penetration of American agents into Russia and the entire Eastern Bloc. In time, the agency had ordered Howard to be posted to an important job in Moscow where he would work out of the American embassy. As part of his daily briefings at Langley headquarters, he was given the names of all the CIA covert agents in Russia and was privy to the types of undercover operations that were scheduled behind the Iron Curtain. For Howard, this was heady stuff, as he was one of a handful of top CIA officers who were given the "keys to the kingdom" as far as Russian operations were concerned.

In 1983, shortly before he was scheduled to leave for Moscow, he was given a routine polygraph test, which showed discrepancies and deceptions in his answers. He admitted that he had been engaged in a series of petty thefts and was unceremoniously kicked out of the CIA. His once promising career at the center of power in Washington was now suddenly over. By 1984 he had been a regular visitor to the Soviet diplomatic mission and was heavy into his second career as a Soviet agent. Once again the "see no evil, hear no evil" mentality at CIA headquarters resulted in the agency not contacting the FBI regarding Howard's potential espionage.

The CIA never revealed to the FBI the fact that Howard was indulging in illicit drugs or that he admitted to petty theft, and the Bureau never put Howard under surveillance.

Howard decided that if the CIA didn't want his services, he would offer them to the Soviet Union. In a brazen act, Howard made covert contact with the Soviets, and his offer to supply them with his expertise was accepted.

He returned to New Mexico where, despite his less than stellar CIA employment resume, he got a job with the New Mexico State Hospital as an economic analyst. In 1984, Howard made a clandestine trip to Austria where he met with his KGB handlers and passed over to them his treasure trove of information.

On August 1, 1985, the case against Edward Lee Howard would take on a dramatic and unexpected twist. On that day a top Soviet KGB officer named Vitaly Yurchenko entered the U.S. embassy in

Rome and decided to defect. He was taken by jet to Andrews Air Force Base outside of Washington where he was met by two CIA officers, Aldrich Ames and the Soviet Divison's CI chief, Colin Thompson. Also on hand to meet Yurchenko was FBI agent Mike Rochford. At the debriefing session, the men asked Yurchenko if he knew the identities of any Soviet moles. Yurchenko said that he knew the codename of a Russian double agent who was secretly working for the KGB. This unnamed man whom he only knew as "Robert," was to be sent to Moscow but his assignment was stopped at the last minute. "Robert," said Yurchenko, had also made a trip to Austria to meet with the KGB. The CIA assigned Gus Hathaway, a veteran of the clandestine service to look into the "Robert" matter. After an intensive investigation, Hathaway was convinced that "Robert" was none other than Edward Lee Howard. The profile supplied by Yurchenko fit perfectly with the operational conduct of Howard.

In an unexpected move, the CIA, for reasons all its own, did not immediately share its information on Howard with the FBI. It was the FBI's job to investigate and arrest any potential traitor but they were left out of the loop. A few days later, the CIA finally brought the Edward Lee Howard case to FBI agent Philip Parker who would now take on the Bureau's investigation.

As the Bureau finally began its probe of Edward Lee Howard, the ex-spy fooled everyone when he suddenly departed for Vienna to meet his Russian handlers. If the FBI had known that Edward Lee Howard was in Austria, they could have mounted an undercover operation and would have had him dead to rights.

Upon Howard's return to the United States, the FBI tapped his home phone and mounted a 24-hour watch on his activities. The CIA also failed to notify the Bureau that one of Howard's best friends was then in contact with Howard, a man named William Bosch, who had once worked for the CIA. The FBI failed to talk with Bosch to find out if he had any information that could have aided them in their investigation of Howard.

The CIA now notified the FBI of the latest news concerning Edward Lee Howard and one month later, the FBI began round-the-clock surveillance of him. With the Bureau now hot on his trail, Howard and his wife returned to their home in Santa Fe, New Mexico to plan their next move. While at the CIA, Howard learned the intricacies of how to detect and foil any surveillance that might be mounted against him. The Howards decided it was time for Edward to flee the country, and a detailed plan was generated to elude the FBI.

In September 1985, Howard and his wife left their home for a drive. The pursuing FBI car was not far behind but they were not close enough to observe the activity in the Howard car. Mary Howard propped up a fully dressed dummy in the front seat where her husband had been sitting. On a darkened stretch of highway, Edward Howard exited the car and made his escape. The trailing feds did not notice that their prime suspect had departed into the night. When Mary Howard arrived home, the FBI agents noticed a person in the next seat, thought nothing of it, and ended their night's vigil.

In a roundabout route, Edward Lee Howard left Albuquerque via Copenhagen and Helsinki, finally ending up in Moscow where he sought refuge. He was welcomed with open arms by the KGB and was treated initially like the prodigal son come home. During his years in Moscow, Howard lived in a spacious apartment not far from the Kremlin. He had people to cook his meals, and was protected from unwanted visitors by state-supplied guards. Life in Russia was not what Howard had envisioned and he desperately wanted to see his wife and 9-year-old son again. The boredom of life in Russia was temporarily lessened by the occasional visits of Mary and their son. Soon though, they both returned to the United States.

In 1991, Howard left Russia for Stockholm, Sweden on a temporary basis. He went into the export business and found life better than his restricted existence in Russia. In August 1986, the Russians held a press conference with Howard, who had returned quietly to the Soviet Union, as the main participant. They said that Howard was given Russian citizenship and that he was entitled to all the rights accorded to any other Russian. In 1995, Howard wrote his memoir called *Safe House* in which he tried to explain his defection and his subsequent life in the Soviet Union.

In the wake of the Howard defection, the CIA began an inquiry into the arrest of two of its highly prized agents inside the Soviet Union: Adolf Tolkachev, codenamed GTVANQUISH, and Paul

Stomaugh.

Adolf Tolkachev had been spying for the CIA in Russia for more than six years, working as a specialist in Soviet missile design. In this capacity, he photocopied hundreds of pages of scientific information and gave them to the CIA.

On June 13, 1985, Paul Stombaugh, a CIA officer who served undercover in Moscow as a second secretary in the U.S. embassy, met with Tolkachev who was to give him his secret cache of documents. Stombaugh carried with him more than $150,000 for Tolkachev, along with miniature spy cameras. Suddenly, KGB men who had been observing the scene from concealed locations, bore down on Stombaugh and Tolkachev and put them under arrest. The CIA man was taken to the infamous Lubyanka Prison where he was interrogated. Tolkachev was given a show trial and was subsequently executed on October 22, 1986. Paul Stombaugh was eventually expelled from Russia and returned to the United States.

The fallout from the Stombaugh/Tolkachev case was immediate. It was originally believed that Edward Lee Howard had betrayed both men but it seems clear that Aldrich Ames was the main culprit in the betrayal of Tolkachev. Others in the CIA believed that both Ames and Howard shared the responsibility of giving the men up, leading to the death of one of the CIA's best plants inside the Soviet Union in the decade of the 1980s.

Edward Lee Howard died in Moscow on July 12, 2002, due to an accidental fall in his apartment.

Chapter 42:
The Harold Nicholson Espionage Case

Two of the most important espionage cases of the 1990s involved two very different men, Aldrich Ames and Harold Nicholson. Ames, an unkempt man who drank excessively, was not a very big fish in the CIA pecking order. Harold Nicholson, a 16-year veteran of some of the most sensitive posts in the CIA, was a man on the fast track to even higher positions in the agency. Some people in the intelligence community believe that if Nicholson's espionage on behalf of the Soviet Union weren't discovered, he probably would have been selected as one of the top officers in the Clandestine Service, that part of the CIA that is involved in undercover work in foreign countries. The men had one thing in common: the desire for money in exchange for supplying the Russians with vital secrets. But the difference between what the Russians paid them was startling. Ames received more than $2,000,000 during his 10-year spying career, while Nicholson received only $120,000 over a two-year period. Both men were also involved in bitter divorce settlements that would cost them thousands of dollars, a circumstance which led them to spy for cash.

Harold Nicholson was born on November 17, 1950 in Woodburn, Oregon. His father was an Air Force officer and brought the family along with him to his various duty posts. Harold graduated from Novato High School while his father was stationed at Edwards Air Force Base in California. He graduated from Oregon State University in 1973 with a degree in geography. He later joined the Army and was discharged with the rank of Captain in 1979. While in the Army, he received his master's degree in education from the University of Maryland.

He joined the ranks of the CIA on October 20, 1980 and would remain in the agency until his arrest in 1996. Harold Nicholson was a fast study, gaining valuable experience in his various agency postings, learning the complexities of tradecraft, and making an instant impression among his peers.

What Nicholson did not know was that at the same time that he was working secretly for the Russians, the Soviets had another mole inside the CIA, Aldrich Ames. There is no evidence to suggest that either man knew of the existence of the other. If that was the case, it seems that the KGB wanted to compartmentalize the two men in order to protect them if one was caught.

Nicholson served at Camp Peary, the CIA's training facility in Williamsburg, Virginia. This was a choice assignment for any person who had higher ambitions in the Clandestine Service. As an instructor, he was privy to the detailed backgrounds of all the men and women who passed through the facility, and he later supplied the Soviets with this vital information. This was solid gold to the KGB as they were now in a position to have detailed knowledge of all CIA officers anywhere in the world.

His first overseas assignment came in 1985 when he was sent to Manila, in the Philippines. In Manila he was given the job of trying to recruit Russian intelligence officers. He managed to learn the native language and was seen as a rising star. His next overseas posting were in Bangkok, Thailand (1985 to1987), and Tokyo, Japan (1987 to1989). His work performance was so exceptional that he was promoted to CIA Station Chief in Bucharest, Romania in 1990, a mere 10 years after joining the CIA. In 1992, he left the cold of Eastern Europe and was posted to Kuala Lumpur, Malaysia as the deputy station chief. It was in Malaysia that Nicholson took his first steps, contacting the Soviet embassy and offering his services for a hefty fee.

On June 30, 1994, one day after secretly meeting with the KGB in Kuala Lumpur, Nicholson wired $12,000 to his personal account and paid $6,000 that was due on his credit card account.

In 1995, Nicholson returned to Malaysia (after being posted back to the U.S.), met once again with the KGB, and paid off debts totaling $23,000.

His decision to spy for the Russians was a direct result of a messy divorce from his wife and his affair with a Thai woman he had met in Southeast Asia. Like Aldrich Ames, he decided that the only way to pay for his divorce and his new, expensive lifestyle was to offer his services to the Soviet Union, thus, his constant trips to such places as Malaysia and Thailand.

Over two years, he passed along intelligence to the Soviet Union. Unlike in the Ames case, the CIA, which had unmasked Ames while

Nicholson was continuing his espionage, took exceptional notice of Nicholson's unexplained sudden wealth. Undergoing a series of lie detector tests, Mr. Nicholson was found to be less than candid, and the CIA began an all-inclusive follow up investigation of his daily activities. His home was bugged, his CIA workstation was monitored, and he was tailed by undercover FBI agents who had now begun cooperating on domestic espionage cases with the CIA. The FBI extracted the mail sent by Nicholson to the Russians, postcards with encrypted messages, signed by Nicholson using his alias "Nevil Strachey."

In order to keep better track of Nicholson's espionage activities, he was given a new assignment, this time in the Counter-terrorism Center where he would have limited access to the kind of information that the Soviets might need. He began his new assignment in July 1996 and in between his official duties, Nicholson began to tap into the CIA's computer for his own use. Computer surveillance of Nicholson saw him enter a word search using the terms "Russia," and "Chechnya," information that was not related to his daily work. The smoking gun on his espionage pursuits for the Soviet Union was discovered when the CIA searched his notebook computer and found a bevy of classified documents bearing on numerous Russian topics that he had no business downloading. These materials concerned the assignment of a CIA officer to Moscow, biographical information on CIA officers bound for Russia, and the attempts of Soviet intelligence officers to recruit Americans. Also found in his notebook were debriefing reports of Aldrich Ames, and the codenames of many CIA officers and their job assignments.

The investigation of Nicholson also revealed that he had in his possession a number of secret internal CIA reports concerning Russian military readiness. Undercover watchers also took pictures of Nicholson photographing sensitive documents relating to Russia while at his workstation.

The FBI now had enough incriminating information on Nicholson to make an arrest and they began their final preparations to bring him in. Nicholson, who had no idea that he was under investigation, made plans for a trip to Zurich, Switzerland to meet with his Russian intermediaries. In November 1996, as he was getting ready to board a plane for Zurich, he was nabbed by FBI agents at Dulles Airport.

While the espionage cases of Aldrich Ames and Harold Nicholson intersected, the fallout from each was vastly different. For instance, Ames had been spying for the Russians for over 10 years and his actions led to with the deaths of over a dozen highly placed U.S. agents working in the Soviet Union. The information Ames passed to the Russians was invaluable, giving them a heads-up on years of CIA intelligence gathering missions inside the Soviet Union during the heyday of the Cold War. Nicholson worked for the Russians for only two years and the intelligence he gave them was limited in nature. John Deutch, who was the DCI at the time of Nicholson's arrest, said of the fallout of the case, "It seems unlikely that the damage he caused in any way approaches that done by Ames."

An institutional change resulting from the Nicholson case was the close-nit relationship between the FBI and the CIA when it came to the sharing of intelligence between the departments. During the Nicholson inquiry, FBI agents worked at the CIA's Counter-terrorism Center. Unfortunately, that involvement did not last into the new century, and that proved a disaster during the events leading up to September 11, 2001.

Harold Nicholson is now serving a life sentence for his espionage activities.

Chapter 43:
The Aldrich Ames Spy Case

The most shocking spy case that hit the CIA toward the end of the 20th century was that of Aldrich Ames, a career CIA officer who should never have been hired in the first place. It was the CIA's own fault that they let him stay in the high positions that he was in for so long, without taking the necessary steps to stop the devastation he was wreaking upon the agency.

The Aldrich Ames spy case went on for 10 long years before he was arrested on February 21, 1994. His career as a spy for the Soviet Union took place largely under the watch of DCI William Webster (Webster had left the FBI to take over the CIA) and ended under the directorship of James Woolsey. During the extended time that U.S. intelligence investigated Ames' treachery, the Cold War ended, and the first bombing of the World Trade Center took place.

The man the FBI and the CIA would pursue over the span of ten years was a 25-year veteran of the CIA, Aldrich Ames. He was not what fiction writers would call a "Master Spy," not the James Bond type who went around shooting the enemy, or seducing the most attractive women. Rather, Ames was unkempt in his appearance, a man who liked to drink on the job—a slack off all the way around. If anyone saw Aldrich Ames, they would not believe the important role he played for, and against, the United States.

Unknown to the FBI and the CIA, Ames had been working for the Russians since 1985, giving them some of the most important classified information that the CIA had. For his efforts, he was paid $2.7 million dollars, much of it spent on a Jaguar X16, a mortgage free home in the Washington, D.C. suburbs, and dressy clothes for his wife, and fellow conspirator, Rosario. But Ames was more than an ordinary double agent. The information he gave to the Soviets resulted in the deaths of 10 undercover agents working for the CIA in Russia.

Ames worked in the Soviet/East European Division, where America's covert agents spied on the Soviet Union, and from where undercover officers were infiltrated into the Soviet Union usually on, one-way trips. The Soviet/East European Division was one of the most valuable areas of the Directorate of Operations, and Ames had full knowledge of all its secrets. Never, in the 10 years that Ames was spying for the Russians, did anyone ever suspect that he was anything but a loyal employee.

Ames' father, Carleton, had been a CIA employee and after college, Aldrich ("Rick") too joined the service. His first assignment began in 1969 when he was sent to Ankara, Turkey. During all his time in this hotbed of international espionage, Ames was never able to recruit a single Russian agent.

Back in Washington, Ames was assigned to the counterintelligence section from which he worked for nine years (1972-81). Ames worked in the CIA headquarters at Langley and then in New York where he was assigned to monitor the Russian delegation. Rick had no better luck in New York than in Ankara, at one time leaving sensitive documents in a briefcase on a New York City subway.

In 1969, Ames married his longtime sweetheart, Nancy. However, his excessive drinking, as well as his secret life, caused a strain in their marriage and they were separated in 1983 and finally divorced in 1985.

Rick Ames' was posted to Mexico City in 1981, and it was here that his downfall began. While in Mexico, Ames met Maria del Rosario Casas who worked at the Colombian embassy as a Cultural Attaché. They soon began to date and after a while they were more than just friends. By having a relationship with Rosario Casas, and not informing the CIA, Ames had broken his first rule of tradecraft—to notify his superiors of any contact with foreigners. The couple was married on August 10, 1985 and would later have a son, Paul. The cost of his divorce and Rosario's profligate spending had Ames doing some creative thinking about how to increase his income.

Ames' had returned to the United States in 1983 where, despite his drinking problem, he was given the sensitive post at CIA headquarters of running counterintelligence operations against the Soviet Union. Ames now had one of the most important jobs at the CIA. But unperceived by his colleagues, he began spying for the Russians.

By April 1985, Ames was working in the Soviet/East European

Division at Langley and was able to learn firsthand where all the moles working for the U.S. in Russia were buried, as well as their identities. That same month, Ames went to the Soviet embassy in Washington, ostensibly as part of his job, and offered his services as a spy. He brought with him a number of highly classified CIA documents and shortly thereafter he received his initial payment of $50,000. In December 1985, Ames flew to Bogotá, Colombia where he met with KGB officers and handed over more material.

The first hint at the CIA that some of their most sensitive missions were being compromised came to light in 1985. A significant number of Russian deep cover men were called in and were summarily shot. A number of CIA analysts believed the cases were blown by renegade CIA officer Edward Lee Howard who eluded CIA surveillance and escaped to Moscow in 1985. With Howard gone, he could no longer be the number one suspect when the executions continued.

After reviewing all the evidence, the CIA came to the conclusion that someone had infiltrated the agency, and a mole hunt was started. It was at this time that the FBI and the CIA began to cooperate in the mole hunt investigation. On orders from DCI William Casey, the agency organized a Special Task Force made up of four officers under the auspices of the CI Staff. The FBI also undertook a probe to see if there was a mole inside the bureau.

For their part, the FBI organized a group to look into the losses at the CIA. The FBI's Deputy Assistant Director for Intelligence appointed a six-member panel called the ANLACE Task Force to monitor events as they progressed. Like the CIA, they said that Edward Lee Howard might have been the culprit but could not definitely say so. The ANLACE investigation ran out of steam and collapsed without any further action being taken.

The joint probe wound down by 1988 as the CIA turned its attention to the creation of a Counterintelligence Center (CIC). The FBI took a lot of flack when they turned down an invitation by the CIA to send a representative to join the new CIC. Tensions between the two agencies continued to erode when the FBI told the CIA that they believed that a mole had probably penetrated the CIA, and that they agency itself would have to uncover that person.

For a period of three years, the former joint FBI-CIA investigation of the mole inside the CIA was moribund. However, by 1991, events changed and cooperation was once more the order of the day. The FBI sent one of its agents to work out of the CIA's mole hunting unit called SIU, Special Investigative Unit. In addition, the FBI's Washington Field Office began its own probe. With all this so-called cooperation going on, it seems strange that FBI Director Webster was never informed by the CIA that FBI personnel had joined the mole hunt investigation.

The CIA Inspector General's report on the Ames case noted that "the FBI could have taken over the Ames case completely in 1991 but apparently concluded it did not have sufficient cause to open an intensive CIA investigation directed specifically at Ames." The FBI was told of Ames' sudden wealth, which coincided with his meetings with the Russians, and their subsequent payoffs to him. However, this information was not sufficient to warrant a full investigation by them.

While the mole hunt sputtered, Ames was transferred to Rome where his secret life gained in intensity. At a diplomatic gathering, Ames met his new Russian contact. Ames was in a strategic position to funnel all manner of intelligence regarding American double agents working inside the Soviet Union and he did so without any second thought. The security inside the U.S. embassy was so lax that all Ames had to do was walk out of the building with his copied material stuffed inside bulging shopping bags. He received $50,000 for his first load and would get more as time went on.

If Ames had success in his secret life as a Russian spy, his overall work performance with the CIA stagnated. He continued to drink heavily, often returning to work drunk and then falling asleep at his desk. His work evaluation suffered and the CIA would write a blunt appraisal of him saying, "His full potential had not been realized here in Rome."

In the summer of 1989, the CIA transferred Ames back to the United States. Before leaving Rome, Ames had one last meeting with his Soviet controller, "Vlad." Vlad thanked Ames for his work and told him that the Russians had deposited two million dollars in his various accounts.

Back at Langley, Ames was assigned to the important post of Western Europe Branch Chief of Soviet counterintelligence. It was during this time period that the CIA began to get wind of Ames' lavish spending and began a quiet, but detailed probe of his personal affairs. When questioned about his new lifestyle, Ames said that the money came from a large inheritance that Rosario got from her family.

On April 12, 1991, the FBI gave Ames a polygraph test, a routine examination often given to agency employees. If Ames had any worry about the outcome of the polygraph, he needn't have. The operator did not delve too explicitly into Ames' personal life. The only red flag came up when he was asked if he had any unauthorized contacts with foreigners, not approved by the CIA. He was able to fool the questioner regarding his secret meeting with Vlad. For all intents and purposes, Ames had passed the test.

By 1992, the CIA and the FBI narrowed down their list of suspects to just over a dozen, with Ames' name still in the mix. When an unidentified CIA officer reported her misgivings about Ames' sudden wealth, a full court press investigation into his personal and professional life began.

The most important evidence linking Ames to being the mole centered on the FBI's correlation between the deposits he made and his operational meetings with the Russians. By tracing the days he made his deposits to the times he met his Soviet handlers; the investigators began to lay culpability at Ames' feet.

Ames unwittingly tipped off the CIA to his secret life when, in October 1992, he told his superiors that he would be traveling to Colombia to visit Rosario's relatives. Instead of going to Colombia, Ames diverted to Caracas, Venezuela. Ames was followed to Caracas by undercover FBI agents who saw him meeting with KGB officers in that city. They now had all the proof they needed to make an arrest.

When Ames was away from his desk, undercover officers searched his workstation, retrieved information from his hard drive and found irrefutable evidence of Ames' treason. At his computer were diskettes and hard copies of top-secret materials that Ames had no business having access to. At night, FBI agents rifled through his trash and found more incriminating evidence. They bugged his home phone, and retrieved the ribbon from his typewriter, which contained letters and messages to his Soviet contacts.

With all the pieces now fitting into place, the CIA reassigned Ames to the Counter-Narcotics Section in order to limit his further entree to sensitive information. On February 21, 1994, as Ames was heading for work, he was arrested by waiting FBI agents. Also arrested that day was his wife, Rosario.

Ames' treachery led to the deaths of 10 double agents in the Soviet Union who were working for the CIA, and the derailment of numerous covert operations.

The subsequent investigation by the Permanent Committee on Intelligence of the U.S. House of Representatives, gave both praise and condemnation to the FBI and CIA in their work on the Ames case. On the upside: "Although proof of his espionage activities was not obtained until after the FBI began its CI investigation of Ames in 1993, the CIA mole hunt team played a critical role in providing a context for the opening of an intensive investigation by the FBI. Moreover, although the CIA and the FBI have had disagreements and difficulties with coordination in other cases in the past, there is ample evidence to support the statements by both FBI and CIA senior management that the Ames case was *a model of CI cooperation between the two agencies* (italics by author)."

The Congressional Investigation of the Ames affair had harsh words for the CIA. Among the areas they described the agency as deficient in were the following:

First, Agency leaders had not moved quickly enough to overcome the distaste for internal security functions, which had been engendered by the excesses of the Angleton years. The CIA did not have a fully functioning internal counterespionage capability when Aldrich Ames compromised the Agency's most important Soviet agents in 1985.

Three major components of the CIA—operations, counterintelligence and security—failed to work together initially as part of the investigation.

Although the level of cooperation between the CIA and the FBI was unprecedented, the sharing of information was not always timely. While several officials interviewed by the Committee had concluded by the late 1980s, that the losses had been caused by a human penetration, some CIA investigators were reluctant to share source information, even with the FBI, although the FBI is the principle government agency responsible for the conduct of espionage investigations.

Aldrich Ames is now serving a life sentence without the possibility of parole.

Chapter 44:
The CIA Hunts the Jackal

On August 16, 1994, the world's newspapers caught the attention of the public by announcing the capture of one of the most important terrorists of the day, Ilich Ramirez Sanchez, a.k.a., "Carlos the Jackal." "Carlos" had been wanted by Western intelligence agencies for numerous crimes, including bombings and assassinations, from Western Europe to the Middle East.

The surprise announcement came from the French Interior Minister, Charles Pasque, who said that Carlos, then 44 years old, had been arrested in Sudan and was flown secretly to France. He told the assembled newsmen in a packed room that his prisoner "was one of the most well known and most dangerous criminals in the world."

For a man of such glamour and celebrity as the paramount terrorist of his day, Carlos spent the last year of his life in seclusion in an apartment in Damascus, Syria, virtually out of the spotlight that he had craved for so long. It was said that he took to drink in order to while away the days that turned into months.

The full circumstances of his arrest were not clear but he was arrested by the government of Sudan and sent to France where he faced a life sentence for the killings of two French policemen in 1975. Who was "Carlos the Jackal" and how did he become one of the most wanted men of the 1970s?

Ilich Ramirez Sanchez was born in Venezuela, but left his home at an early age to seek out the militant, pro-revolutionary groups then in vogue throughout the world. In September 1968, Ilich and his brother Lenin arrived at the Patrice Lumumba University in Moscow. But the cold, hard Russian winters were not what the young Ilich expected and he soon turned to drinking and street demonstrations. During one altercation with Russian police he was arrested but soon released.

He came from two very different parents. His father, Jose Altagracia Ramirez Navas, was an admirer of Lenin and saw to it that one of his sons was named after the famous revolutionary.

285

His mother was Elba Maria Sanchez who wanted her sons to be educated in a Christian environment, something her husband was not fond of. Ilich got his political education from his lawyer father who endowed him with the Marxist/Leninist system, something he'd carry with him all his life.

By 1958, his parents were undergoing a personal crisis and Elba took her three sons to Kingston, Jamaica before going to Mexico, and then returning to Venezuela. Soon, Elba and Jose were divorced but continued to live apart in Caracas.

As a dedicated Marxist, it was said that his father sent Ilich to Cuba in late 1966 to finish his education under the auspices of Fidel Castro's authoritarian regime. It is believed that Carlos underwent training at Camp Mantanzas, outside of Havana, that was run by the DGI (Cuban intelligence) and the KGB under the command of General Viktor Semenov, of the KGB. Years later, a member of the French intelligence service said that Ilich underwent "terrorist training in Cuba (automatic arms, explosives, bombs, mines, destruction of pipelines, cryptography, photography, falsification of documents, etc.). Later, Carlos denied the story that he had been in Cuba. "I read that I went to the Mantanzas camp," said Carlos, "and was trained in terrorist methods. All that is fable." Documents later revealed that General Semenov was appointed head of the KGB in Havana in 1968, not 1966 when Carlos was supposedly in Cuba.

It seems that the reports that Carlos was in Cuba were fabrications on the part of the CIA. The CIA said that the information they got on Carlos' presence in Cuba came from a DGI defector named Orlando Carlos Hidalgo. Hidalgo said that Carlos was one of as many as 1,500 Latin Americans who were trained in Cuba each year. A member of the CIA's counter-terrorism task force said that he had no official documentation that placed Carlos in Cuba at that time.[1]

The French intelligence services echoed the false reports that Carlos had been in Cuba by saying, "U.S. intelligence gives it to be understood that Ilich may have been sent to Cuba by his father in 1966. The recruitment of Ilich by the DGI, it concludes, is at best difficult and at worst impossible to establish."

In 1966, the Ramirez brothers (and their mother) moved to

[1] Follain, John, *Jackal: The Complete Story of the Legendary Terrorist, Carlos the Jackal,* Arcade Publishing Company, New York, 1998, Page 9-10.

England where Ilich attended classes at the Stafford House Tutorial College in Kensington, where he took classes in English, physics, and math. It was through the efforts of his father that Ilich and his brother Lenin moved to Moscow in 1968, where they attended Patrice Lumumba University. There has been much speculation at the time whether or not the KGB had anything to do with the transfer of Ilich to Moscow. He later said about his attendance at the university, "Even before I arrived in Moscow, I got in touch with the KGB in London through the resident at the Soviet embassy. Thanks to this contact I was able to get a visa for Moscow and a plane ticket, despite the fact that I hadn't been granted a scholarship that year because it had gone to my brother Lenin. This gave me a certain weight in Moscow."

At the university he studied the Russian language, Marxist teachings, and submerged himself in Russian culture. If he wasn't a dedicated Marxist before arriving at the university, he was now.

During his time at Patrice Lumumba University he made contacts with many of the militant Palestinian students who also attended the school. For a short time in 1969, he visited his parents who were now living in England, but he soon disappeared, heading for the Middle East. While visiting Jordan, he was expelled from the university. Amid the terrorist training camps in Jordan, Ilich became "Carlos," a code name he'd used for the rest of his life.

Carlos moved to Lebanon where he made contacts with Dr. George Habash, the founder of the PFLP (the Popular Front for the Liberation of Palestine) whose organization worked hand-in-glove with him, and taught him the necessary terrorist skills he'd put to good use throughout the decade of the 1970s. Carlos' first mission was to hijack a train carrying Jews en route from Czechoslovakia to Austria.

Soon, Carlos flew to Beirut, where the PFLP had moved during the Jordanian-Palestinian civil war of September 1970. He then took training with the group's special operations unit. It was rumored in certain intelligence circles that Carlos, as his reputation grew, took part in the killings of Israeli athletes at the 1972 Munich Olympics. The bloody incident was carried out by Black September, a Palestinian terrorist group.

His next victim was Joseph Sieff, the president of the Marks and

Spencer stores in London. Sieff, a prominent British Jew was in his home on the night of December 7, 1973 when Carlos barged past Sieff's butler and shot him in the head at close range. Somehow, Sieff survived and Carlos managed to slip away. Now acting on his own, Carlos traveled to Paris where he sent a grenade spinning into a crowd at a Latin Quarter drugstore, killing two and wounding 34 more.

His next act of terror was to shoot a rocket-propelled grenade at an El Al airliner at Orly Airport in January 1975. However he missed, hitting a Yugoslav plane instead.

By now, the Israeli Mossad was hot on Carlos' trail, and working closely with the French security service, DST, they were led by a double agent named Michel Murkobal to the home in Paris where Carlos was hiding. As the police entered Carlos' flat, he killed three DST men, including Murkobal.

But his most daring escapade took place during Christmastime, 1975. The object of his attack was the annual summit meeting of the ministers of OPEC (Organization of Petroleum Exporting Countries) in Vienna, Austria. Security was minimal at the headquarters site and within minutes Carlos and his trained crew had taken more than 70 hostages. Carlos began negotiations with the Austrian police who had surrounded the building. In the end, Carlos and his band were given safe passage out of the country, taking 15 OPEC ministers with him on his getaway plane. When his plane landed in Algiers, he let the hostages go free. Carlos' share of the ransom was a cool $1 million.

By the late 1970s, Carlos had established a covert relationship with Edwin Wilson, an ex-CIA agent turned arms dealer who was supplying Libyan leader Muammar Qaddafi with illegal plastic explosives. In a public broadcasting interview on *The McNeil-Lehrer News Hour,* former KGB General Oleg Kalugin, once chief of the KGB counterintelligence unit, said that Carlos was never employed by the KGB and might have been working for the Libyans.

The SDECE, the French intelligence service, was hell bent on finding Carlos, no matter the cost. In 1977, the job of finding Carlos was given to Phillipe Rondot, a graduate of the French military academy Saint-Cry. In military circles, Rondot was called the French Lawrence of Arabia due to his brilliance and daring in the field. Members of the Action Service were sent to Colombia where

Carlos' mother Elba now lived. In 1977, Carlos was spotted in a café in Colombia and Action officers were seated near him, hoping for a chance to extract him back to France. Carlos was within earshot of the officers, and one of them made the mistake of speaking French. Carlos heard the man speak and bolted from the café.

Another crazy scheme called for Action Service officers to make contact with Carlos' father, Ramirez Navas who was then living in San Cristobal, Venezuela. It is believed that Rondot went to San Cristobal where he was to befriend Ramirez Navas and slip into his drink a concentrate of the hepatitis virus. It was thought that Carlos, upon hearing of his father's illness, would rush to his side and would be captured. The go-ahead, however, never was given.

If any plan to assassinate Carlos had been given, it would have to have been approved by then French President Valery Giscard d'Estaing. When he was asked by a reporter if he had ever given any such order, President d'Estaing said, "There was no question of shooting him down. The order was never given. The order was to identify him, to follow him, to become intimate with his family and thus to find out his movement and to intercept him when he came to Europe. There was no plan for an operation over there. The officers did not suggest one to me. We respected international law and justice, we wanted to try him." But the former President confided: "If there had been an attack, if Carlos had been armed, things would have been different."[2]

In December 1982, the CIA's Paris station chief John Siddel made a call to the head of the DST, Yves Bonnet. He told Bonnet that the CIA received a tip from a Syrian informant that Carlos was sighted in Damascus and that he was planning to travel under a Swiss passport in the very near future to the Swiss city of Gstaad over the Christmas holidays. Siddel said he had the name of the hotel where Carlos was staying and the date of his arrival. The Interior Minister of France, Gaston Defferre gave the OK for his men to try to get Carlos. The DST was like the American FBI and was not allowed to take action outside of the territory of France. However, Defferre decided to carry out the mission without informing the French President of his impending actions.

The job of actually taking down Carlos in Gstaad went to a Colonel Christian Prouteau who headed France's new antiterrorist

[2] Ibid, Page 115.

unit. Colonel Prouteau and a number of his men went to Gstaad to intercept Carlos. Much to their bitter disappointment, Carlos was not to be found.

Back in Paris, Bonnet was livid with John Siddel, berating him for giving them false intelligence on Carlos. Siddel responded by saying that his source was given a polygraph test and passed.

In 1984, the ambassadors to Washington from a number of Warsaw Pact countries-Bulgaria, Czechoslovakia, East Germany, Hungary and Romania—met at the State Department with Mark Palmer, the deputy assistant secretary responsible for Eastern Europe and the Soviet Union. Palmer told the ambassadors that the United States had information that those countries were protecting Carlos and his men. Palmer said that if they wanted to continue to be on good terms with Washington, they'd have to cut their ties with Carlos. The ambassadors flatly denied any association with Carlos.

What Palmer failed to tell the ambassadors was that the CIA had documented proof of Carlos' whereabouts in Eastern Europe and knew when and where he was going to be at a certain time. Palmer urged his superiors to mount a plan to either capture or kill Carlos. However, Bill Casey, then DCI, rejected the idea. The CIA also hired a man with a checkered past to find Carlos. This man had been a terrorist but the agency decided to use him anyway. Dewey Clarridge said of the CIA's use of this unidentified man, "Sometimes in the spy business you don't have a choice with whom you deal; unfortunately, it is often the unsavory individuals who have the critical information."

The CIA was however, still hot on his trail. After the First Gulf War, Carlos went to Sudan where a Syrian contact told the agency of his arrival. The CIA sent an undercover team to Khartoum and the men made covert contact with him, even having drinks with him at a local club. The team managed to get Carlos' fingerprints and had them analyzed. The prints came back positive, but orders from Washington said not to attempt to kidnap the Jackal.

By 1994, with Carlos now in residence in Sudan, his luck finally ran out. He was no longer considered a major threat and was turned over to French authorities. Carlos' exploits hit the big screen with the 1973 movie *The Day of the Jackal,* based on the novel by Frederick Forsythe.

Chapter 45:
George H.W. Bush Arrives at Langley

No other CIA director has had the pedigree that George Herbert Walker Bush brought with him when he took over the scandal-ridden CIA in 1976. Although he was to serve as DCI for less than one year, he became one of the most popular leaders among the rank and file at Langley headquarters. To his bevy of opponents, Bush was a caretaker who aligned the CIA with the most notorious regimes, whose intelligence services ran rampant across the world, disregarding the rule of law.

George H.W. Bush arrived at the CIA at a time when the agency was in the throes of a wide-open scandal that allowed the American public access to all its dirty laundry. By the time Bush took over the reigns at the CIA, the Watergate affair, in which the CIA was implicated, was still a lingering memory. President Nixon had tried to use the CIA to cover up his association with the Watergate burglars, and a number of the men who took part in the Watergate break-in were former members of the agency (Howard Hunt, James McCord).

In 1976, the Senate, under the leadership of Idaho Senator Frank Church, was conducting open hearings on past CIA abuses, including foreign assassination plots, illegal CIA domestic mail openings, and the revelation of the so-called "Family Jewels" which detailed numerous agency misdeeds over the years. The American public was growing skeptical of the way the agency was operating and called for the abuses to stop. The Congress decided to conduct oversight activities over the CIA, and intelligence committees in both the House and the Senate were formed.

After Gerald Ford replaced Richard Nixon in 1974, the new President decided to keep DCI William Colby in place. But as the scandals erupted, President Ford determined to replace Colby with someone less controversial. The man he finally chose was not his number one pick (the influential Washington lawyer Edward Bennet Williams turned down the job). The position went by default to George H.W. Bush; a conservative Texan who had impressive job resumes in both the social and political worlds. He was also a real-life World War II hero.

George H.W. Bush was the son of a former Senator from Connecticut, Prescott Bush. He was a graduate of Yale and was a member of the close-knit society called Skull and Bones. Although his family had its roots in the Texas soil, George Bush was at home at Yale, and at the family summer home at Kennebunkport, Maine. In 1948, George, his wife Barbara and their small son, George W., headed home to the Midland-Odessa section of Texas where Bush would begin his career in the vast booming Texas oil business. In 1953, Bush opened up his own oil company called Zapata Petroleum with money backed up by both family and Wall Street executives, including those at the firm of Brown Brothers Harriman. Zapata drilled dozens of wells and soon moved their growing enterprise to Houston where they organized another venture called Zapata Offshore Company. Bush used his powerful father's political connections to his full advantage and he soon became a millionaire, making friends with both Americans and the growing international cadre of foreign investors who were flooding Texas, including many members of the Royal Saudi government. He would use these connections with the Saudis later in his presidency during the 1991 Gulf War.

In 1966, George Bush made a decision that would affect the rest of his life: he sold his controlling shares in Zapata Oil, cashed in $1 million in profits, and set upon a new career, politics.

The Bush story involves oil, politics, and spying. Over the years there had been rumors that George Bush was working in some informal capacity for the CIA. It is not inconceivable that during his travels throughout Latin America on his oil exploring business, that Bush did favors for the CIA, reporting the political and economic conditions in the countries he'd visited.

The early Bush-CIA connection is spelled out by Joseph Trento in his book *Prelude to Terror: The Rogue CIA and the Legacy of America's Private Intelligence Network*. He writes that while Bush had no prior knowledge of the Bay of Pigs invasion of Cuba in April 1961, the CIA used his Zapata Offshore Company to place certain counterintelligence people across the Caribbean to try and protect the invasion plan from being leaked. Trento quotes a man named

John Sherwood, a former CIA agent, as saying that Bush's role was to "provide cover to allow our people to set up training facilities and invasion launch points against Cuba in the 1960-61 period. We had to pay off politicians in Mexico, Guatemala, Costa Rica, and elsewhere. Bush's company was used as a conduit for these funds under the guise of oil business contracts. We used his company to find Cuban refugees jobs. Bush wasn't even told what the money was for, although he damn well knew what we were up to."[1]

Like John F. Kennedy before him, George Bush used his status as a World War II hero to his advantage. He was the youngest pilot in the Navy and had his plane shot out from under him in the Pacific theater. He was elected to Congress in 1967 and would serve two terms in the House of Representatives. In 1970, Congressman Bush gave up his seat and ran against Lloyd Bentsen for the Texas Senate seat and was defeated. Bush did not have long to ponder his fate and was soon on his way, thanks to President Richard Nixon, to a further career in national and international politics. The following years saw Bush becoming the American Ambassador to the United Nations, the American Representative to China, a return home to become the head of the Republican National Committee, and in 1976, he was nominated by President Ford to become CIA Director.

Bush, who had his own post-CIA presidential ambitions always in the back of his mind, did everything he could to deflect any wrongdoing on the part of the CIA away from the director's chair. Bush moved to make peace with the congressional oversight committees, structuring a deal whereby he would be more receptive to congressional mandates, and in return, the committees would give the agency a freer hand in conducting its business.

While his tenure at the CIA did not involve any important covert operations, he used the CIA in the new war against America's enemies in third world countries in Africa, the Middle East, and Latin America. His detractors also complained that he used known thugs and gangsters, many of whom were allied with the United States (including Manuel Noriega) without regard to their past abuses. Conspiracy theorists went so far as to accuse Bush of being in the CIA at the time of the Kennedy assassination, and having

[1] Trento, Joseph, *Prelude To Terror: The Rouge CIA and the Legacy of America's Private Intelligence Network,* Carroll & Graf Publishers, New York, 2005, Page 17.

something to do with the events of November 22, 1963.

Unlike previous DCIs, Bush came to the agency without any prior intelligence experience. That did not stop him from becoming a favorite of the career intelligence bureaucrats, who saw Bush as a non-threatening boss who would let them run the shop.

As DCI, Bush first turned his attention to the proxy war then going on in Angola between factions allied with the United States and the Soviet Union. Using American friends in Africa, the CIA oversaw a covert supply of arms to the pro-Western forces in that country. America's main objective in Angola was to curb the ever-growing military aid going to the rebels from their Soviet and Cuban allies.

Bush relied heavily on his DDCI (Deputy Director Central Intelligence) for his assistance and expertise, Henry Knoche. Knoche had served as a naval officer in World War II and Korea but he had little or no intelligence experience. He replaced General Vernon Walters, who was very well versed in intelligence matters and took part in the Watergate affair when the Nixon administration tried to put the blame for the break-in on the CIA. Knoche was not very well liked in the CIA and he was soon relegated to a post where he had little day-to-day say in running the agency. He resigned his post four months after Bush left the CIA.

Another person of some note who Bush appointed to a position of importance during his tenure was Theodore Shackley, who became the associate deputy director for operations. Shackley gained his reputation during the 1960s when he was part of the CIA's efforts to kill Fidel Castro. Working out of the Miami station, he helped run Operation Mongoose, the Kennedy administration's hit and run raids against military targets inside Cuba. Shackley would later team up with the disgraced CIA renegade agent Edwin Wilson in his schemes to sell military equipment to Libya.

The problem of Edwin Wilson and his links with the Qaddafis of Libya posed a potential problem for Bush in the early 80s. By now, the agency had full knowledge of Wilson's arrangement with Qaddafi, as well as the fact that certain former CIA officers including Thomas Clines, Kevin Mculahy, and Rafael Quintero had been working with Wilson in his illegal schemes. The last thing that Bush needed was another CIA scandal, and he took the extraordinary step of ridding the CIA of this problem by notifying the FBI about Wilson and letting them run with the ball. Wilson would ultimately be lured back to the United States where he was arrested for his illegal activities with Libya.

As the new DCI, Bush also sent a memo to all CIA employees notifying them that it was the stated policy of the agency not to engage in political assassinations. The revelations coming from the Church Committee about previous CIA assassination attempts on foreign leaders was not to be repeated during Bush's watch. Bush was a professional politician and he knew the realities of realpolitik in the 1980s. On Bush's watch, the CIA faced its first terrorist attack on American soil, an event that few people even knew about. The incident revolved around a number of Cuban American groups called the Coordination of United Revolutionary Organizations (CORU). Many of these men had previously been associated with the CIA during the 1960s, when the agency targeted Castro for elimination. A number of these Cuban dissidents set off bombs at the Cuban United Nations building in New York, as well as other locations in the Americas.

The man at the center of these hemispheric terrorist attacks was a doctor named Orlando Bosch who joined forces with CORU to foment anti-Castro terror throughout Latin America. To the CIA's and Bush's credit, they learned of a plot hatched by Bosch to kill Henry Kissinger and notified the government of Costa Rica, who picked Bosch up before he could carry out the plot.

The biggest strike against Bush during his time at Langley was the assassination of Orlando Letelier, the former Chilean Ambassador to the United States. Letelier, a harsh critic of the repressive regime in Chile, was killed, along with an American woman named Ronnie Moffitt, along the busy streets of Washington, D.C. The killers of Letelier were part of a hit squad made up of intelligence agents from various Latin American countries dubbed Operation Condor. It was soon ascertained that the government of Chile was responsible for the attack, and that two of its hit men were allowed inside the United States to carry out the assassination.

The investigation of the Letelier-Moffitt killings was handed over to a federal prosecutor named Eugene Propper. Propper contacted Bush and asked him for a meeting. At the meeting were Bush and his general counsel, Anthony Lapham. Bush stunned Propper by telling him that for security and operational reasons involving ongoing CIA sources and methods, the agency would not cooperate with the feds' investigation of the murders. Bush covered up the fact that the assassination was carried out by DINA, the Chilean intelligence service, with the approval of its security chief, Manuel Contreras, who at one time was a paid CIA asset. Bush also knew that the man who came to the U.S. to carry out the assassination was Michael Townley and that Townley was in Washington. However, nothing was done to intercept Townley.

Bush also had a covert relationship with General Manuel Noriega of Panama, a known drug dealer and overall thug. Panama was an important American ally in Latin America, thanks in large part to the vital Panama Canal. Bush and President Reagan determined to overlook Noriega's illicit drug dealings in favor of his support for American policies. As President, Bush would invade Panama and remove Noriega from power.

Noriega had a long-standing relationship with the CIA, having been recruited by the agency in Lima, Peru in 1959. He was paid for his services until 1962 when he returned to Panama from other military duties. Noriega served as a paid informer for the CIA until 1976 while serving as an important military figure in Panama under the regime of General Omar Torrijos.

Noriega became a problem for the CIA (and for Bush) in March 1976 when he came under investigation by the U.S. Defense Intelligence Agency; they mounted an investigation of him for buying secret intelligence information from three U.S. Army soldiers in Panama. The men were called "The Singing Sergeants" by DIA officers. Noriega gave the information to General Torrijos to help him blackmail the United States into making concessions to Panama in the negotiations over the Panama Canal treaty that were then going on. The DIA feared that Noriega gave the information to Fidel Castro.

Bush decided not to prosecute the "Singing Sergeants" for fear that their revelations, if made public, would seriously wound the CIA, as well as relations between Panama and the United States. Bush was in a precarious position over the incident. The possibility existed that there was a mole inside the CIA and that information had to be kept secret at all costs. The CIA did not need another "mole hunt" that could, once again, wreak havoc inside Langley.

Bush also had to cover up the fact that Noriega, a known drug dealer, was one of the most important CIA assets inside Panama and throughout Latin America. The Noriega secret had to be kept quiet at all costs.

With the election of Jimmy Carter to the presidency in 1976, George Bush's days at the CIA were numbered. The new President decided not to rehire Bush and replaced him with Admiral Stansfield Turner.

In 1980, Republican presidential nominee Ronald Reagan picked Bush to be his vice presidential candidate and they were elected in a landslide over President Carter. Bush won the 1988 Republican presidential nomination and handily defeated Massachusetts Governor Michael Dukakis in the election. He served for one term in the White House and was defeated by Governor Bill Clinton in 1992.

In recognition of his service at the CIA, Congress passed a law in 1998 naming CIA headquarters the "George H.W. Bush Center for Central Intelligence," a rather nice payoff for a man who had little intelligence experience to begin with.

Chapter 46:
The CIA-Iran Contra Connection

The Iran-Contra affair had all the necessary ingredients for a good novel: arms traded for hostages, an illegal diversion of funds to a rebel force fighting the communists in Central America, and a rogue spy operation being run by the President's own men, right in the basement of the White House. The "Enterprise," the name by which the entire Iran-Contra operation was called, was staffed by a number of ex-CIA officers who played a vital role in the sordid affair that almost destroyed the Reagan administration.

The Iran-Contra affair was not fiction, but a large-scale covert operation that dominated the last few years of the presidency of Ronald Reagan. It involved not only the United States but also other nations, such as Israel, Saudi Arabia, and a number of governments in Central America. The people who participated in the arms-for-hostages negotiations, and the subsequent diversion of funds to the Contras in Nicaragua were an assorted lot that would make any spy novelist proud. Among them were CIA agents, Middle Eastern arms dealers of varied political persuasions, top White House officials and cabinet officers, and a little-known Marine Lt. Colonel named Oliver North, who would play a central role in the affair.

The roots of the scandal lay in the Middle East, where Iran, once the United States' most trusted ally in the region (with the exception of Israel), had gone through a revolutionary period in which its ruler, the Shah of Iran, was deposed by the revolutionary government headed by the Ayatollah Khomeini. During the Carter administration, the Khomeini government seized the United States embassy and held our citizens in total isolation for 444 days. In November 1979, President Carter ordered a halt to U.S. arms shipments to Iran in response to the illegal takeover of the embassy. The unsuccessful attempt by American Special Forces to free the hostages resulted in a military disaster in the sands of the Iranian desert. The American public, weary of the lack of resolve by the Carter administration vis a vis the Iranian situation, fired the President and elected Ronald Reagan in 1980.

Once the hostages were released on January 20, 1981, the day that Ronald Reagan took office, a new phase in the hostile relationship between the United States and Iran began. In the early 1980s, a number of American civilians working in Lebanon and other Middle Eastern countries were taken captive by anti-U.S. radical groups. Among those held hostage was William Buckley, the CIA Station Chief in Lebanon. Buckley was later killed by his kidnappers.

With the ban on official U.S. arms shipments to Iran in place, a number of private American firms illegally tried to cut deals with the Khomeini regime but were unsuccessful. Israel, in the early 1980s (and before), had been secretly supplying arms to the Shah of Iran on a private basis, with tacit American approval. In 1982, Israeli Defense Minister Ariel Sharon proposed that Washington look at the possibility of selling arms to Iran in order to open a channel of communications between the two countries (the deal was rejected).

The events at the origin of what would become the Iran-Contra affair took place in 1985 when Adolph Schwimmer and Yaacov Ninrodi, men who had covert ties to then Israeli Prime Minister Shimon Peres, were negotiating their own arms deal with Iran. They were contacted by an arms dealer, known to the CIA, named Manucher Ghorbanifar who said that Iran was interested in buying American TOW missiles.

In the Reagan White House, a new policy was being developed to stop the Russian influence in Iran. National Security Advisor Robert McFarlane's staff recommended that the U.S. proceed with a limited policy of allowing a small amount of American-produced armaments to be sold to Iran.

While all these backchannel dealings were going on, the Reagan administration was backing the Nicaraguan exiles, the Contras, rebels who were fighting to overthrow the communist-backed Sandinista government.

The CIA had by now gotten into the secret arms supply operation vis a vis the Israelis and the Contras. In 1983, the U.S. and Israel made a deal to allow captured arms seized from the Palestine Liberation Organization (PLO) to be sent to the U.S. Department of Defense with the CIA as the intermediary. This secret deal was called Operation Tipped Kettle and was developed by ex-Air Force

Major General Richard Secord and Israeli General Menachem Meron. This plan would, in 1985, join the United States and Israel together in a common pact to supply American-built arms to Iran in exchange for the release of Americans being held captive in the Middle East.

At CIA headquarters, DCI William Casey took the reigns of the Contra supply effort. In March 1981, President Reagan granted the CIA permission to spend $19 million on covert activities directed against the Nicaraguan government, and gave permission to the agency to create a 500-man paramilitary force and a political "action team" that would work exclusively inside Nicaragua. During testimony to the congressional oversight committees, Casey deliberately withheld the fact that the stated purpose of the U.S. was to dethrone the Sandinista regime.

The CIA began its secret war against the Sandinista government by mining Nicaraguan harbors, and began intensive training of the ragtag Contra army. The agency developed a Contra manual that recommended the murder of certain members of the Sandinista government, in a direct violation of a law passed by Congress that prohibited assassination as an instrument of American foreign policy.

The now not-so-secret war in Nicaragua was a growing concern for Congress, which, in December 1983, passed a bill that put an official limit of $24 million that could be used to supply the Contras. In a further effort to curb the war in Nicaragua, a bill sponsored by U.S. Representative Edward Boland was passed that prohibited the U.S. government from supplying funds for the overthrow of the Nicaraguan government.

But that impediment did not stop the Reagan administration from backing the Contras. A high intensity campaign to aid the Contras, and buck the Boland Amendment, was taken away from the CIA (not really), and diverted to the National Security Council (NSC) under the direction of a little-known Vietnam veteran, Lt. Colonel Oliver North. The war against the Sandinistas would now take a major turn: the diversion of funds from the sale of arms to Iran and the use of the profits to fund the Contras. This covert campaign would be run by numerous CIA officers, who would play their own, unique roles in the burgeoning scandal.

Despite the passage of the Boland Amendment, the Reagan administration decided on an extralegal operation that would funnel military aid and cash to the Contras. President Reagan's secret emissaries approached such countries as Saudi Arabia, Israel, and South Africa to provide aid to the Contras. Saudi Arabia funneled millions of dollars in aid to the Contras for the purpose of purchasing needed military supplies.

As mentioned before, the day-to-day operations of the Contra war were transferred from the CIA to the NSC. DCI William Casey oversaw the entire project and handed over the operational reigns to Lt. Colonel North who worked hand in glove with Casey and the CIA agents on the ground in Nicaragua. Oliver North was taken to neighboring Honduras where he met the leadership of the Contra army and pledged continued United States assistance.

One of the key players in what became known as the "Enterprise" was Robert McFarlane, President Reagan's National Security Advisor. He contacted many rich Americans who were sympathetic to the Reagan cause of backing the Contras and persuaded them to donate large amounts of money. This money was to be funneled through the NSC, under the direct supervision of Lt. Colonel North. North brought others into his scheme, including former U.S. Air Force Major General Richard Secord, who had his own widespread contacts with ex-CIA officers whom he brought into the game. Also in the "Enterprise" was Albert Hakim, an Iranian businessman who established a covert network of dummy corporations around the world that would launder and collect the private funds going to the Contras.

By 1985, the flow of arms bought by the "Enterprise" started heading to the Contras. In order to facilitate the shipment of arms to the rebels, the government of Israel was brought in to act as a middleman. The U.S. would send TOW missiles and other arms to Israel for further transshipment to the Contras. Later, the U.S. would reimburse Israel for its efforts by sending new arms that were taken out of our stockpiles. The person who acted as the official go-between in the arms for hostage talks was Manucher Ghorbanifar, even though the CIA did not trust him. When the agency rejected his earlier efforts to aid them as an international arms and information broker, Ghorbanifar retaliated against the CIA by providing false information to them via other conduits. In 1984, Ghorbanifar failed a polygraph test given to him by the CIA in which he said he had information on a possible assassination attempt on the men running for President in the 1984 United States national elections. In a final affront, the CIA sent out a worldwide "burn notice" telling all friendly government agencies and intelligence services not to have anything to do with him.

As the Contra-CIA connection began to take shape, General Secord brought into the action a former CIA operative who had ties to the Bay of Pigs invasion of 1961, Rafael "Chi Chi" Quintero. Quintero, who worked for the agency in its Central American division, was a native of Cuba who came to the United States in 1959. He was captured at the ill-fated Bay of Pigs invasion, was ransomed with the rest of the invaders, and spent 10 years in various CIA capacities. Secord used Quintero to transport military supplies by air to the Contras. For his vital services he was paid $4,000 a month, earning more than $200,000 from 1985 to 1986 (he didn't pay taxes on this money to the IRS).

Back in Washington, Lt. Colonel North's team at the NSC came up with an ingenious plan to further help the Contras. They would divert some of the profits from the "Enterprise" and give the funds to them for the purchase of arms and ammunition.

On October 5, 1986, the "Enterprise" came crashing down. On that day an American cargo plane ferrying supplies to the Contras was shot down over Nicaragua. Two of the crewmembers died upon impact but a third member of the crew, Eugene Hasenfus, survived. He was captured by Sandinista forces in the region and was taken in for interrogation. Once in captivity, Hasenfus said that he was employed by the CIA and the entire covert arms operation was in shambles.

Soon thereafter, a small Lebanese newspaper reported the arms for hostage deal that was brokered by the Reagan administration. President Reagan, in a nationwide news conference, denied that he was trading arms for hostages, but the charade failed dismally.

There have been many questions as to just what Vice President George H.W. Bush knew about the Iran-Contra affair and the diversion of funds to the Contras. In his campaign biography published in 1987, before he ran for President the next year,

Bush said that he was first informed about the particulars of the case from Dave Durenberger who was the chairman of the Senate Intelligence Committee. "What Dave had to say left me with the feeling, expressed to my chief of staff, Craig Fuller, that I'd been deliberately excluded from key meetings involving details of the Iran operation. In retrospect there were signals along the way that gave fair warning that the Iran initiative was headed for trouble. As it turned out, George Schultz and Cap Weinberger had serious doubts, too. If I'd known that and asked the President to call a meeting of the NSC, he might have seen the project in a different light, as a gamble doomed to fail."[1]

But that is not the entire story. Bush knew quite a lot about the Iran-Contra affair, even if he did not know all the details. Bush was present at a vital White House meeting on November 10, 1986 during the height of the scandal. Also present in the room was President Reagan, Secretary of State George Schultz, Secretary of Defense Cap Weinberger, and National Security Advisor John Poindexter, among others. The meeting was about what kind of statement the President would make to the nation regarding the affair. Poindexter spelled out a detailed account of the Iran-U.S. connection for the past two years. He also reported on the sale of weapons to Iran.

In 1986, Bush and Craig Fuller, his chief of staff, met with an Israeli by the name of Amiram Nir who was a confidant of Israeli Prime Minister Shimon Peres. Nir was a former military correspondent, and was Peres' advisor on counter-terrorism in 1984. He was also a confidant of Lt. Colonel Oliver North. North told Nir about the pending arms for hostages deal and the possible role of Israel in the operation. Bush and Fuller met with Nir in Jerusalem in July 1986 at which time Nir told them of the extent of the covert dealings between Iran and the United States. Bush later said he didn't understand what Nir was telling him regarding the arms for hostages deal. Bush later told Dan Rather, "I went along with it—because you know why, Dan, when I saw Mr. Buckley, when I heard about Mr. Buckley being tortured to death, later admitted as a CIA Chief. So I erred. I erred on the side of trying to get those hostages out of there."

Congress began hearings on the Iran-Contra affair and called

---

[1] Draper, Theodore, *A Very Thin Line: The Iran-Contra Affairs,* Hill and Wang Publishers, New York, 1991, Page 573.

numerous witnesses to testify, including all the principal players from the NSC staff. President Reagan also appointed an independent commission to report on the scandal headed by the late Texas Senator John Tower. The "Tower Report" offered a comprehensive narrative on all aspects of the arms for hostage affair and how the "Enterprise" operated. In the end, a number of the prime suspects involved in the Iran-Contra affair, (Oliver North, John Poindexter, Robert McFarlane and others) were convicted of crimes related to their participation in the scandal. President Reagan escaped further political embarrassment and completed his last term unscathed.

The man made most famous by the scandal was Oliver North. North testified before the congressional committee, ramrod stiff in his Marine uniform, and told the senators that he was proud of what he did, and had no qualms about the illegal nature of the work he took part in. He later became a nationally-known radio talk show host and a darling of the conservative right wing of the Republican Party. In his case, crime did indeed pay.

Chapter 47:
The Noriega Connection

Before the likes of Saddam Hussein and Osama bin Laden, the man who vexed the United States the most was Manuel Noriega of Panama, a brutal thug, drug dealer and overall bad guy with whom the United States made an unholy alliance in its fight against communist influence in Central and South America. Not only was Noriega a brutal dictator to his own people, he was a CIA informant going back to the 1960s. As happens with most dictators who lose the respect of the United States, Washington mounted a military invasion of Panama in order to remove him from power.

Manuel Noriega was born on February 11, 1938 in Panama City, Panama. He came from a poor family of Colombian heritage and as a young man went to the Chorillos Military School in Lima, Peru. Upon graduation, Noriega was commissioned as a sublieutenant in Panama's National Guard and was stationed in Colon. While at Colon he met the future President of Panama, Omar Torrijos, whom he would later help to overthrow. While at the academy he attracted the attention of the CIA, who put him under their wing. In 1967, he attended classes at the School of the Americas at Fort Gulick, Panama, as well as attending classes at Fort Bragg, North Carolina where he took courses in psychological operations.

Manuel Noriega was first recruited by the CIA's chief of station in Lima, Peru in 1959 when he was asked to give information on some of his fellow students at the Peruvian military school. He was given only a limited amount of money until his return to Panama in 1962. He stayed on the CIA's payroll in one form or another until 1976. For the CIA, Noriega was a good find as he rose in the ranks of Panama's Defense Force and supplied the agency with important information.

Among the information he supplied to the CIA was the political situation in the country the names of those men in the Defense Force who had received training in Moscow and his relationship with President Omar Torrijos. He backed Trujillo after the 1968 coup that led Torrijos to power. After that, Noriega was promoted to the rank of lieutenant colonel and was named chief of military intelligence. By the early 1970s the CIA was paying him the handsome sum of one hundred thousand dollars a year.

Noriega caused problems when he came under investigation by the U.S. Defense Intelligence Agency; they mounted a probe of him for buying secret intelligence information from three U.S. Army soldiers stationed in Panama. Noriega gave the information to General Torrijos to help him blackmail the United States into making concessions to Panama in the negotiations over the Panama Canal treaty that were then going on. The DIA feared that Noriega gave the information to Fidel Castro.

Revelation of Noriega's connection with the CIA would seriously wound the CIA, as well as relations between Panama and the United States. Then DCI Bush had to cover up the fact that Noriega, a known drug dealer, was one of the most important CIA assets inside Panama and throughout Latin America. The Noriega secret had to be kept quiet at all costs.

In 1981, President Torrijos died in a mysterious plane crash and Noriega took over the reins of power in Panama, becoming its unelected President. He promoted himself to the rank of general in 1983.

Noriega also played a part in the Reagan administration's secret Contra war against the Sandinista government in Nicaragua. He allowed the U.S. to set up listening posts in Panama and covertly allowed the U.S. to use his nation as a supply base for aid to the Contra rebels.

The Noriega-Contra connection was a topic of a communication on August 23, 1986 from President Reagan's National Security Advisor John Poindexter to an unidentified person regarding the Iran affair. The note said, "On Noriega, I wonder what he means about helping him to clean up his act? If he is really serious about that, we should be willing to do that for nearly nothing. If on the other hand, he just wants to get us indebted to him, so that he can blackmail us to lay off, then I am not interested. If he really has assets inside, it could be very helpful, but we can not (repeat not) be involved in any conspiracy on assassination. More sabotage would be another story. I have nothing against him other than his illegal activities. It would be useful for you to talk to him directly to find out exactly what he has in mind with regards to cleaning up his act."[1]

As Noriega's ties to the international drug cartel and money laundering began to mount, the CIA found itself in a pickle as far as what to do with him. If word was leaked publicly that Noriega had ties to the drug cartel, the CIA could find itself in another major scandal, one it did not need. However, that scenario did not take place due to a congressional investigation of Noriega started by Senator Jesse Helms, who publicly charged Noriega with the above-mentioned crimes. Helms' charges were politically motivated because he opposed President Carter's plan to turn over the Panama Canal to Panama. When the treaty was ratified, Helms backed down.

However, in December 1985, Senator Helms asked the Senate to begin an investigation of Noriega's ties to the drug cartels after he had a visit from Winston Spadafora, the brother of a well-known Panamanian political leader named Hugo Spadafora, who had been brutally murdered near the border between Panama and Costa Rica. Winston said that his brother had been murdered on orders of Noriega because he was going to reveal Noriega's ties to money laundering schemes and his ever-growing drug deals. Helms asked the Senate Foreign Relations Subcommittee on Western Hemisphere Affairs, which he chaired, to hold hearings regarding Noriega's ties to the cartels. The subcommittee called witnesses but they could produce no solid evidence tying Noriega to the cartels.

The hearings, however, gained national attention, and Seymour Hersh of the *New York Times,* began his own investigation of Noriega and his drug ties. On June 12, 1986, Hersh wrote a big story in the *Times* with the headline "Panama Strongman Said To Trade In Drugs, Arms And Illicit Money." The next day, the *Washington Post* followed up on Hersh's piece, running a story saying that the CIA had written a study revealing that Noriega was involved in the drug and arms trade and had ties with Castro's intelligence services. The CIA wrote the study because they believed that Noriega had knowingly compromised the names of U.S. undercover operatives in Central America and that these secrets would wind up in the hands of the Russians. The information that the CIA had was received through intercepts obtained by the National Security Agency. The State Department believed that the roughshod tactics used by

[1] Reply to note of 8/23/86, National Security Archive on worldwide web.

Noriega's cohorts tipped the presidential election in Panama to Nicholas Ardito Barletta, a supporter of Noriega, when the election was really won by Arnulfo Arias by 30,000 votes.

If Noriega was bothered by the charges, he did not show it. In June 1986, he paid a visit to the United States, stopping off in Washington where he met a number of people including NSC aide Oliver North and CIA Director William Casey, and spoke at a meeting at the Inter-American Defense Board at Fort McNair. Casey told Noriega that the United States was beginning to take the charges being leveled against him seriously, but the CIA refused to cut off all contact with him.

In a secret meeting, Senator Helms and Senator John Kerry of Massachusetts decided to consolidate their investigations on Noriega, (Helms on the drug charges, and Kerry on Noriega's connection to the Contras). They had a small staff consisting of four people, including Kerry aides Jack Blum, Richard McCall, and Jonathan Winer, all of whom had excellent intelligence connections as well as having a reputation of being dogged in unearthing secrets hidden in plain sight.

At one of the first hearings of the Kerry-Helms committee, they called as a witness a noted drug trafficker, Jorge Morales, who testified about his knowledge of the drug trade in Panama. Morales said, "I get the money in the briefcase, take a plane, a personal plane, a private plane and I fly to Panama—I would meet these guys who work for the [Panamanian] government, and they will take care of the situation with customs, and immigration people. The authorities, and the airport." Morales did not have to mention Noriega's name but the committee now had enough information, gleaned from him and the CIA, to verify Noriega's drug and money laundering connections.

On February 26, 1989, an American named Colonel Gerald Clark, a top-flight American diplomat/soldier in Panama, was killed in a hit-and-run accident on a deserted stretch of highway. An investigation was conducted by the U.S. military, the State Department's Office of Diplomatic Security and the DIA in Panama. The driver of the car that hit Colonel Clark gave conflicting information regarding the incident and was not charged.

What made the incident of Colonel Clark's death so interesting was the fact that he was part of the 470th Military Intelligence Brigade located in the Canal Zone. His primary job was to find out as much as he could about the political opposition to Noriega, and if possible, aid them in their efforts. The Noriega regime refused to cooperate in any way with the U.S. investigation of Colonel Clark's death and there were constant rumors that the regime was behind his death.

Senator Alfonse D'Amato of New York learned of the strange circumstances of the death of Colonel Clark and had his staff conduct its own study. The senator believed that Colonel Clark had been murdered and suspected that Noriega was part of the cover-up. Senator D'Amato had been calling for an official investigation into Noriega's drug ties, and when he learned of a possible link between Noriega and Clark's death, the senator said about Noriega, "That son of a bitch."

The case of the death of Colonel Clark was summed up by Colonel James Conigilo, who was a friend of Clark's. He said, "I would be very, very careful if I were a reporter about printing allegations of Clark's murder. I know that there are people in this government who would like it known that Colonel Clark was killed by Noriega. They need a reason to get him." The death of Colonel Clark was one of the last straws leading to the plan by the U.S. to finally get rid of Manuel Noriega.

The CIA was so frustrated with its inability to force Noriega out that they decided to try a psychological operation against his regime. However, they could not muster enough opposition within the anti-Noriega forces and all they could accomplish was a drop of leaflets printed in the Canal Zone, which amounted to nothing.

However, the bad press against Noriega stemming from the Helms-Kerry investigations led two U.S. federal grand juries in Florida to indict Noriega on charges of drug trafficking and racketeering. After the charges were filed, the CIA finally removed him from its payroll.

In 1989, Noriega cancelled the presidential elections scheduled for that year. Following the cancellation of the elections, there was an attempted coup by some opposition forces, but it failed.

In Washington, the Bush administration had finally had enough of Noriega and his ties to the cartels. There had also been some incidents of harassment of soldiers in the Canal Zone. In December 1989, on Bush's orders, the United States mounted a military operation to depose Noriega from power. In a speech to the nation announcing the military operation, the President said, "General Noriega's reckless threats and attacks upon Americans in Panama created an imminent danger to the 35,000 American citizens in Panama. As President, I have no higher obligation than to safeguard the lives of American citizens."

The codename for the campaign was "Operation Just Cause." As the scope of the American invasion became clear, Noriega sought refuge in the residence in the Apostolic Nunciature in Panama. Using loud rock music on a continuous basis and a neighboring field as a helicopter landing pad, U.S. forces harassed Noriega. He finally surrendered to U.S. troops. The invasion was a total success with the loss of only 24 troops, and three civilian casualties. Panama suffered about 200 casualties.

On January 3, 1990, Noriega was taken back to Miami where he was arraigned on many different charges relating to his drug dealings. In 1992, he was convicted in U.S. federal court on charges of cocaine trafficking, racketeering, and money laundering. He was given a 40-year jail term which was reduced. He served 17 years and was released on September 9, 2007. He stayed in prison while he was appealing his extradition to France, where in 1999, he had been tried in absentia and convicted of money laundering and other serious crimes. The U.S. Supreme Court failed to take up his appeal and he was sent to France where he was put on trial, was convicted, and spent seven years in prison. In 2011, France agreed to extradite Noriega to Panama. On December 11, 2011, Noriega came back to Panama and began serving three 20-year prison terms.

Manuel Noriega was just one of the many corrupt dictators the CIA agreed to work with during the era of the Cold War. The United States used him for its own purposes, and when it was convenient, we jettisoned him as fast as possible, hoping to forget his, and our, mistakes.

Chapter 48:
Barry Seal and Mena

The town of Mena, Arkansas is like other small villages in that mostly rural state; nothing of serious consequence usually goes on. Located near Rich Mountain in the beautiful Ouachita hills, Mena would become one of the hotspots in the U.S. government's covert supply of military equipment to the Contra rebels fighting the government of Nicaragua during the administration of President Reagan. But what happened was not just the secret supplying of arms to the U.S.-backed rebels; it also involved the transshipment of illegal drugs from South America in exchange for arms from the U.S.

According to people involved in the Mena affair, three U.S. Presidents — Ronald Reagan, George H.W. Bush and Bill Clinton — were all deeply involved in the scheme (and all three denied any ties). In time, the secrets of Mena would play a minor part in the Iran-Contra scandal, and would also be investigated by the Whitewater Special Prosecutor looking into President Clinton's alleged participation in a loan scandal during his terms as Arkansas governor.

The story of what happened at Mena must start with a burly, ex-CIA contract agent, gunrunner, dope smuggler turned DEA informant, and all-around bad guy named Alder Berriman "Barry" Seal. From the late 1970s until his assassination by drug dealers out for revenge, Barry Seal was responsible for the importation of billions of dollars worth of illegal cocaine and other drugs from Latin America. In return for his enormous profits from the drug trade, Seal, with the backing of the CIA, would fly large amounts of guns bound for the Contra guerillas from Mena.

Barry Seal grew up in Baton Rouge, Louisiana, and was interested in flying from an early age. He took his first solo flight at the age of 15 and was soon able to make a living by towing advertising banners. In 1955 he joined the Civil Air Patrol in Baton Rouge and it was rumored that he took CAP training in New Orleans with David Ferrie, who was a rabid anticommunist in whose squadron Lee

Harvey Oswald participated. It was also rumored that at an early age, Seal began working in some capacity for military intelligence, but what he did was not disclosed.

In 1958, Seal began taking weapons to Fidel Castro who was then fighting the regime of Fulgencio Batista in Cuba. The following year, Seal became a CIA contract pilot in Guatemala and was supposed to have taken some training with the exiles in the Florida Keys, as well as at Lake Pontchartrain in Louisiana.

In 1964, Barry Seal went to work for TWA and became its youngest 707 captain, and later, its youngest 747 captain. He was fired by TWA after his arrest on July 1, 1972, in New Orleans on charges of flying explosives to anti-Castro Cubans in Mexico. His plane, a DC-4, contained seven tons of C-4 plastic explosive, 7,000 feet of primer cord and 2,600 electric blasting caps. Three other men were arrested at the same time.

Seal's trial began two years later (in June 1974) but interestingly enough, government prosecutors decided to drop the charges on "national security" grounds.

A number of writers who studied the Seal case, including Pete Brewton who wrote the book *The Mafia, CIA & George Bush,* said that after his mistrial he began working full time for the CIA, making numerous trips from the United States to Latin America. Daniel Hopsicker, who wrote extensively on Barry Seal, said he was "sheep-dipped" into the Drug Enforcement Administration (DEA) as an agent for the Special Operations Group. Hopsicker also alleged that Seal worked for Lucien Conein, a CIA agent who operated on behalf of the Nixon White House.

On December 10, 1979, Seal and Steve Planta were arrested in Honduras where they arrived from Ecuador with 40 kilos of cocaine, worth $25 million. Seal spent nine months in jail in Honduras. While there, he met a man who would affect his life for the next several years. William Reeves was a fellow prisoner who worked for the Ochoa crime family of Medellin, Colombia. Reeves was Ochoa's New Orleans business manager and he brought Seal into the most dangerous narcotics cartel of the time, run by Jorge Ochoa and Pablo Escobar. They united their forces in 1982 and formed a 2,000-man army to battle M-19, the Marxist revolutionary group that was causing them major problems.

In 1982, Seal, now a prime player in the Ochoa crime network, began making trips on behalf of the Medellin Cartel, bringing tons of cocaine into the United States. One of the places he brought the drugs was the small airstrip in Mena, Arkansas. Seal's profits were so huge that he made a cool $1.5 million profit in one trip.

In time, Seal would use the Intermountain Regional Airport facility that was part of the Mena complex to become a big time arms broker, hiding his illegal arms trafficking business behind a legitimate shell game of a successful plane broker. With a staff of mechanics to work on the planes, he went to South America to do his dirty work.

According to the private papers obtained by author Roger Morris revealed in his book called *Partners in Power: The Clintons and Their America,* Seal was on the CIA payroll before and after his criminal activities began in Mena.

As the U.S. involvement in the Contra supply began in earnest, Seal would use the surrounding area around Mena as a training ground for hundreds of Contra rebels flown into the country. In order to aid in this covert exercise, the CIA would send down aircraft from its own secret fleet (Air America) to Mena, including helicopters and large cargo planes.

By 1984, Seal's once flourishing business began to come to an end. He was indicted on charges of selling Quaaludes by the DEA, which had finally come to the end of its rope with Seal. He served a limited prison sentence but by 1985 his use by the CIA had also come to an end. Seal was abandoned by the boys at Langley and became a double agent for the DEA. He would now become an informer against the same drug czars he was hobnobbing with for years.

After he was indicted on the Quaaludes charge and facing a 10-year prison term, Seal asked for a deal with the feds, but they said no. Taking matters into his own hands, Seal went to Washington where he met with two members of Vice President George Bush's Task Force on Drugs. He told them that the Medellin Cartel had made a secret deal with the Sandinistas in Nicaragua. The pact called for the cartel to give part of their cut of their drug profits to the Sandinistas in exchange for the use of an airfield in Managua, Nicaragua as a transshipment point for narcotics.

With the blessing of the DEA, Seal now bought a C-123 cargo plane that he called *The Fat Lady,* which was used to transport tons of coke on behalf of the cartel. Seal placed a hidden camera inside the plane in order to take photos of Pablo Escobar, who was helping a squad of soldiers from Nicaragua load 1,200 kilos of cocaine at the Managua airport. In a televised address to the nation regarding the cartel's involvement in the sale of drugs in South America, President Reagan used some of the photos taken by Seal to attack the Sandinistas and their alliance with the Ochoa family.

With Seal now cooperating with the DEA, the judge who oversaw his conviction in the Quaaludes case reduced his sentence to six months' probation. Seal was lucky that the judge reduced his sentence because in December of 1984, he was arrested in Louisiana for taking into the United States a cargo of marijuana. U.S. District Judge Frank Polozola had no choice but to allow Seal's six-month probation to stand instead of throwing the book at him. Judge Polozola called Seal one of, "the lowest, most despicable people I can think of." One of the conditions that he imposed on Seal was that he spend every night, from 6:00 p.m. to 6:00 a.m., at the Salvation Army's halfway house on Airline Highway in Baton Rouge. The judge also forbade him from carrying a weapon.

The Mena, Arkansas connection to the Contra supply effort soon came crashing down. Flying out of Mena in October 1986, on one of the Contra supply runs, was a plane carrying the pilot Eugene Hasenfus. Hasenfus's plane was shot down over Nicaragua, he being the only survivor. Papers found in the plane clearly documented the U.S.-sponsored arms shipment to the Contra guerillas. This incident was to play a crucial role in the unraveling of the Iran-Contra scandal.

Throughout the Mena-Seal scandal, then Governor Bill Clinton's role in the affair was hotly debated. Numerous participants who knew about Seal's illegal dealings placed Clinton "in the loop" as far as his knowledge of what was going on there. Among those who told of Clinton's direct knowledge was one of his most trusted bodyguards at the time, Larry Douglas Brown, who told of Clinton's then secret ties to the CIA (it was Clinton, then Governor of Arkansas, who made a phone call to someone at the CIA in order to get Brown a job with the agency). Clinton had publicly said that he had little or no knowledge of the Mena operation.

Unknown to Barry Seal, time was running out. His violent end came on February 19, 1986 when he arrived at the Salvation Army headquarters at 6:00 p.m. After parking his car, he was approached by a man armed with a machine gun. The man pumped two shots into Seal's head and body. A friend of Seal's, Russ Eakin, said he saw three men near his body when he was shot. He was found dead by the police, slumped over the steering wheel of his car.

Who murdered Barry Seal? Was it a hit sanctioned by someone in the Ochoa crime family who believed that Seal had ratted them out? Or had some other, unidentified person or group got to him first?

Soon after his murder the police arrested several men suspected of killing Barry Seal. They included Miguel Velez, Bernardo Vasquez, Luis Quintero-Cruz, John Cardona, Elberto Sanchez and Jose Renteria. Another man who was implicated in the crime, Rafa Cardona, escaped the country and made his way to Colombia. Over time, Sanchez and Cardona were deported. Jose Coutin, the man who supplied the weapon used in the Seal murder was not charged in the crime. However, he testified against the other defendants, Velez, Quintero-Cruz, and Vasquez. At the trial, Velez, Quintero-Cruz and Vasquez were found guilty of Seal's murder and were sentenced to life terms in jail.

Shortly after Seal's death, William Guste, Jr., the Attorney General of Louisiana, wrote a letter to U.S. Attorney General Ed Meese asking that a formal U.S. Justice Department investigation in the Seal murder be undertaken. Attorney General Guste related Seal's past history, including his association with the Ochoa cartel. Guste had previously been the Chairman of the Subcommittee on Narcotics and Drug Interdiction of the President's Commission on Organized Crime, at which Seal testified.

In his letter to the Attorney General, Guste wrote:

> His purpose there was to inform the Commission and top United States officials of the methods and equipment used by drug smugglers. I give this information to establish that he was a heinous criminal. At the same time, for his own purposes, he had made himself an extremely valuable

witness and informant in the country's fight against illegal drugs. He had cooperated with the government in testifying before federal grand juries, the President's Commission and was scheduled to be a key witness in the government's case against Jorge Ochoa-Vasques, the head of the largest drug cartels in the world. Barry Seal's murder suggests the need for an in-depth but rapid investigation into a number of areas.

WHY WAS SUCH AN IMPORTANT WITNESS NOT GIVEN PROTECTION WHETHER HE WANTED IT OR NOT?

Barry Seal refused to go into the Federal Witness Protection Program. But he could have been imprisoned in some town in America under an assumed identity.

Instead, he was given sentences in cases against him in Florida and in Louisiana that permitted him to live in a Halfway House in Baton Rouge and required him to report daily to the Salvation Army there. Why did the government permit this after it was made aware of the fact that Ochoa investigators had been following Seal and that these investigators were actually in court at the time his sentence was announced.

Prior to his death, Seal said that having to report to the Salvation Army everyday at the same time made him a "clay pigeon." He virtually predicted his assassination.[1]

Attorney General Meese took no action following Mr. Guste's letter.

The case of who killed Barry Seal took on a new twist when the attorney for the Colombian defendants in the penalty phase of their trial, Sam Dalton, subpoenaed the CIA about what they knew about Seal's demise. During the discovery phase of the investigation, Dalton found out that the FBI went to the Baton Rouge police department and "literally and physically seized the contents of that trunk [Seal's car] from the Baton Rouge Police. In fact, the Baton Rouge Police would have to draw their guns to keep possession of that trunk." When Dalton tried to subpoena the CIA and FBI to give

[1] The Crimes of Mena: Barry Seal set up for murder. Whatreallyhappened.com.

him the information he asked for, the subpoena was not complied with. However, a state judge forced the two agencies to comply with the subpoena and what they found was most interesting. Inside Seal's wallet was the private phone number of George Bush.

Lewis Unglesby, a noted lawyer in Louisiana, at one time represented Barry Seal. "I sat him down one time," recalls Unglesby, talking about his relationship with Seal, "and I said: I cannot represent you effectively unless I know what is going on. Barry smiled and gave me a number, and told me to call it, and identify myself as him. I dialed the number, a little dubiously, and a pleasant female voice answered: Office of the Vice President."

Unglesby said into the phone that he was Barry Seal. Soon, an admiral came on the line and Unglesby said he was Barry Seal's lawyer. The next minute, the phone connection was canceled.

There are still so many questions to be answered regarding Barry Seal's life and death. What was his true role in the Iran-Contra affair, and what really went on at the Mena Airport? What was his true connection with the CIA? And what was he doing with the private phone number of Vice President George Bush? The answers to those questions are still to be determined.

Chapter 49:
Murder At CIA Headquarters

All was calm at the entrance to the CIA headquarters in the early morning of January 25, 1993. Agency employees were lining up in their cars waiting to clear security at Langley headquarters, a routine that went on every day. Suddenly, the early morning stillness was shattered as a man carrying an AK-47 rifle left his car and began shooting randomly at the people sitting in their automobiles. The shooting spree lasted only a few seconds, but when it was over, two CIA employees were dead. The victims were Frank Darling, 28, an employee of the Directorate of Operations, and Lansing Bennett, a 65-year-old doctor. Inside the car with Mr. Darling was his wife Judy, who, upon spotting the gunman, luckily ducked down in the vehicle and was spared any harm. Besides Darling and Bennett, three other people were wounded, but would live.

In the furious commotion that followed the shooting, the gunman, to his surprise, was able to elude his pursuers and flee the scene. What followed was one of the most intense manhunts in CIA history, forming a path that would lead American intelligence agents to Pakistan where, four years later, they would nab the assassin and bring him back to face justice.

In the months following the incident, the CIA focused its attention on a 33-year-old Pakistani citizen named Mir Aimal Kasi who came to the United States in 1991. Mir Kasi lived with his roommate Zahed Mir in an apartment in nearby Reston, Virginia. Shortly after the attacks, Mir notified the police that Kasi was missing. When the police came to his home to investigate, they found the smoking gun that would link Kasi to the killings at CIA headquarters: an AK-47, 600 rounds of ammunition, and a bulletproof vest. Mr. Mir told the police that he had helped his friend purchase the items by allowing him to use his credit card. Mir also told the authorities that Kasi had complained to him of the way many Muslims were being treated in the United States and promised to take some sort of action.

While the police were starting their probe, Mir Kasi fled the United States and returned to his home in Pakistan via New York on a Pakistani International Airlines flight to Karachi. Kasi's family lived in the province of Quetta in southwest Pakistan where they owned a building contracting company. Kasi grew up in Quetta and received a Master's degree in English literature from Baluchistan University. Once in Quetta, Kasi was on familiar ground and was protected by a local network of fellow Muslims who shared his anti-American views.

At CIA headquarters, the hunt for Mir Kasi took shape at the newly created Counter-terrorist Center. In a well-coordinated and detailed plan, the CIA recruited a number of Afghans from one family who lived in the city if Kandahar. They were given the cryptonym FD/TRODPINT, and were supplied with all-terrain vehicles for use in the rugged Afghan mountains. The focal point of the search for Kasi was Karachi, Pakistan where the CIA was to develop a unit of American Special Forces, which would be infiltrated into Afghanistan upon the capture of Kasi by the FD/TRODPINT team. A secure landing strip was located and a special U.S. plane would fly the fugitive back to U.S. soil.

It was an open secret along the streets of Quetta that the U.S. had placed a $2,000,000 reward on Kasi's head and soon, legitimate tips were being called in concerning his whereabouts. In May 1997, a man entered the U.S. consulate in Karachi, Pakistan and said he had information regarding Kasi. In further talks with CIA men in the embassy, the informer gave them information regarding Kasi and gave them an application for a Pakistani driver's license that had been requisitioned by Kasi using a phony name. The person also had a real picture of Kasi. With irrefutable proof now in their hands, American authorities began their final plans to capture the killer.

Since the abduction of Kasi was to be a covert operation, it needed the approval of the Clinton administration's National Security Council. The President was persuaded to sign a National Intelligence Finding in order to carry out the mission. Now, all the plans were set in motion.

CIA and FBI teams were covertly sent to Pakistan and, working with the Pakistani intelligence (the ISI), were able to locate Kasi at the Shalimar Hotel in Der Ghazi Kahn. On June 15, 1997, FBI agents swarmed down on Kasi's room and took him to a safe location. He was swiftly taken out of Pakistan and was returned to the U.S. for trial.

On November 10, 1997, a jury in Fairfax County convicted Mir Kasi of murder and sentenced him to death.

During his incarceration, Kasi told reporters that he originally wanted to kill CIA Director James Woolsey, but settled on the people waiting to gain entrance to CIA headquarters. "I wanted to shoot James Woolsey but was not able to find him, or his timing of coming or going to CIA. If I had found Gates [Robert Gates, the former head of the CIA], I would have attacked him, as these people who make up policies for CIA or U.S. government. The genesis for this hatred for the American government came after the 1991 Persian Gulf War and the continued allied air campaign that followed. I wanted to punish those who do wrong things against Muslim countries like Iraq," commented Kasi.

On November 14, 2002, Mir Kasi was executed in Virginia for the brutal murders of Frank Darling and Lansing Bennett.

Tales From Langley

Chapter 50:
The CIA and Abdul Haq

On October 25, 2001, six weeks after the September 11 attacks on the United States, a team of lightly armed men made their way into Afghanistan in an attempt to rally the anti-Taliban tribesmen into a cohesive force and overthrow the government that gave sanctuary to Osama bin Laden. The leader of the team was a veteran of the Afghan-Soviet war, an assert of the CIA, Abdul Haq. In a carefully laid ambush, the Taliban fighters spotted Haq's band and in a fierce firefight, killed him and others in the party. With the death of Abdul Haq, the United States had lost one of its main allies in the war against the Taliban regime in Afghanistan. The U.S. relationship with Abdul Haq went back to the early days of the Soviet-Afghan war when the CIA supplied military equipment to the Mujahedin in their war against the invading Soviet army. His death left a gaping hole in the anti-Taliban resistance and left a number of Haq's American benefactors shaking their heads as to why the CIA did not do enough to insure his safety.

The CIA first came into contact with Abdul Haq in 1979, and an on again, off again relationship ensued. His family came from eastern Afghanistan near the city of Jalalabad. Haq was instrumental in garnering a fighting force to battle the Soviets and he did not share the most virulent, anti-American views being espoused by the other, more militant Mujahedin. In time, Haq was the middleman between the CIA, the British MI6, and the Afghan fighters.

Haq was recruited in Afghanistan by CIA officer Howard Hart, a veteran of the Philippine campaign during World War II. Hart served in the Directorate of Operations, finding himself in such places as Iran, Bahrain, and India. When the Soviets invaded Afghanistan in 1979, Hart was sent to Pakistan where the United States ran its not-s-secret war against the Soviet's. Hart's job was to train the Afghan freedom fighters and supply them with the latest American weaponry, including the STINGER missile that the rebels used to shoot down Soviet aircraft. Hart met Haq in the Pakistani city of Peshawar and their covert alliance was established. As hundreds of thousands of pieces of military equipment began flooding into the hands of the Mujahedin, the CIA used Haq to clandestinely monitor the price these guns were selling for, and let the U.S. know if they were being siphoned off for resale among the warring tribesmen.

In order to further cement his ties with Haq, Hart, disregarding CIA orders not to enter Afghanistan, made a secret trip with Haq to inspect his headquarters and monitor Soviet forces in the mountains.

As the bond between Haq and the agency grew, the CIA put him on its payroll and Haq in turn, provided invaluable information on battlefield progress in the areas he controlled.

As the war wound down in the late 1980s, the CIA began to reconsider its one time favorable relationship with Haq, who seemed to be creating his own agenda as to who would rule a post-Soviet Afghanistan. Some officers in the CIA began calling him "Hollywood Haq." By the time the war ended, Haq had been noticed by the highest members of the Reagan administration, including National Security Advisor, Robert McFarlane, and even by British Prime Minister Margaret Thatcher.

When the last Soviet soldier left Afghanistan in 1988, the United States had accomplished its goal: the end of Soviet influence in Afghanistan (the U.S. got was an added bonus—the collapse of the Soviet Union—one year later). With the end of the Russian empire and the halting of the Cold War, the United States turned a blind eye toward its Mujahedin allies and let the region return to its ages old policy of intertribal warfare. The gap left by the United States affected its erstwhile friends, including Ahmed Shah Massoud and Abdul Haq.

In the aftermath of the Soviet exodus from Afghanistan, Haq was appointed to the post of Police Chief in the capital of Kabul. His brother, Haj Abdul-Qadeer, was named the Governor of Nangarhar Province. In 1996, the paths of Osama bin Laden and Haj Abdul-Quadeer crossed deadly paths when the Saudi fugitive entered Nangarhar. By 2000, the Taliban had taken control over Afghanistan, with Haq fleeing to the United Arab Emirates (where he would start a carpet business), while his sibling wound up in Dubai.

Haq was living in Dubai at the time of the 9-11 attacks and, in the immediate aftermath of the destruction in New York and Washington, the U.S. contacted him once more, asking his help in once again ridding Afghanistan of the Taliban, and seeking his aid in forming a new government in that nation.

Haq had influential American backers including former Reagan administration National Security Advisor Robert "Bud" McFarlane. McFarlane had first met Haq during the 1980s when the Reagan administration began supplying the Afghan rebels with CIA- supplied munitions. Over the years, Haq and McFarlane would keep in touch. Haq was also backed by two wealthy Chicago businessmen, Joe and Jim Richie, who had spent part of their childhood in Afghanistan. The brothers were friends with McFarlane, and the three men tried to influence the U.S. government to back Haq in the years after the end of the Soviet-Afghan war. Haq also used his considerable influence to begin a process that he hoped would lead to a free Afghanistan.

While Haq was working with his U.S. allies to draft a plan to rid Afghanistan of the Taliban, he was a target of the powerful and corrupt Pakistani intelligence service, the Inter-Services Intelligence. The ISI had longstanding ties with the Taliban, and they viewed Haq as a first-rate troublemaker who was capable of destroying the alliance (with the Taliban) that had been crafted over many years.

On January 12, 1999, a hit team entered Haq's home and killed not only his bodyguards, but also his wife and children. No one took responsibility for the killing of Haq's family but American diplomats in the region placed the blame on agents of the ISI. After the deaths, reliable information came in saying that the killers were probably trained at a bin Laden military compound in Afghanistan called Tarnak Farm.

After the 9-11 attacks, Haq publicly called for the United States to refrain from conducting a massive aerial attack on the Taliban. Rather, he asked for a stepped up psychological warfare campaign against them.

During this hectic time, Haq received support from the exiled Afghan king Mohammed Zahir Shah who was living in Rome. A few weeks before his death, Haq traveled to Rome where he met, and held discussions with, the ex-King. At their meeting, Haq informed the King that he planned to assemble a small group of men to head into Afghanistan to gather up an anti-Taliban force. The King pleaded with Haq not to take any premature military action on his own.

In late October 2000, Haq and about 20 lightly armed men entered Afghanistan. They planned to meet with as many tribal leaders as possible and recruit them to topple the Taliban. His plan called for the group to wind up in the city of Jalalabad and then return to Pakistan. Unfortunately, Haq's team wound up near his home village of Azra, a long distance from Jalalabad. It was there that the Taliban ambushed Haq and his followers.

No one knows the exact circumstances of just how Haq was found. Under intense fire from the Taliban, Haq made hurried calls to his nephew in the Pakistani city of Peshawar. The nephew called his contacts in Washington, and the CIA was immediately notified of Haq's perilous situation. American military officials monitoring the situation were unable (or unwilling) to redirect any military assets to aid Haq. They did, however, divert an unmanned Predator drone with Hellfire missiles to Haq's position. The drone fired a missile on the Taliban forces but it was too late. Haq and his long time friend Muhammad Doran were captured, and summarily executed days later.

If the Pakistani ISI did in fact tip off the Taliban to Haq's whereabouts, that fact alone did not derail the alliance of convenience between the Bush administration and the government of Pakistani President Pervez Musharraf in the war against Osama bin Laden and international terrorism.

Haq's benefactors in the United States however, point the finger of blame directly at the CIA, saying the agency did not do enough to aid Haq in his last hours. In the final analysis, "Hollywood Haq's" luck had run out.

Chapter 51:
Pakistan's ISI

Often in its long history, the CIA has had to make alliances of convenience with disreputable individuals or organizations in order to further its own ends. During the decades of the 1970s and 1980s, the CIA worked closely with Pakistan's main intelligence agency, a group not noted for its democratic tendencies, a group with links to the heroin trade in Central Asia and radical, terrorist groups throughout the region, a group called the Inter-Services Intelligence Agency, or ISI. The ISI, the CIA, and Saudi intelligence worked in conjunction to train and supply the Afghan rebels in their war against the Soviet Union. Information following the 9-11 attacks against the United States revealed a possible sinister connection between the head of the ISI and one of the prime movers in the assaults against America.

The foundation of the ISI goes back to 1948 when it was created by a British army officer, Major General R. Cawthome, who was the deputy Chief of Staff in the Pakistani Army. After the partition of India and Pakistan into two different nations, the President of Pakistan, Ayub Kahn, expanded the role of the ISI to cover internal espionage, and the monitoring of Khan's potential enemies. The duties of the ISI subsequently expanded into both foreign and internal intelligence collection, the coordination of intelligence gathering among the various military departments, and the use of its agents to keep the prevailing military strongman of the time in power. Critics of the ISI have called it "a state within a state," or the invisible government. Since its inception, the ISI has been linked to drug smuggling and the assassination of political opponents of the ruling government; it was instrumental in the founding of the Taliban regime in Afghanistan.

During the decades-long engagements between India and Pakistan over the sovereignty of Kashmir (which is currently recognized as being part of India), the ISI has provided insurgents battling the Indian army with training and equipment. It has been estimated by Indian government officials that by 1995, the ISI had trained more than 5,000 men to battle its forces in Kashmir.

Over the years, the ISI took as much power and influence as the various prime ministers would allow. The most influential director, as far as this narrative is concerned, was Lt. General Hamid Gul who worked closely with Western intelligence agencies in ousting the Russians from Afghanistan. During the height of the Soviet-Afghan war, Gul worked hand-in-glove not only with the CIA but the Saudi Arabian intelligence service called the General Intelligence Department, or GID. Gul got his marching orders from Pakistan's President, Mohammed Zia-ul-Haq, who took control of Pakistan's government in July 1977 when he deposed the regime of Zulfikar Ali-Buttho, the father of a latter day Prime Minster, Benazir Bhutto. President Zia ordered the execution of the elder Bhutto, despite warnings from the United States, and other Western nations.

In time, Zia canceled national elections, and was instrumental in the development of the radical political movement called Jamaaet-e-Islamia, which shunned modern dress and politics, and called for an absolute Islamic government in Pakistan.

Despite his pro-Islamic penchant, the new Reagan administration saw President Zia as an ally in Central Asia especially after the 1979 Russian invasion of Afghanistan. Without Zia's permission, the United States would not be able to funnel military aid to the Afghan rebels via the CIA. In the end, the Reagan administration made a deal with the devil whereby Zia was fundamentally in charge of all covert CIA/U.S. military aid to the rebels. Zia forbade the CIA to meet on a regular basis with its Afghan rebel allies, but the agency did so anyway,

The CIA agent who had the most contact with the ISI Chief, Akhtar Abdul Rahman, was Howard Hart. The ISI Chief told Hart in no uncertain terms that no CIA officer would be allowed to enter Afghanistan to set up shop or meet with any potential assets. All weapons shipments would pass through ISI hands, the CIA would be forbidden to directly train the Mujahedin, and all training would be held in Pakistani camps.

While the Reagan administration knew all about the illegal activities of the ISI, they turned a blind eye toward these transgressions. CIA Director Casey made a number of clandestine trips to Pakistan where he assessed the military situation, and met with Akhtar and planned strategy. Casey said Akhtar "is completely involved in this war and certainly knows better than anyone else about his requirements. We have to support him."

As the war progressed, the CIA under Casey let the ISI arm and train its Afghan clients, who were known to have engaged in illegal activities such as drug smuggling, murder and torture, and who were known to have made any number of anti-American, anti-Western statements.

ISI agents took the war to the streets of Kabul in 1983, killing nine Soviets by detonating a briefcase bomb near Kabul University. Russian soldiers felt the wrath of the ISI/CIA connection, and many were killed by car bombs and other means of assassination.

A rift soon opened up between the CIA and ISI over the agency's relationship with Ahmed Shah Massoud, an Afghan chief who was allied with the United States. The ISI did not trust Massoud and did everything in its power to undermine his authority among the anti-Soviet groups. They even went so far as to intercept a CIA arms shipment to Massoud. Massoud would be killed on September 9, 2001 by assassins sent to his mountain headquarters by Osama bin Laden. There have been unverified reports that the ISI had a hand in the Massoud assassination, even if one of its agents did not actually pull the trigger.

By 1992, the Afghan rebels had managed to do the impossible — outlast the mighty Soviet army and force them to leave Afghanistan in full retreat. For the United States, the main objective had been accomplished, and by 1992 the CIA had all but closed up shop in Pakistan. The CIA and the United States, in effect, washed their hands of the entire mess and left Afghanistan to sort out its own affairs.

Big changes also took place in Pakistan when, in October 1999, General Pervez Musharraf took power in a coup. The Clinton and Bush administrations decided to overlook the anti-democratic way Musharraf came to power and threw in their lots with him. From 1999 through September 11, 2001, Musharraf claimed to be reining in the power of the ISI, but they still had considerable influence in his government.

After 9-11, President Bush gave Musharraf an ultimatum: work with the United States in its war against bin Laden or face the consequences. Musharraf decided to cooperate with Washington and opened up his borders to the largest CIA base since the beginning of the Afghan war.

Despite Musharraf's pledge to aid the United States, the fundamental fact was that for years, the ISI had been openly aiding the Taliban in Afghanistan with intelligence and military equipment during the Afghan-Soviet war. Once the Taliban was safely in power in Afghanistan, elements of the ISI did all they could to beef up the radical, Islamic government, despite the pressure put on them by Musharraf to end their ties.

In 1999, when the Clinton administration was gearing up for a snatch operation in Afghanistan to capture bin Laden, the Pakistani government ordered the ISI to aid the CIA in the planning of the operation, but in reality, the ISI did nothing significant to push the plan along.

The ISI had a checkered past to say the least, and that included murder when necessary. They may have been involved in the abduction and murder of *Wall Street Journal* writer Daniel Pearl. Pearl and his French-born wife, Marianne, arrived in the Pakistani city of Karachi to do a story on Islamic militants and their relationship with the ISI. Pearl also planned to do a story on Richard Reid, the shoe bomber who was caught when he tried to bomb a jet using an explosive device hidden in his shoe.

Daniel Pearl's contact in Karachi was an English-speaking man who said his name was Chaudhry Basheer. In fact, Basheer was Omar Saeed Sheikh, as British-born citizen with ties to the ISI. Days before the Pearl kidnapping, Sheik had met Pearl in Karachi, befriended him, and said that he could deliver the reporter to his contacts who would be able to help him write his expose. That Sheik did deliver Pearl to his contacts is without question. What happened next was simply pure murder. Pearl was kidnapped by unnamed people, who made a video of his last moments before killing him in a brutal execution. In the investigation that followed the death of Daniel Pearl, detectives unraveled the role played by Sheikh, and his ties to the ISI.

Sheikh grew up in London, and attended the London School of Economics. He stayed one year before dropping out. He then traveled to Bosnia in conjunction with an Islamic charity. He then joined other radical Islamic fighters in Pakistan where he took all sorts of military training. He was arrested for plotting the kidnapping of three Westerners, and spent five years in jail. The ISI is reported to have supplied him a lawyer, something that would not have been done if he were not someone high up in the ISI pecking order. After serving time in jail he was finally released on New Years Eve 1999, in return for the freedom of 154 passengers of a hijacked Indian Airlines plane. After his release from jail, Sheikh was in the hands of the ISI, traveling to various camps in Afghanistan, and possibly carrying out missions in India.

Sheikh was complicit in the Pearl kidnapping case and soon Pakistani authorities, under intensive pressure from Washington, pulled out all the stops in the effort to find him. He was traced to Karachi where he was finally taken into custody, not by the police, but by members of the ISI. One week after his arrest, he was finally handed over to the police. Sheikh admitted that he was a participant in the Pearl abduction, and then confirmed that the reporter was already dead.

Further investigation into the background of Sheikh showed that he was in constant contact with General Mohammad Aziz Kahn, who once served as the deputy director of the ISI, whose responsibility was the training for covert operations in Afghanistan and India. Sheikh's involvement in the murder of Danny Pearl puts to rest any fallacy that there was no connection between his death and the ISI.

A more troubling circumstance that has yet to be fully documented is a report linking ISI chief Lt. General Mahmoud Ahmad to the ringleader of the 9-11 attacks, Mohammad Atta.

One week before the 9-11 attacks, Lt. General Mahmoud Ahmad, the ISI Director, paid an official visit to Washington where he met with high-ranking Bush administration officials in the State Department and Deputy Secretary of State Richard Armitage. He also met with individuals from both the Pentagon and the CIA, and members of the U.S. Senate (including then Senator Joe Biden). The reason for his visit to Washington was "routine consultations" between the Pakistani armed forces and the United States.

Lt. General Ahmad remained in Washington on 9-11 due to the grounding of all commercial aircraft after the attacks. No one knows what business was conducted between Lt. General Ahmad and American authorities, but right after the blasts in New York and Washington, the government of Pakistan pledged to cooperate fully in apprehending bin Laden. In a further, curious development, Lt. General Ahmad was in Washington when Ahmed Shah Massoud, the leader of the Northern Alliance mentioned above, was killed in his home by two men linked to bin Laden and, possibly, the ISI.

In the wake of 9-11, the Bush administration decided it had to work closely with Pakistan and the ISI to rout out the terrorists in Afghanistan, despite the well-known fact that the ISI (with the CIA) had helped create the Taliban in the first place, and did all they could during the Afghan war to help their ally with military supplies and intelligence. In the end, the Pentagon and the State Department decided to pay the devil they knew (once again) to aid their own ends.

The first signs of the new cooperation between Washington and Karachi came on September 13, 2001, when President Pervez Musharraf sent Lt. General Ahmad to meet with the Taliban government in Afghanistan to seek the extradition of Osama bin Laden to the United States. Lt. General Ahmad met in the Afghan city of Kandahar with the Taliban leader, Mohammad Omar. The ISI chief passed on his instructions but his mission was a failure. With the task a nonstarter, the United States now could pursue its planned attack on Afghanistan in retaliation for 9-11.

In an about-face that caught many observers by surprise, President Musharraf fired Ahmad as ISI chief just as the United States began its counteroffensive in Afghanistan. But the real reason for the dismissal of General Ahmad might not be so cut-and-dried as it may seem.

In an article in the *Times of India* from October 10, 2001 that was given very little attention in the United States in the wake of the attacks, the paper revealed information linking General Ahmad to the ringleader of 9-11, Mohammad Atta.

Citing Indian intelligence reports that were transmitted to the United States, the article said, "The evidence we [the Government of India] have supplied to the US is of a much wider range and depth than just one piece of paper linking a rogue general to some misplaced act of terrorism."

It is worth quoting a part of the *Times of India* piece in order to fully convey the possible ramifications of the charges in the wake of 9-11:

> While the Pakistani Inter Services Public Relations claimed that former ISI director-general Lt. General Mahmoud Ahmad sought retirement after being superseded on Monday 8 October, the day the US started bombing Afghanistan, the truth is more shocking. Top sources confirmed here on Tuesday [October 9], that the general lost his job because of the "evidence" India produced to show his links to one of the suicide bombers that wrecked the World Trade Centre. The US authorities sought his removal after confirming the fact that $100,000 was wired to WTC hijacker Mohammad Atta by Amad Umar Sheikh at the insistence of General Mahmoud [Amad]. Senior government sources have confirmed that India contributed significantly to establishing the link between the money transfer and the role played by the dismissed ISI chief. While they did not provide details, they said that Indian inputs, including Sheikh's mobile phone number, helped the FBI in tracing and establishing the link.

The reference to Ahmad Umar Sheikh (really Omar Saeed Sheikh) is to the same person who was held on charges of abducting Danny Pearl.

In a subsequent article by reporter Manoj Joshi published in the *Times of India* on August 1, 2003 under the title "9-11 funds came to Pakistan says FBI," we learn that John Pistole, the deputy assistant director of the FBI's counter-terrorism division, had "traced the origins of the funding of 9-11 back to financial accounts in Pakistan." The original *Times of India* article linking General Ahmad to Mohammad Atta said that $100,000 was sent by Omar Saeed Sheikh to Atta in the weeks before 9-11. The FBI has estimated that the cost of the 9-11 attacks was about $175,000 to $250,000, and that the money came from unknown accounts and individuals in both Germany and the United Arab Emirates.

If any segment of the *Times of India* story is correct, the smoking gun linking the head of the Pakistani ISI and the leader of the 9-11 attacks, Mohammad Atta, may have huge consequences on how we look at the events of that tragic day.

Chapter 52:
The CIA, bin Laden and 9-11

Early on, while the CIA had some operatives following Osama bin Laden's activities, the FBI had its own man on the inside who provided vital information on him. He was an American soldier named Ali Mohamed who had quite a checkered past. What U.S. authorities did not know was that Ali Mohamed was also secretly working for bin Laden.

Ali Mohamed was an Egyptian by birth and entered the Egyptian army, taking training in the elite Egyptian Special Forces. He served as an intelligence officer, and was a devoted Muslim. In 1981 he came to the United States and took extensive training with the Green Berets at Fort Bragg, North Carolina. While in Egypt, Ali Mohamed attended sermons by The Blind Sheik, Omar Abdel-Rahman, who would later be tried for plotting to destroy bridges and tunnels in New York City. Ali joined Sheik Rahman's Egyptian Islamic Jihad.

After leaving the Egyptian army in 1984, Ali got a job with the Egyptian airlines. He then contacted the CIA and proffered his extensive services, and was hired on a temporary basis. When the agency learned that he was having unauthorized contacts with certain Middle Eastern terrorist groups such as Hezbollah, he was let go. The State Department then put him on a watch list, but when he applied for a visa to enter the United States in 1986, no one noticed and he slipped through the cracks.

In a bizarre set of circumstances, Ali Mohamed joined the U.S. Army, despite his radical ties to Hezbollah and his entry on the State Department Watch List. He was reassigned to the JFK Special Operations Warfare School where he was a supply sergeant. In an ironic twist, it would be the men of this elite unit who would be part of any American attack on bin Laden.

In 1987, Ali took a 30-day leave and, without the permission of his superiors, made his way to Afghanistan to fight the Russians. According to Ali's account, while in Afghanistan he engaged the Russians, learned their battlefield tactics, and killed a number of men. After his 30-day tour was over, he abruptly left Afghanistan and returned to Fort Bragg. He recounted his experiences to his army bosses but they chose not to fully debrief him on what he learned or saw.

Ali Mohamed, as mentioned above, was a member of the Egyptian Islamic Jihad. This unit had been linked to the 1981 assassination of President Sadat of Egypt. Mohamed was not indicted in the Sadat killing because he was in the United States at that time. More troubling was that, on weekends, he went to New York to a shooting range located in Calverton, Long Island where he met with certain members of the team that was planning to blow up the World Trade Center (the first attempt in 1993). Among the men whom he met at Calverton were El Sayyid Nosair, Mohammed Abouhalima, Mohammed Ajaj, and Mohammed Salameh. El Sayyid would later kill the firebrand Jewish Rabbi Meyer Kahane in Manhattan on November 5, 1990.

What is more damaging in the story of Ali Mohamed is that an elite team of FBI agents called SOG followed Ali to the Calverton shooting range and took pictures of the team practicing on targets. These shooting sessions continued until July 23, 1989 when they were ended.

The FBI now had proof that a number of Islamic men were taking part in practice shooting sessions, including a member of the U.S. Army who had "Secret" clearance, but the FBI did not report Ali Mohamed's alliance with these men and no action was taken against him.

When his tour of duty was over, he moved with his wife to Sacramento, California where he secretly became an informer for the FBI (despite his links to the Calverton shooting cell). While working for the Bureau, Ali clandestinely worked for and met with bin Laden's number two man, Ayman al-Zawahiri, the leader of the Egyptian Islamic Jihad, who was allowed into the United States. He served as al-Zawahiri's security guard on trips. He also failed to tell the FBI that while he was in Afghanistan, he aided bin Laden with the security layout when the al-Qaeda leader moved to Sudan. Years later Ali told U.S. intelligence agents that he took part in military and explosive training with bin Laden's forces. In 1993, with the help of Ali Mohamed, the CIA got its first real glimpse of bin Laden and his al-Qaeda network, including knowledge of the fact that bin

Laden had set his sights on toppling the Saudi regime, and attacking American targets across the globe.

It wasn't until the late 1990s, that the Justice Department put out an order for Ali's arrest. He subsequently became a government informant, passing on whatever information he had on bin Laden.

The year 1997 turned out to be a pivotal one in the United States' war on Osama bin Laden and the Taliban regime that was harboring him. Three years previously, the Taliban received its biggest boost when the Pakistani ISI all but created the new regime, giving all necessary aid in its bid for power. On May 25, 1997, Pakistan formally recognized the Taliban as the legitimate government of Afghanistan. For the United States, the recognition by its erstwhile ally in the hunt for international terrorists was a blow that could not go unanswered. A further blow to U.S. interests vis a vis the Taliban came the following day when Saudi Arabia officially recognized the government. Soon, the United Arab Emirates would become the last of the only three nations in the world to give the Taliban a nod.

Given this situation, it was decided by President Clinton to re-enter Afghanistan in a covert way and unleash the CIA in an effort to kill or capture bin Laden. Cruise missiles were also released on four targets said to be terrorist training camps. Rather than keeping quiet, bin Laden continued to urge his followers to attack Western targets across the globe.

The United States decided it was time for an unofficial plan to get bin Laden, and in 1998, in a secret move, allied with the government of Uzbekistan, once a former Soviet republic. A covert plan was developed in which the U.S. and troops from Uzbekistan conducted joint military operations against the Taliban.

At Langley headquarters, the CIA was burning the midnight oil trying to capture or kill bin Laden. Earlier, while he was still in the Sudan, the CIA instituted an "Issue Station" which would exclusively track every movement bin Laden made. The CIA named their bin Laden watch the "TFL," or terrorist financial links. With bin Laden back in Afghanistan, the CIA now put him in another category as a main terror suspect, not just the financier that he had originally been thought to be. The watch now took the simple name OBL. In secret, the CIA began to try to cultivate new assets inside Afghanistan to monitor bin Laden's every move.

In an attempt to conquer bin Laden, the CIA's Counter-terrorist Center came up with a daring plan that called for the capture of bin Laden at his main headquarters called Tarnak Farms located near the city of Kandahar. The CIA was able to lay out with precision all the main buildings at Tarnak Farms, and by 1997, were training with local allies in the region to implement the attack.

DCI George Tenet briefed National Security Advisor Sandy Berger about the plan and the CIA was given permission to put the operation in motion. The operation called for a group of Afghan allies to snatch bin Laden from Tarnak Farms and take him to a location near Kandahar where he would be turned over to another group. From that location, bin Laden was to be flown to the U.S. When discussing the plan, it was noted by those involved that if anything went wrong, innocent people, or the men directly involved in the mission, might be killed. One of the principals involved in the decision justified the job by saying, "Sooner or later, bin Laden will attack the U.S., perhaps using WMD [weapons of mass destruction]."

In March 1998, the CIA had begun mock drills for the attack plan. Soon, the operation was modified whereby the second group of agents on the ground in Afghanistan would hold bin Laden for up to a month, not take him immediately to the U.S.

While the CIA had no problem with the raid, other high-ranking special operations officers had qualms. The commander of the Delta Force team was "uncomfortable" with the fact that bin Laden would be held on the ground for so long. Another person who had trouble with the operation as it stood was Lt. General Michael Canavan, the commander of the Joint Special Operations Forces. General Canavan bluntly said that the proposed mission could not be carried out by the CIA as planned. It was "out of their league."

In April 1998, while the capture/assassination plans were being implemented against bin Laden, the Clinton administration sent U.N. Ambassador Bill Richardson on a fact-finding trip to South Asia that included a stop in Afghanistan. Ambassador Richardson was the first official of the U.S. government to travel to that nation in years, and more to the point, while bin Laden was being given sanctuary by the Taliban. In a tense meeting with Taliban leaders, Richardson asked that bin Laden be expelled (which was denied), and asked that the civil war between the Taliban and the various Afghan factions be stopped (another failure). Why Richardson went to talk with the Taliban to begin with is questionable, as his journey just resulted in failure.

In May 1998, a Memorandum of Notification, a legal document that authorized the bin Laden snatch operation was reviewed by the CIA. They said that they believed it had a 30% chance of success, and the plan was run by Attorney General Janet Reno and FBI Director Louis Freeh. Also in the meeting was John O'Neil, the head of the FBI's New York Field Office, as well as Mary Joe White, the U.S. Attorney for the Southern District of New York.

The date for the raid was scheduled for no later than July 23, 1998.

On May 20, DCI Tenet met with Sandy Berger. Tenet said that he believed that many people would be killed in the attack on Tarnak Farms, including innocent tribesmen and others not involved in the raid. Without consulting anyone else in the administration, Tenet called off the mission. "Mike," a CIA officer who was deeply involved in the mission's progress said, "We were told to stand down on the operation for the time being." The reason for the cancellation, said Mike, was fear of "collateral damage," or the loss of innocent lives. The 9-11 Commission wrote with regard to the cancellation of the attack, "They [the administration] were concerned about the tribal safety, and had worried that the purpose and nature of the operation would be subject to unavoidable misinterpretation—and probably recrimination—in the event that bin Laden, despite our best intentions and efforts, did not survive."

In the final analysis, all the participants involved said that DCI Tenet was the one who cancelled the operation, and did not really push for it within the Clinton White House. The CIA field officers were the ones who were most disappointed in the mission's scrubbing. Gary Schroen, a CIA officer with deep experience in Afghanistan said, "It was the best plan we were going to come up with to capture bin Laden while he was in Afghanistan and bring him to justice."

Reflecting on the failed capture mission, the 9-11 Commission wrote of the event, "It was the duty of Tenet and the CIA leadership to balance the risks of inaction against jeopardizing the lives of their operatives and agents. And they had reason to worry about failure; millions of dollars down the drain; a shoot-out that could be seen as an assassination; and, if there were any repercussions in Pakistan, perhaps a coup. The decisions of the U.S. government in May 1998 were made, as Berger has put it, from the vantage point of the driver looking through a muddy windshield moving forward, not through a clean rearview mirror."

A new plan to get bin Laden took shape after the August 7, 1998 East Africa embassy bombings that killed hundreds of people, among them, Americans. The White House and the CIA tasked the agency with recruiting as many as possible Afghan tribesmen from the various tribes who wanted to work for the U.S. in an effort to capture bin Laden. On a number of occasions, these informants gave the CIA details of where bin Laden would be on a given day. However, no attack took place, as bin Laden was so well protected that it would have been foolish to attempt a strike. One time, bin Laden suddenly changed his route so when the attack team got to the location, he was already gone.

To show just how serious the Clinton administration was in getting to bin Laden, the President, in August 1998, signed a Memorandum of Notification that gave the CIA permission to capture bin Laden or better yet, kill him. A basic lack of intelligence forced the CIA to abandon its plan to kill bin Laden. Those CIA officers who took part in the covert plan to get bin Laden said the administration accepted the policy of "risk avoidance" when it came to killing him.

After the 1998 embassy bombings, the U.S. ordered the Navy to station two submarines equipped with cruise missiles in strategic positions in the Indian Ocean awaiting a chance to kill bin Laden. But once intelligence agents on the ground pinpointed bin Laden's position, it would take up to ten hours to program the missiles, more than enough time for him to get away. On a few occasions, the CIA had bin Laden in its sights and was ready to unleash the missiles. At the last minute, DCI Tenet decided that there was not enough detailed information to authorize a strike and they were not carried out.

One such strike did take place after the 1998 embassy bombings, but bin Laden was apparently tipped off (possibly by the ISI) and while a number of his followers were killed, the main target eluded the CIA once again. After the 1998 attack, Richard Clarke, the President's Counter-terrorism "czar," said that if the ISI wanted to fully cooperate with the CIA about bin Laden's location, they could have easily picked up the phone. Unfortunately, no call ever came.

In the wake of the U.S. retaliation for the embassy bombings, the Clinton administration decided on a full tilt strategy to target bin Laden. The President asked Richard Clarke to come up with a plan. Clarke came up with a far-ranging structure called "Delenda," which name was derived from the Latin "to destroy." It was Clarke's job to lay out the potential strategy and report to the higher-ups in the White House, who would accept or reject his proposals. The goal of the plan was the elimination of any threat from the "bin Laden organization." Other pertinent parts of the plan were to prevent any further threat from al-Qaeda against Americans worldwide.

The strategy for Delenda was the following:

•Diplomacy to eliminate the sanctuary in Afghanistan and bring terrorists to justice.
•Covert action to disrupt terrorist cells and prevent attacks. The highest priority was to target the enemy in Afghanistan.
•Financial measures, beginning with the just-adopted executive order to freeze the funds of bin Laden related businesses.
•Military action to attack targets as they were developed. This would be an ongoing campaign, not a series of responses in retaliation to particular provocations.

Despite Clarke's extensive work on Delenda, the influential powers in the Clinton administration decided not to implement the plan.

The decision not to implement Delenda left the United States without any effective covert action program to eliminate bin Laden. Efforts by the United States to get Saudi Arabia and Pakistan to aid in the disruption of bin Laden's finances were not effective. Also, neither Pakistan nor the Saudi government would yield in their support of the Taliban regime that gave sanctuary to bin Laden in Afghanistan. With little foreign help coming, Clarke grudgingly told the President that in his opinion it was a "virtual certainty" that bin Laden's followers were likely to hit the Unites States at some future date.

By October 1998, an analyst for the Defense Intelligence Agency, a brave agent named Julie Sirrs, made a covert trip to Afghanistan to see for herself the conditions on the ground and report back her findings. Sirrs met with Ahmed Shah Massoud who pleaded for more money to carry on the fight against bin Laden. Massoud told Sirrs that bin Laden was the prime financier of the Taliban, and that if it weren't for his aid, they would not be able to stay in power. She also reported that the Afghan airline called Ariana Airlines was the principal facilitator of the delivery of drugs and arms to the Taliban from other countries.

Upon her return to D.C., her reports were met with skepticism and downright hostility on the part of the State Department. Sirrs said," the State Department didn't want to have anything to do with Afghan resistance, or even, politically, to reveal that there was any viable option to the Taliban."

In another affront to her character, all of the material she brought back from her trip was taken away and her security clearance was yanked. In the end, she was exonerated of any wrongdoing but eventually quit the DIA. That the State Department and the CIA refused to cooperate with Julie Sirrs after her dangerous trip to Afghanistan, with her life potentially on the line, is outrageous.

At various times during the CIA's hunt for bin Laden, DCI Tenet terminated any U.S. strike against bin Laden for lack of "actionable intelligence." Actionable intelligence was put to the test in December 1998 when the U.S. located bin Laden in Afghanistan and was preparing to take him out in a missile strike. The attack was not recommended because of worries about collateral damage to civilians in the immediate area. While the cruise missiles were nixed, another proposal to use precision-guided bombs fired from aircraft over the target was also rejected by General Anthony Zinni, who was the chief of the U.S. Central Command. General Zinni did not want the U.S. to use our warplanes over Afghanistan.

A meeting was held in the spring of 1999 between Richard Clarke and his aides in the White House to discuss a preemptive attack on bin Laden's terrorist camps in Afghanistan. Why wait for another al-Qaeda attack when the camps would be empty, was their way of thinking. Why not strike now, when we knew where bin Laden would be with a fair amount of certainty? The group discussed attacking a number of bin Laden's infrastructures but this tack was rejected as not militarily feasible.

By the summer of 1999 it was obvious that a new plan was needed to disrupt bin Laden. At CIA headquarters, Cofer Black, a veteran of the CIA-Afghan wars, took control of the Counter-terrorism Center. He developed a new plan that relied less on the CIA's Afghan allies, and included more trained CIA agents who would be able to infiltrate Afghanistan. The plan also called for a new pact with the Northern Alliance that had been allowed to fade away after the U.S. pulled out after the Soviet-Afghan war ended.

In the spring of 2000, shortly before Clinton was to leave office, Clarke's members of the Principles Committee met in the White House to plan further strategy. Clarke asked permission to use cruise missiles against bin Laden if he or any of his men were spotted by the Predator unmanned drone that was now being flown by the CIA over Afghanistan. He was told by National Security Advisor Sandy Berger that before any decision was made authorizing cruise missiles, a verified sighting of bid Laden would be necessary. Thus, the phrase "actionable intelligence" was brought into the lexicon of the war on terror.

When the 9-11 Commission began its work, it was decided, in an unorthodox move, to hire a young woman by the name of Alexis Albion to work on its counter-terrorism policy team. Alexis Albion was then at Harvard University doing her PhD in history. Her case was unusual as she read spy books in order to write her doctoral dissertation. She was especially interested in Ian Fleming's fictional spy, James Bond, or 007. At Harvard she wrote a paper called "The Global Historical Moment of Bond in the mid-1960s." The title of her dissertation was "The Spy in All of Us: The Public Image of Intelligence."[1]

Ms. Albion was hired by Philip Zelikow, who was the executive director of the 9-11 Commission. She was appointed to Team 3, the counter-terrorism team. She would be the commission's chief investigator of the CIA and its vast archives. She would be

[1] Shenon, Philip, *The Commission: The Uncensored History of the 9/11 Investigation,* Twelve Publishing Co., New York, 2008, Page 135.

responsible for reading all the CIA files at Langley on al-Qaeda and the CIA's response to terrorist threats.

At 33, this was a chance of a lifetime and she approached in her work with vigor. She was soon a familiar face at Langley headquarters, and she spent most of her days reviewing past CIA case files on terrorist attacks on the United States. Supervised by an agency lawyer, her notes were checked and, once cleared, were sent to the 9-11 Commission staff.

One of the things she was able to read was "the Scroll," a huge chronology that was prepared after 9-11 that documented all elements of the CIA's antiterrorist efforts before 9-11. "The Scroll" was estimated to be about 150 feet across, " a day-by-day, hour-by-hour, almost minute-by-minute chronology on the agency's battles against al-Qaeda."

The most important information came from the CIA's Alec Station, the office they set up in 1996 to find out all they could on Osama bin Laden and al-Qaeda. The director of Alec Station was a veteran agency officer named Michael Scheuer. Scheuer was a 22- year veteran of the CIA who was called "the Prophet" by his co-workers for his relentless warnings about al-Qaeda and bin Laden. Alec Station was not located at Langley, rather it was in a nondescript office in Tysons Corner, Virginia in the middle of a shopping center. Remarking on its location, Scheuer said, "It was a good idea because it kept us away from all the crap" at Langley. He said that he first came to believe that bin Laden was a threat to America after he released his fatwa—a declaration of war against the United States—in 1996. Bin Laden's fatwa attacked the royal family in Saudi Arabia for allowing the U.S. to use its land at the beginning of the 1991 Persian Gulf War. In December 1996, Alec Station prepared a 50-paragraph memo regarding bin Laden's efforts to acquire WMD. Scheuer asked his superiors to distribute the entire memo to the proper people at Langley but they only sent two paragraphs along, saying that he was an "alarmist" regarding bin Laden.

Clearly, the agency did not take Scheuer's warnings about the dangers of bin Laden seriously. Speaking before the 9-11 Commission he said, "I am big on personal accountability. I'm not sure we could have stopped the attack, but I know for a fact that we didn't do everything we could. I do think that if we had killed bin Laden in the desert, this never would have happened," referring to 9-11.

Scheuer was so incensed at the agency's failure to take bin Laden seriously, he sent an e-mail to DCI Tenet listing the 10 things that needed to be changed if the CIA was ever to effectively confront al-Qaeda. For his insubordination, he was fired. He was sent back to Langley headquarters where he worked in the CIA's library.

When Albion was working on the final draft of the 9-11 report, she discovered that President George W. Bush did not mention al-Qaeda or bin Laden often in his public speeches compared to President Clinton in his. She asked Zelikow if she could have this piece of information published in the final report. He said no.

Both the FBI and the CIA were complicit in fumbling the ball as far as the warning signs of the 9-11 attack are concerned. Their sins of omission are too numerous to mention, but here are just a few warnings ignored:

•The arrival of a number of Arab speaking men taking flight training in Phoenix, Arizona which was reported by FBI agent Harry Ellen.

•In Phoenix, FBI agent Ken Williams was becoming worried regarding the activities of certain Middle Eastern men who took classes in airport management at the Embry-Riddle Aeronautical University in Prescott, Arizona.

•The FBI did not know that two Arab men who took part in 9-11, Khalid al Midhar and Nawaf Hazmi, who arrived in the U.S. in January 2000, were in San Diego. At the time that al Midhar and al Hazmi lived in San Diego they were in constant contact with an unnamed FBI informant who provided the Bureau with information on them. Both men had previously attended an al-Qaeda summit in Malaysia in which planning for the 9-11 attack was hatched. Adding to the CIA's sins, it wasn't until August 2001 that the agency asked that the two men be placed on a watch list in order to prevent them from entering the United States.

•Planning for the 9-11 attack took place in Hamburg, Germany. Among the participants were Mohammad Atta,

Ramzi Binalshibh, Marwan al Shehhi, and Ziad Jurrah. In late 1999, they went to Afghanistan for terrorist training. Both the CIA and German intelligence monitored the men for months but had no clue as to what these men were up to.

In the end, 9-11 was waiting to happen.

Chapter 53:
The CIA and Saddam Hussein

When United States forces captured Saddam Hussein in December 2003 hiding in his rat hole, the top administrator in Iraq, Paul Bremer, informed the world by saying at a press conference, "Ladies and gentlemen, we got 'im." The fact is that Saddam was: everything the world said he was, a tyrant who killed thousands of his own citizens, a mass torturer who took pleasure in maiming and killing anyone who opposed his rule, a man who invaded a neighboring country (Kuwait) because he believed that Kuwait was the lost province of Iraq, and a man who ignored all international sanctions imposed upon him by the world community despite the fact that his nation was starving to death.

The big story, all but ignored in the flush of the moment, was that for more than 40 years, Saddam Hussein was used by the United States and the CIA for their own purposes, mainly as a bulwark against Soviet domination in the Middle East. In its long history, the CIA made relationships of convenience with various military strongmen in the world, mainly in the Cold War years. For example, we supported Batista in Cuba, Diem in South Vietnam, the Shah of Iran, Trujillo in the Dominican Republic, and Noriega in Panama. All these men were ruthless dictators who were eventually overthrown or killed. Saddam Hussein, too, was used by the United States, although he began his life as nothing more than a rabble-rouser and an ineffective assassin.

The United States first began its ties with a very young Saddam Hussein when he took part in a CIA attempt to kill Prime Minister Abd al-Karim Qassim. On July 14, 1958, Qassim and his followers overthrew the Iraqi monarchy of King Faisal II. Iraq, in the 1950s, was seen by the United States as a bulwark against Soviet communism, especially in the Middle East. Iraq's strategic position was heightened by the fact that the country was rich in oil. Iraq also joined the anti-communist Baghdad Pact that included such nations as the United States, Turkey, Britain, Iran, and Pakistan.

In time, Washington was startled to notice that the Qassim

government was purchasing arms from the Soviet Union, and putting communist sympathizers in various governmental positions. The situation got so bad that then CIA Director Dulles said, "Iraq today is the most dangerous spot on earth." As Washington got more and more fed up with Qassim's ruling Baath Party, they began covert steps to overthrow him.

Saddam Hussein joined the Baath Party at age 20 and would rule in its name until his overthrow in 2003. The attempt on Qassim took place on October 7, 1959 while he was en route to the East German embassy in Baghdad. Qassim was to travel along al-Rashid Street, and it was along this route that the gunmen would await their target. Saddam Hussein was to render covering fire for the four shooters who would take out Qassim. As Qassim passed by in his car, the assassins opened fire, killing his driver and wounding another person in the car. Qassim himself was shot in the shoulder and was taken to a hospital in a taxi. As far as Hussein was concerned, he got so excited when the car passed, he began firing and was himself wounded in the frenzy. In the ensuing melee, Hussein, disguised as a Bedouin, crossed the hot Iraqi desert and spent the next three years in Egypt and Syria. While in Egypt, Hussein was befriended by the country's ruler, Gamal Abdul Nassar who was no friend of Qassim's.

According to various intelligence reports of the day, Hussein was under the control of both the CIA and Egyptian intelligence. One report had him in Beirut, Lebanon where he took training under the aegis of the CIA. CIA officers who knew Hussein in those days said he "was known as having no class. He was a thug—a cutthroat." In Cairo, Saddam often dined at the Andiana cafe and rarely paid his bills.

Qassim's luck finally ran out on February 8, 1963 when Baath Party supporters staged a coup that resulted in his ouster from power. Qassim had made the Kennedy administration angry when he took Iraq out of the Baghdad Pact, threatening to allow the Soviets into Iraq. In 1961, he also threatened to invade Kuwait and nationalized a part of the Iraq Petroleum Company.

In the end, Qassim was killed and the Baath Party indulged in an orgy of violence and killing.

Throughout much of the 1960s and 1970s, the United States was beset with problems at home and abroad, fighting a non-winnable war in Vietnam, and supplying military equipment to the rebels fighting the Russians in Afghanistan. In Iraq, Saddam Hussein had taken power and ran that country like his own personal fiefdom. However, the United States once again turned its attention to Iraq when Iraq and Iran began a years-long, bloody war that would leave thousands dead on both sides.

In 1984, the United States and Iraq repaired their mutual diplomatic relations and the first Bush administration looked to Iraq to contain Iran in the Persian Gulf. The United States knew full well who Saddam Hussein was, a ruthless dictator who had no compunction when it came to killing his own people. However, realpolitik dominated Washington and the Bush administration decided it was better to keep Saddam Hussein in power, where we could at least try to control him, than take the chance that an Iranian victory would carve up large chunks of Iraq, thus allowing the Soviet Union an entryway into the region.

The U.S. even went one step further when it lifted Iraq from the list of nations who harbored international terrorists, even though Abu Nidal was then living in Baghdad.

In Washington, President Bush gave CIA Director William Casey Carte Blanche to aid Iraq with whatever military/intelligence it needed. During the war, the CIA provided Iraq with aerial photographs of the battlefield taken from Saudi Arabian AWACS surveillance planes overhead. Teams of CIA agents arrived in Baghdad to monitor the transfer of information and meet with members of Iraq's intelligence service. One of Saddam's highest-level intelligence agents to meet regularly with the CIA was General al-Samarrai, the deputy head of the Istikbarat (military intelligence).

Once the decision was made to aid Iraq, DCI Casey contacted Jordan's King Hussein and asked if he could take on the role of middleman in supplying American arms to Iraq. The King was glad to comply, and Casey even met with King Hussein on his visits to Jordan. The CIA station chief in Amman, Jordan oversaw the transfer of war material, much of which traveled from Jordan's port of Aqaba to Iraq. At one point in the war, when Iraq faced defeat, King Hussein personally went to Baghdad to present Saddam with U.S. satellite photos.

351

In 1989, the lengthy, merciless conflict between Iran and Iraq ended, along with the CIA-U.S. presence in Iraq. No longer wanted or needed, the U.S. would let Iraq face its own miserable problems. The two nations would meet next, barely two years later, when Saddam took over Kuwait and began the First Persian Gulf War.

Dozens of books have been written about the Persian Gulf War, which began in 1991, and its political/military consequences, and it is not necessary in this text to go into the fine points of the invasion. Suffice it to say that the United States missed a golden opportunity after the ceasefire to march into Baghdad and remove Saddam from power. But that was not part of the U.N. mandate, which called for the coalition to remove Iraq from Kuwait. With that feat accomplished, the United States allowed Saddam to keep a good part of his army intact, allowed him to continue to operate helicopters in parts of the country, and pulled out the vast majority of its troops from the region. In order to protect the minority Kurds, the U.S. and Great Britain imposed a no-fly zone, which was constantly patrolled by aircraft from both nations. These operations would continue right up to the 2003 war.

With the CIA now removed from Iraq after the First Persian Gulf War, the United States got limited intelligence from reports from our Kurdish allies who sent their messages via Iran to Damascus, Syria.

After the war, the prevailing attitude in Washington was that somehow Saddam would be toppled either by his own military or by a revolt inside the country. Nothing of the sort happened and the United States had to find another way to topple Hussein. President George H.W. Bush made a speech in which he encouraged Iraqi dissidents to mount an insurrection against Saddam, but did nothing militarily to back up his call to arms.

With no sign that Saddam's hold on power was slipping, President Bush signed a finding that allowed the CIA to step in and see if they could provoke any kind of covert mischief against Saddam. The person at Langley headquarters ordered "to create the conditions for the removal of Saddam Hussein from power" was Frank Anderson, chief of the Near East division of the agency's Directorate of Operations. Anderson had a most difficult task ahead of him; if a coalition of over a half million troops from many nations could not topple Hussein from power, what was Anderson supposed to do with a limited budget and a few resources on the ground? Most of Anderson's work entailed the spreading of propaganda that would wind up in he hands of Saddam and his loyalists, describing the horrid fate that awaited them if they continued in office.

Iraq was what was called a "denied area"; no CIA agent could enter the country to meet any dissidents. Saddam had such a tight-fisted rein on the opposition that no Iraqi military official was allowed to travel outside of Iraq, thus causing major headaches for any agency personnel willing or able to meet with the resistance.

From the mid 1990s under the Clinton administration, right up to the 2003 war against Iraq, the CIA mounted a number of clandestine operations inside Iraq. One such CIA effort was described in a book by ex-CIA officer Robert Baer called *See No Evil: The True Story of a Ground Soldier in the CIA's War on Terrorism* (Crown, 2002).

As Baer describes his covert actions inside Iraq, he and his small team entered the country in January 1995 in order to meet with General Wafiq al-Samarrai in the town of Zakhu. The general had defected from Saddam's army in November 1994 to plot against him. Al-Samarrai told Baer that he represented a number of disgruntled Iraq generals who wanted to oust Saddam. In their discussions, the general asked Baer if the U.S. government would grant diplomatic recognition to the new leader if the coup succeeded.

Another opposition leader Baer met while in Iraq was Ahmed Chalabi, then the head of the Iraqi National Congress, an anti-Hussein group. Chalabi hoped to become the new head of the Iraqi government once Saddam was gone. He urged Baer to set up a secret CIA team in Iraq after the defection of General al-Samarrai. Chalabi further told Baer that he was planning to lead the Kurdish opposition in a revolt on March 4, 1995. After Baer contacted his superiors, the word came back that the U.S. would not give the go-ahead for the proposed revolt.

Chalabi came from a wealthy Shia banking family that moved to London. He attended M.I.T. and the University of Chicago, where he got a PhD in mathematical theory. He moved to Jordan where he founded the Petra Bank. A banking scandal enveloped the Petra Bank and Chalabi was accused of "questionable foreign exchange dealings." The bank failed and he fled to Jordan in the trunk of a car headed for Damascus. He was convicted in absentia of misappropriating $60 million, charges that he denied. In time, the CIA began funding his Iraqi National Congress to the tune of $326,000 per month.

He was a prime mover in the Bush administration's decision to invade Iraq in 2003, pleading the case that Saddam had WMD—weapons of mass destruction—in the months leading up to the war. When no WMD were found in Iraq in the year following the invasion, Chalabi was denied any further funding, and in the spring of 2004, his offices in Baghdad were looted by Iraqi forces, with the full cooperation of the U.S.

As the United States geared up for war against Iraq in 2003, the CIA was given its marching orders by President Bush to shake Saddam's tree and finally right the wrong that had been left over from the 1991 Persian Gulf War.

After 9-11, President George W. Bush declared a war on international terrorism, singling out Iraq, which he believed was one of the prime movers on the world stage. If Richard Clarke is to be believed, days after the World Trade Center was destroyed, the President asked Clarke to find out if Saddam had anything to do with the attacks on New York and Washington. Clarke told the President that all the evidence pointed to al-Qaeda and Osama bin Laden. Unmoved, the President unleashed the CIA against Iraq.

At CIA headquarters, DCI George Tenet appointed "Saul" (his real identity is still secret), the Chief, Iraq Operations Group—bluntly called by its detractors "The House of Broken Toys," for its lack of success in toppling Saddam—to oversee agency operations inside Iraq. "Saul" was born in Cuba and worked for years in the Directorate of Operations; he had also served as the executive assistant to Tenet's number two, John McLaughlin.

After 9-11, Saul met with President Bush and Vice President Dick Cheney and told them that covert action would not overturn Saddam. The only thing that would work was a military invasion.

Saul's proposal was approved and on February 20, 2002, a CIA study team arrived in Kurdish-held northern Iraq to pave the way for the later arrival of CIA paramilitary teams. The name given to the group was NILE, "Northern Iraq Liaison Elements." Over time, the CIA would infiltrate two paramilitary teams inside Iraq, with Saul in charge back at headquarters. They began recruiting teams who were supplying them with good intelligence on Saddam's army.

On March 15, 2003 Saul's men went into action, destroying trucks along the Mosul-to-Baghdad rail line. The rail line was destroyed and a troop train was demolished. Unknown to the American public, the destruction of the rail line set off a number of insurgent attacks on separate military and civilian targets inside Iraq. The CIA had finally been unleashed.

Another covert CIA network set up inside Iraq prior to major military engagement was called ROCKSTAR, which operated in Kurdish-held northern Iraq. One of ROCKSTAR's main agents on the ground was a person called "Rokan" who was the security chief at Dora Farms, a complex near Baghdad on the Tigris River. Rokan radioed the paramilitary teams saying that he had seen Saddam at Dora Farms and he wanted the CIA to know about it. Before the war began, the ROCKSTAR web would prove instrumental in providing the CIA with valuable intelligence on the possible whereabouts of Saddam Hussein.

In the end, it was not the CIA who captured Saddam; a tip from someone on the ground led U.S. troops to Saddam's rat hole in Dawr, a town near Tikrit, Saddam's ancestral home.

Chapter 54:
Kill Bin Laden

It was May 1, 2011, and on the east coast of the United States, the viewing public was getting ready for bed. The Sunday night baseball game of the week had just ended and people were heading off to sleep, just a typical weekend night in the United States. Then, news broadcasts across the country began to interrupt the late night shows, saying that something important was about to be broadcast over the networks. The early word was that it had something to do with Osama bin Laden, the mastermind of the 9-11 attacks that killed more than 3,000 Americans in Washington and New York. A few minutes later, most of the newscasters had reported that Osama bin Laden had possibly been killed in some sort of American military operation. Was it really true? Soon, President Barack Obama came to the podium in the White House and gave the public the word that they had been waiting to hear for 10 long years. In a stern voice, not showing any emotion, the President reported, "justice had been done. For more than two decades, bin Laden has been al-Qaeda's leader and symbol. The death of bin Laden marks the most significant achievement to date in our nation's effort to defeat al-Qaeda. But his death does not mark the end of our effort."

What the President did not tell the world was how difficult and painstaking it had been to finally track down bin Laden, and how all facets of the U.S. intelligence community took part in the operation. When the story was finally told, it was clear that bin Laden had been tracked down by the most sophisticated eavesdropping and electronic communications intelligence on hand. It was a multifaceted effort, using the resources of the CIA, the NSA, and the Navy Seals to pull off the most daring operation in years.

While there was no doubt that bin Laden was responsible for the attacks on 9-11, he never made a public statement taking responsibility for his actions. However, a videotape of his that was found in the Afghan city of Kandahar a few weeks after the attack made that point moot. On the tape he said, "We calculated in advance the number of casualties from the enemy, who would

357

be killed based on the position of the tower. We calculated that the floors that would be hit would be three or four floors. I was the most optimistic of them all." He further said, "The brothers who conducted the operation did not know what the mission would be until just before they boarded the planes."

A few months after the 9-11 attacks, President George W. Bush ordered the United States military to invade Afghanistan, the home of the Taliban who were probably harboring Osama bin Laden. Following the first attacks, bin Laden fled into the Tora Bora Mountains, trying to evade U.S. forces who were hot on his trail. For days, the Air Force bombed the rugged mountains and the administration was sure that they had bin Laden cornered. However, the wily bin Laden was one step ahead of his pursuers and he somehow managed to escape. Whatever chance the United States had in the days following the 9-11 attacks to capture bin Laden was now lost.

For most of the decade after 9-11, there were persistent rumors that bin Laden was hiding in a cave in Afghanistan, or maybe in the tribal areas of Pakistan, being protected by his loyal followers. After a long time of not knowing where he was, the U.S. intelligence community appeared to lose interest in bin Laden's whereabouts, as we geared up for war in Afghanistan and Iraq.

While bin Laden was nowhere to be seen, his terrorist network was still active. On October 12, 2002, a bomb was set off in Bali, killing 202 people. On July 7, 2005, four suicide bombers killed themselves and 52 others in London, England. On July 11, 2006, more than 200 people were killed in explosions that took place in Mumbai, India. On December 25, 2009, a Nigerian man who had links to al-Qaeda, tried to blow up a plane landing in Detroit, Michigan. One month earlier, an American military doctor stationed at Fort Hood, Texas, killed 13 people on the base. All these incidents had links to bin Laden's al-Qaeda networks.

Even while bin Laden's whereabouts were unknown in the early years after September 11, 2001, the U.S. intelligence community was still actively looking for clues as to where he might be. The entire gambit of U.S. intelligence collection operations were centered on a worldwide hunt for any tidbit of information leading to bin Laden's hiding place. The CIA interrogated many captives held in its secret prisons in Eastern Europe, plus the NSA culled e-mails from the Middle East and eavesdropped on telephone calls from known people who were affiliated with bin Laden.

One of the first leads came from CIA interrogations of high level al-Qaeda operatives who had been captured, including the mastermind of 9-11, Khalid Sheikh Mohammed, and al-Qaeda's operational chief, Abu Faraj al-Libi. CIA officers wanted to know the name of bin Laden's chief courier. They gave them his pseudonym, but the man who brought information to and from al-Qaeda to bin Laden both men said they did not know his true identity. CIA interrogators did not believe them, saying that the men were purposely hiding the courier's true identity.

In the years since the attacks, new information on the true identity of the courier has come forth. His real name is Abu Ahmad al-Kuwaiti, a citizen of Kuwait. The first inkling of just who this man was came from detainees at the U.S. prison in Guantanamo Bay, Cuba. Al-Kuwaiti was very close to Khalid Sheikh Mohammed, the mastermind of 9-11. Documents on him say, "[he] received computer training from an al-Qaeda facilitator and subordinate of Mohammed. The assessment added, Al-Kuwaiti worked in the al-Qaeda house operated by KU-10024 [Khalid Sheikh Mohammed] in Kandahar and served as a courier."

U.S. forces spotted Al-Kuwaiti just after 9-11 with bin Laden in the Tora Bora Mountains but he, too, escaped. A U.S. intelligence assessment of him says, "He had access to the inner circle of al-Qaeda through his interactions with senior al-Qaeda members including UBL [bin Laden], Ayman al-Zawahiri, and KU-10024 [Mohammed]."

As the hunt for bin Laden grew cold, the CIA reorganized its efforts to find him. This resulted in a new operation called "Operation Cannonball" that placed more CIA agents inside Pakistan and Afghanistan. These agents were the ones finally able to get the name of the courier. They gave it to the analysts at the National Security Agency who began intercepting his e-mails and phone calls to and from his family in Pakistan. CIA agents on the ground began trailing him and in July 2010, spotted him driving his car in the city of Peshawar, Pakistan. After following him for several weeks, they saw him enter a huge, walled off residence in the city of Abbottabad, Pakistan, near a sprawling military complex. The CIA had no idea who the courier was visiting, but they knew whoever lived in the sprawling place must have been important.

Instead of living in a cold cave in the mountains, bin Laden was staying in a huge compound that was built by an unknown person in 2005. The compound was triangular in shape on a one-acre piece of land. The walls ranged from 10 feet to 18 feet, with a barbed wire fence. The compound was only one mile from Pakistan's elite military academy, comparable to our West Point. There were locked gates in the front, and only people who were known by the inhabitants were allowed to enter. The people living in the home burned their own garbage and refused to allow any strangers to enter. Bin Laden had been living in the home for five years, along with many of his relatives, his children and his wives. Satellite photos of the walled compound often showed a picture of a tall man walking around the area but they could not identify him.

It is interesting to note that no one from the military academy just a few miles from the walled compound tried to find out who was living in the building. John Brennan, a top advisor to President Obama, said of the strange goings-on inside the compound, "Once we came across this compound, we paid close attention to it because it became clear that whoever was living here was trying to maintain a very discreet profile. It had the appearance of sort of a fortress."

In the summer of July 2011, a high level meeting took place at the White House between President Obama, Vice President Joe Biden, Secretary of State Hillary Clinton, CIA Director Leon Panetta, and Defense Secretary Robert Gates. The topic of discussion was the mysterious compound and who might be living there. Director Panetta brought up the possibility that it was bin Laden. Highly sophisticated electronic assets were put in the field to monitor all communications at the Abbottabad residence. U.S. spy satellites took high-resolution pictures of the area. Dozens of receivers were aimed over Pakistan to collect what is called SIGINT—Signals Intelligence—for months at a time. Some of this information was revealed by Edward Snowden, who leaked hundreds of documents on the inner workings of the National Security Agency (Snowden is now living in Russia). The documents came from a "black budget" for U.S. intelligence agencies, including the NSA and the CIA.

These documents were obtained by the *Washington Post,* but they had only a few tidbits of information regarding the bin Laden raid.

About eight hours after the raid to kill bin Laden was over, say the documents, a forensic intelligence laboratory run by the Defense Intelligence Agency in Afghanistan had analyzed the DNA from the body of bin Laden, which provided a "conclusive match" confirming his identity. The Snowden documents also say that satellites run by the National Reconnaissance Office took more than 387 "collects" of high resolution and infrared scans of the Abbottabad compound one month before the raid took place.

Another secret asset of the intelligence community that played a part in the operation was an arm of the NSA called the Tailored Access Operations Group. This highly secret unit's duties were the "specialization of surreptitiously installing spyware and tracking devices on targeted computers and other 'persons of interest' in the hunt for bin Laden."[1]

In February of 2011, Director Panetta had a meeting with Vice Admiral William H. McRaven, commander of the Pentagon's Joint Special Operations Command, at CIA headquarters. Panetta told the admiral of the information coming out of Pakistan and asked that he come up with a series of plans regarding a possible military operation on the compound. McRaven came up with three options: a helicopter assault using U.S. commandos, an air strike with B-2 bombers that would destroy the compound, or a joint raid with Pakistani intelligence operatives who would be told about the raid only hours before the operation began.

By March, the President had asked his most senior military/ intelligence advisors about what they thought would be the best approach. Defense Secretary Gates said that a helicopter attack would be took risky, and recommended the use of smart bombs. That idea was nixed, as there would be no body to be retrieved after such an attack. Meanwhile, the prevailing attitude among most of the officials was that bin Laden was probably in the Abbottabad building. Why would such an elaborate edifice be built to hide someone who was not important? The President weighed his options, and by May, he had made a decision about what action to

---

[1] Whitlock, Craig and Gellman, Burton, *"To hunt Osama bin Laden, satellites watched over Abbottabad, Pakistan, and Navy SEALs," Washington Post,* August 20, 2013.

take. After much reflection, he decided it was worth the risk to take military action. The President knew his decision would have huge ramifications not only for the nation, but also for his presidency. If it succeeded, he'd be the President who finally got bin Laden. If, on the other hand, the raid took place and bin Laden was not there, Obama would have to face the American public and report his failure. Not far in the back of his mind was the failure of U.S. forces to free the American hostages being held in Iran under the presidency of Jimmy Carter. That botched raid ruined Carter's reputation and was one reason for his defeat in the 1980 presidential election by Ronald Reagan.

Before the raid, the CIA employed a Pakistani doctor and other public health officials in Abbottabad. They were to go to the complex and ask the inhabitants to donate blood samples as part of a "vaccination program," to see if the people who lived there might be related to bin Laden. After the raid, the doctor, Shakil Afridi, was arrested and a Pakistani court convicted him of "conspiring against the state." He was given a 33-year prison term but that was later overturned.

Months before the raid took place, the Navy SEALs began practicing assaulting a compound that was much like the one in Abbottabad. They were not told the nature of what their training was for; that information would be given to them at a later date.

On the day of the attack, all White House tours were cancelled, the administration acting under an abundance of caution. On the night before the raid, the President attended the annual White House Correspondents' Dinner where he sparred and traded jokes with the celebrities in the room. While he made jokes at the expense of such people as Donald Trump, who had previously made a stink about the legitimacy of the President's birth certificate, the Navy SEALs were boarding their assault helicopters from a base in Jalalabad, Afghanistan en route to Abbottabad. The assault force consisted of four helicopters and about 80 men. They would land at night, in darkness so as to avoid any unwanted contact with people in the area.

At the White House, the President and all his major national security aides huddled in the Situation Room where they would get real-time information on the progress of the raid.

In the early morning darkness, the SEAL team landed in the compound and headed into the building. Upon entry, they met resistance and firing began on both sides. As the SEALs made their way into the home, they killed three men and one woman, one of the men being bin Laden's son. The SEALs rounded up the other women and children in the home and left them unharmed. Among those killed in the raid was the courier the CIA had initially traced to the Abbottabad compound. The SEALs found bin Laden on the third floor and shot him twice. There was no word if he tried to resist. The SEALs had a picture of bin Laden with them and his wife confirmed his identity. They put his body in a body bag for transport out of the country. Before leaving, they found a treasure trove of computers, computer disks and other electronic equipment, which they retrieved. As they were about to depart, one of the helicopters had mechanical problems, and because of the sensitive nature of the machine, the SEALs blew it up so it would not fall into the hands of the Pakistanis.

By now, the Pakistani army had been alerted to what was happening at the compound, and they began moving their forces into the area. The Americans took off at 1:10 a.m. local time, with the body of bin Laden aboard one of their choppers. A few hours later they arrived back at their base in Afghanistan, the job done.

The next day, the body of Osama bin Laden was taken aboard the U.S. warship *Carl Vinson* where it was prepared for burial, according to Muslim tradition. The body was then sent overboard.

It took 10 years, but retribution for 9-11 had been achieved.

However, the story does not end there. In August 2011, 22 members of SEAL Team 6, some of the same men who killed bin Laden, along with seven Afghan fighters, were killed when their Chinook helicopter was shot down by Taliban fighters. Shortly after the bin Laden raid, word had leaked out that SEAL Team 6 was responsible for his demise. That was supposed to have been a secret, and the families of the SEAL Team, as well as some of the members themselves, felt betrayed. No one knows just what really happened to the Chinook and its passengers in the assault on the chopper. It seems like the Taliban was waiting in ambush for the helicopter. If so, how did they find out where the chopper would be?

After the crash, unnamed senior American military officials

ordered the bodies of the dead soldiers to be cremated, before getting permission from the families. Anther interesting fact concerning the attack is that the black box inside the helicopter was not found. The military said it was destroyed in a flood. Also, according to written reports, the seven Afghan men who were on board the helicopter were not the same men who were on the original flight manifest. Who were they? Congressional Republicans have stated that they will begin hearings in the foreseeable future to find out what really happened to the ill-fated helicopter. So far, nothing concrete has been revealed.

Chapter 55:
What Happened at Benghazi

If you believe that things happen for a reason, then the terrible events at Benghazi were the fault of the late Libyan leader, Muammar Qaddafi. When the erratic and paranoid dictator ran Libya with an iron fist, there was no one who dared to take him on. To do so meant a certain bullet to the head. After Qaddafi began to slaughter his own people in 2011, the Western powers decided they had had enough of his brutal, unpredictable rule and mounted an air campaign to oust him from power. Qaddafi had been a thorn in the side of the United States since the Reagan administration, when we decided to launch an air campaign in retaliation for Libya's support of terrorism in Western Europe in which a number of Americans were targeted. As the air campaign of 2011 grew in intensity, Libyan forces crumbled under the assault, and Qaddafi himself was captured and killed by his own people. What followed in Libya was nothing more than another failed state in the hectic Middle East, one that did not have the stable, solid government the U.S. and its allies hoped it would develop.

Instead Libya became home to numerous terrorist groups in the region who hoped to make that country their new place for jihad. In the city of Benghazi, the second largest in the country, bands of men bearing all sorts of weapons roamed the streets, making it similar to the Wild West of 19th century America. Many of them were supporters of al-Qaeda, which hoped to use Libya as a new jumping off point for their attacks against American targets in the region.

Most Western governments pulled their diplomats out of Benghazi, as did Iran, which was no stranger to terrorism.

For its part, the United States owned Libya after the successful removal of Qaddafi, and our embassy in Tripoli was reopened. Another mission was opened in Benghazi. The man who represented the United States in Libya was Ambassador Christopher Stevens, a well-heeled diplomat with years of experience in the Middle East. Stevens was born in Grass Valley, California in 1960 and had served in the Peace Corps in Morocco, where he began a love affair with the Middle East and its people. Most of his diplomatic postings were in North Africa. In April 2011, Stevens was sent to Benghazi as the special representative of the U.S. by Secretary of State Hillary Clinton. He was sent to Libya at the time of the insurgency against Qaddafi, and he soon forged relationships with many of those elements on the ground who were trying to oust the dictator. He was a likeable person and soon even the militants who were working against Qaddafi decided that Chris Stevens was someone they could trust.

Once Qaddafi was gone, President Obama appointed Stevens as the new U.S. Ambassador and he took up residence in the embassy in Tripoli. He soon cemented good relations with all the various factions in the country, and he was an admired friend of ordinary Libyans he met on the street. For once, America was the good guy in Libya.

The United States also had another diplomatic compound in Libya, in Benghazi where we operated a U.S. Special Mission, a consulate that took on all the duties of the main embassy in Tripoli. Ambassador Stevens spent many a day in Benghazi, meeting with local officials as well as the Americans under his command. He was in Benghazi when his life ended. What happened at Benghazi revealed the CIA's involvement in an as-yet undisclosed undercover operation that has yet to be fully explained, and embroiled the Obama administration in a controversy that still has legs as of this writing.

The group responsible for security at all U.S. embassies in the Middle East and elsewhere is the Diplomatic Security Service, which is part of the Bureau of Diplomatic Security (DS), which is run by the U.S. State Department. Part of the DS's job is the physical security of all our embassies, including providing blast proof doors and other means by which an embassy could be protected from attacks aimed at the buildings. In one of their most successful operations, DS and FBI agents mounted a raid to capture Ramzi Yousef, the man who was responsible for the 1991 bombing of the World Trade Center. In a coordinated operation, they found Yousef holed up in an apartment in Islamabad, Pakistan and whisked him back to the United States to stand trial.

On September 11, 2012, 11 years after the attacks on the U.S., there were only five DS agents assigned to the Benghazi consulate, not really enough to protect the building from a well coordinated attack. The Libyan government (what was left of it) was not able to provide any real security to augment the DS officers on the ground. Ambassador Stevens was in residence at that time, doing his work as he had always done. Two of the men in the compound were Stevens' personal security guards who had flown in with him from Tripoli.

All seemed quiet on the night of September 11. Inside the compound the Americans slept or were getting ready for bed. A Libyan security guard (who was unarmed) was stationed at the main gate, more of a lookout than anything else. At around 9:30 p.m., a tan Toyota pickup truck belonging to a group of militias known as SSC (Supreme Security Council) pulled up near the main gate. The truck was armed with twin Soviet-built 23mm anti-aircraft guns, which were used against jet fighters. Suddenly, the driver of the pickup left the scene, as if on cue. After the attack, a report by the Accountability Review Board said of the incident, "This hints that the SSC knew an attack was imminent; that it did not warn the security assets in the Special Mission Compound implies that it and elements of the new Libyan government were complicit in the events that transpired."

A dozen heavily armed men poured into the Special Mission Compound seeking their targets. Also pouring in were heavily armed Toyota and Nissan pickups loaded with multi-barreled 12.7mm, and 14.5mm heavy machine guns. As the shooting began, the Americans in the compound tried to assess the unfolding situation as best they could. At that point they had no idea how many men were in the area, and took up defensive positions to the best of their ability. One troubling incident was, when the attack first took place, the U.S.-allied February 17 Martyrs Brigade took flight and began running away.

As the firing began, one of the DS agents found Ambassador Stevens and his communications specialist Sean Smith, a 34-year-old Air Force veteran and computer specialist, and began taking them to a safe room in the building. Wearing protective vests, the men hid in a steel-reinforced room with limited access of entry and egress. Ambassador Stevens made two calls, the first to Gregory Hicks, his deputy chief of mission in Tripoli. Hicks did not immediately respond. The second call went to members of a local militia brigade. The ambassador, however, did not call members of the U.S.- allied Libya Shield Force, a group of fighters which was a paramilitary force associated with the Libyan Defense Ministry. Neither of these two groups rendered any assistance. In the ensuing chaos 35-armed members of the rebel forces lobbed grenades and fired heavy weapons into the building, making escape for the Americans trapped inside almost impossible.

As described in an article in *Vanity Fair* magazine called "40 Minutes in Benghazi" by authors Fred Burton and Samuel Katz, the attackers were well coordinated in the maneuvers, split into small, effective groups, and wore different kinds of uniforms. The authors assert that the attackers were people from different cities, including Derna, Benghazi and Tobruk. They write, "It was clear that *whoever* the men who assaulted the compound were, they had been given precise orders, and impeccable intelligence. They seemed to know when, where, and how to get from the access points to the ambassador's residence and how to cut off the DS agents as well as the local guard force and the February 17 Martyrs Brigade militiamen on duty that night. The moment notifications and requests went out to the Libyan Transnational Council and the militias in advance of Steven's arrival, it was basically like broadcasting the ambassador's itinerary at Friday prayers for all to hear."[1]

The assailants picked up fully loaded fuel cans they found in the compound and began pouring the combustible fuel on the floor of the compound. They then lit the cans, sending a huge pillar of fire rumbling throughout the building, trapping Ambassador Stevens and the DS agents inside.

As the compound burned, one of the DS agents, whom the writers referred to as "R," sent a hurried communication to the CIA Annex in Tripoli, as well as the Diplomatic Security Service Command Center in Virginia.

Twelve attackers breached the building where the Americans were hiding, firing RPG munitions. The building was now completely engulfed in fire, and agent "A" tried desperately to locate Sean Smith and Ambassador Stevens, to no avail. In the end,

---

[1] Burton, Fred and Katz, Samuel, "40 Minutes in Benghazi," *Vanity Fair,* August, 2013. Page 141.

four Americans were killed, including Sean Smith and Ambassador Chris Stevens. The attack on Ambassador Stevens' compound was a monumental intelligence failure on many fronts. However, the story does not end there. In the wake of the attack, the CIA came under intense scrutiny as to just how many of its agents were in the Benghazi area at the time of the attack, and their possible role in a covert mission that may have involved the sale of rockets to the rebels fighting in Syria.

At the time of the attack, there were 35 CIA officers in Benghazi about a mile from the consulate. In the months after the attack there were persistent allegations that certain people in Washington and elsewhere deliberately held back these men from aiding Ambassador Stevens and his DS agents while the attack was going on. Top-level CIA officers said that the reason they didn't give the immediate order to aid the ambassador was because they were trying to contact their Libyan allies in the region to give assistance. As we have seen, these groups never did render assistance, for whatever reasons. After it was obvious that no outside help was available, the CIA officers moved toward the embattled compound. One CIA contractor said he made calls on the radio asking for air cover but there were no planes in the immediate area. One unnamed U.S. army ranger who was at the secret base said that he was told to "wait" two times by his superior and was not able to help his comrades. According to congressional testimony, when seven CIA officers made it to the compound, they had to fight their way into the area under intensive fire. Once inside the building, they found five DS officers and took shelter with them. As they made their way into the building, they found Sean Smith dead, but did not locate Ambassador Stevens. Republican Congressman Lynn Westmoreland, who headed the House Intelligence subcommittee investigating the Benghazi attack, said that when the CIA team returned to their base they were attacked by militants and returned fire, which then ended the skirmish.

Months after the attack, the national press began an intensive inquiry into what really happened in Benghazi the night Ambassador Stevens was killed. The *Wall Street Journal* wrote an article saying, "The U.S. mission in Benghazi was at its heart a CIA operation."

In her testimony before the committee, former Secretary of State Hillary Clinton told Congress "that the CIA was leading a concerted effort to try to track down and find and recover MANPADS [man-portable air defense systems] looted from the stockpiles of toppled Libyan ruler Muammar Qaddafi." It is alleged that the compound in Benghazi served as a diplomatic cover for a hidden annex. The presence of a secret agency base in Benghazi was disclosed by Charlene Lamb, a top official in the State Department's Bureau of Diplomatic Security. In her testimony, Ms. Lamb showed a photograph of the secret compound, which she should never have done. She was interrupted in her testimony by two congressmen, Jason Chaffetz and Darrell Isa who asked that her revelation be stricken from the record. Congressman Chaffetz said during the hearing, "I totally object to the use of that photo. I was told specifically while I was in Libya I could not and should not ever talk about what you're showing here today."

According to *Business Insider.com,* on the day of his death, Ambassador Stevens met with the Turkish Consul General Ali Sait Akin; Ambassador Stevens had gone to Benghazi "to negotiate a weapon transfer in an effort to get SA-7 missiles out of the hands of the Libya-based extremists." It is said that the reason Ambassador Stevens met with the Turkish official was to broker a deal whereby these SA-7 missiles would be transferred to the Syrian rebels battling the government of Bashir Assad. Soon thereafter, the rebels were successful in shooting down numerous Syrian helicopters and a few fighter jets. Coincidence or not?

The question that must be asked is this: Did the CIA run a covert operation out of Benghazi to funnel SA-7 missiles that were supposed to be destroyed to the Syrian rebels? It is a well-known fact that Turkey was sending huge amounts of ammunition to the rebels in Syria over a long period of time. Were the SA-7s part of the deal? Was Ambassador Stevens' last talk with Consul General Ali Sait Akin part of the missile transfer? Those questions, among many others, are still open to debate and need to be decided before we know what really happened at Benghazi on that terrible September night.

Appendix:
The Directors of the C.I.A.

Name	Date of Service
Rear Admiral Sidney Souers, NSNR	Jan 23, 1946-June 10, 1946
Lt. Gen. Hoyt Vandenberg, USA	June 10, 1946-May 1, 1947
Rear Admiral Roscoe Hillenkoetter, USN	May 1, 1947-Oct. 7, 1950
Gen. Walter Bedell Smith, USA	October 7, 1950-Feb. 9, 1953
Allen W. Dulles	Feb. 26, 1953-Nov. 29, 1961
John A. McCone	Nov. 29, 1961-April 28, 1965
Vice Admiral William Rayborn, Jr. USN	April 28, 1965-June 30, 1966
Richard Helms	June 30, 1966-Feb. 2, 1973
James Schlesinger	Feb. 2, 1973-July 2, 197
William Colby	Sept 4, 1973-Jan. 30, 1976
George H.W. Bush	Jan 30, 1976-Jan 20, 1977
Adm. Stansfield Turner	March 9, 1977-Jan. 20, 1981
William Casey	Jan. 28, 1981-Jan 29, 1987
William Webster	May 26, 1987-Aug 31, 1991
Robert Gates	Nov. 6, 1991-Jan 20, 1993
R. James Woolsey	Feb 5. 1993-Jan 10, 1995
John Deutch	May 10, 1995-Dec. 15, 1995
George Tenet	July 11, 1997-July 11, 2004
Porter Goss	Sept 24, 2004-May 26, 2006
Gen. Michael Hayden, USAF	May 30, 2006-Feb. 13, 2009
Leon Panetta	Feb. 13, 2009-June 13, 2011
David Petraeus	Sept. 6, 2011-Nov. 9, 2012
John Brennan	March 8, 2013-

Bibliography
Books

Allen, Thomas & Polmar, Norman, *Merchants of Treason*. Delacorte Press, New York, 1988.

Ambrose, Stephen, *Ike's Spies: Eisenhower and the Espionage Establishment,* University of Mississippi Press, Jackson, 1981.

Andrew, Christopher, *For the President's Eyes Only,* Harper Collins, New York 1995.

Ashley, Clarence, *CIA Spy Masters,* Pelican Publishing Co., Gretna, LA, 2004.

Bagley, Tennet, *Spy Wars: Moles, Mysteries and Deadly Games,* Yale University Press, New Haven, CT, 2007.

Bearden, Milton & Risen, James, *The Main Enemy: The Inside Story of the CIA's Final Showdown with the KGB,* Random House, New York, 2003.

Brown, Anthony Cave, *Treason in the Blood,* Houghton Mifflin Co., New York, 1994.

Carlisle, Rodney, *The Complete Idiots Guide to Spies and Espionage.* Alpha Books, New York, 2003.

Clarridge, Duane, with Drehl, Digby, *A Spy for All Seasons,* Scribner, New York 1997.

Cockburn, Andrew & Cockburn, Patrick, *Out of the Ashes: The Resurrection of Saddam Hussein,* Harper Collins, New York, 1999.

Coll, Steve, *Ghost Wars: The Secret History of the CIA, Afghanistan, and bin Laden, From the Soviet Invasion to September 10, 2001,* The Penguin Press, New York, 2004.

Corn, David, *Blond Ghost: The Shackley and the CIA's Crusaders,* Simon & Schuster, New York, 1994.

Corson, William, Trento, Susan, & Trento, Joseph, *Widows,* Crown Books, New York, 1989.

Draper, Theodore, *A Very Thin Line: The Iran-Contra Affairs,* Hill and Wang, New York, 1991.

Dulles, Allen, Edited by, *Great True Spy Stories,* Castle Books, Secaucus, NJ, 1968.

Epstein, Edward Jay, *Deception: The Invisible War Between the KGB and the CIA,* Simon & Schuster, 1989.

Freedman, Lawrence, *Kennedy's Wars: Berlin, Cuba, Laos and Vietnam,* Oxford University Press, 2000.

Friedman, Alan, *Spider's Web: The Secret History of How the White House Illegally Armed Iraq,* Bantam Books, New York, 1993.

Gentry, Curt, *J. Edgar Hoover: The Man and the Secrets,* W.W. Norton Co., New York, 1991.

Hart, John Limond, *The CIA's Russians,* Naval Institute Press, Annapolis,

MD, 2003.

Hickle, Warren, & Turner, William, *Deadly Secrets: The CIA-Mafia War Against Castro and the Assassination of JFK,* Thunder's Mouth Press, New York, 1992.

Higgins, Trumbull, *The Perfect Failure: Kennedy, Eisenhower and the CIA at the Bay of Pigs,* W. W. Norton & Co., New York, 1987.

Hillsman, Roger, *To Move a Nation,* Doubleday & Co., New York, 1967.

Holtzman, Michael, *James Jesus Angleton: The CIA & the Craft of Counterintelligence,* University of Massachusetts Press, Amherst, 2008.

Hopsicker, Daniel, *Barry & The Boys: The CIA, the Mob and America's Secret History,* Trine Day, 2006.

Hougan, Jim, *Secret Agenda: Watergate, Deep Throat and the CIA,* Random House, New York, 1984.

Hunt, Linda, *Secret Agenda: The United States Government and Project Paperclip 1945-1990,* St. Martins Press, New York, 1991.

Hurt, Henry, *Shadrin: The Spy Who Never Came Back,* Berkeley Books, New York, 1981.

Jones, Howard, *The Bay of Pigs,* Oxford University Press, New York, 2008.

Kessler, Ronald, *Spy Vs. Spy: The Secret Campaign Against Terror,* St. Martin's Press, New York, 2003.

Ibid, *The Bureau: The Secret History of the FBI,* St. Martin's Press, New York, 2002.

Ibid, *Escape from the CIA,* Pocket Books, New York, 1991.

Kross, Peter, *Oswald, the CIA and the Warren Commission: The Unanswered Questions,* Bridger House Press, Hayden, ID, 2011.

Ibid, *Spies, Traitors and Moles: An Intelligence and Espionage Quiz Book,* Illuminet Press, Lilburn, GA, 1988.

Ibid, *Target Fidel: A Narrative Encyclopedia of the US Government's Plots to Kill Fidel Castro, 1959-1965,* Privately Published, 1999.

Ibid, *The Encyclopedia of World War 2 Spies,* Barricade Books, 2001.

Ibid, *JFK: The French Connection,* Adventures Unlimited Press, Kempton, IL, 2012.

Ibid, *The Secret History of the United States: Conspiracies, Cobwebs and Lies,* Adventures Unlimited Press, Kempton, IL, 2013.

Lane, Mark, *Plausible Denial: Was the CIA Involved in the Assassination of JFK?,* Thunder's Mouth Press, New York, 1991.

Mangold, Tom, *Cold Warrior: James Jesus Angleton: The CIA's Master Spy Hunter,* Simon & Schuster, New York, 1991.

Marin, David, *Wilderness of Mirrors,* Harper & Row, New York, 1980.

Miller, John, Stone, Michael, & Mitchell, Chris, *The Cell: Inside the 9-11 Plot, and Why The CIA Failed to Stop It,* Hyperion, New York, 2002.

Minter, Richard, *Losing Bin Laden,* Regnery Publishing Inc., 2003.

Nash, Jay Robert, *Spies: A Narrative Encyclopedia of Dirty Deeds & Double Dealing, From Biblical Times to Today,* M. Evans & Co., New

York, 1997.

Newman, John, *JFK and Vietnam,* Warner Books, New York, 1992.

Ibid, *Oswald and the CIA,* Carroll & Graf Publishers, New York, 1995.

O'Leary, Brad & Seymour, L.E., *Triangle of Death,* WND Books, 2003.

O'Toole, G.J.A., *The Encyclopedia of American Intelligence and Espionage,* Facts on File, New York, 1988.

Perry, Mark, *Eclipse: The Last Days of the CIA,* William Morrow & Co., New York, 1992.

Polmar, Norman, & Allen, Thomas, *Spy Book: The Encyclopedia of Espionage,* Random House, New York, 1994.

Prados, John, *President's Secret Wars,* Ivan Dee Publisher, 1996.

Ibid, *Lost Crusader: The Secret Wars of CIA Director William Colby,* Oxford University Press, 2003.

Ranelagh, John, *The Agency: The Rise and Decline of the CIA,* Simon & Schuster, New York, 1986.

Reeve, Simon, *The New Jackals: Ramiz Yousef, Osama bin Laden and the Future of Terrorism,* Northeastern University Press, 1999.

Reibling, Mark, *The Secret War Between the FBI and CIA,* Alfred Knopf, New York, 1994.

Richelson, Jeffrey, *A Century of Spies: Intelligence in the Twentieth Century,* Oxford University Press, 1995.

Russell, Dick, *The Man Who Knew Too Much,* Carroll & Graf Publishers, New York, 1992.

Russo, Gus, *The Secret War Against Castro and the Death of JFK,* Bancroft Press, 1998.

Schecter, Jerrold & Deriabin, Peter, *The Spy Who Saved the World,* Charles Scribner's Sons, New York, 1992.

Seale, Patrick, *Abu Nidal: A Gun for Hire,* Random House, New York, 1992.

Shenon, Philip, *The Commission: The Uncensored History of the 9-11 Investigation,* Twelve Publishing, New York, 2008.

Smith, W. Thomas, Jr., *Encyclopedia of the Central Intelligence Agency,* Facts on File, New York, 2003.

Schlesinger, Arthur, Jr., *A Thousand Days: John F. Kennedy in the White House,* Houghton Mifflin Co., Boston, MA, 1965.

Sorensen, Theodore, *Kennedy,* Harper & Row, New York, 1965.

Stockton, Bayard, *Flawed Patriot: The Rise and Fall of CIA Legend Bill Harvey,* Potomac Books, Washington, D.C., 2006.

Swenson, Allan & Benson, Michael, *The Complete Idiot's Guide to the CIA,* Alpha Books, New York, 2003.

Thomas, Evan, *The Very Best Men,* Simon & Schuster, New York, 1995.

Trahair, Richard, *Encyclopedia of Cold War Espionage, Spies and Secret Operations,* Greenwood Press, Westport, CT, 2004.

Trento, Joseph, *The Secret History of the CIA,* Prima Publishing Co., 2001.

Troy, Thomas, *Wild Bill and Intrepid: Donovan, Stephenson, and the*

Origins of the CIA, Yale University Press, New Haven, CT, 1996.

Unger, Craig, *House of Bush, House of Saud: The Secret Relationship Between the World's Two Most Powerful Dynasties,* Charles Scribner & Sons, New York, 2004.

Von Tunzelmann, Alex, *Red Heat: Conspiracy, Murder, and the Cold War in the Caribbean,* Henry Holt & Co., New York, 2011.

Waldron, Lamar & Hartmann, Thomas, *Legacy of Secrecy: The Long Shadow of the JFK Assassination,* Counterpoint, New York, 2008.

Ibid, *Ultimate Sacrifice: John and Robert Kennedy, the Plan for a Coup in Cuba, and the Murder of JFK,* Carroll & Graf Publishers, New York, 2005.

Weiner, Tim, Johnson, David, & Lewis, Niel, *Betrayal: The Story of Aldrich Ames, An American Spy,* Random House, New York, 1995.

Wise, David, *NIGHTMOVER,* Harper Collins, New York, 1995.

Woodward, Bob, *Veil: The Secret Wars of the CIA 1981-1987,* Simon & Schuster, New York, 1987.

Ibid, *Plan of Attack,* Simon & Schuster, New York, 2004.

Magazines and Journals

Anderson, John Lee, *The Assassins,* The New Yorker, June 10, 2002, Page 72-81.

Burton, Fred, & Katz, Samuel, *40 Minutes in Benghazi,* Vanity Fair, August 2013.

Coll, Steve, *Flawed Ally Was Hunt's Best Hope,* Washington Post, February 23, 2004.

Ibid, *A Secret Hunt Unravels in Afghanistan,* Washingtonpost.com, February 22, 2004.

Chossudovsky, Michel, *The Role of Pakistan's Military Intelligence (ISI) in the September 11 Attacks,* globalresearch.ca, November 2, 2001.

Epstein, Edward Jay, *The Spy Who Came Back from the Dead,* Live, September, 1986.

Friedman, Robert, *The CIA and the Sheik,* The Village Voice, March 30, 1993.

Hersh, Seymour, *Saddam's Best Friend: How the CIA made it a lot easier for the Iraqi's to rearm,* The New Yorker, no date, Page 32-41.

Hopsicker, Daniel, *CIA Linked to Seal's Assassination,* The Washington Weekly, August 18, 1997.

Johnston, David & Weiner, Tim, *On the Trail of a CIA Man, From Asia to Bank Accounts,* New York Times, November 21, 1996.

Johnston, David, *The CIA Dug for Moles but Buried the Loyal,* New York Times, March 8, 1992.

Joshi, Manoji, *9/11 Funds Came from Pakistan, Says FBI,* Times of India, August 1, 2003.

Kross, Peter, *Death on the Chesapeake: Paisley and the CIA,* Critique, Vol. 14, No. 13 & 14, Fall/Winter 1983-84, Page 100-103.

Ibid, *The behind the scenes story of how a World War I hero helped to strengthen U.S.-British ties and forged the beginnings of today's CIA,* World War II Quarterly, Winter, 2013.

Leiby, Richard & Priest, Dana, *The Spy Next Door,* Washington Post, October 8, 2003.

Loeb, Vernon, *CIA Had Covert Tie to Letelier Plotter,* Common Dreams News Center.

Ibid, *CIA Operative Becomes First Combat Casualty,* Washingtonpost. com, November 28, 2001.

Marshall, Tyler, *Last Minute Attempts Failed to Save Anti-Taliban Leader,* LATimes.com, October 28, 2001.

Mass, Peter, *Selling Out: How an Ex-CIA Agent Made Millions Working for Qaddafi,* New York Times Magazine, April 13, 1986, Page 26-40.

Mazzetti, Mark, Cooper, Helene, & Baker, Peter, *Behind The Hunt for bin Laden,* New York Times.com, no date.

Morley, Jefferson, *The Good Spy,* The Washington Monthly, December, 2003.

Parry, Robert, *A Case of State Terrorism,* www.davidicke.com.

Powell, Bill, *Inside the CIA,* Fortune, September 29, 2003.

Prados, John, *JFK and The Diem Coup,* National Security Archive, world-wide web.

Riding, Alan, *Carlos the Terrorist Arrested and Taken to France,* New York Times, August 16, 1994, Page 1-2.

Risen, James, & Johnston, David, *FBI Rejected Spy Warnings 2 Years Before Agent's Arrest,* New York Times, April 22, 2001.

Starobin, Paul, *Agent Provocateur,* George Magazine, October 1997, Page 86-91.

Thomas, Gordon, *The Spy Who Never Came in from the Cold,* world-wide web, October 25, 2006.

Tran, Mark, *Manuel Noreiga-From US Friend to Foe,* The Guardian. com, April 27, 2010.

Von Drehle, David, *Death Comes for the Terrorist,* Time, May 20, 2011.

Ward, Vicky, *Double Exposure,* Vanity Fair, January, 2004.

Whitlock, Craig, & Gellman, Burton, *To Hunt bin Laden Satellites Watched Over Abbottabad, Pakistan and Navy Seals,* The Washington Post, August 20, 2013.

Wise, David, *The Spy Who Got Away—Again,* Newsweek, September 7, 1992, Page 46-47.

No author, *Manuel Noreiga,* Encyclopedia Britannica, www.britannica. com.

No author, *Barry Seal.* Spartacus, schoolnet.co.uk.

No author, *CIA Officials Testimony Sheds Light on Benghazi Consulate Attacks,* The Guardian.com.

Tales From Langley

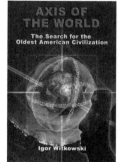

ANCIENT ALIENS ON THE MOON
By Mike Bara
What did NASA find in their explorations of the solar system that they may have kept from the general public? How ancient really are these ruins on the Moon? Using official NASA and Russian photos of the Moon, Bara looks at vast cityscapes and domes in the Sinus Medii region as well as glass domes in the Crisium region. Bara also takes a detailed look at the mission of Apollo 17 and the case that this was a salvage mission, primarily concerned with investigating an opening into a massive hexagonal ruin near the landing site. Chapters include: The History of Lunar Anomalies; The Early 20th Century; Sinus Medii; To the Moon Alice!; Mare Crisium; Yes, Virginia, We Really Went to the Moon; Apollo 17; more. Tons of photos of the Moon examined for possible structures and other anomalies.
240 Pages. 6x9 Paperback. Illustrated.. $19.95. Code: AAOM

ANCIENT TECHNOLOGY IN PERU & BOLIVIA
By David Hatcher Childress
Childress speculates on the existence of a sunken city in Lake Titicaca and reveals new evidence that the Sumerians may have arrived in South America 4,000 years ago. He demonstrates that the use of "keystone cuts" with metal clamps poured into them to secure megalithic construction was an advanced technology used all over the world, from the Andes to Egypt, Greece and Southeast Asia. He maintains that only power tools could have made the intricate articulation and drill holes found in extremely hard granite and basalt blocks in Bolivia and Peru, and that the megalith builders had to have had advanced methods for moving and stacking gigantic blocks of stone, some weighing over 100 tons.
340 Pages. 6x9 Paperback. Illustrated.. $19.95 Code: ATP

THE ILLUSTRATED DOOM SURVIVAL GUIDE
Don't Panic!
By Matt "DoomGuy" Victor
With over 500 very detailed and easy-to-understand illustrations, this book literally shows you how to do things like build a fire with whatever is at hand, perform field surgeries, identify and test foodstuffs, and form twine, snares and fishhooks. In any doomsday scenario, being able to provide things of real value—such as clothing, tools, medical supplies, labor, food and water—will be of the utmost importance. This book gives you the particulars to help you survive in any environment with little to no equipment, and make it through the first critical junctures after a disaster. Beyond any disaster you will have the knowledge to rebuild shelter, farm from seed to seed, raise animals, treat medical problems, predict the weather and protect your loved ones.
356 Pages. 6x9 Paperback. Illustrated. $20.00. Code: IDSG

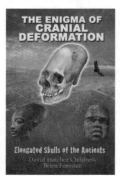

THE ENIGMA OF CRANIAL DEFORMATION
Elongated Skulls of the Ancients
By David Hatcher Childress and Brien Foerster
In a book filled with over a hundred astonishing photos and a color photo section, Childress and Foerster take us to Peru, Bolivia, Egypt, Malta, China, Mexico and other places in search of strange elongated skulls and other cranial deformation. The puzzle of why diverse ancient people—even on remote Pacific Islands—would use head-binding to create elongated heads is mystifying. Where did they even get this idea? Did some people naturally look this way—with long narrow heads? Were they some alien race? Were they an elite race that roamed the entire planet? Why do anthropologists rarely talk about cranial deformation and know so little about it?
250 Pages. 6x9 Paperback. Illustrated. $19.95. Code: ECD

LOST CITIES & ANCIENT MYSTERIES OF THE SOUTHWEST
By David Hatcher Childress

Join David as he starts in northern Mexico and searches for the lost mines of the Aztecs. He continues north to west Texas, delving into the mysteries of Big Bend, including mysterious Phoenician tablets discovered there and the strange lights of Marfa. Then into New Mexico where he stumbles upon a hollow mountain with a billion dollars of gold bars hidden deep inside it! In Arizona he investigates tales of Egyptian catacombs in the Grand Canyon, cruises along the Devil's Highway, and tackles the century-old mystery of the Lost Dutchman mine. In Nevada and California Childress checks out the rumors of mummified giants and weird tunnels in Death Valley, plus he searches the Mohave Desert for the mysterious remains of ancient dwellers alongside lakes that dried up tens of thousands of years ago. It's a full-tilt blast down the back roads of the Southwest in search of the weird and wondrous mysteries of the past!

486 Pages. 6x9 Paperback. Illustrated. Bibliography. $19.95. Code: LCSW

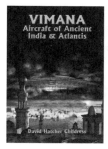

TECHNOLOGY OF THE GODS
The Incredible Sciences of the Ancients
by David Hatcher Childress

Childress looks at the technology that was allegedly used in Atlantis and the theory that the Great Pyramid of Egypt was originally a gigantic power station. He examines tales of ancient flight and the technology that it involved; how the ancients used electricity; megalithic building techniques; the use of crystal lenses and the fire from the gods; evidence of various high tech weapons in the past, including atomic weapons; ancient metallurgy and heavy machinery; the role of modern inventors such as Nikola Tesla in bringing ancient technology back into modern use; impossible artifacts; and more.

356 PAGES. 6x9 PAPERBACK. ILLUSTRATED. BIBLIOGRAPHY. $16.95. CODE: TGOD

VIMANA AIRCRAFT OF ANCIENT INDIA & ATLANTIS
by David Hatcher Childress, introduction by Ivan T. Sanderson

In this incredible volume on ancient India, authentic Indian texts such as the *Ramayana* and the *Mahabharata* are used to prove that ancient aircraft were in use more than four thousand years ago. Included in this book is the entire Fourth Century BC manuscript *Vimaanika Shastra* by the ancient author Maharishi Bharadwaaja. Also included are chapters on Atlantean technology, the incredible Rama Empire of India and the devastating wars that destroyed it.

334 PAGES. 6x9 PAPERBACK. ILLUSTRATED. $15.95. CODE: VAA

LOST CONTINENTS & THE HOLLOW EARTH
I Remember Lemuria and the Shaver Mystery
by David Hatcher Childress & Richard Shaver

Shaver's rare 1948 book *I Remember Lemuria* is reprinted in its entirety, and the book is packed with illustrations from Ray Palmer's *Amazing Stories* magazine of the 1940s. Palmer and Shaver told of tunnels running through the earth—tunnels inhabited by the Deros and Teros, humanoids from an ancient spacefaring race that had inhabited the earth, eventually going underground, hundreds of thousands of years ago. Childress discusses the famous hollow earth books and delves deep into whatever reality may be behind the stories of tunnels in the earth. Operation High Jump to Antarctica in 1947 and Admiral Byrd's bizarre statements, tunnel systems in South America and Tibet, the underground world of Agartha, the belief of UFOs coming from the South Pole, more.

344 PAGES. 6x9 PAPERBACK. ILLUSTRATED. $16.95. CODE: LCHE

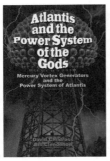

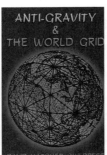

COVERT WARS AND BREAKAWAY CIVILIZATIONS
By Joseph P. Farrell
Farrell delves into the creation of breakaway civilizations by the Nazis in South America and other parts of the world. He discusses the advanced technology that they took with them at the end of the war and the psychological war that they waged for decades on America and NATO. He investigates the secret space programs currently sponsored by the breakaway civilizations and the current militaries in control of planet Earth. Plenty of astounding accounts, documents and speculation on the incredible alternative history of hidden conflicts and secret space programs that began when World War II officially "ended."
292 Pages. 6x9 Paperback. Illustrated. $19.95. Code: BCCW

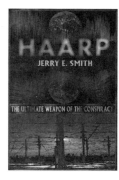

PRODIGAL GENIUS
The Life of Nikola Tesla
by John J. O'Neill
This special edition of O'Neill's book has many rare photographs of Tesla and his most advanced inventions. Tesla's eccentric personality gives his life story a strange romantic quality. He made his first million before he was forty, yet gave up his royalties in a gesture of friendship, and died almost in poverty. Tesla could see an invention in 3-D, from every angle, within his mind, before it was built; how he refused to accept the Nobel Prize; his friendships with Mark Twain, George Westinghouse and competition with Thomas Edison. Tesla is revealed as a figure of genius whose influence on the world reaches into the far future. Deluxe, illustrated edition.
408 pages. 6x9 Paperback. Illustrated. Bibliography. $18.95. Code: PRG

HAARP
The Ultimate Weapon of the Conspiracy
by Jerry Smith
The HAARP project in Alaska is one of the most controversial projects ever undertaken by the U.S. Government. At at worst, HAARP could be the most dangerous device ever created, a futuristic technology that is everything from super-beam weapon to world-wide mind control device. Topics include Over-the-Horizon Radar and HAARP, Mind Control, ELF and HAARP, The Telsa Connection, The Russian Woodpecker, GWEN & HAARP, Earth Penetrating Tomography, Weather Modification, Secret Science of the Conspiracy, more. Includes the complete 1987 Eastlund patent for his pulsed super-weapon that he claims was stolen by the HAARP Project.
256 pages. 6x9 Paperback. Illustrated. Bib. $14.95. Code: HARP

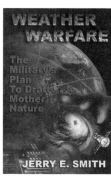

WEATHER WARFARE
The Military's Plan to Draft Mother Nature
by Jerry E. Smith
Weather modification in the form of cloud seeding to increase snow packs in the Sierras or suppress hail over Kansas is now an everyday affair. Underground nuclear tests in Nevada have set off earthquakes. A Russian company has been offering to sell typhoons (hurricanes) on demand since the 1990s. Scientists have been searching for ways to move hurricanes for over fifty years. In the same amount of time we went from the Wright Brothers to Neil Armstrong. Hundreds of environmental and weather modifying technologies have been patented in the United States alone – and hundreds more are being developed in civilian, academic, military and quasi-military laboratories around the world *at this moment!* Numerous ongoing military programs do inject aerosols at high altitude for communications and surveillance operations.
304 Pages. 6x9 Paperback. Illustrated. Bib. $18.95. Code: WWAR

ORDER FORM

**10% Discount
When You Order
3 or More Items!**

One Adventure Place
P.O. Box 74
Kempton, Illinois 60946
United States of America
Tel.: 815-253-6390 • Fax: 815-253-6300
Email: auphq@frontiernet.net
http://www.adventuresunlimitedpress.com

ORDERING INSTRUCTIONS

✓ Remit by USD$ Check, Money Order or Credit Card

✓ Visa, Master Card, Discover & AmEx Accepted

✓ Paypal Payments Can Be Made To:

   info@wexclub.com

✓ Prices May Change Without Notice

✓ 10% Discount for 3 or More Items

SHIPPING CHARGES

United States

✓ Postal Book Rate { **$4.50 First Item**
50¢ Each Additional Item

✓ POSTAL BOOK RATE Cannot Be Tracked!
   Not responsible for non-delivery.

✓ Priority Mail { **$6.00 First Item**
$2.00 Each Additional Item

✓ UPS { **$7.00 First Item**
$1.50 Each Additional Item

NOTE: UPS Delivery Available to Mainland USA Only

Canada

✓ Postal Air Mail { **$15.00 First Item**
$2.50 Each Additional Item

✓ Personal Checks or Bank Drafts MUST BE

   US$ and Drawn on a US Bank

✓ Canadian Postal Money Orders OK

✓ Payment MUST BE US$

All Other Countries

✓ Sorry, No Surface Delivery!

✓ Postal Air Mail { **$19.00 First Item**
$6.00 Each Additional Item

✓ Checks and Money Orders MUST BE US$
   and Drawn on a US Bank or branch.

✓ Paypal Payments Can Be Made in US$ To:
   info@wexclub.com

SPECIAL NOTES

✓ RETAILERS: Standard Discounts Available

✓ BACKORDERS: We Backorder all Out-of-
   Stock Items Unless Otherwise Requested

✓ PRO FORMA INVOICES: Available on Request

✓ DVD Return Policy: Replace defective DVDs only

ORDER ONLINE AT: www.adventuresunlimitedpress.com

**10% Discount When You Order
3 or More Items!**

Please check: ✓

☐ This is my first order   ☐ I have ordered before

Name			
Address			
City			
State/Province		Postal Code	
Country			
Phone: Day		Evening	
Fax		Email	

Item Code	Item Description	Qty	Total

Please check: ✓

	Subtotal ▶	
	Less Discount-10% for 3 or more items ▶	
☐ Postal-Surface	Balance ▶	
☐ Postal-Air Mail Illinois Residents 6.25% Sales Tax ▶		
(Priority in USA) Previous Credit ▶		
☐ UPS Shipping ▶		
(Mainland USA only) Total (check/MO in USD$ only) ▶		

☐ Visa/MasterCard/Discover/American Express

Card Number:

Expiration Date: Security Code:

✓ SEND A CATALOG TO A FRIEND: